OUT OF IRRELEVANCE:
A socio-political introduction to Indian affairs in Canada

by

J. Rick Ponting
University of Calgary

and

Roger Gibbins
University of Calgary

with a contribution by

Andrew J. Siggner

Butterworths
Toronto

© 1980 Butterworth and Company (Canada) Limited
2265 Midland Avenue
Scarborough, Ontario, Canada M1P 4S1

The Butterworth Group of Companies:
Canada: Butterworth & Co. (Canada) Ltd., Toronto, Vancouver
United Kingdom: Butterworth & Co. (Publishers) Ltd., London,
        Borough Green
Australia: Butterworth Pty. Ltd., Sydney, Melbourne, Brisbane
New Zealand: Butterworths of New Zealand, Ltd., Wellington
South Africa: Butterworth & Co. (South Africa) Pty. Ltd., Durban
United States: Butterworth Inc., Boston
        Butterworth (Legal) Inc., Seattle

Canadian Cataloguing in Publication Data

Ponting, J. Rick.
  Out of irrelevance

Bibliography: P.
Includes index.

ISBN 0-409-85915-X

1. Indians of North America—Canada—Government relations. 2. Indians,
Treatment of—Canada. 3. National Indian Brotherhood. 4. Canada.
Dept. of Indian Affairs and Northern Development. I. Gibbins, Roger,
1947- II. Siggner, Andrew J. III. Title.

E92.P66   323.1'197'071   C80-094282-5

For Nelson Small Legs Jr.
and the many other Indians
for whom suicide seemed the only way out

Table of Contents

List of Abbreviations

ADM	Assistant Deputy Minister
AIM	American Indian Movement
CAP	Career Assignment Program (of the Public Service Commission)
CARC	Canadian Arctic Resources Committee
CASNP	The Canadian Association in Support of the Native Peoples (formerly IEA)
CCCB	Canadian Catholic Conference of Bishops
CIRC	Canadian Indian Rights Commission
CMHC	Central Mortgage and Housing Corporation
CMS	Canadian Metis Society
COPE	Committee for Original Peoples Entitlement
DIAND	The Department of Indian Affairs and Northern Development
DM	Deputy Minister
FPRO	Federal-Provincial Relations Office (federal government)
IEA	Indian-Eskimo Association of Canada (later CASNP)
IEDF	Indian Economic Development Fund (of IIAP)
IIAP	Indian/Inuit Affairs Program (of the Dept. of Indian Affairs and Northern Development)
IIRDP	Indian and Inuit Recruitment and Development Program
IPDS	Indian Policy Development Secretariat (of NIB)
IRIW	Indian Rights For Indian Women
ITC	Inuit Tapirisat of Canada
JNCC	Joint NIB/Cabinet Committee
JSC	Joint Sub Committee of JNCC
JWG	Joint Working Group of JNCC
MIB	Manitoba Indian Brotherhood
MP	Member of Parliament
NCC	Native Council of Canada
NCIC	National Commission on the Indian Canadian
NCIRT	National Committee on Indian Rights and Treaties
NGO	Non-Governmental Organization (of the United Nations)
NIC	National Indian Council

NIB	National Indian Brotherhood
ONC	Office of Native Claims (of DIAND)
ORLC	Ontario Regional Liaison Council
PCO	Privy Council Office
PLU	Parliamentary Liaison Unit (of NIB)
PMO	Prime Minister's Office
PSG	Program Support Group (of IIAP)
PTO	Provincial and Territorial Member Organizations (of NIB)
RDG	Regional Director-General (of IIAP)
SCIAND	House of Commons Standing Committee on Indian Affairs & Northern Development
WCC	World Council of Churches
WCIP	World Council of Indigenous Peoples

Preface

The writing of this book has been at once a source of challenge, frustration, and pleasure. The challenge came in defining the task and reducing it to manageable proportions for the time and space available. There was also a challenge involved in penetrating the rhetoric and defensiveness of some respondents aand in negotiating the participation of others. The frustration arose in the necessity for reining in scientific curiosity and submitting to a discipline which precluded the pursuit of so many details which were of such considerable personal interest. Two other major frustrations stemmed from having to exclude such important topics as land claims and from experiencing the interdependencies of so many issue areas in Indian affairs, yet having to ignore them because of limitations of space and resources.

The writing of this book produced many pleasures as well. Particularly noteworthy here are the many gratifications of the interview phenomenon itself—the meeting of new people and the construction of a relationship with them, the feeling of satisfaction after a productive interview, and the positive feedback from them. The experience of being able to piece together the jigsaw puzzle (or more accurately, parts of it) which is Indian affairs was also rewarding.

A few words might be in order here about the origin of the book and the contributions of the respective authors. The book originated in the intent to make available, in readily readable form and to a broad audience, the findings of a national survey which Gibbins and Ponting conducted in 1976. Pursuant to a comment by University of British Columbia political scientist Alan Cairns, the decision was eventually made to expand the book to deal with the Ottawa bureaucracy, with the result that in the final format the survey data now constitute only one chapter (Chapter Three) among eleven.

Chapter One and part of Chapters Nine and Eleven were written by Gibbins. He also extensively rewrote an earlier co-authored (Gibbins and Ponting) version of Chapter Three, edited Chapter Ten, and served as a close consultant to the senior author throughout the project from the data collection phase onwards. Chapter Two was written by a longstanding friend, Andy Siggner, who also made important contributions in terms of suggesting research directions, indentifying important contacts in the bureaucracy, commenting upon the manuscript, and with his wife, providing generous hospitality for Ponting during five lengthy research trips to Ottawa. As senior author, Ponting conducted most of the field research, wrote approximately eight chapters, and edited all but Chapter

Ten. Various colleagues and interviewees provided comments upon some or all of the first draft of the manuscript, but the responsibility for the final version must of course rest with the senior author.

In a book such as this, which relies so heavily upon field research rather than upon library research or armchair theorizing, a long list of indebtedness is incurred. First and foremost, we are indebted to the hundreds of interviewees without whose kind co-operation and generous giving of time this book would not have been possible. These interviewees include not only the respondents in the national survey, but also the many respondents and "informants" in various organizations. Almost as great is our indebtedness to the Donner Canadian Foundation which financed the major portion of the expensive national survey. The Samuel and Saidye Bronfman Family Foundation provided a particularly helpful grant in support of the preparation of the manuscript, and the Clifford E. Lee Foundation provided a grant to underwrite publication costs, thereby reducing the price of the book to you, the reader.

The University of Calgary and the Killam Resident Fellowship Program were also instrumental in the completion of the book. The university helped fund the national survey and provided computing funds for the data analysis. A Killam Resident Fellowship and accompanying support grant during the 1978 fall academic term enabled Ponting to assume the senior authorship responsibility for the book. The opportunity to devote full time to the book for four months without the distractions of regular departmental responsibilities was invaluable, and the support of the university sociology department head, Robert Stebbins, and the Killam Fellowship Program are gratefully acknowledged.

We are grateful to Judy Tregaskis and particularly to Gloria Hall for their patience and perserverence in turning twelve hundred handwritten pages into typewritten manuscript, while simultaneously discharging other demanding duties. Cathy Caldwell's painstaking efforts in compiling the index are greatly appreciated. The support and co-operation of the Butterworth's editorial staff, and their show of confidence in the authors, was also much appreciated.

The undertaking of a task as major as the writing of a book inevitably entails familial sacrifices, and for these the senior author extends his sincere appreciation to the Gibbins and Siggner families. To Patricia Ponting go special thanks for her patience and understanding during the five years of virtual "widowhood" surrounding this project. To Susan and Michael Ponting, an apology for the paternal unavailability you were too young to understand.

J. R. P. and R. G.
Calgary,
January 1, 1980.

Introduction

This book takes as its point of departure the assumption that there is in the social science literature a dearth of base-line descriptive data about Canadian society and that such a deficiency can only foster stereotyping and non-constructive criticism. The focus of the book is upon Indian affairs in Canada at the national level, and through the book we aim to help rectify that deficiency in this complex and widely misunderstood sector of Canadian society. The book is therefore heavily descriptive, although our attempts to provide a basic understanding of the phenomena under study certainly take us beyond the description and into analysis as well.

The book has several intended audiences, foremost among which are students and members of the general public, Indian and nonIndian alike. For students and the general public the book seeks to show both how Indians came to occupy a position of virtual irrelevance for the rest of Canadian society and what has been and is being done to change that situation. In addition, the book seeks to prepare the reader for further social change in the directions discussed.

Practitioners in the field and academics are our other two intended audiences. For practitioners, whether they be in Indian organizations, Indian bands, in government, or elsewhere, the book seeks to provide an overview of the context in which are formulated the general constraints faced daily on the job. It is hoped that among academics this book will provide the impetus for a more informed critique of various aspects of Indian affairs and that it will prompt academics to be less rhetorical and more empirical in their pronouncements on Indian affairs. This, we feel, is very important, for the complexity of Indian affairs is so great that commentators who lack a grasp of that complexity may well come to be seen as irrelevant by, and lose credibility with, Indian and government policy makers alike. A very real danger of such uninformed critiques is that they may generate pressures for change in directions which are not in the best interests (as defined by Indians) of the Indian people whom they are usually intending to help. There is also danger that such uninformed critics will get drawn into the Indian political arena in the service of an Indian political elite against other Indian social classes or other Indian political interest groups. Finally, as events surpass the uninformed critics and moralizers, they may awaken to find themselves in a position which is very little different from the "we know what is best for Indians" stance which has for so long prevailed in the minds and acts of paternalistic "do-gooders."

For those who wish to take up this challenge for a more empirically grounded analysis of Indian affairs this book is intended as a starting point, an elementary atlas of the socio-political terrain of Indian affairs. We hope that the book will stimulate much research and that it will generate theoretical interest in Indian politics and in an organizational approach to the study of race and ethnic relations in Canada.

Having identified our purposes, mention should be made of what the book is and is not. First, the book is not a comprehensive treatment of Indian affairs. It is merely an introduction, for a comprehensive treatment would require volumes, as Hawthorn (1967a, 1967b) found even during a much less complex period. Instead we focus upon the apex of Indian-government relations, which is to say the relations between the National Indian Brotherhood and the federal government or its representatives. In this sense Chapters Four through Nine are the core of the book, although important contextual information is also included. If Indian affairs in Canada be likened to a jigsaw puzzle, we have assembled but a few pieces. To even begin to do justice to these important pieces, other important pieces have necessarily been neglected and left for other researchers. Thus, the reader will find only passing reference to land claims, economic development, aboriginal rights, and the status of Indian women. In their place we focus on the federal arena where circumstances conveniently permit the researcher to "get a handle" on what is emerging as the central struggle for Indians in the 1970s and 1980s, namely the struggle for authority over Indian affairs. Indeed, in light of the diversity of Indian affairs from one part of the country to another, a national-level overview is not only convenient but, we contend, a necessary first step. Similarly, the difference in circumstances between status and nonstatus Indians, Metis, and Inuit (Eskimos) dictates that for the task to be at all manageable, we must restrict our focus to but one of these "groups." We have chosen status Indians.

The book is also not neo-Marxist in its orientation. In eschewing this approach which is in vogue in Canada today, we will likely disappoint or antagonize some of our readers. We believe, however, that an understanding of the organizational actors involved in a conflict arena is an important adjunct to any Marxian analysis, and that for some purposes it should actually come prior to a Marxian analysis.

On a positive note, the book can be described as historical, contextual, and data-based. The authors are firm believers in the merit of the call by van den Berghe (1967:149) and others for a social science of race relations which is both historical and contextual, and in this most neo-Marxists would surely agree. Accordingly, to the extent that space has permitted we have devoted attention, especially in Chapter One, to the historical background which helps us understand contemporary aspects of Indian affairs. Our concern with context is manifested in Chapters Two and Three, as well as in discussions of the external environments of our focal organizations. In Chapter Two we call upon the senior demographer in the government's Indian and Inuit Affairs Programme (IIAP) to describe the socio-demographic-economic situation of Indian people themselves. While we preoccupy ourselves in Parts II and III with power and structure and function and politics in Ottawa, Chapter Two should serve to remind us about the "little guy" for whose benefit the politicians and administrators claim to be working. In Chapter Three we provide further context by describing the attitudes and perceptions which are held by members of the general public and which are sometimes perceived to impose certain constraints on the freedom of action of the main protagonists in Indian affairs.

Chapters Two and Three are rich in quantitative data, while Chapter Four through Ten are rich in qualitative data. In those latter chapters we deal with the main protagonists—the National Indian Brotherhood, representing its provincial-level member organizations, and the Indian and Inuit Affairs Programme (IIAP) of the Department of Indian Affairs and Northern Development (DIAND), representing the federal government. We approach NIB and DIAND/IIAP as organizations which: are characterized by certain structures and functions; procure and deploy certain resources; are directed by live human beings; and are constrained and supported by, and act upon, an external environment.

These seven chapters are based upon nearly two hundred hours of interviews with key individuals in these organizations and in organizations which are part of their external environment. These interviewees ranged widely in their responsibilities and roles, from a cabinet minister to religious ministers (e.g., the head of the Anglican Church of Canada), from senior bureaucrats to low level functionaries, from modern Indian politicians to traditional Indian elders, from "detached" Ottawa technocrats to field veterans, from policy makers to policy executers and policy evaluators, from Indian bureaucrats to Indian activists, and from the political and bureaucratic elite to the economic and religious elite. Altogether, discussions were held between July 1978 and October 1979 with over eighty such interviewees (apart from the 1,832 interviews upon which Chapter Three is based) including forty in DIAND and IIAP, thirteen in NIB, eight in three national churches (Anglican, Catholic, and United), and twenty-two in other nonIndian support organizations (including an average of one in each of nineteen philanthropic foundations). Six interviews were over four hours in length, including one conducted from midnight to 4:00 a.m. and another which stretched to eleven hours over four sessions. Most, however, were from one and one-half to three hours in duration. In addition, heavy use was made of written documents. It should also be noted that to enhance the quality of the manuscript, the opportunity to comment upon an earlier draft was given to several key respondents and informants who are currently or were previously associated with DIAND, IIAP, or NIB.

The enormous amount of data generated has placed us in a position to do some prognosticating about the nature of Indian affairs in the future, which we do in Part V, at times with relative assurance and at times only on the basis of informed "guestimation." In Part V we also summarize the highlights of our findings and develop parallels between Indians and French Québécois in their dealings with the dominant society.

Throughout the book we use various terms and abbreviations which are more or less peculiar to our subject area. For the reader's convenience a list of abbreviations has been provided. With regard to terminology, we have made a concerted effort to minimize the amount of academic jargon. However, other terms are unavoidable. Consequently, prior to wrapping up this Introduction with an explanation of the book's title, we digress to make some key terminological distinctions.

First and foremost the reader must understand the difference between status (registered) Indians and nonstatus Indians. Status Indians, who are the main concern of this book and of whom there were about 309,000 in 1980, are persons who fall under the legal jurisdiction of the federal Indian Act and therefore have their names included on a register kept by IIAP. Nonstatus Indians are either (1) former registered Indians who have lost their registered status by marriage to a nonIndian or by a process (discussed later) known as enfranchisement, or (2) the off-spring of such persons. Metis are the off-spring of a mixed (Indian and white) marriage. Metis are sometimes known as "half-breeds" and sometimes identify themselves as nonstatus Indians. However, as Sealey and Lussier (1975) have demonstrated, many Metis have a distinct Metis self-identity which contrasts sharply with an Indian identity, and is sometimes based in part upon the denial to Metis of rights and privileges which are extended to status Indians.

In addition to Metis, status Indians, and nonstatus Indians, there is the Inuit population in Canada, who number about 17,000, including about 4,000 (mainly in northern Quebec) who fall under the jurisdiction of IIAP.

Athough all of the foregoing may be described as "Native people," and although any given pair of status and nonstatus Indians may be indistinguishable in terms of the cultural and physical attributes of "Indianness" (Frideres, 1974:3), the term "Native people" is not one which they prefer. Status Indians are particularly vocal in their objections to being called "Natives," for it is felt that policies based upon such a term will seriously erode the special rights (e.g., treaty rights) and special constitutional status of status Indians and will lead to status Indians being "lumped in" with other aboriginal peoples in Canada and treated like "merely another ethnic group." Indeed, this concern was a central motif for many of the events in Indian affairs in the 1970s and will likely continue to be in the 1980s. Accordingly, and in light of the fact that many status Indians consider themselves to be the only group which can legally call itself Indians, in this book we shall reserve the term Indian to denote registered (status) Indians.

All registered Indians are members of a band, which is a political-administrative unit created by the federal government. However, contrary to the frequent usage of the term in the popular media, not all registered Indians are treaty Indians. Indeed, in many parts of Canada, treaties were never signed (nor offered), such that today only about 57% of all status Indians are also treaty Indians.

Registered Indians may live on a reserve ("reservation" is the American term), on crown-owned land, or elsewhere off-reserve. Since sociologically speaking, Indian settlements on crown land are closely akin to settlements on reserves, we follow a common convention and include Indians living on crown land among Indians living on reserves.

Another distinction which must be made is that between DIAND and IIAP, and throughout the book, we employ great care in our selection of one or the other term. Indeed, it is hoped that one of the contributions of this book will be a reinforcement of the fact that IIAP is just one part of the larger DIAND and that the two cannot be equated because of conflicting views and interests which sometimes emerge between the Assistant Deputy Minister (ADM) of IIAP and the head of DIAND (the Deputy Minister) or between the ADM of IIAP and the ADM of one of the other two programmes in DIAND. Having said that, however, we note that DIAND is the more inclusive term and that we sometimes refer to "a senior DIAND official" when we wish to protect the anonymity of that official (e.g., when reporting on information provided on a "not for attribution" basis) by leaving it ambiguous as to whether that official works in IIAP or elsewhere in DIAND.

Another distinction we make is between *programme* and *program*. The former is used to refer to one of the major organizational subunits of DIAND, such as the Indian/Inuit Affairs Programme or the Northern Affairs Programme. Our use of the term "program" is restricted to particular operational endeavours of one of the programmes, such as a housing or education or economic development program of IIAP.

Another important distinction is that between DIAND or IIAP on the one hand, and "the government" on the other hand. By "the government" we usually refer to the federal Cabinet, which is by no means synonymous with a particular department such as DIAND. To equate "the government" with DIAND is to gloss over important conflicts and differences of interest and opinion.

Another distinction worth noting is that between Indian *A*ffairs and Indian *a*ffairs. The former is synonymous with IIAP, while the latter refers to Indian issues, Indian problems, and to relations between Indian representatives and representatives of the government, as defined above.

Finally, we wish to stress the difference between our use of the terms "bureaucracy", and "bureaucrat" and the popular usage of those terms. The popular usage carries with it strong connotations of a negative value judgement (e.g. red tape, delay, lack of concern for the client, etc.). However, when we use the term "bureaucracy" we are using it in the same sense as the famous sociologist Max Weber (1944:329ff), to describe a particular type of organization—that is, one which is characterized by hierarchical authority relations: specialization of roles and tasks; formalization of acts, decision, rules, and procedures in writing; hiring on the basis of technical qualifications; separation of organizational and personal property; an orientation towards the efficient and rational attainment of specific goals; etc. Similarly, by "bureaucrat" we refer simply to one who works in that type of organization. Our usage is in no way intended to carry a pejorative connotation, whether we be referring to Indian bureaucracies or nonIndian bureaucracies.

To conclude this Introduction, an explanation of the title of the book is in order. When Europeans first came to what is now Canada they were outnumbered by Indians and were dependent upon Indians in learning how to cope with the harsh physical environment. Over time the relationship came to be more symmetrical, as the Europeans needed the Indians as military allies (e.g., against the Americans in the War of 1812) and needed their labour in the fur trade. In return, Indians mainly received European technology (including weapons), but also food, money, whiskey, and trinkets. As the demographic balance tipped and the fur trade was eclipsed by other forms of industry and commerce, Europeans needed Indians less and less but needed Indians' land more and more. Finally, with the clear establishment of Eurocanadian military superiority and the acquisition of Indian lands and of Indian acquiescence through the signing of the treaties in the mid-nineteenth century, the nature of dependency in North America completed its one hundred and eighty degree shift. Indians were pushed onto reserves and, in the words of historian E. Palmer Patterson (1972, Ch. 3), were relegated to a position of irrelevance vis-à-vis the Eurocanadian society. Simply put, Indians were no longer needed by Eurocanadians for their labour, their land, their technology, or their military might. Nor were Indians needed for their votes.

The post-World War II era has seen changes in the position of Indians. With the widespread acquisition of the English language, Eurocanadian education, and on the heels of a war that accentuated the contrast between their plight and the professed ideals of Canadian society, Indians began to organize nationally to improve their lot in life. Events abroad provided an added impetus, as the colonized people of Africa proved that the colonial yoke could be thrown off and as the civil rights movement in the United States galvanized blacks and whites alike to take action. The mass media carried to Indians news of these events and of the surge of nationalistic ideologies in Quebec, Africa, Latin America and the United States. Finally, in the late 1960s there came together a battery of factors which were to propel Indians out of their state of irrelevance, probably permanently.

These factors included a soaring level of federal expenditures on Indians, a sham-like series of consultative meetings which insulted Indians, and then a government proposal (the 1969 White Paper) for a formal and official policy of assimilation of Indians—a policy which was highly consistent with the climate of the times as far as individual freedoms and civil rights were concerned, but which flew in the face of the times as far as considerations of nationalism and decolonization were concerned. Thenceforth, Indians exhibited levels of determination, organization, and sophistication in the ways of Eurocanadian politics and media manipulation such as had not been seen for over a century, if ever. Simultaneously, Indian lands once again took on high value in the nonIndian economy, and various favourable court rulings (especially the one by the Supreme Court in 1973 on the Nishga Indians' aboriginal land claim) demonstrated to the government that Indians could no longer be ignored. Indians had once more become a power to be reckoned with and negotiated with. In large part this book is a portrayal of the nature and development of that new order in the 1970s and of its prospects for the 1980s.

Part I

The Context of Indian Affairs

Chapter 1

The History of Indian-Government Relations

Although the central focus of this book is upon Indian affairs during the 1970s, the issues of that decade were firmly embedded in the past history of Indian-nonIndian relations in Canada. The rights and obligations under dispute, the administrative agencies and policy goals of the national government, and the ideologies that shape public opinion and public policy all have deep roots in that history. Thus the present chapter will provide an historical prologue to the seventies, a prologue that will culminate with the government's 1969 "White Paper" on Indian policy. Our concern will rest with the history of Indian-nonIndian relations as these have become embodied in legislation, bureaucratic agencies, and more nebulous policy goals. Particular attention will be paid to the Indian Act which, having served as the central pillar of Indian-nonIndian relations for the past hundred years, fittingly serves the same role for the concerns of this chapter.

HISTORICAL BACKGROUND TO THE 1876 INDIAN ACT

The early French settlements in the territory that was to become Canada were of such a character that there were few impediments to the integration of the small French and Indian communities (Guillemin, 1978: 320). The French government had little interest in permanent agrarian settlement, the agriculture that was practised was not intensive, property boundaries were loose, and many economic pursuits—particularly the fur trade—required the cooperation of Indians. On the other hand the pattern of English settlement, with its emphasis on agricultural homesteading, was not compatible with the Indian's indigenous occupation of the land.

As English settlement advanced, Indian-nonIndian relations became a pressing matter of public policy. As early as 1670 the British government passed legislation that placed the conduct of Indian affairs in the hands of the colonial Governors and laid out what were to be the principal components of British policy in the future: a) protection of Indian people from unscrupulous whites, b) introduction of Christianity, and c) an activist role for the Crown as a protector of Indians (Miller et al., 1978:2). A milestone in British policy and hence in the Canadian policy that eventually followed was the Royal Proclamation of 1763. That Proclamation, Harper argues (1947:134),

> . . . laid the foundations of four great principles which became embedded in Canada's treaty system: that the Indians possess occupancy rights to all land which they have not formally surrendered; that no land claimed by Indians may be granted to whites until formally surrendered; that the government assumes the responsibility of evicting all persons unlawfully occupying Indian lands; and that surrenders of Indian land may be made only to the Crown, and for a consideration.

Thus, the Royal Proclamation not only recognized aboriginal rights to the land but also established the government as a middleman in the settlement process; the transference of land from Indians to the incoming flood of whites could only come about through the intervention of the government. However, the recognition of Indian sovereignty had some important limitations: sovereignty rested with poorly delineated individual tribes and nations rather than with Indians as a broader cultural entity; missionaries and fur-traders were admitted to Indian territory; the pursuit of fugitives from justice was allowed; intoxicants were forbidden; and nonIndians charged with civil or criminal offenses within Indian territory were tried before British court (Smith, 1975: xv-xvi).

In the century surrounding the 1763 Proclamation, Indian policy was preoccupied by the need to maintain Indians as military allies. Treaties and documents referred explicitly to the Indians as allies, and Indian policy ". . . sought aid or neutrality from Indians in war, and their friendship in peace" (Miller et al., 1978:1). The Indian Department formed in 1755 was an arm of the colonial military with the Superintendent-General reporting directly to the Commander-in-Chief of the British forces. The Department remained in military hands until 1799 when civil authority was established. As it turned out, military control was reasserted in 1816 at a time when the military value of, or threat by, Indians had come virtually to an end in Canada. The conclusion of the War of 1812 had ended the prospects for continued military conflict between British and American Forces and the stage was set for the emergence of new policy directions.

By 1830 when civil control of the Indian Department was re-established, the British Empire no longer needed the Indians (Upton,

1973:51), although the same could not be said of Indian lands. In the earlier days of exploration, trapping, and settlement, the skills and environmental knowledge of Indians were of great importance to whites. Soon, however, the Indians had little left to give (Jenness, 1960:264). It was also becoming clear that the rate of white settlement was overtaking earlier attempts to push Indians back into what had been assumed to be an unlimited interior wilderness, and it was recognized therefore that Indians would have to be incorporated into, rather than simply excluded from, areas of white settlement.

The evolution of Indian policy reflected the missionary activities of the churches and the climate of social reform that prevailed in Britain. In 1838 Lord Glenelg, British Colonial Secretary, established *civilization* and *protection* as the guiding principles of British policy. He stated that the primary goal of British policy was "to protect and cherish this helpless Race . . . [and] raise them in the Scale of Humanity" (Upton, 1973:59). This goal was to remain largely intact for the next one hundred and thirty years. Complementary policies were designed to protect Indians from the evils apparently inherent in contact with white settlers and traders, and to encourage the settlement of Indians in villages where the instruments of civilization and Christianity—schools, churches, and agriculture—could be brought into effect. The eventual target was the assimilation of Indians into the general society. These religious and reformist inputs provided the "moral premise" of Canadian Indian policy.

The union of Upper and Lower Canada in 1840 had no impact on Indian affairs for at this time there was no *Canadian* legislative framework for Indian affairs, which remained an Imperial concern in 1840 and largely stayed so until 1860. However, in the intervening two decades the foundations of a Canadian legislative framework were slowly put into place. In 1850 the first Canadian acts were passed to protect Indian land from trespass. All Indian land and property came under the control of a Commissioner of Indian lands who could exercise and defend all rights of the landowner, including the right to lease land and collect rents. A year later, additional legislation indirectly excluded from Indian status whites living among Indians and nonIndian males married to Indian women (Miller et al., 1978:26). Thus, important Canadian precedents began to be set, such as this one distinguishing between "status" and "nonstatus" Indians, that would eventually be incorporated in the Indian Act of 1876.

In 1856 two special commissioners were appointed by the colonial government to report on objectives that were to serve as mainstays of public policy in the years to come: ". . . the best means of securing the future progress and civilization of the Indian Tribes in Canada" and ". . . the best mode of so managing the Indian property as to secure its full benefit to the Indians, without impeding the settlement of the country" (Miller et al., 1978:28). Here we see the primary policy components of civilization and protection, the latter constrained by the recognition that white settlement would proceed regardless. In their report the commissioners were optimistic about the eventual civilization and assimilation of the Indian people, and predicted the end of the Indian Department. To further the goal of assimilation they recommended a number of steps to encourage economic development.

A year later, in 1857, the colonial government introduced legislation that clearly set out the assimilationist character of public policy and put in place some of the methods by which assimilation could be achieved. The preamble to the *Act for the Gradual Civilization of the Indian Tribes in the Canadas* reads as follows:

> Whereas it is desirable to encourage the progress of Civilization among the Indian Tribes in this Province, the gradual removal of all legal distinctions between them and her Majesty's other Canadian subjects, and to facilitate the acquisition of property and of the rights accompanying it, by such individual Members of the said Tribes as shall be found to desire such encouragement and to have deserved it . . . (Miller et al., 1978:26).

The Act offered monetary, property and enfranchisement inducements to Indians who would choose assimilation and cut their ties with tribal societies—inducements that were to remain important components of Indian policy for the next one hundred years.

A central concern of Indian policy in the pre-Confederation period was the disposition of Indian lands. Here it should be stressed that the principal intent of legislation was not the protection of Indian lands per se but rather the protection of Indians in the land conveyance process. This distinction is critical. While some land was to be retained for the exclusive use of Indians, the more pressing intent of legislation was to establish orderly procedures by which Indian-occupied land could be opened up for white settlement. For example, the Management of Indian Lands and Property Act passed by the colonial government in 1860 dealt primarily with the procedures by which Indian lands could be surrendered. Land could only be surrendered to the Crown and the distribution of liquor to Indians at surrender meetings was prohibited.

The 1860s witnessed two important transfers in the legislative responsibility for Indian affairs. In 1860 responsibility was transferred from the Imperial government to the Province of Canada. Then in 1867 the British North America Act (section 91, subsection 24) gave the new federal government the authority to legislate on matters relating to "Indians and Lands Reserved for Indians." The Secretary of State for the Provinces became the Superintendent-General of Indian Affairs. The delegation of Indian affairs to the federal government rather than to the provinces can be traced to an earlier concern of the Imperial government (Manuel and Posluns, 1974:162):

> A Committee of the English House of Commons in 1837 stressed the need to keep Indian affairs under strict Imperial control. They observed that the chief exploitation of Indians came from neighbouring land-hungry colonists who also controlled local and provincial governments. Only an Imperial intervention in favour of the Indians could help maintain the balance and keep the peace.

In 1867 the federal government was most distant from local affairs and was thus presumably better able than the provincial governments to protect Indian interests (Sanders, 1978:2). At the same time, there was no option to federal government control in the western territories where provincial governments did not yet exist, and where federal control of land was deemed essential to the settlement policies of the national government. It is also worth noting that although the power to legislate for the administration of Indian *lands* was exclusively federal, this was not so for Indians themselves. Thus, Lysyk (1969:696) concludes that

> . . . the withholding of provincial services from Indians on reserves has never been dictated by constitutional necessity, and that whatever justification existed for such provincial policy must be found in historical and political—not constitutional—considerations.

Whether this was realized and then ignored by provincial governments, or whether provincial governments indeed perceived constitutional constraints, is difficult to determine.

Predictably, the early legislative activity of the new federal government pursued the pre-existent policy of assimilation. For instance, the Enfranchisement Act of 1869 laid out a process of enfranchisement as a lure to assimilation and sought to establish some measure of individual Indian property rights that would be analogous to those prevalent in the nonIndian society. That Act also expanded upon the status-nonstatus distinctions set out in the amended Indian Protection Act of 1850 (Miller et al., 1978:54):

> Clause six stipulated that, if an Indian woman married a nonIndian, she and her offspring would neither be entitled to collect annuities, be members of her band, nor be Indians within the meaning of the Act. If she married an Indian from another band, however, she could receive annuities as a member of his band.

In 1872 the General Council of Ontario and Quebec Indians sought to amend this clause in order that "Indian women may have the privilege of marrying when and whom they please without subjecting themselves to exclusion or expulsion from the tribe" (Miller et al., 1978:54). This position, which incidentally runs counter to the contemporary stance of the National Indian Brotherhood, had no effect on government policy.

To summarize, prior to the passing of the 1876 Indian Act the major policy components that were to be imbedded within it had already been determined. The policy cornerstone was assimilation to which end education, Christianization, and settlement on reserves were means. At the same time the government undertook a guardianship role in which it acted to protect Indians from the evils of the white society. Despite the desire to have Indians assimilate, the white society was viewed with rather a jaundiced eye. It was not that the Indian cultures were deemed worthy of preservation but rather that the warts on the frontier white society were readily apparent. Government officials saw themselves standing between Indians and the colonizing whites, acting as buffer in the clash of cultures and values. However, in terms of Indian lands, protection was only partial. No serious attempt was made to limit the expansion of white settlement, and the buffering role of the government became one of blunting the impact of white settlement on Indians—of easing while at the same time promoting the transition to a new social order. Rather than protecting Indian land, the government acted to protect the interests of Indians in the process of land conveyance. Although government officials frequently showed considerable sympathy for Canadian Indians, the direction of social change on the northern half of the continent was never challenged.

THE INDIAN ACT OF 1876

The 1876 Indian Act consolidated rather than departed from pre-existing legislation in the provinces and territories that dealt with Indians. The Act clarified, codified and to some degree revised existing practice and in so doing delineated the responsibilities of the federal government that had been established by the BNA Act. Its importance comes from the fact that it pulled together existing legislation and policy directives and cast them in a document that was to dominate Indian affairs for the next century. For Indians the Act is of great importance because it touches, and not lightly, virtually every aspect of their lives. As Dr. Munro, former assistant deputy minister (ADM) of the Indian Affairs Branch, describes it (Doerr, 1974:40):

> The Indian Act is a Lands Act. It is a Municipal Act, an Education Act and a Societies Act. It is primarily social legislation, but it has a very broad scope: there are provisions about liquor, agriculture and mining as well as Indian lands, band membership and so forth. It has elements that are embodied in perhaps two dozen different acts of any of the provinces and overrides some federal legislation in some respects. . . . It has the force of the Criminal Code

and the impact of a constitution on those people and communities that come within its purview.

Thus, in the scope of its impact upon the lives of individuals, the Indian Act approximates what sociologists call a "total institution" (Goffman, 1959). Furthermore, it is the Indian Act and not the treaties that defines the relationship between Indians and the broader Canadian society (Cardinal, 1977:95). Yet it is the treaties and not the Act that protect land, hunting, fishing and trapping rights, to the extent that this is done at all. The treaties and the Act are not two sides of the same coin—while the former provide a limited form of protection, the latter provides a comprehensive mechanism of social control.

DEFINITION OF INDIAN

It was imperative that "Indian" be defined within the Indian Act. Here legislative precedents were followed; an "Indian" became any male person of Indian blood reputed to belong to a particular band, any child of such person, and any woman who is or was lawfully married to such a person. Excluded from Indian status were persons living continuously five years or more in another country, Indian women marrying non-Indian men and, in some cases, illegitimate children. Through this definitional exercise the Indian Act fragmented the Native population in Canada into legally and legislatively distinct blocs experiencing quite different rights, restrictions and obligations. The contemporary conflicts among status Indians, nonstatus Indians, and Indian women married to nonIndian men are today's legacy of this definitional approach. However, it should be kept in mind here that while the Indian Act only applies to Indians as defined by the Act, the responsibilities and legislative prerogatives of the federal government are not so limited. In contrast to our usage in this book, the term "Indian" has been more broadly interpreted with respect to the BNA Act than it has been within the Indian Act (Lysyk, 1967:515). Furthermore, because the Indian Act is a Canadian statute it cannot amend or limit the terms of the BNA Act so as to exclude nonstatus or enfranchised Indians from federal government jurisdiction (Green, 1969:29). Thus, Manuel and Posluns (1974:242) argue that while Parliament has the power to legislate for all Natives, under the Indian Act Parliament chooses to make laws only for some.

INDIAN LANDS

Clause 25 of the Act retained the government's guardianship of Indian lands: "no reserve or portion of a reserve shall be sold, alienated or leased until it has been released or surrendered to the Crown for the purposes of the Act." Surrender procedures were put in place by the Act to protect Indian interests in the conveyance process. In this and related sections, the Act establishes what might be termed "boundary-maintenance" mechanisms for the Indian societies, mechanisms that Indians were unable to provide internally (Weaver, 1973:5). These mechanisms protected Indian societies by inhibiting assimilation.

Indian land was also protected in part through clauses which ". . . excluded Indian people from taxes, liens, mortgages or other charges on their lands and from loss of possessions through debt or through pawns for intoxicants" (Miller et al., 1978:66). However, while protecting Indian land these provisions have made it difficult for Indians to enter the modern debtor society. More importantly, they have made it next to impossible for Indians to raise outside investment capital, for potentially valuable Indian land cannot be mortgaged (Cardinal, 1977:104). Thus, Indians must usually rely on the federal government for the capital needed to promote economic development. These provisions of the Act, necessary as they may once have been, now serve as a shackle on Indian self-reliance.

ENFRANCHISEMENT

The Indian Act set forth a process of enfranchisement whereby Indians could acquire full Canadian citizenship by severing their ties to the Native community. The Department's summary of the process is as follows (Miller et al., 1978:68):

> Any Indian who was "sober and industrious" could go to an agent appointed for that purpose, to see whether or not he was qualified for the franchise. If qualified, he received a ticket for land, and after three years was entitled to receive a patent (title deed) for it. This would give him absolute control of the land during his life and he could then will it to whomever he chose. During this three-year period, he retained his share in band funds. After an additional three years, he could make application and gain possession of his share of the invested funds of the band. Thus, after six years of "good behavior" he would cease in every respect to be an Indian according to Canadian laws and would then be an ordinary subject of Her Majesty.

The Act also laid down the framework for a limited form of local government and for the election of chiefs and councils: "the Government no doubt assumed that substitution of limited local administration for existing tribal organizations would accelerate the assimilation process" (Miller et al., 1978:66).

CONCENTRATION OF AUTHORITY

Over the long run the most contentious aspect of the Indian Act was the sweeping power that it gave to administrators and to the federal government. The Indian Act extended the regulatory reach of the government into virtually every nook and cranny of Indian life. Indians, unlike other Canadians, were not faced with a plurality of governments and government departments but rather with a single government and a single department. Although the Act presented a veneer of self-government and Indian participation in the control of their lives, even the veneer was an illusion. As Harper (1946:313) notes,

> . . . at every point at which there is a potential contradiction of Indian wishes and government authority, the issue may be resolved by the latter by overcoming the folly to which Indians seem expected to succumb. In this sense, the Act is a non-democratic document, because it reflects so little faith in the Indians.

The Indian Act was administered in the Indian communities by the Indian Agent. In the words of Manuel and Posluns (1974:54), "it was the job of these new white chiefs to displace our traditional leaders in their care over our day-to-day lives in order to bring our way of life into line with the policies that had been decreed in Ottawa." To assist him in this task the agent, like the head of other total institutions (e.g., the prison warden) had an extraordinary range of administrative and discretionary powers; he was an instrument of social control par excellence. Because of his sweeping powers the agent inevitably generated a state of dependency among his Indian clientele. Also, because the agent personified the Indian Act and the character of the relationship between Indians and the government, he became the focal point for Indian hostility and anger, no matter how repressed. Despite the admirable personal qualities of some agents, few Indian leaders today would contest Manuel and Posluns' (1974:69) description of the Indian Agent as a destructive force within the Indian community.

In large part it is the social control features of the Indian Act that have led to the charge that Indians are in the position of a colonized people. Cardinal (1969:43-4), for example, asserts that the Indian Act, ". . . instead of implementing the treaties and offering much-needed protection to Indian rights, subjugated to colonial rule the very people whose rights it was supposed to protect." He goes on to argue (1969:45) that the Indian Act, ". . . enslaved and bound the Indian to a life under a tyranny often as cruel and harsh as that of any totalitarian state." Paradoxically, however, the Act is also perceived by Indians today as one of the major protections for Indian rights (Weaver, 1973:2).

Through the Indian Act legislators tried to pursue two frequently incompatible policy goals. Although the principal policy goal of the Indian Act is assimilation, the Act also sought to protect Indians by restricting their contact with the white society. The resulting isolation could only inhibit assimilation, as Chamberlin (1975:90) has observed:

> From its initial promulgation, there have been those who have questioned the sanity of a piece of legislation which actively discouraged, and indeed in some areas positively prohibited, the assimilation of the Indian into the social and economic life of the non-native population, while at the same time being the centerpiece of a broad policy of moving the Indians towards full citizenship and full participation in Canadian life. By existing to regulate and systematize the relationship between the Indian and the majority society, the Act codifies and often exaggerates the distinctions which it is its function eventually to eliminate.

LEGISLATIVE EVOLUTION OF THE INDIAN ACT

The Indian Act was not cast in bronze and was subjected to frequent legislative fine-tuning and amendment. Throughout, however, its basic features were not altered and the legislation governing Indian affairs in the 1970s bore a close resemblance to the Act passed in 1876.

The ink of the 1876 Act was scarcely dry before a series of amendments was introduced. In 1880 an amendment declared that any Indian with a university degree would ipso facto be enfranchised and therefore no longer be an Indian under the Act. Four years later the Indian Advancement Act transformed tribal regulations into municipal laws and tried to introduce a limited system of band self-government. Also in 1884 an amendment to the Indian Act imposed two to six months imprisonment for anyone participating in the Potlach or Tawanawa dance, ". . . a landmark amendment for it represented the first in a long series of attempts by Parliament to protect Indians from themselves as well as from unscrupulous whites" (Miller et al., 1978:82). A final amendment of 1884, the year before the Riel Rebellion, made the inciting to riot of Indians, non-treaty Indians or "half-breeds" an offense under the Act. The 1885 Electoral Franchises Bill gave the vote under very limited conditions to a small number of Indians, primarily assimilated Indians in Central Canada.

The passage of amendments to the Indian Act in 1889 demonstrated a move to greater government control over Indian education, morality, local government and land (Miller et al., 1978:99). For example, the government was given the power to override a band's reluctance to lease reserve land. Superintendent-General Daly advised the House of Commons that the amendment would overcome a band's refusal to lease reserve land "through spite or pique," terms that were left undefined (Miller et al., 1978:97).

In 1920 the Conservative government, led by Arthur Meighen and displaying his same insensitivity to minority views that had already won the lasting antipathy of French Canadians, passed legislation empowering the government to order the enfranchisement of qualified Indians without any such request from individuals concerned. The power of compulsory enfranchisement was removed by an amendment two years later when the Liberals were in office, but was then reinstated by the Conservative government in 1933. This sequence of events reveals one of the very few significant policy differences between Liberal and Conservative governments with respect to Indian affairs.

The Indian Act was amended in 1924 to give the Superintendent-General of Indian Affairs responsibility for Canada's Eskimo (Inuit) population. Interestingly, though, the Indian Act itself was not applied to Eskimos, in part due to the feeling that the Act was doing little to help Indians and that the problem should not be compounded by extending its coverage to other groups.

The most substantial changes occurred in 1951 with the passing of a new consolidated Indian Act. From the onset of the Depression to the end of the Second World War, little legislative adjustment had occurred in Indian affairs. Then from 1946 to 1948 Indian administration was subjected to a detailed review by a Special Joint Parliamentary Committee that went to unprecedented lengths to solicit Indian representations. As a consequence of the Committee hearings, a new Indian Act was introduced by the Liberal government in 1950, although it was withdrawn when Indians did not have enough time to react to the proposals. Following additional consultation with Indian groups, a revised act was passed a year later.

The 1951 Indian Act, like its predecessors, was framed to promote the integration of Indians into Canadian society (Dunning, 1962:210). The main features of the 1876 legislation had not been altered, although the revised Act reduced the degree of government intrusion into the cultural affairs of Indians. The prohibition on the Potlach was repealed, Indians were now allowed to consume liquor in public places, and the 1933 provision that allowed an Indian to be enfranchised without his consent was dropped, as was a 1927 ban on political organizing. In general the powers of the Minister were curtailed, although they remained formidable. Under the previous Act the Minister had the power to initiate action under 78 sections of the Act; this was reduced to only 26 sections (Miller et al., 1978:149).

A change of at least major symbolic significance occurred in 1960 when legislation prohibiting residents of reserves from voting in federal elections was repealed. Enfranchisement ceased to be held out as an enticement for assimilation. Citizenship and assimilation were no longer equated—one could be both an Indian and a full-fledged Canadian citizen, a combination that had been largely prevented by previous federal legislation.

In the 1960s the Indian Act still dominated Indian affairs in Canada. However, it should be noted that with the general expansion of government activity since the end of the Second World War, Indians came to be affected by an array of federal and provincial legislation from which the Indian Act and the treaties offered little shelter. As Cardinal (1977:97) has written, "it is difficult for Indian people to understand that many decisions that vitally affect them are made for reasons totally unrelated to the Indian scene and without regard to their effect on the Indians." Thus, as Indians today try to redefine their relationship with the government and with the nonIndian society, more than the Indian Act is at issue. To mention but a few illustrations, the Fisheries Act, the Migratory Birds Convention, and provincial fish and game regulations all come into play.

To conclude, although the Indian Act has been subjected to frequent review and amendment since 1876, at the end of the 1960s it did not differ greatly from the original form. Throughout the years a relatively consistent set of goals had prevailed, preventing any fundamental restructuring of the Act.

THE ADMINSTRATIVE EVOLUTION OF INDIAN AFFAIRS

The administration of Indian affairs in Canada has been less than straightforward throughout its long history. Canadian bureaucratic structures were built on the foundations laid down by the British colonial administration of Indian affairs. When the responsibility for Indians and Indian lands was assigned to the federal government in 1867, an Indian Affairs Branch was established within the Department of the Secretary of State for the Provinces. The post-Confederation administrative history of Indian affairs has been marked by frequent shifts in ministerial responsibility and by a slow evolution in departmental status and autonomy.

The Indian Affairs Branch remained within the Department of the Secretary of State for only a few years. In 1873 the Department of the Interior was created within the federal government and, as the new department was responsible for the administration and disposal of Crown lands, the responsibility for Indian lands seemed a natural extension of its mandate. Moreover, Interior was responsible for orchestrating the settlement of the West, an undertaking in which negotiations with western Indians would be of great importance. Therefore in 1874 Indian Affairs became a branch within the Department of the Interior and the Minister of the Interior became the Superintendent-General of Indian

Affairs. (From 1878 to 1895 Macdonald, acting as President of the Privy Council, and not the Minister of the Interior, served as Superintendent-General.)

Although Indian Affairs was now a branch within the Department of the Interior, settlement remained the principal responsibility, goal, and preoccupation of that Department. There was thus an inherent conflict lodged within the Department—that between expanded white settlement and the protection of Indian interests. In practice the conflict was attenuated as officials in the Indian Affairs Branch appear to have functioned not as advocates for Indians but as facilitators for the inevitable process of assimilation. Whether or not an independent Department of Indian Affairs would have defended Indian interests more successfully is difficult to assess; the answer may lie more in the goals that bureaucrats were trying to achieve than in the departmental context within which they worked. It is interesting to note though that some very powerful politicians served as Superintendents-General of Indian Affairs in large part because that post was occupied by the Minister of the Interior. Men such as Edgar Dewdney, Clifford Sifton, Frank Oliver, Arthur Meighen, Sir James A. Lougheed, H. H. Stevens, R. B. Bennett and T. A. Crerar would have been unlikely candidates for Superintendent-General had that post not been tied to the Department of the Interior. It might also be noted that the potential advantages and disadvantages of an autonomous Department of Indian Affairs are still being debated.

The evolution of Indian Affairs can be briefly summarized in the following chronology:

—1880: Indian Affairs Branch accorded departmental status although remaining under the control of the Minister of the Interior.

—1902: independent Deputy Superintendent of Indian Affairs established, ending the system whereby the Deputy of the Interior held the post.

—1936: Department of Indian Affairs transferred from Interior to the Department of Mines and Resources.

—1945: Indian Health Services transferred to the Department of National Health and Welfare.

—1949: Indian Affairs transferred to the Department of Citizenship and Immigration, thus lodging responsibility for the assimilation of new Canadians and Native Canadians within the same department.

—1965: Indian Affairs transferred to the Department of Northern Affairs and National Resources.

—1966: Department of Indian Affairs and Northern Development created.

The year 1966 also witnessed the release of the Hawthorn report, an extensive examination of the conduct of Indian affairs that had been commissioned by the Department in 1963. The Hawthorn report recommended a much more activist, and in a sense more partisan, role for Indian Affairs. The Department was urged to act as the national conscience, to be an advocate for Indian needs within the government and within the society.

THE EVOLUTION OF INDIAN POLICY

The confinement of legislative activity in Indian affairs to the national government and the legislative dominance of the Indian Act—compared to over 4000 separate and unsystematized statutory enactments in the United States (Harper, 1946:298)—make the evolution of Indian policy relatively easy to follow. There are, of course, some complications. In British Columbia, for example, provincial politicians routinely frustrated and undermined the actions of the national government (Miller et al., 1978:74). In addition the policies of the national government, particularly in the early decades after Confederation, were often different in Eastern Canada than they were in the West. Prime Minister Macdonald, for instance, in discussing 1880 legislation that restricted the sale of agricultural products by the Indians of Western Canada, commented (Miller et al., 1978:80) that the "wild nomads of the North-West" could not be judged on the same basis as the Indians of Ontario. Nevertheless, the major threads of public policy can be readily followed. Six major goals or policy motifs can be isolated and these will now be discussed in turn.

PROTECTION

The officials who forged Canadian Indian policy were not imbued with an overly noble view of white society. While they may have believed on balance that European civilization was unsurpassed in the advantages it had to offer, they were acutely aware of the evils of drink, greed, dishonesty and prostitution that flourished in great abundance, particularly on the edge of the frontier. Thus, one of the earliest and most humanitarian goals of Indian policy was the protection of Indians from the manifest evils of the white society. This goal led to laws prohibiting the private sale of Indian land, Indian consumption of alcohol, and the prostitution of Indian women. The reserve system itself (Harper, 1945:132) was in part a device to isolate and protect Indians, while at the same time becoming ". . . the cradle of the Indian civilizing effort and the means of securing the white man's freedom to exploit the vast riches of a growing dominion." The prominence of protection as a policy goal, however, faded over time, although as late as 1930 there was an amendment to the Indian Act restricting the use of poolrooms by Indians, and it was not until the sixties that all prohibitions on Indian use of liquor were removed.

The policy of protection, guardianship, or wardship fostered an air of paternalism in the administration of Indian affairs that has been difficult to dispell. The development of paternalistic attitudes was understandable given the early history of Indian-nonIndian contact in North America. Indians had not been successful in defending themselves or their land in the face of advancing nonIndian settlement and the government had become a buffer between the Indians and the crush of settlement. However, rather than acting as an impregnable wall the government pursued the more limited goal of temporarily protecting Indians until they could be assimilated into the white society. This protective stance led in turn to the attitude that Indians' views on their own welfare were not to be given much weight, that the government knew the best interest of the Indian people in the long run. Thus, for example, the Minister of the Interior, Clifford Sifton, advised Governor-General Minto in 1899 that while the Department of Indian Affairs would consider Indian views as far as possible, the right of Indians to control the action of the Department would not be recognized "under any circumstances" (Miller et al., 1978:100). This outlook, coupled with the sweeping powers of the Indian Act and the high proportion of former military men and clergymen with Indian Affairs, entrenched paternalism within the Department. As a target for Indian protest it has persisted to this day.

ASSIMILATION

If there has been a central pillar to Canadian Indian policy, it has been the goal of assimilation. While the terminology has varied among "assimilation," "integration," "civilization," and "moving into the mainstream," the policy has remained virtually unaltered; Indians were to be prepared for absorption into the broader Canadian society. It was expected that eventually Indians would shed their Native languages, customs and religious beliefs, and would become self-sufficient members of the modern Canadian society and labour force. In 1880 Sir John A. Macdonald, speaking as Minister of Indian Affairs, stated (Miller et al., 1978:191) that government policy towards Indians was

. . . to wean them by slow degrees, from their nomadic habits, which have become almost an instinct, and by slow degrees absorb them on the land. Meantime, they must be fairly protected.

In 1950 the then-Minister Walter E. Harris announced a new Indian policy that echoed the words of Macdonald seventy years earlier (Miller et al., 1978:191):

The ultimate goal of our Indian policy is the integration of the Indians into the general life and economy of the country. It is recognized, however, that during a temporary transition period . . . special treatment and legislation are necessary.

In the intervening years interpretations of Indian policy followed the same theme. In 1920, for instance, the Deputy Superintendent-General of Indian Affairs spoke as follows to a Special Committee of the House of Commons on proposed changes in the enfranchisement provisions of the Indian Act:

. . . our object is to continue until there is not a single Indian in Canada that has not been absorbed into the body politic and there is no question, and no Indian Department, that is the whole object of this Bill (Miller et al., 1978:114).

After the end of the Second World War when the period of settlement and treaty-making was long past, and when the process of assimilation was well underway, the complete assimilation of Indians into the Canadian mainstream became a less pressing concern. In the post-war years there was an increased acceptance of cultural pluralism (Palmer, 1976), and the positive aspects of Indian traditions began to receive greater recognition. The idea that a common Canadian citizenship was compatible with ethnic and cultural distinctiveness began to be entertained. Nevertheless, the principle of assimilation that had guided Indian policy over the past hundred years was neither abandoned nor fundamentally modified.

The goal of assimilation raises the very touchy charge of cultural genocide. Genocide, one of the most emotionally charged words in the English language, must be used with caution. Nevertheless, the primacy of assimilation as a policy goal gives credence to Indian claims that cultural genocide has been at least an implicit goal in the administration of Indian affairs. When an outside observer (Harper, 1945:127) concludes that "the extinction of the Indians as Indians" is the ultimate end of Canadian public policy, the charge of genocide cannot be lightly brushed aside.[1]

Despite the zeal with which assimilation was pursued, the policy largely failed. Due to Indians' isolation, racial and linguistic distinctiveness, marginality to the labour force, and the gulf between Native and European cultural patterns, Indians proved to be a difficult group to assimilate. A large part of the responsibility for the failure of assimilation must be laid at the feet of the broader Canadian society. Ironically, the government's pursuit of assimilation did little to create a receptive climate for assimilating Indians within the Canadian public. In fact, the obstacles posed by societal discrimination and prejudice were immense;

Indians attempting to leave their traditional society encountered little by way of reward, compensation, or encouragement for their efforts. Government policy tried to induce Indians into a mainstream that was unwilling to receive them.

Assimilation was also impeded by the conflict between the policy goals of protection and assimilation. As mentioned, the Indian Act formed a major barrier to assimilation by setting Indians apart from the society they were expected to join. The desire to protect Indians, the reserve system, the laws discouraging social interaction and some forms of inter-marriage, and the special provision of federal government services all impeded assimilation. Not uncharacteristically, the government tried simultaneously to achieve conflicting policy goals. In the end assimilation—not to mention Indians—was the victim.

CHRISTIANITY

The policy of assimilation was buttressed by a number of supporting policies, one of which was the spread of Christianity to the Indian population. As Harper (1945:122) observed:

> In Canada the civilization of the Indian is made synonymous with his Christianization. Indian missions, in fact, enjoy government favour; the aboriginal religious and ceremonial practices are officially discouraged. Next to the attainment of the goal of self-support, the Indian's conversion from pagan belief to Christianity is the most important criterion for judging his fitness to assume an equal place in the white man's society.

It must be remembered here that the entwinement of the Christian church with the administration of Indian affairs was virtually inevitable. In many cases missionaries spearheaded the first white contact with Indians in the interior of the continent and the missionaries were frequently the most successful in learning Indian languages and mores. Many missionaries worked vigorously to protect Indians and often found themselves serving as intermediaries between government officials and the Indians. It must also be borne in mind that the early church and missionary work in North America attracted some individuals of outstanding character and drive who were bound to leave their stamp on the policies of their times.

The church came to play a very important role in the education of Indians. In the early years education was viewed, as it still is, as an essential tool of assimilation. The responsibility for Indian education, however, was largely left by the government to the churches. Regardless of its short term merits, in the long run this strategy was to prove unsatisfactory. Because the religious residential schools isolated Indians from other students, assimilation was impaired. Because their curricula served as much as a vehicle for Christianization as for secular education, the secular education of Indians suffered in comparison to that received by nonIndians. The small number of graduates from the residential schools found themselves at a disadvantage when moving on to advanced secular education or when moving into the larger society. Finally, the residential schools were a source of great disruption and antagonism within the Native communities and did little to enhance the value of education in the eyes of Native students (Cardinal, 1969:87-95).

By the 1960s the traditional role of the church in Indian affairs was drawing to a close. As a result of the increased secularization of the Canadian society and of the almost total separation of church and state, Christianization flagged as a policy goal. The education of Indians passed into secular hands and by the mid-sixties the denominational residential school system was being abandoned. Although education remained a vehicle for assimilation it was no longer a vehicle driven by the churches.

RESERVES AND SELF-SUFFICIENCY

An important means of assimilation was the settlement of Indians into agriculturally-based communities. Settlement allowed other instruments of assimilation such as churches, schools and limited local government to be more readily brought into effect. Moreover, to the extent that settlement proceeded, large tracts of land formerly held by Indians could be freed for nonIndian settlement, for the exploitation of natural resources, and for the development of lines of communication stitching together the new country (Upton, 1973:51). The success of Indian settlement was of great importance in western Canada where Indian land holdings were large and where settlement pressure from nonIndians was building steadily as the nineteenth century drew to a close. Indeed, the immigration boom of the early twentieth century increased pressure even on the newly-founded Indian reserves and the government began to actively encourage Indian land surrenders and moved to make "excess" Indian reserve land available for nonIndian settlement. In 1911 the Indian Act was amended to allow for the expropriation of reserve lands for public works. Speaking to the amendment, Minister of the Interior, Oliver (Miller et al., 1978:108) ". . . claimed that the *whim* of a band would no longer obstruct a provincially-chartered railroad company from developing a certain part of the country" (our emphasis). In the clash between nonIndian settlement and the protection of Indian interests, public policy clearly came down on the side of the former, although Indian interests were by no means totally abandoned.

In the pursuit of assimilation the government tried to make Indians as self-supporting as possible. Harper (1945:120), in noting the importance of self-sufficiency in both the Indian Act and the administration of Indian affairs, quoted the first page of administrative instructions sent to every Indian agent in 1933:

> It may be stated as a first principle that it is the policy of the Department to promote self-support among the Indians and not to provide gratuitous assistance to those Indians who can provide for themselves.

It should be stressed in this regard that the policy of encouraging self-support was not motivated solely by the desire to limit public expenditures in support of Indians; the desire to promote the integration of Indians into the Canadian economy was also an important motivation. Yet here again the policy was frustrated by the legislative restrictions of the Indian Act. The prohibition of mortgages on Indian land and restrictions on the ability of outside creditors to collect debts from reserve residents curtailed the infusion of outside capital into the Indian economy. Self-support and fiscal self-management were also frustrated by the paternalism of Indian Affairs. Not only were band funds under the control of the Department, but even the most straightforward financial and entrepreneurial enterprises by Indians required Departmental approval if they involved contact with the nonIndian society. The government "red-tape" inherent in this process posed yet a further obstacle.

An interesting step towards greater self-sufficiency was taken by the community development program launched by Indian Affairs in the early 1960s. This program sought to mobilize the Indian population, to create conditions of economic and social progress for the whole community by encouraging the maximum amount of community participation, initiative, and self-reliance. The program called for a change in emphasis from people *administration* to people *development*. To this end sixty-two community development officers were hired by Indian Affairs to work as resource persons and coordinators in the Indian communities. However, despite, or because of, its early successes the program quickly disintegrated in a welter of bureaucratic infighting and conflicts among the community development staff, Indian agents, senior bureaucrats, and factions in the Indian communities. The community development staff, torn between loyalty to their employer and to the Indian people, frequently found themselves as partisans on the side of the Indians against the government, and as such their support and effectiveness within the Indian Affairs bureaucracy rapidly dissipated. Concluding that the community development program threw sand in the gears of efficient administration, IIAP moved to terminate the program.

ENFRANCHISEMENT

The principal reward held out to Indians contemplating assimilation was enfranchisement. The equation of assimilation with enfranchisement and full citizenship was not an unexpected policy in a young country faced with the absorption of a large and polyglot immigrant population; in this sense Indian policy reflected a more general policy perspective within the society. However, the costs to be paid by an Indian seeking enfranchisement far surpassed those paid by non-British immigrants to Canada.

The enfranchisement provisions of the Indian Act equated citizenship with cultural characteristics; only Indians who fit the dominant cultural mode could be full citizens. Indians who clung to Native traditions or to reserve land clearly did not fall into this category. We can assume that in the eyes of policy makers, "rights" as we know them today were associated with enfranchisement. Here we would include such things as the right to vote, freedom of speech, the right to organize, and so forth. The "rights" imbedded in the Indian Act and the treaties, on the other hand, were seen more as transitory means of protection rather than as inalienable rights as we would perceive such today. According to that line of thought, these lesser rights could be justifiably trimmed away when they were no longer needed as a means of protection. For example, reserve land that was not needed to support the Indian population could be made available for nonIndian settlement or farming; the Indian right to the land in this case was not equated with the more basic property rights associated with enfranchisement and citizenship. In effect, the types of Indian rights under debate today were probably not recognized as such in the nineteenth century.

As a lure for assimilation, enfranchisement clearly failed. The rate of assimilation remained extremely low, much lower in fact than the rate of Indian population growth. As Hawthorn (1960:482) found in British Columbia, the great bulk of adult enfranchisement was involuntary, coming from Indian women marrying nonIndian males. Among the adult male Indians in British Columbia who sought enfranchisement, the principal lures were the eventual pursuit of American citizenship and the right to gain access to liquor stores and thus engage in bootlegging. The right to vote itself offered little attraction, in part because it was already available to Indian veterans, Indians living off reserves, and Indians living on reserves who waived taxation privileges.

In 1960 all Indians were enfranchised for federal elections. It was recognized at last that full citizenship in the Canadian state need not be conditional upon complete assimilation into the Canadian society. The legitimacy of cultural pluralism and cultural distinctiveness for Canada's aboriginal inhabitants had been recognized.

THE TREATIES

The first treaty between Indians and colonial officials in North America was signed in 1670 and the last Canadian treaty (by such name) was signed in 1923; the last American treaty was signed in 1871. During the intervening years a multitude of treaties of varying format and complexity were concluded. These generally included many or most of the following: an agreement of peace and amity, the cession of land, initial payments to Indians, small annual payments in cash and/or goods, the designation of chiefs and councillors to negotiate and administer the treaty, guarantee of land reserved for Indians and/or right to use unoccupied territory in its natural state, and promises of government services such as education and health care (Smith, 1975:xxvii). Perhaps the major treaties in Canada have been the numbered treaties on the prairies (starting with Treaty One in 1871 and ending with Treaty Ten in 1906) which opened the western territories for settlement and the construction of the CPR.

Although this is not the place for a thorough examination of the Indian treaties, there are some policy perspectives entailed in the treaties that should be mentioned. For example, as the treaties were signed to extinguish Indian title to the land, they carried with them the explicit recognition of Indian ownership rights. Treaty Seven, to cite but one illustration, calls for Indians to "cede, release, surrender, and yield up to the Government of Canada . . ." traditional lands in the then North-West Territories. Lands not so released remained as Indian reserves, the land being held in trust for Indian people by the Crown.

As mentioned earlier, there is considerable room for confusion between rights that derive from treaties and those that come from the Indian Act. Here it should be kept in mind that the various treaties are by no means identical in content and that no treaties were signed with Indians in Quebec, the Maritimes, and most of British Columbia. For registered Indians not under treaty—almost half of the registered Indian population—the only claim they have to their land is that based on aboriginal rights, that is, the rights of occupancy of the first settlers of the land which have never been officially yielded to the Canadian government. The legal character and potency of treaty and aborigial rights cannot be equated.

There is also room for confusion about the conception of "rights" that was brought to the treaty-making process by Indians and whites. As Smith (1975:xxviii) points out, while the treaties

. . . clearly reflect national policy towards Indians, especially when viewed in historical perspective, it can never be assumed that these truly reflect the agreement and understanding of Indians.

The Indian perspective is set out by Harold Cardinal (1969:29); the treaties were

. . . the beginning of a contractual relationship whereby the representatives of the Queen would have lasting responsibilities to the Indian people in return for valuable lands that were ceded to them.

In this respect the National Indian Brotherhood argues that free Indian education in perpetuity has been paid for by the lands released by treaty. The government perspective at the time of the signings was quite different, although this conclusion is deduced from the Indian policies of the time rather than from the letter of the treaties themselves. To government officials, the critical feature of the treaties was that they ceded Indian ownership of the land; the treaties were more important for what Indians gave up than for the concessions given to Indians. Government officials also viewed the treaties as a means of providing transitional protection of an indigenous people who were faced with eventual assimilation or extinction. It is unlikely that officials at the time read into the treaties the scope and duration of responsibilities that Indians are claiming today.

It is also unlikely that the treaty-making process had the bilateral quality that is frequently assumed or asserted today. As MacInnes (1946:387), Green (1969:11), and others have argued, the treaties were approached by the government less as a matter of negotiation than as a take-it-or-leave-it proposition. Finally, it should also be noted that the conditions surrounding the signing of the treaties were often less than equitable and were not such as to ensure that Indian interests were fairly protected (Cardinal, 1969:36).

The policy interpretations applied to the treaties have taken on a moral rather than a legal character (Green, 1969:14). For example, the Indian Chiefs of Alberta (1970:8) argued in *Citizens Plus* that treaty clauses promising machinery and livestock symbolized a lasting government commitment to economic development, a commitment that is not easily read into the letter of some of the treaties themselves. Medicine chest clauses provide another example of legal interpretation. Treaty Six, signed near Fort Carlton and Fort Pitt in 1876, provides that "a medicine chest shall be kept at the house of each Indian agent for the use and benefit of the Indians at the direction of such agent." The scope of this and similar clauses in other treaties has come under considerable debate. In 1935 the Treaty Six clause was interpreted by the Exchequer Court of Britain (*Draver vs The King*) to mean that all drugs or medical supplies required by Indians should be supplied to them free of charge. However, in this decision testimony from Indians who were actually present at the signing of the treaty and at related discussions was critical; the letter of the treaty alone did not form the basis of the court decision (Macdonald, 1970:177). During the 1970s the scope and perpetuity of government obligations with respect to medicine chest clauses have come under frequent debate. In a broader sense the policy implications of treaty rights appear likely to remain a matter of controversy for the foreseeable future.

The evolution of Indian policy in Canada has been shaped by changes in the larger society which have exerted very significant pressure on Indians, the administration of Indian affairs, and the direction of this policy. A striking example of the impingement of external societal developments on the evolution of Indian policy is provided by the 1969 White Paper.

THE 1969 WHITE PAPER

During the 1960s Indian affairs in Canada came to be so buffetted by the winds of social change that a climate of confusion and near turmoil prevailed. Inside the bureaucracy IIAP had been experimenting with community development programs, the transfer of programs and responsibilities to provincial governments, increased grants to bands, and the creation of regional and national Indian Advisory Boards. The experiments were at best a mixed success and IIAP came under heavy criticism from other agencies within the national government (Weaver, 1978:2-3). The Hawthorn report, released in the mid-sixties, raised further searching questions about the direction of IIAP and of Indian policy.

Externally, the sixties witnessed the initial stirrings of Indian activism both in Canada and the United States. The American civil rights movement indirectly called into question the legal segregation of Canadian Indians through the Indian Act, and civil rights advocates in Canada began to pay increased attention to the plight of Indians. Many Canadians felt that advances in civil rights, such as the provisions of the new Bill of Rights outlawing discrimination on the basis of race, colour or creed, should apply equally to Indians as to other Canadians. Politically, a new Liberal government led by Pierre Trudeau, with his promise of a "just society," was elected in 1968 and Canadians within and outside the government tried to reconcile the promise of the "just society" with the conditions faced by Canadian Indians. These various forces were not to leave Indian affairs untouched.

The new Liberal government was imbued with a strong liberal ideology that stressed individualism and the protection of individual rights. Reflecting a combination of North American ideological tenets that can be traced back to the American Revolution, Trudeau's personal ideological beliefs, and his deep antagonism to ethnic nationalism in Quebec, the government quickly adopted a new approach to Indian affairs that emphasized individual equality and de-emphasized collective ethnic survival. Indians as individuals were to be helped at the expense of Indians as a people. On June 25, 1969 Jean Chrétien, Minister of Indian Affairs and Northern Development, tabled ''A Statement of the Government of Canada on Indian Policy'' in the House of Commons. The statement, or White Paper as it quickly became known, advocated far-reaching changes in the administration of Indian affairs and in the legislative framework that governed Indian-white relations. As the White Paper (Government of Canada, 1969:5) stated:

> The Government believes that its policies must lead to the full, free and non-discriminatory participation of the Indian people in Canadian society. Such a goal requires a break with the past. It requires that the Indian people's role of dependence be replaced by a role of equal status, opportunity and responsibility, a role they can share with all other Canadians.

More specifically the White Paper proposed that the legislative and constitutional bases of discrimination be removed; the Indian Act was to be repealed. Rather than being legislatively set apart, Indians were to receive the same services as other Canadians and these were to be delivered to Indians through the same channels and from the same government agencies as serviced other Canadians. The unique federal government responsibility for Indians was to end. The Indian Affairs Programme within DIAND was to be abolished and any residual responsibilities that were not transferred to provincial governments or to bands were to be transferred to other departments within the federal government.

The White Paper sought an end to paternalism and discrimination, and the abolition of the Indian Affairs Programme was to be a major step in that direction. In addition the White Paper proposed that the control of Indian lands be transferred to the Indian people; land would no longer be held in trust for Indians by the Crown. The White Paper also recognized that any lawful obligations that the government had incurred through the signing of the treaties must be recognized, although here the government expressed the very limited interpretation of treaty rights discussed above (Government of Canada, 1969:11):

> The terms and the effects of the treaties between the Indian people and the Government are widely misunderstood. A plain reading of the words used in the treaties reveals the limited and minimal promises which were included in them . . . the significance of the treaties in meeting the economic, educational, health and welfare needs of the Indian people has always been limited and will continue to decline. The services that have been provided go far beyond what could have been foreseen by those who signed the treaties.

The government also proposed that the Indian bands that were the farthest behind economically should receive special assistance. Universal aid programs were to be discontinued in favour of selective aid to particular bands, aid that would come from a wide range of government departments. Finally the White Paper called for a "positive recognition by everyone of the unique contribution of Indian culture to Canadian life" (Government of Canada, 1969:6).

The White Paper clearly reflected the contemporary tide of social change in North America. Those concerned with civil rights in Canada, people who were perhaps more sensitive to the winds of social change that were sweeping the United States and the Third World than they were to the reality of Canadian Indian conditions, had begun to label the reserve system and the Indian Act as Canada's apartheid policy. The facts that the Canadian government still drew legislative distinctions on the basis of race and that Indians fell largely outside the coverage of the Bill of Rights were intolerable to many people. As Weaver (forthcoming) points out, the White Paper was also a response to values within the policy-making arena of the national government. It was designed more to protect the government from external criticism than to meet the aspirations of Canadian Indians as these were perceived by Indians themselves.

In its stress upon achieving contemporary equality for Indians the White Paper paid scant attention to the liabilities that had been accumulating for Indians from the inequalities of the past. Nor did the White Paper acknowledge that discrimination in fact may exist even when discrimination in law has been abolished, and that as a consequence the special legal protection of minority rights may be necessary (Green, 1979:2-3). As Weaver (1973:3) points out, the problem of reconciling demands for special status with the principle of equality is an old and enduring one for democratic societies; the White Paper solution was to come down on the side of equality. The rights of the individual were placed above the collective survival of the group.

Prime Minister Trudeau was one of the most articulate defenders of the White Paper. The following is from a speech that Trudeau delivered in Vancouver on August 8, 1969, shortly after the White Paper had been released (Macdonald, 1970: Appendix 8):

> We can go on treating the Indians as having a special status. We can go on adding bricks of discrimination around the ghetto in which they live and at the same time perhaps helping them preserve certain cultural traits and certain ancestral rights. Or we can say you're at a crossroads—the time is now to decide whether the Indians will be a race apart in Canada or whether it will be Canadians of full status. And this is a difficult choice. . . . It's inconceivable, I think, that in a given society one section of the society have a treaty with the other section of the society. We must all be equal under the

laws and we must not sign treaties amongst ourselves . . . What can we do to redeem the past? I can only say as President Kennedy said when he was asked what he could do to compensate for the injustices that the Negroes had received in American society: "We will be just in our time." This is all we can do. We must be just today.

The White Paper departed very significantly from the Hawthorn report which had been released only three years earlier and which had been generally well-received by the Indian community (Weaver, 1976). The Hawthorn report had recommended that the Department act as a more forceful advocate of Indian interests within the government. This role, which had been rejected by the Department, was also rejected by the White Paper recommendation that the Indian Affairs Programme be abolished. The Hawthorn report recommended the retention of a modified Indian Act; the White Paper sought the Act's abolition. Both agreed, however, that provincial services should be extended to Indians and that the exclusive federal responsibility for Indian affairs should be discontinued. Here the White Paper was reinforcing a legal critique of provincial abstention from Indian affairs that had been developing for some time (Lysyk, 1967:553):

. . . where Parliament has not legislated, and putting aside matters relating to Indian lands, the provinces have a relatively free hand in legislating for the well being of the Indian, and this is so with respect to reserve Indians no less than for those who have moved off the reserve into the mainstream of non-Indian society.

The Hawthorn report, because it had been well-received by Indians and because it disagreed with the White Paper in several key areas, became a focal reference point for Indian opposition to the White Paper as that opposition mobilized.

It took some time for the nascent Indian organizations to gauge the response of their memberships to the White Paper, but as the Indian reaction was mobilized and orchestrated the rejection of the White Paper took on landslide proportions. Wuttunee's (1971:23) description of the White Paper as "a dramatic breakthrough for the Indian people" was clearly a minority perspective. Indian hostility to the White Paper was crystallized in a number of documents, one being Cardinal's *The Unjust Society*. Cardinal (1969:1) charged that the new Indian policy was ". . . a thinly disguised programme of extermination through assimilation," that the White Paper postulated that "the only good Indian is a non-Indian." Cardinal was particularly angry with the proposal to turn over the responsibility for Indians to the provincial governments (1969:30-31):

We will be fearful of any attempt by the federal government to turn over to provincial governments responsibility for Indian affairs. We will be certain that the federal government is merely attempting to abandon it's responsibilities. Provincial governments have no obligations to fulfill our treaties. They never signed treaties with the Indians. We could not expect them to be concerned with treaty rights. In our eyes, this new government policy merely represents a disguised move to abrogate all our treaty rights.

A second document, *Citizens Plus*, was presented by the Indian chiefs of Alberta to Prime Minister Trudeau in June, 1970. *Citizens Plus* was introduced by the following excerpt from the Hawthorn report:

> Indians should be regarded as 'Citizens Plus'; in addition to the normal rights and duties of citizenship, Indians possess certain additional rights as charter members of the Canadian community.

Stating that the White Paper offered "despair instead of hope," *Citizens Plus* (p. 4) went on to reject the central proposal of the White Paper:

> The White Paper Policy said "that the legislative and constitutional bases of discrimination should be removed". We reject this policy. We say that the recognition of Indian status is essential for justice. . . . justice requires that the special history, rights and circumstances of Indian people be recognized.

Citizens Plus reiterated Cardinal's rejection of the transfer of responsibilities to the provincial governments; again this was seen as an attempt to renege on the treaties and responsibilities set forth in the BNA Act. The White Paper proposal that Indian Affairs be abolished was also rejected. Instead the authors called for the creation of a full-time Minister of Indian Affairs: "we are insulted because it is clear that the Government does not intend to regard its Indian people as deserving proper cabinet representation" (1970:10). In the face of continued and virulent Indian opposition the White Paper proposals were formally retracted by the Trudeau government in 1971, although the legacy of suspicion and mistrust which they left in their wake remains strong to this day.

CONCLUSIONS

The 1969 White Paper was the capstone of a policy of assimilation that can be traced back to the pre-Confederation years. Its rejection by Indians and its formal retraction by the government in 1971 thus marks a watershed in the evolution of Indian affairs in Canada. Assimilation was at least officially placed aside as an explicit policy goal, although it may well continue as a socio-economic and cultural process. The page was being turned on what had been the central theme of Indian policy over the past one hundred and thirty years. The rejection of the White Paper therefore opened up a new and confused policy era; the direction of Indian policy in the seventies was suddenly "up for grabs." Yet while the policies of the past were being put aside, the development of alternative policies was to prove to be an incredibly complex process, the complexity in part coming from a basic change in the composition of the policy makers. Through to the publication of the White Paper, Indian policy in the past had been formulated with very little Indian input and frequently in opposition to Indian goals and interests. In the seventies Indians were to be deeply involved.

NOTES

1. In addition Patterson (1972:63,74) notes that not only were bounties placed on the heads of the Beothuk Indians in Newfoundland, but the British General Jeffrey Amherst waged biological warfare against the Indians. He distributed to Indians blankets known to be infected with smallpox, when it was also known that the disease was often fatal to Indians due to their lack of natural immunity to it.

Chapter 2

A Socio-Demographic Profile of Indians in Canada*

contributed by
Andrew J. Siggner

INTRODUCTION

With the development in recent years of the "policy sciences," policy formulation in the realm of Indian affairs has become increasingly systematized and professionalized. It is now widely recognized that a thorough understanding of the demographic structures and processes of the population under consideration is fundamental to most policy development assignments. Thus, one of the main purposes of this chapter is to present a basic demographic and socio-economic profile of the Indian population in Canada. A second objective is to extract from the data implications about the structures of opportunity—or lack thereof—which are available to Indians, for the opening of opportunities to Indians is clearly going to be one of the main preoccupations of policy makers in governments and Indian organizations alike during the 1980s. In so doing we must exercise caution so as to avoid falling into the trap of assuming that Indians' goals and values are all identical to those of other Canadians. However, inasmuch as Indian leaders have made well known some of the opportunities which Indian people seek, and inasmuch as there is a certain amount of overlap in the goals and values of Indians and nonIndians, we can nevertheless cautiously use the concept of opportunities or enhanced "life chances" as a motif for this chapter.

---

* Views, opinions, and interpretations expressed in this chapter are those of the author and do not necessarily represent those of the Department of Indian Affairs and Northern Development.

SIZE, DISTRIBUTION, AND CULTURAL
COMPOSITION

Historical records on the size of the Indian population are sketchy.[1] Kroeber (1939) estimates that prior to the arrival of Europeans, the total Indian population of North America was about 900,000 people, of whom about 220,000 were in what is now Canada. The introduction of firearms from Europe was one of several factors contributing to a subsequent decline in the Indian population. By the seventeenth century both intertribal warfare and English-French warfare, into which Indians were drawn as allies of the Europeans, were also taking their toll on the Indian population. Particularly devastating were the famines (e.g., that of 1879-80 on the Prairies) and epidemic diseases such as smallpox, scarlet fever, tuberculosis, and influenza, against which Indians had no natural immunity. Epidemics of these diseases were numerous and sometimes literally decimated the population they struck. For instance, Fumoleau (1976) estimates that the smallpox epidemics of 1781-84 eliminated nine-tenths of the Chipewyans.

With the advent of Confederation in 1867, record-keeping improved somewhat. Shortly after Confederation the Indian population of what is now Canada was approximately 102,000. Over the next seventy years (to 1941), the Indian population apparently fluctuated between that level and about 122,000,[2] which in turn represented from 2.5% to 1.1% of the total Canadian population. It was not until 1941 that the Indian population began to show a pattern of sustained growth and it was not until 1966 that the Indian population of Canada again reached the size it had been just prior to European contact.

By the end of 1979 the registered Indian population stood at about 309,000, which was 1.3% of the total Canadian population. The distribution of the population across Canada is shown in Table 2.1. There we observe that Indians are most numerous in Ontario and British Columbia, which between them account for four of every ten Indians in Canada. The Prairie provinces account for another four out of ten and Quebec for one out of ten. However, as Table 2.1 shows, when we rank the provinces according to the proportion of the total provincial population composed of Indians, a quite different ordering from that cited above emerges. In the Northwest Territories and Yukon, registered Indians constitute a larger share (17% and 13%, respectively) of the population than they do in any of the ten provinces. In fact, when all aboriginal peoples are combined together in the Northwest Territories, they make up the majority of the Territorial population. This fact could take on added importance in the 1980s as the Territories gain greater political autonomy from DIAND. In the western five provinces, registered Indians constitute less than 5% of the respective provincial

TABLE 2.1
Regional Distribution of The Indian Population and Indian Lands, 1977

REGION	INDIAN POPULATION*				INDIAN LANDS			
	Number	Percent of Canadian Indian Population	Percent of Total Provincial Population, 1977	Percent off Reserve**	Number of Bands	Number of Reserves and/or Settlements	Approximate Area (1977) of Reserves (x 1000 Hectares†)	Average Area of Reserve or Settlement (x 1000 Hectares†)
	(A)	(B)	(C)	(D)	(E)	(F)	(G)	(H)
Atlantic	11,093	3.7	0.5	26.2	29	64	24	0.4
Quebec	30,175	10.2	0.5	18.1	39	39	77	1.9
Ontario	66,057	22.3	0.8	31.6	115	171	691	3.6
Manitoba	43,349	14.6	4.4	25.2	57	103	215	2.1
Saskatchewan	44,986	15.2	4.4	29.8	68	124	551	4.1
Alberta	35,162	11.9	2.7	21.9	41	96	653	6.7
British Columbia	54,318	18.4	2.4	36.1	194	1,629	335	0.2
N.W.T.	7,541	2.5	17.4	3.6	16	29	13	0.03
Yukon	3,217	1.1	12.7	17.6	14	26	<.5	0.1
Canada	295,898	99.9	1.3	27.6	573	2,281	2,559	1.1

* The registered Indian population has not been adjusted for late-reported births. However, such an adjustment would be unlikely to significantly alter the percentages shown in this table.

** Here and in the text "off reserve" is used to mean "off-reserve, off crown land".

† 1 hectare = 2.5 acres; 1000 hectares = 2500 acres = 3.91 square miles. Thus, from the bottom of column (H), the *average* size of a reserve in Canada is 4.3 square miles. Many, however, are much larger.

Sources: —Statistics Division, *Registered Indian Population by Sex and Residence, 1977*. Ottawa: Programme Reference Centre, IIAP, 1979, (columns A, B, D, and E).
—*Census of Canada, 1971*, (calculations for column C).
—James Frideres, *Canada's Indians*. Scarborough: Prentice Hall, for columns F and G.

populations, while in the separate provinces of Central and Eastern Canada, Indians account for less than one percent of the population. Clearly, then, Indians on their own do not have the force of numbers to be able to sway the electoral system.

Table 2.1 also contains data bearing upon a major controversy of the 1970s, namely which level of government shall have jurisdiction over registered Indians living off-reserve and off-crown land (hereafter referred to as "off-reserve"). In question here, as of 1977, is the well-being of about eighty-two thousand individuals (up from 36,000 in 1966), or 28% of the status Indian population (compared to 16% in 1966). Since we shall consider in Chapter Six the jurisdictional controversy in which these people are caught, suffice it to say here that the pronounced inter-provincial variation in the proportion of the population living off-reserve is likely, in large part, a reflection of the opportunities which Indians perceived to exist on and off-reserve. In particular, during the last half of the 1960s many reserves were experiencing severe economic depression and over-crowding in housing. On the other hand, the urban industrial areas of Ontario and British Columbia appeared to offer one of the few remaining sources of hope for young, largely unskilled, English-speaking Indians in those regions.[3] Then, as urban industrial growth slackened in the early 1970s and as Indians encountered the barriers of discrimination in employment, housing, and social life, data suggest that a movement back to the reserves occurred, along with a diminution of the out-migration from reserves. The result was that the proportion living off-reserve ceased its rapid increase and stabilized around 1975 at about 27%. Other relevant factors in the opportunity structure of the 1970s which might have contributed to this stabilization would be increases in the on-reserve housing supply, new economic development projects, and the government's official endorsement of a policy of Indian control of Indian education.

Two highly relevant characteristics of Indian bands for any understanding of the opportunity structure which they offer, are their population size and geographic location. Table 2.2 shows the distribution of Indian bands on these two characteristics. From the left panel of that table it can be seen that most Indian bands are rather small in size. Indeed, only about thirteen percent of all bands in Canada have a membership in excess of one thousand people, and almost all of the "large" bands of more than two thousand population are concentrated in just three provinces, namely Ontario, Manitoba, and Alberta. Almost half of all bands have a population of three hundred people or less, and some regions, notably British Columbia and the Yukon, have the vast majority of their bands falling in this category. When this fact is considered in the light of our earlier observation that over a quarter of the status Indian population now lives off-reserve, one must conclude that the on-reserve popula-

TABLE 2.2
Numerical and Percentage Distribution of Indian Bands by Size and Geographic Location, for Regions, 1977

REGION	TOTAL BANDS		DISTRIBUTION OF BANDS BY POPULATION SIZE										DISTRIBUTION OF BANDS BY GEOGRAPHIC LOCATION*							
			0-100		101-300		301-1000		1001-2000		2000+		Remote		Rural		Semi-Urban		Urban	
	#	%	#	%	#	%	#	%	#	%	#	%	#	%	#	%	#	%	#	%
Atlantic	29	100	5	17	10	35	12	41	2	7	—	—	—	—	13	45	10	34	6	21
Quebec	39	100	5	13	6	15	17	44	10	26	1	3	14	36	5	13	15	38	5	13
Ontario	115	100	20	17	40	35	40	35	10	9	5	4	34	30	52	45	21	18	8	7
Manitoba	57	100	3	5	6	11	32	56	12	21	4	7	25	44	26	46	5	9	1	2
Sask.	68	100	2	3	11	16	41	60	12	18	2	3	10	15	43	63	13	19	2	3
Alberta	41	100	4	10	9	22	18	44	6	15	4	10	7	17	19	46	12	29	3	7
B.C.	194	100	54	28	81	42	53	27	6	3	—	—	53	27	77	40	41	21	23	12
N.W.T.	16	100	—	—	6	38	9	56	1	6	—	—	8	—	7	—	1	—	—	—
Yukon	14	100	2	14	10	71	2	14	—	—	—	—	13	—	—	—	—	—	1	—
Canada	573	100	95	17	179	31	224	39	59	10	16	3	164	29	242	42	118	21	49	9

* For definitions of geographic location categories, see the text.

Source: Statistics Division, Registered Indian Population By Sex and Residence, 1977. Ottawa: Programme Reference Centre, IIAP, 1979.

TABLE 2.3
Percentage Distribution of Registered Indian Population
by Residence and Band Location, 1977

RESIDENCE	BAND LOCATION†				
	Urban	Semi-Urban	Rural	Remote	Total
On Reserve*	14.9%	19.8%	37.4%	27.9%	100.0%
Off Reserve	13.9%	22.6%	41.6%	21.9%	100.0%
Total	14.6%	20.6%	38.6%	26.2%	100.0%

† See definitions in the text.
* Includes on Crown Land.

Source: Statistics Division, *Registered Indian Population By Sex and Residence,*
1977. Ottawa: Programme Reference Centre, IIAP, 1979.

tion of hundreds of Indian bands is so small as to itself create major
problems. For instance, many such small bands lack the minimum
population, especially in the labour force age group, to sustain viable
economic development enterprises. Also, their populations are too small
to permit the band to realize economies of scale in the delivery of services, which is to say that the per capita cost of services for such bands is
high.

In the right hand panel of Table 2.2, we observe that almost a third of
all bands in Canada—representing over a quarter of the Indian population (Table 2.3)—are geographically remote. In some regions these proportions are much higher. Altogether, over 70% of all bands—representing 65% of the Indian population—have either a remote or a rural location, where "remote" is defined as lacking access by road, and "rural"
is defined as having at least one access road and being more than forty
miles commuting distance from an urban centre of at least 10,000 people.
Less than ten percent of the bands are situated in or contiguous to urban
areas (of ten thousand people or more). Yet, along certain dimensions it
is the urban and adjacent areas which offer the most opportunities to Indians. For instance, reserves in these areas can develop their lands for
one or more of a variety of purposes, including shopping centres, light
industry, residential accommodation, and recreation—all of which can
cater to both an Indian and a nonIndian market. Furthermore, the
delivery of services to such reserves is also much easier than to remote
reserves.

Turning briefly to the cultural realm, it is important to bear in mind
the cultural diversity of the Indian population. Prior to contact with
Europeans there were at least six distinct cultural types among the "Indian" population. The different groups for the most part lived in quite different ecological environments and consequently pursued quite different

economies and life styles. In turn, differences and variations appeared in their spiritual beliefs and larger cultural systems. Across these six cultural areas there were a total of ten major linguistic groupings. The most common nowadays are the Algonkian, Athapaskan, Iroquoian, and Salishan, which respectively encompass 64%, 9%, 9%, and 8% of the registered Indian population. In addition, the ten major linguistic groupings are broken into a total of over fifty dialects of which the most commonly spoken are Cree (spoken by 30% of registered Indians), Ojibway (21%), Mohawk (6%), and Micmac (4%). Although most Indians now also speak English, this has been a relatively recent development characteristic only of the post-World War II era. Thus, when we consider this cultural-linguistic diversity, it is not surprising that Indians' efforts to organize at the national level met with little success prior to the 1960s.

BIRTHS AND DEATHS: THE GROWTH OF THE INDIAN POPULATION

One useful model for describing population change is called the "demographic transition" model. This model identifies three major stages of population change. In Stage I both birth rates (fertility) and death rates (mortality) are high. Indeed, for the population to survive, fertility levels must be high in order to counter the high mortality rates which result from famine, disasters, and poor sanitation, nutrition, and medical care. In Stage II, fertility rates remain high but advances in sanitation and medicine bring down the mortality rates. Finally, in Stage III the fertility rates have dropped to a level only slightly above the already low mortality rates, as the influences of urbanization and modernization (including more effective birth control techniques) are brought to bear. Assuming, as the model does, that the population does not experience in-migration or out-migration,[4] then Stages I and III will result in a low rate of population growth by "natural increase" (excess of births over deaths), since in both of these stages the fertility and mortality rates are quite close to each other. However, in Stage II, which is known as the transitional growth stage, the wide discrepancy in fertility and mortality rates produces a high rate of population growth. The model is portrayed in Figure 2.1.A.

From the beginning of this century until the early 1960s the birth rate for registered Indians remained relatively stable at around 39 per 1,000 population (Romaniuk and Piché, 1972:18). This birth rate was almost identical to that exhibited by countries in the developing world and was markedly higher than that of Canada as a whole throughout the period. After a "baby boom" which peaked in 1965 (pushing the Indian birth rate that year up to 44 per 1,000 population), the registered Indian birth

FIGURE 2.1A The Demographic Transition Model

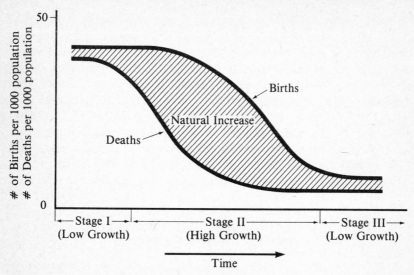

FIGURE 2.1B Crude Birth and Death Rates of the Registered Indian Population, 1925-75

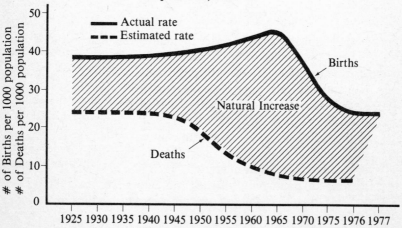

rate began a decline which has continued ever since. By 1976 for instance, it had plummetted to 28.5 per 1,000 population.

In examining the mortality component of the model we are handicapped by the unavailability of reliable data prior to the 1960s. However, in light of our knowledge of Indian fertility rates and rates of growth in Indian population, we are probably fairly safe in assuming that over the first part of this century the death rate among registered Indians was quite high, probably in the range of 20 to 30 deaths per 1,000 population. By 1961 that death rate had dropped to 10 per 1,000 population, which is quite low and fairly similar to that of Canada as a whole at that time. By 1976 the Indian death rate had declined further to 7.5 per 1,000 population. Thus, in comparing Figures 2.1.A and 2.1.B, it appears as though the demographic transition model, painted in broad strokes, does apply to the Indian population of Canada. The Indian population can be said to be in the second or transitional stage, where the birth rate, although declining, is still significantly higher than the mortality rate. In correspondence with this stage of the model, the decade of the 1960s was one in which the Indian population experienced a high rate of natural increase. Indeed, the population grew at an average annual rate of 3.5% during that decade—a rate which, had it persisted, would have made the Indian population double in just twenty years. However, in accordance with the model, the annual growth rate had declined to 2.0% by 1976, largely as a result of the precipitous decline in the birth rate.

To this point, we have relied upon very crude measures of fertility and mortality. For long range planning purposes administrators in IIAP and in Indian associations need to have more refined measures (particularly for fertility), for planning which is based on crude data is itself rendered crude, with the result that the opportunity structures created may not match the population's needs. Thus, we now turn to a more detailed analysis of birth rates.

Both the Indian and the nonIndian populations of Canada have experienced a "baby boom" in the second half of the twentieth century, although the Indian boom lagged behind the nonIndian one by several years.[5] An indication of the magnitude of the Indian boom and the depth of the subsequent decline can be gained by examining the so-called "general fertility ratio," which is the number of births per 1,000 women in the childbearing years (age 15 to 44 years old). In 1966, near the height of the Indian baby boom, the Indian general fertility ratio was 222 births per 1,000 women aged 15 to 44. By 1976, this ratio had declined to a mere 132.[6] This decline in this birth *rate* is very significant in light of the substantial increase during that period in the *number of women* in the 15 to 44 age bracket. Had the 62,500 women of these ages in 1976 exhibited the same high birth rates as the 41,700 women in the childbearing age group did in 1966, the result would have placed extremely heavy demands upon the labour force sector of the Indian population and upon the IIAP budget.

Although both the absolute number of births and the birth rates have been declining for the overall population of Indian women (of childbearing age), certain sectors of that population have not conformed to the pattern. Of particular significance is the pattern among *un*married Indian women living *off*-reserve. Between 1971 and 1976 the absolute number of babies born to them increased by 28% (i.e., 848 babies born in 1971 and 1,089 born in 1976), while the number of babies born to *un-married* *on*-reserve women increased by only eight percent.[7] Babies born to their married counterparts on- and off-reserve decreased by 22% and 24%, respectively. Data not shown here clearly demonstrate that, as might be expected, the increase in births among unmarried off-reserve women is attributable to women under the age of thirty. In particular, the increase is attributable to teenagers, to whom births increased by 52% over the five-year period. Apropos our concern with opportunities available to Indians, it is possible that the social and economic opportunities available to such young women will be reduced, in light of the presence of their child (or children) and the paucity of low-priced day care facilities in our society. Mitigating this, however, is the fact that to many young women, having a baby is itself highly rewarding. Also, it is not uncommon for friends or relatives of these young mothers to care for their children.

Interestingly, since 1976 the majority of Indian births has been to *un-married* women, while for the total Canadian population only one birth in nine is out-of-wedlock. Many factors underlie this increase in births among unmarried Indian women, but one stands out. This is the fact that under Section 12(1)(b) of the Indian Act a registered Indian woman and her offspring forfeit legal status as registered Indians if the woman marries a nonIndian male. Indian women, as we shall observe in a later section, became increasingly reluctant to make such a sacrifice after 1973 and the proportion of common-law relationships increased accordingly. Thus, by maintaining her status, an Indian woman and her children will not lose access to the various programs which are available to registered Indians but not to the general population (e.g., education and training programs). This obviously has a bearing upon certain opportunities which these women will face in the long term. Thus, the increased proportion of births to unmarried Indian women—from 33% of all Indian births in 1971 to just over 50% in 1976—may stem in part from rational economic calculations on the part of those women.

Turning now to mortality, the reader will recall from the earlier discussion of the demographic transition that great reductions have occurred in Indian death rates during this century. A case in point is the infant mortality rate, which is internationally used as an indicator of the overall standard of living in a population. In 1960 this rate stood at 79 deaths of Indian infants before reaching age one, per 1,000 live births. By 1976 this rate had dropped to 32, but was still significantly higher than the rate exhibited by the overall Canadian population in either 1960 (27) or 1976 (16). Other measures of mortality among Indians reveal a somewhat similar picture, which we have depicted in Table 2.4.

Although we have shown the crude death rate in Table 2.4 (column 'A'), it is by definition crude. A more informative measure, which is available only for 1976, is the standardized death rate. It is used to com-

TABLE 2.4

Specific Measures of the Improving Mortality Situation Among Canadian Indians, With Comparisons to the Total Canadian Population*

	(A) Crude Death Rate	(B) Infant Mortality Rate	(C) Average Age at Death	(D) Male Life Expectancy at Birth	(E) Female Life Expectancy at Birth
1960					
Indians	10.9	79.0	—	59.7	63.5
All Canadians	8	27.3		68.5	74.3
1965					
Indians	8.7	52.6	36	60.5	65.6
All Canadians	7.5	23.6	64	68.8	75.2
1970					
Indians	7.5	43.2†	42	60.2	66.2
All Canadians	7.5	18.8	66	69.3	76.4
1976					
Indians	7.5	32.1	43	—	—
All Canadians	7.4	16.0	67		

* Due to the difficulty in getting data, the data in any given cell above may be for a different year than for that shown. The difference is never more than two years and usually only one, and in any such cases of discrepancy the data is more recent than the date shown.

— not available

† This figure is an average of the rates for 1969 and 1971, since the 1970 data are unreliable due to incomplete reporting that year.

A — Deaths per 1000 population.

B — Deaths of children in first year of life per 1000 live births.

C — Sum of the age at death of all persons dying in a given year ÷ the number of people dying that year.

D & E — Age to which a person can be expected to live, calculated at time of birth.

Source: Medical Services Branch, *Health Data Book*, Ottawa: Department of National Health and Welfare, 1978.

pensate for the fact that the crude death rate is biased by the age structure of the population for which it is calculated. Thus, the fact that the age structure of the Indian population is much younger than that of the Canadian population results in the crude death rate for the Indian population being deceptively low in comparison with the crude death rate of the Canadian population. Hence, we use the standardized death rate, which is based upon the death rates in the various age groupings in the Indian population ("age-specific death rates").[8] In calculating the standardized Indian death rate those age-specific Indian death rates are applied to the age structure of the Canadian population and the weighted average is calculated. The resultant standardized death rate is interpreted as the death rate (per 1,000 population) which the Indian population would have if it had the same age structure as the overall Canadian population. The Indian and total Canadian rates will be different because the respective Indian age groups each face different risks than their counterparts in the total Canadian population. Indeed, at 13.0 deaths per 1,000 population the Indian standardized death rate in 1976 was almost twice as high was the crude death rate of the overall Canadian population[9] (and almost twice as high as the crude death rate of the Indian population).

Striking Indian-nonIndian differences appear not only in the foregoing general measures of death rates, but also in the rates of death due to various specific causes. For instance, the major cause of death among Indians and Inuit is listed by the Department of National Health and Welfare (Medical Services Branch, 1978) as being "accidents, violence, and poisoning" (including suicides). This accounts for one-third of all Indian/Inuit deaths but for only one-tenth of all nonIndian deaths. Among the major causes of accidental death among Indians/Inuit in 1976 were motor vehicle accidents, drowning, and suicides.[10]

Diseases of the circulatory system (e.g., heart disease) are the second most frequent cause of Indian/Inuit deaths. These account for one-fifth of Indian/Inuit deaths, but for one-half of the deaths in the overall Canadian population. Diseases of the respiratory system are the third major cause of Indian/Inuit deaths, at eleven percent, after which come cancer-related diseases ("neoplasms") at eight percent.

To summarize the mortality patterns among Indians, it can be said that Indian death rates have dropped significantly in recent years, but that both general indicators and most "cause-specific" measures still compare unfavourably with those of the overall Canadian population. Indeed, in one of the most striking comparisons of opportunities in our data set, life expectancy tables show that as a consequence of health, social, and environmental conditions, life expectancy at birth for Indians is still nine or ten years less than that for the nonIndian population.

SOCIAL AND ECONOMIC CHARACTERISTICS

AGE COMPOSITION

Closely related to some of the trends in birth and death rates discussed above is the age composition of the Indian population. Figure 2.2 portrays the age structure of the Indian and the Canadian population at three different points in time. Major and important changes in the shape of the Indian population pyramid occurred over that fifty-year period, while the Canadian population pyramid remained virtually static by comparison. In the Indian population we observe a sizable expansion between 1924 and 1966 in the proportion of the population composed of dependent children (age 0-14), as infant mortality declined and then the baby boom of the 1960s set in. The labour force age group of 15-64 year old Indians, never as large (proportionately speaking) as its Canadian counterpart, over this same period experienced a shrinkage in its share of the Indian population. In fact, by 1966 this potentially economically productive sector of the Indian population was actually out-numbered by its youthful and aged dependents. By 1976 the first of the Indian "baby boomers" had come of labour force age, thereby producing a swelling in the labour force age group, although it was still markedly smaller than its Canadian counterpart, proportionately speaking.

FIGURE 2.2 Age Distribution of the Indian and Total Canadian Populations (Selected Years)

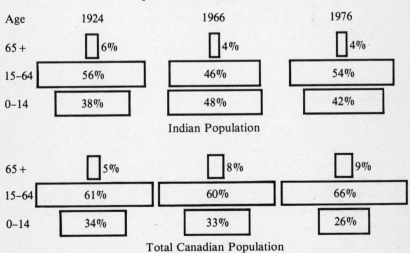

Indian Population

Total Canadian Population

Source: Census of Indians, 1924 Registered Indian Population by Age, Sex, and Residence, 1966, 1976 Indian Affairs Annual Reports

It is important to note that the entry of the baby boom children into the labour force was an important contributing factor to the high unemployment levels experienced by the overall Canadian population during the 1970s. Significantly, the Indian labour force will not experience the full brunt of the Indian baby boom until the 1980s. Thus, the already astronomically high levels of Indian unemployment are likely to be exacerbated by the changing age structure of the Indian population unless major improvements occur in economic opportunities for Indians on- and off-reserve. Furthermore, data not shown here indicate that the young adult age group (age 15-29) increased in absolute numbers more rapidly than any other age group between 1966 and 1976. This growth is not expected to slacken in the 1980s, such that between 1976 and 1986 it will likely match the increase of 30,000 people which it exhibited between 1966 and 1976. This age group will not only be entering the labour force seeking employment, but will also be entering the family formation stage of the life cycle. Thus, the already extremely poor Indian housing situation (to be discussed below) will come under increased demographic pressure. With housing playing such a pivotal role in the "vicious cycle" of poverty, the outlook is not encouraging.

MIGRATION

Migration, as a phenomenon, is also influenced by trends in the birth rate and by population pressure on the scarce housing and other resources of the reserves. Our earlier-cited figures on the large increase in the proportion of the Indian population living off-reserve are but one concrete indication of the upsurge in Indians migrating elsewhere in search of better opportunities for themselves and their children. Unfortunately, in analyzing this phenomenon and the subsequent reverse flow of migrants back to the reserves, we are handicapped by a lack of current and detailed data. However, the 1971 census does provide some insights which likely still have some relevance.

It is widely believed that Indians are highly mobile. Interestingly though, the 1971 census data which examines the migration of the population in the 1966-71 period, reveals that a smaller proportion of the Indian population (20%) than of the overall Canadian population (25%) had moved one or more times during this period. Yet the aforementioned belief is actually not totally incorrect, for those Indians who did move exhibited a higher frequency of migration than the nonIndian population. More specifically, in Figure 2.3 we present a percentage breakdown of the Indian migrant population classified in terms of place of residence in 1966 ("origin") and in 1971 ("destination"). In that figure we observe that urban areas were the destination of slightly more than half (52%) of the migrants. Inspection of the "Total" columns reveals that they gained

FIGURE 2.3 **Percentage Distribution of All Registered Indian Migrants According to 1966 Place of Origin and 1971 Destination**

1966 Origin	1971 Destination				
	Indian Reserves[1]	Rural Non-Reserve	Urban Non-Metropolitan (1,000– 99,999 Pop.)	Urban Metropolitan Area (≥ 100,000 Pop.)	Total
	%	%	%	%	%
Indian Reserves	12	3	3	3	21
Rural Non-Reserve	6	10	9	7	32
Urban Non-Metropolitan (1,000– 99,999)	5	5	10	6	26
Urban Metropolitan (≥ 100,000 Pop.)	4	3	4	10	21
Total	27	21	26	26	100

Note: Among the percentages of migrants as shown along the diagonal above, 11 percent of all migrants were living on the same Indian Reserves in 1966 and 1971 and 1 percent on different Indian Reserves in 1966; 4 percent in the same Rural Non-Reserve Areas and 6 percent in different Rural Non-Reserve Areas; 3 percent in the same Urban Non-Metropolitan Areas and 7 percent in different Urban Non-Metropolitan Areas; 7 percent in the same Urban Metropolitan Areas and 3 percent in different Urban Metropolitan Areas.

Source: Unpublished 1971 Census tabulations

more of the migrant population through this in-migration than they lost through out-migration ([26% + 26%] – [26% + 21%] = +5%). Interestingly, Indian reserves also gained more in-migrants than they lost through out-migration (27% – 21% = +6%). The big losers were the rural non-reserve areas, which lost population amounting to eleven percent (21% – 32% = –11%) of the migrating Indians.

The footnote in Figure 2.3 highlights a major component of Indian migration, namely the phenomenon which in demographers' jargon is called "quasi-return migration." In the data presented here, a quasi-return migrant would be illustrated by a person who, say, lived on a Northern Manitoba reserve in 1966, then left to take up residence in Winnipeg, but returned to take up residence again on that same reserve and was living there in 1971. Thus, the quasi-return migrant is one who lived in the same municipality (or reserve) in 1966 and 1971, but who moved two (or more) times during that period. This, then, is a so-called "reverse-flow" migration stream whose members constitute twenty-seven percent of all Indian migrants, an important element of the migration stream into or out of any given type of area in Figure 2.3, especially Indian reserves and metropolitan areas.

One of the concerns which community leaders and planners harbour about migration is that it can create or exacerbate social problems in an area, particularly where there are high levels of both in-migration and out-migration. However, data not shown here suggest that at the national level the total impact of in- and out-migration on reserves was not great. At the time of the 1971 census it was found that less than five percent of the total Indian population residing on-reserve were in-migrants who had not lived there in 1966 and the equivalent of only three percent of the 1966 population was lost to out-migration. On the other hand, in the metropolitan areas about twenty-eight percent of the Indian population living there at the time of the 1971 census were in-migrants who had not lived there in 1966 and the equivalent of nineteen percent of the 1966 Indian population moved away prior to the 1971 census.[11] Thus, as compared to the reserves, in the metropolitan areas we find both a higher differential and a higher absolute value in the percentages. These metropolitan figures are indicative of considerable change in the population, which itself generates special needs and difficulties to be addressed in the planning of programs and services.

Two final highlights of our research on Indian migration patterns should be mentioned. First, we found that almost one-quarter of all Indian migrants had moved four or more times during the five-year period, which may suggest that this large minority of the Indian migrant population had little success in finding or plugging into satisfactory opportunity structures.[12] Second, we found that Indians also conformed to a pattern which has been widely discussed in the migration literature on other populations. That is, those falling in the age group 20-29 are not only particularly likely to be migrants, but are also particularly likely to make several moves within a five-year period. It appears that many of these people are not single, but rather are parents who are moving with their young families. This comment is based on the fact that the 5-14 year old age group is the second most heavily represented age group among all Indian migrants. Inasmuch as more recent data suggest that return migration to reserves has increased since 1971, this finding of a heavy representation of young families in the migration stream could have important consequences for the availability of on-reserve services and facilities.

One consequence of the foregoing migration patterns of Indians is that the Indian population in Canada's metropolitan areas has increased dramatically since the mid-1960s. Unfortunately, reliable and recent data on this are not available. For instance, the 1971 census reports the total *Native* population of Regina to be about 2,900. This is almost certainly an under-enumeration. Indeed, by 1979 the Native population in Regina was probably in excess of 20,000.

ENFRANCHISEMENT AND MARITAL STATUS

As Indian women migrate from the reserves, their chances increase of meeting a nonIndian male. At the time of writing, if such a relationship resulted in marriage the Indian woman would lose her legal status as an Indian and with it her right to live on her reserve, her right to receive services offered by IIAP, and her right to a share of any wealth that her band might subsequently acquire. IIAP records show that between 1953 and 1971 there was an average of 720 enfranchisements per year. Prior to 1960, Indians had to become enfranchised if they were to be legally allowed to vote and drink liquor. Thus, in that period about 40% of enfranchisements were upon request and the remaining 60% resulted from the marriage of Indian women to nonIndian men. However, after the vote and liquor rights were granted to Indians in 1960 and 1969, respectively, enfranchisement by request all but disappeared—in the *five-year* period from 1971 to 1975 there were only 74 such enfranchisements, which represented a mere 4% of all enfranchisements (Statistics Canada, 1977:285). The remaining enfranchisements, therefore were brought about through marriage.

In 1972 in the Lavell-Bedard case, there was a challenge in the Supreme Court of Canada to the section of the Indian Act which requires an Indian woman to forfeit her registered Indian status upon marriage to a nonIndian man. The basis of the challenge was that the Indian Act contravened the Canadian Bill of Rights by discriminating on the grounds of sex, which is to say that Indian men were not required to give up their registered Indian status upon marriage to a nonIndian. Although Lavell and Bedard lost their case,[13] the issue created a much greater awareness among Indian women as to the advantages of keeping their Indian status. Thus, after the Supreme Court decision was announced in 1973, Indian women began to exhibit greater reluctance towards marrying nonIndian men and often chose instead to enter into common-law relationships with

TABLE 2.5
Total Enfranchisements of Registered Indians, Selected Years

Year	1953	1961	1966	1971	1976
Enfranchisements	788	716	658	652	302

Source: Membership Division, IIAP.

such men so as not to forfeit their Indian status. Lachance-Brulotte (1975:135), for instance, estimated that one-quarter of all single Indian women are living in common-law unions. Between 1971 and 1976 the proportion of the Indian female population who were single increased from 43 to 48 percent, and the percentage of all Indian marriages accounted for by Indian women marrying nonIndian men dropped from 29 to 21 percent.[14] Consequently, a similar drop in total enfranchisements also occurred during this period, as we observe in Table 2.5.[15]

HOUSING

Demand for Indian housing grew during the 1970s and can be expected to increase well into the 1980s. Among the various factors contributing to this growing demand are several demographic ones, including: (1) the increase in the size of the family formation age group (20-29 years old) as a result of the Indian baby boom; (2) a stabilization in the percentage of the young adult age group living on-reserve; (3) an increase in single female parent families; and (4) the aforementioned trend toward common-law relationships among Indian women who, by retaining their registered Indian status also maintain their eligibility for Indian housing programs offered by bands and IIAP.

The most recently available national Indian housing survey data are from 1977 (Community Services Branch, 1979). Those data, shown in Table 2.6, indicate that while the vast majority (90%) of Indian houses on-reserve had electricity, for various reasons such was not the case with other basic modern facilities. For instance, only half of Indian houses had potable water, less than half had indoor plumbing, and less than half were linked to a sewage disposal system. As Table 2.6 shows, these conditions were particularly acute in rural and remote reserves, and for all three types of reserve these conditions did not compare favourably with conditions in the overall Canadian population. Other available data are no more encouraging. For instance, in 1977 twenty-six percent of reserve houses stood in need of major repairs and a further thirteen percent needed to be replaced entirely. The 1977 survey also documented a severe over-crowding situation whereby one-third of the on-reserve housing

TABLE 2.6
Selected Housing Conditions for Registered Indian Reserves (1977) and for the Total Canadian Population (1971)

PERCENTAGE OF HOUSES BY TYPE OF FACILITIES

GEOGRAPHIC AREA	ELECTRICITY		POTABLE WATER		SEWAGE SYSTEM		INDOOR PLUMBING	
	Registered Indian (1977)	Total Canadian (1971)	Registered Indian (1977)	Total Canadian (1971)	Registered Indian (1977)	Total Canadian (1971)	Registered Indian (1977)	Total Canadian (1971)
Urban*	96%	99%	74%	99%	71%	98%	71%	98%
Rural†	93%	95%	49%	84%	38%	64%	38%	76%
Remote	79%	—	22%	—	17%	—	18%	—
Total	90%	98%	50%	96%	45%	90%	45%	94%

* Urban area includes reserves in urban and semi-urban locations.
† The 1971 housing conditions for the total population derive from the 1971 Census which used different definitions for urban and rural areas. However, it was assumed that these definitional differences would not detract from the general comparisons being made between Indian and Canadian housing conditions.
— not available

Sources: —Statistics Canada, 1971 Census Bulletins: Cat. No. 93-738.
        —Community Services Branch, *Housing Needs Analysis Survey, 1977*, Ottawa: IIAP, 1979.

units either have two or more families living in them, or require an addition to accommodate large families.

Such over-crowding, which is exacerbated by housing starts not keeping pace with the aforementioned social and demographic changes in the Indian population, is but one of several factors contributing to the deterioration of Indian housing. Another factor has been that the subsidy ($12,000 as of 1977) made available for the construction of any given new house usually falls far short of what is needed to complete a house adequately.[16] Furthermore, as NIB and the President of the Central Mortgage and Housing Corporation have noted (Canadian Press, 1975), government-designed Indian housing has tended to reflect the values and life styles of middle class nonIndians (e.g., the compartmentalization inherent in numerous interior walls and partitions) rather than of Indians. And finally, construction materials and practices have often been substandard.

The inadequacy and deterioration of housing conditions caused by the above factors is a source of major concern among Indians. This is because housing occupies an important position in the so-called "vicious circle" of poverty. For instance, over-crowded housing poses a major obstacle to the Indian student attempting to study at home at the end of the school day, thereby hampering his/her efforts to escape from poverty through education. In addition, drafty or otherwise substandard housing poses health risks, and over-crowding facilitates the spread of contagious illness and disease, with the result that valuable time may be lost from school or employment. Also of major concern is the reliance upon oil-fired space heaters, which are highly dangerous but much less expensive than forced air furnaces, for this sometimes results in tragic deaths by fire in winter. Figures available for 1976, for instance, show that sixty-one reserve Indians (half of whom were under the age of six) died in fires that year, for a rate of over 34 per 100,000 residents, as compared to a rate of 4 per 100,000 residents for Canada as a whole (Sellar, 1977).[17] Forty percent of those reserve fires were caused by overheated stoves or stove pipes, or by faulty electrical installations.[18]

POVERTY AND WEALTH

The income situation of Indians has traditionally been dismal. For example, Hawthorn's (1967a: 45) report on the results of a 1964 IIAP survey of 35 bands revealed the average per capita Indian income to be $300, as compared to an average of $1,400 for the total Canadian population.[19] Average yearly earnings per Indian worker were a mere $1,361, while for all Canadians the figure was almost $4,000. More recently, the 1971 census showed that almost two-thirds (62%) of the

TABLE 2.7
Social Assistance to Indians Residing on Reserves and Crown Lands, 1973-1974

REGION	REASON FOR ASSISTANCE				AVERAGE MONTHLY NUMBER OF PERSONS[4] RECEIVING ASSISTANCE		Annual Assistance Per Person	Total Assistance
	Health[1]	Social[2]	Economic[3]	Total	Total	As Percentage of 1974 Reserve and Crown Lands' Population	Dollars	
	Percent of Persons Receiving Assistance							
Maritimes	11.2	27.5	61.3	100.0	6,453	83.4	513	3,311,179
Quebec	10.7	19.7	69.6	100.0	6,348	27.3	461	2,927,077
Ontario	29.5	—	70.5	100.0	7,611	18.7	475	3,615,077
Manitoba	21.1	20.9	58.0	100.0	14,763	47.6	464	6,844,827
Saskatchewan	11.7	29.7	58.6	100.0	16,743	56.7	541	9,065,093
Alberta	17.2	28.1	54.7	100.0	15,400	57.9	488	7,515,127
British Columbia	17.1	41.7	41.2	100.0	11,102	32.3	727	8,072,260
Yukon	16.3	26.1	57.6	100.0	1,018	44.6	502	511,100
Canada[5]	16.8	24.3	58.9	100.0	79,438	40.7	519	41,861,740

[1] A family head or single person is unable to work or has inadequate earnings because of physical or mental disability, including advanced age.

[2] A family head or single person is unable to work or has inadequate income because he or she is giving care to an incapacitated spouse or parent, or is giving care and supervision to the dependent children in the family. Health and social reasons are combined in Ontario.

[3] A family head or single person does not come within either of the first two categories but is unable to work or has inadequate earnings because of a lack of employment opportunities.

[4] Includes family members dependent on the head of the family (See Note 20 in text.).

[5] Excludes Northwest Territories.

Source: Statistics Canada, *Perspective Canada II*. Ottawa: Department of Industry, Trade and Commerce, p. 291.

Native labour force working full-time *for at least forty weeks* earned less than $6,000 per year. This proportion is twice as high as the thirty-three percent of the total Canadian labour force which fell into the same category. Furthermore, it should be borne in mind that only slightly more than half (57%) of the Indian labour force was classifed as having worked at least forty weeks in that year prior to the 1971 census.

An insight into the extent of poverty in the Indian population can be gained from data in Table 2.7 showing social assistance payments to Indians residing on-reserve during the 1973-74 fiscal year.

This, however, does not tell the full story, inasmuch as it does not include off-reserve Indians. What it does show is that 41% of the on-reserve population was receiving social assistance payments, although in some regions this figure was much lower (e.g., 19% in Ontario[20]) and in some regions it was much higher (e.g., 83% in the Maritimes). By way of comparison, we note that in the overall Canadian population, only six percent of the people were receiving assistance in 1974 under the Canada Assistance Plan. Of particular interest in the Indian data is the fact that only 59% of those who were receiving social assistance payments were doing so because of a lack of employment opportunities. The remainder were recipients due to health reasons (17%) which prevented them from working, or due to having to stay at home to care for a dependent child or an incapacitated spouse or parent (24%).

The geographic area of Indian reserves provides us with an indicator— albeit an extremely crude one—of the potential which the exploitation of Indian land offers for generating revenue that could help pull Indian bands out of poverty. In Table 2.1 we noted that the average reserve in Canada, at about 1100 hectares (4.3 square miles), is rather small and therefore not likely to hold great economic potential, especially since the vast majority (70%) of reserves are situated in either remote or rural areas. Furthermore, despite the implicit policy of the treaty-makers that Indians should become agriculturalists, most Indian land is suitable neither for crops nor for livestock grazing (Frideres, 1974:168). Thus, for some bands there is little prospect that their reserve lands will generate major revenue flows.

However, Table 2.8 shows that during the 1977-78 fiscal year, Indian bands received an income of $96.9 million from such sources as band enterprises, oil and gas royalties, and interest on funds held in trust for them by government. Over four-fifths of this revenue was derived from oil and gas royalties, which themselves accrued almost entirely to five bands (all in Alberta). After taking into account the balance at the beginning of the fiscal year and expenditures[21] by bands during the year, the total year-end bank balance across all depositing bands was about $138 million. The oil and gas revenues of Alberta bands in the 1980 fiscal year are expected to increase to about $200 million, and it is estimated that

TABLE 2.8
Indian Band Funds Held in Trust, 1977-78 Fiscal Year
(in millions of dollars)*

Receipts

Dues, Royalties, and Minerals (mainly oil and gas)	79.7
Government Interest on Band Funds	10.3
Leasing (agricultural, residential, commercial, and industrial)	4.2
Sales (land and other)	1.3
Forestry (including timber dues)	0.4
Other Band Enterprises	0.1
Miscellaneous	0.7
Total Receipts	96.9
Total Expenditures	69.0
Excess of Revenue Over Expenditures	27.9
Balance at Beginning of Fiscal Year	110.5
Balance at End of Fiscal Year	138.4

Source: Department of Finance, *Public Accounts of Canada, 1977-78*, Volume II, Section 9, Appendix 2. Ottawa: Department of Supply and Services.

* Figures may not exactly equal totals due to rounding errors.

there is at least two billion dollars worth of royalties left in current known oil and gas pools on Alberta reserves (Warden, 1979b). The way in which this money is spent and invested has the potential for becoming a source of controversy in the 1980s, in a fashion parallel to that surrounding the Heritage Trust Fund of the Government of Alberta. On the one hand we would speculate that pressures will arise for the sharing of these revenues with less fortunate bands (e.g., through low interest loans), while on the other hand some of the rich bands may well argue that such is the proper role of government under the treaties and the Indian Act (Warden, 1979c). Regardless of the outcome of the debate, the exploitation of these and perhaps other non-renewable natural resources (e.g., uranium in Saskatchewan) can offer the opportunity for some bands to cross the economic threshold and acquire considerable economic power—a development which could have ramifications in internal Indian politics.

EMPLOYMENT[22]

Census tabulations are available comparing various ethnic origin groups in terms of their distribution in Canada's occupational structure. An interesting comparison is that between persons of British ethnic origin and persons of Native origin. When compared to people of British origins, Natives are over-represented in the so-called "unskilled" and "semi-skilled" areas (e.g., service occupations, construction, forestry and logging, and fishing) and under-represented in the managerial, professional, clerical, and sales areas. Other tabulations from the IIAP economic activity survey of 211 Indian bands in 1974-75 point in the same general direction. For instance, the majority of approximately 5,900 economic operations surveyed fell in the realm of primary or extractive industries (wildlife, agriculture, fishing, forestry) and about one-third of the total number of persons employed in the bands surveyed were employed in this primary or extractive sector. Another interesting finding from that survey is that arts and crafts still provide employment for a substantial portion (16% in this survey) of the Indian work force, although the revenue generated therefrom makes only a very minor contribution (4% in this survey) to the total employment income received by Indians. Finally, it was noteworthy that this survey reveals over 600 industrial, commercial, and real estate operations owned by Indians.

There are no scientifically gathered data available on Indian unemployment. However, "guestimates" have variously placed the level of unemployment in the national Indian population in the forty to eighty percent range, although on some reserves even these levels are exceeded.[23] The most recent of such estimates comes from IIAP regional offices in June 1979 and places the on-reserve Indian unemployment rate at forty-eight percent.

A crude measure of the economic burden borne by the labour force age group is the dependency ratio. This is simply the number of people in the dependent age groups (under age 15, and age 65 and over) per 100 people in the labour force age group (15-64 years old). In 1976 the respective dependency ratios for the Indian and Canadian populations were 86 and 53 dependents per 100 persons in the labour force age group. If the Indian birth rate continues to decline, it is projected that by 1986 the dependency ratio of the Indian and of the total Canadian population will have nearly converged at around 56. However, the Indian population of labour force age, it must be remembered, contains a large proportion of unemployed and unemployable persons. By 1986 that proportion may be significantly higher if jobs are not found for persons who were born during the Indian baby boom of the early 1960s but who do not enter the job market until the 1980s. If sufficient employment opportunities are available to the growing Indian labour force of the 1980s, the aforementioned decline in the dependency ratio could facilitate efforts to ameliorate the economic conditions of Indian families and raise their per capita standard of living. However, such results cannot be attained by the force of demographic changes alone; what is necessary is a substantial commitment of time, effort, money, imagination, talent, and goodwill on the part of Indians and governments alike.

EDUCATION

By 1980 Indian education was in the midst of a radical change. For most of a century, Indian education had been in the hands of the missionaries and other employees of the Christian churches, whose orientations of paternalism and moral rectitude exacted a heavy toll on Indian students (See Chapter Ten). Then, in 1969 the Anglican Church of Canada terminated its contract with the federal government and removed itself from the residential school business in the north. In the south, Canada's nonIndian population had long since established nonIndian communities and schools in relative proximity to Indian reserves. In the mid-1960s, with racial integration in education having already been heralded in the United States, Indian parents in growing numbers forsook the on-reserve federal "day schools" and enrolled their children next to nonIndians in the schools in nearby off-reserve communities. In this they were encouraged by nonIndian school authorities who would receive per capita grants from IIAP for each Indian enrollee. Indeed, IIAP moneys even went towards the construction of schools off-reserve.

Between 1965 and 1972, the enrollment of Indian students in federal schools fell from 61% to 39%. By 1976, 623 agreements had been signed with off-reserve nonIndian school boards, and almost all federal secondary schools had been closed (Frideres, 1980). But around this time the trend started to reverse itself, as Indians came to appreciate the problems of attending integrated schools, such as alienating curricula, the prejudices of nonIndian school children, and a lack of input in the decision-making processes which so profoundly affected the lives of the Indian children. At about this time, too, a major political breakthrough was made as the National Indian Brotherhood won the Indian Affairs Minister's acceptance of a new policy for Indian control of Indian education (See Cardinal, 1977:56ff). By 1978, with more and more Indian teachers and teacher's aides in place in reserve schools, the percentage of Indian students in federal schools had climbed to forty-five. School construction on reserves increased such that in fiscal 1977, IIAP spent $22.5 million constructing schools, including high schools for the baby boom children of the 1960s. Unfortunately, the IIAP dollars spent helping to construct off-reserve schools in nonIndian communities were non-liquidable investments that could not follow the Indian children back to the reserves when the tide changed. (IIAP is still trying to recover some of those funds from the provinces in question.)

Traditionally, an important characteristic of Indian education has been the phenomenally high failure and drop out rate of Indian students. Data from IIAP and Statistics Canada comparing grade two enrollments in a given year with grade twelve enrollments ten years later provide startling measures of the retention powers that school has had for Indians compared to nonIndians. In the 1965-66 school year, for instance,

Indian enrollments in grade twelve were a mere eleven percent of Indian enrollments in grade two in 1955-56. However, between 1969-70 and 1977-78 (the year of the most recently available grade 12 enrollment data), the ten-year retention rates for Indians have fluctuated in the 15 to 19% range. Yet that retention rate is still far below that for the Canadian population as a whole, which climbed from 51% in 1966-76 to 75% in 1975-76.

IIAP data also show that formal education is now nearly universal among Indian primary school age children. At the secondary education level, however, there are some indications that as a percentage of the 14-18 year old age group, secondary school enrollments are declining. For instance in 1969-70, 60% of this age group was enrolled in secondary school. Three years later the figure had climbed to 76%, but by 1977-78 it had again dropped to 60%. Some of this decline may result from the fact that some Indian students are not included due to being in attendance at schools which do not receive federal funding. However, it seems likely that the Indian figure has dropped significantly below the figure of 72% for Canada as a whole in 1977-78. At the time of writing it was, unfortunately, too soon to know if the policy of Indian control of Indian education, which was being gradually implemented, has had any effect on Indian secondary school enrollments.

At the post-secondary level there has been a marked increase in both numbers and percentages of the Indian population enrolled, as Table 2.9 demonstrates. Enrollments in post-secondary educational institutions grew phenomenally during the first half of the 1970s, but then virtually stabilized, except in the universities. By 1975, over eleven thousand post-secondary Indian students were enrolled, including over two thousand in university. As a percentage of the Indian population aged 18-24 in 1965, university students represented only one-half of one percent as compared to 9% of the same age group in the general population. By 1975, the percentage for the Indian population had risen by a factor of ten to 5%. Yet, it still lagged well behind the percentage in the general population (12%). This gap will not close by much more without a substantial increase in the aforementioned retention rates.

The alienation of Indians from the nonIndian education system is reflected in data on educational attainment. Census data, for instance, reveal that four-fifths of all Natives aged twenty and over had only an elementary (grade eight or less) school education at the time of the 1971 census, while only about a third (37%) of that age group in the overall Canadian population had that level of education. At the other end of the education spectrum, about 5% of Indians in that age group and 27% of their counterparts in the overall Canadian population had attained some level of post-secondary education (Statistics Canada, 1977:290).

In concluding these remarks on Indian education, two points should

TABLE 2.9
Full Time Post-secondary and University Enrolment of Registered Indians, for Canada, 1965, 1970, 1975

YEAR	POST-SECONDARY ENROLMENT*		UNIVERSITY ENROLMENT		UNIVERSITY ENROLMENT AS A PERCENTAGE OF THE POPULATION AGED 18-24	
	Number	Five-Year Growth	Number	Five-Year Growth	Registered Indian	Total Canadian
1965	3,103	—	131	—	.5	8.7%
1970	10,946	252.8%	432	229.8%	1.4	11.8%
1975	11,103	1.4%	2,071	379.4%	5.3	12.2%

* includes university and teaching courses, nursing, vocational, auxiliary, pre-vocational formation, and special courses.

Sources: —Programme Reference Centre. Post-Secondary Courses for Indian Students, 1965, 1975. Ottawa: IIAP.
—Statistics Canada, Cat. No. 81-229.
—Programme Reference Centre. Registered Indian Population by Age, Sex, and Residence for Canada, 1965, 1970, 1975. Ottawa: IIAP.

be borne in mind. First, the formal education system of nonIndians is just one type of education, and the more traditional Indian methods of teaching and learning (such as learning from community elders) will continue to be important to Indian children. It is in this regard that the policy of Indian control of Indian education offers so much potential.

Second, although at the post-secondary level the nonIndian educational system remains highly alienating to many Indian students, it is there that they will learn many of the technical and managerial skills which they must possess if Indians are to direct and manage their own affairs. As a community college level of education becomes the norm for the adult Canadian population, the 1980s may well witness more community college programs being offered on the reserves and tailored to Indian needs.

CRIMINAL JUSTICE[24]

In relation to their proportion of the Canadian population, Native people are somewhat over-represented in federal prisons. Natives constitute between 6 and 10% of the total inmate population, but only about 4% of the Canadian population. However, in provincial prisons and jails, where inmates are serving sentences of less than two years, a study conducted by the Law Reform Commission of Canada found that Natives are grossly over-represented among inmates in the Prairie provinces (Schmeiser, 1974). To cite but one example, in Manitoba, where Natives constitute an estimated 12% of the general population, yearly figures between 1966 and 1972 show that Natives regularly account for about 45% of the inmate population of provincial correctional institutions.[25] In British Columbia, Natives are less heavily over-represented in provincial prisons, while data from the rest of Canada do not permit reliable generalizations to be drawn.

The Law Reform Commission data focused upon the late 1960s and early 1970s. It found at the time that Native offenders were usually involved in less serious crimes than were nonNative offenders. Many Natives were found to be incarcerated for breaches of provincial and municipal statutes, particularly liquor (e.g., causing a disturbance, disorderly conduct) and vehicles (e.g., driving with license suspended) offences. The most common federal offences committed by Native offenders were assault, theft, breaking and entering, causing a disturbance, and driving offences involving alcohol. Narcotics and sexual offences were quite rare. More recent data contained in Table 2.10 suggest that violent crimes against persons, as opposed to crimes against property, have increased. It should be emphasized that the vast majority of such

TABLE 2.10
Selected Characteristics of Native and Non-native
Inmates in Federal Penitentiaries, 1979

SELECTED CHARACTERISTICS	INMATES	
	Native*	Non-native
Number*	802	8,442
Percent	8.7%	91.3%
Age Group		
Under 20	6%	4%
20–34	76%	66%
35 and Over	18%	30%
*Offence Type***		
Violent	48%	27%
Non-Violent	52%	73%
No. of Previous Commitments		
0	62%	65%
1	19%	21%
2	12%	9%
3+	7%	5%
Length of Sentence		
Under 2 yrs.	7%	4%
2–3 yrs.	24%	18%
3+ yrs.	69%	78%

* Includes registered and non-status Indians, Metis and Inuit except in the number of Native inmates which excludes Inuit.
** Violent offences include murder, rape, assault, etc.; non-violent are offences not against persons.

Source: Information Systems and Statistics Division, Minister of the Solicitor General, July, 1979.

violent crimes are likely committed against other Natives, especially friends and family members, and are likely committed while under the influence of alcohol. Indeed, in the study of race relations it is commonplace that subordinate group members turn their aggression inward onto themselves or their own people. The Indian suicide data reported earlier are but one illustration of this.

Unpublished computer tabulations provided by the federal Solicitor-General's Department permit comparisons to be made between Native and nonNative offenders according to certain specific federal offences for which they were in prison in 1979. For instance, 14% of all Native inmates, but only 5% of all nonNative inmates were convicted of manslaughter. A robbery conviction was the reason for incarceration of 21% of Native inmates but 31% of nonNative inmates. And as a final example, only 2% of Native inmates, compared to 11% of nonNative inmates were convicted of narcotics offences.

It is highly likely that Natives and nonNatives receive different treatment at various stages of their encounters with the criminal justice system, as a result of various factors, some of which are personal in nature (e.g., racial prejudice) and others of which are characteristics of institutions rather than individuals. For instance, the sociological literature indicates that the physical visibility and low socio-economic status of members of subordinate racial groups is likely to increase their chances of being arrested (rather than ignored or warned). A low level of formal education makes Natives more likely to plead guilty. A low income means that Natives are less likely to be represented by experienced and sophisticated counsel which has major implications for plea bargaining, sentencing, etc. The Law Reform Commission study also found in Saskatchewan that Natives sentenced to jail are less likely than non-Natives to have received a pre-sentencing report and that Natives were more likely (in terms of percentage of admissions) than nonNatives to have been incarcerated for failing to pay a fine for an earlier offence. The Commission also found in Saskatchewan that, proportionately speaking, Natives were less likely than nonNatives to be sentenced to probation (rather than jail or fined), even though Natives' offences were generally of a "less serious" nature. Finally, by way of further concrete example, Statistics Canada has reported federal prison data which show that during 1976, 27% of nonNative inmates, but only 14% of Native inmates, were granted parole (Canadian Press, 1979a).

Most Indian crime is a direct result of alcohol abuse, and efforts at various levels inside and outside government are being made to combat Indian alcoholism and alcohol abuse. Some efforts are rehabilitative, while others—such as sports and recreational programs for youths and programs of cultural awareness and cultural pride—are more preventative in nature. The point, of course, is that Indian crime is inextricably related to the broader social, economic, educational, and cultural problems facing Indians. If and when real progress is made in combatting the underlying causes of those problems, significant reductions can be expected in the incidence of Indian crime. In the interim, major institutional innovations could assist in reducing both the incidence of Indians coming into conflict with the law and the adverse effects experienced by Indians within the criminal justice system.[26] These innovations include Indian control and staffing of on-reserve policing, accompanied by a heavily preventative emphasis (such as is being done in southwest Manitoba). Also important are Native court-workers programs (such as is being funded by the Law Foundation of British Columbia) to advise Native defendants, a greater representation of Natives on the staffs of the various branches of the criminal justice system, and Native inmates' organizations through which Native inmates can keep themselves from being destroyed by the prison experience.

SUMMARY

The present chapter has presented a barrage of facts and figures which carries with it the danger of leaving the reader too preoccupied with the individual "trees" to be able to discern the "forest." Thus, we close this chapter with a brief summary of highlights of its findings.

The registered Indian population of Canada encompasses little more than one percent of the total Canadian population. It is distributed throughout the country, but by no means evenly from province to province. The population is organized into policital-administrative units, called bands, which themselves are usually small and are, in effect, made smaller by about a quarter of the band population living off-reserve. Most reserves are located in remote or rural areas to which the delivery of services is costly and problematic.

Historically, the Indian population was highly fragmented, not only along the aforementioned dimensions, but also culturally. However, English is now emerging as a shared language.

The population is now in the second stage of the demographic transition. Death rates are declining, although by most measures significant differentials do exist with the mortality rates of the nonIndian population. Since the "baby boom" which peaked in 1965, Indian fertility levels have been declining, although not among unmarried women living off-reserve. As birth and death rates change, so too does the age structure of the Indian population. The population has carried the weight of a heavy dependency ratio (children and aged in relation to persons of labour force age) which will lighten in the 1980s. However, the scarcity of employment opportunities for the expanding labour force sector of the Indian population may militate against significant gains being made in the material standard of living. The impact of demographic pressures will be particularly pronounced on the already poor Indian housing situation in the late 1980s.

Many Indians have migrated off-reserve in search of opportunities in urban areas, although they represent but one of several migration streams and there is also a sizable reverse flow. Those Indians who do migrate tend to be more frequent movers than their nonIndian counterparts. Unfortunately, reliable data on the number of Indians in specific cities do not exist.

Most enfranchisements since 1960 have been due to marriage rather than request. However, enfranchisements have declined since the Lavell-Bedard challenge to the Indian Act, as Indian women are now reluctant to forfeit their Indian rights in order to marry a nonIndian. Accordingly, common-law relationships are becoming quite numerous among Indian women, although they are by no means yet the norm.

Socio-economically, although small pockets of considerable wealth do exist among Indians, poverty is the norm. Unemployment and underemployment are rampant and Indians living on economically impotent reserves find themselves in a classic state of "welfare dependency." Those who do find employment find that it is often seasonal or short-term in nature, and is likely to be of the low-paying, unskilled or semi-skilled type in the primary (extractive) sector. There is, however, the possibility that programs such as Indian control of Indian education will reduce the high rate of Indians dropping out of school. There was also a huge increase in the 1970s in the numbers and percent of Indians attending various types of post-secondary educational institutions where knowledge and skills can be acquired that will permit Indians to manage and direct the future development of Indian communities. However, there are fewer grounds for optimism for the near future in the matter of Natives' experiences in the "criminal justice" system, for the problems Indians encounter here result from a very complex set of factors involving features of the system and those who staff it, the actions of Indians themselves, and the more deeply rooted social problems of Indian communities.

Throughout much of this chapter we have concerned ourselves with the implications of our data for the opportunity structures available to Indians, although this has been far from a definitive analysis of Indians' life chances. The data lead us to conclude that in many respects the plight of Indians is extreme. Some of the conditions (e.g., housing, health) described in this chapter are precisely what policy makers in the 1980s are attempting to change. However, other conditions (e.g., the age structure of the population) described in this chapter serve as constraints or parameters within which policy makers must operate. Another set of constraints for them consists of the attitudes, opinions, and perceptions which nonIndians hold vis-à-vis Indians. That is, major policies cannot be changed or adopted without the co-operation of the politicians, and the politicians in turn must usually keep policy within the bounds of acceptability to the electorate. Thus, the next chapter will examine the orientations towards Indians as held by the electorate.

NOTES

1. Most of the data presented in this chapter are taken from various sources within IIAP. As such, they pertain to the registered Indian population only, unless the term "Native" is used, in which case the data include status and nonstatus Indians, Metis, and Inuit. Although certain refinements have been introduced into the data, the regrettable fact remains that not all of the data is of impeccable reliability. For instance, historical comparisons are hampered by changing legal definitions of who is and who is not considered to be an Indian. Overall, one should not attribute too much significance to small differences when comparisons are made. Also, whenever data for the overall Canadian population are cited, the reader should bear in mind that the data for the Canadian population include the registered Indian population.

2. It is not certain whether this apparent fluctuation was due to actual shifts in the size of the population as a result of epidemics, etc., or whether it was due to changes in the definition of an Indian, problems in reporting, or some combination of these.

3. In Quebec, where employment in unskilled industrial jobs is predominantly in the French language, and where most Indians do not speak French, the proportion of status Indians living off-reserve is lower than that for any of the other regions in southern Canada.

4. The only significant way in which the Indian population experiences "in-migration" is through the marriage of nonIndian females to Indian males. "Out-migration" occurs through a small number of people becoming enfranchised or leaving the country (e.g., in search of employment opportunities in the U.S.A.).

5. Whereas the nonIndian baby boom peaked in the late 1950s to early 1960s, the Indian baby boom began its decline in 1965.

6. The general fertility ratio (GFR) does vary considerably by region. For instance, in 1976 the range in the ten provinces was from 178 in Saskatchewan to 84 in British Columbia and the Atlantic Region.

7. Definitive data do not exist on the actual number of unmarried Indian women living in common-law relationships. However, one study (Lachance-Brulotte, 1975:135) has estimated the percentage of common-law relationships among Indian women living on-reserve with two or more children as being forty-one percent in 1974.

8. Comparing the age-specific death rates for the Indian and total Canadian populations over the four year period 1973-1976, we obtain the following average annual rates per 1000 population in each age group:

	Age 1-4	Age 5-19	Age 20-44	Age 45-64	Age 65+
Indian	3.1	1.9	6.0	15.7	57.0
Canadian	0.8	0.7	1.5	9.0	55.0

9. The Department of National Health and Welfare (Medical Services Branch, 1978) provides provincial breakdowns for the Indian standardized death rate in 1976. These are shown below, with the 1974 death rates for the

respective total provincial populations in parentheses: Atlantic, not available; Quebec 7.3 (7.0); Ontario 9.1 (7.5); Manitoba 10.2 (8.3); Saskatchewan 15.9 (8.6); Alberta 15.9 (6.6); and British Columbia 12.4 (8.0). Thus, the main source of the difference in the Indian and Canadian national level figures is to be found in the three most westerly provinces.

10. In recent years the Indian suicide rate has fluctuated at levels about two to three times as high as that of the overall Canadian population (Medical Services Branch, 1978). Drawing from an unidentified source, the Canadian Association in Support of the Native People (1978) identifies the 1974 status Indian suicide rate to be 40.6 per 100,000 population, compared to 12.9 for the overall Canadian population. Other data published by the Pacific Region of Health and Welfare Canada revealed the status Indian suicide rate in British Columbia to have fluctuated from 14.6 to 48.3 per 100,000 persons during the ten year period 1968-77, while the rate for the total British Columbia population ranged from 15.2 to 18.5 per 100,000 during that same period (Medical Services Branch, n.d.).

11. Figures cited here do not correspond with those cited in Figure 2.3, since different bases are being used. That is, for Figure 2.3 the population base is all those who migrated at least once between 1966 and 1971. In the discussion of migrant flows as it relates to community stability and social problems, the bases used are the 1971 reserve population, 1966 reserve population, 1971 Indian population in metropolitan areas, and 1966 Indian population in metropolitan areas, respectively.

12. It is recognized that this interpretation of the data reflects a particular value bias which is favourable to residential stability and unfavourable to residential transience.

13. On August 27, 1973, the Supreme Court of Canada announced a 5-4 decision against Jeanette Corbiere Lavelle and Yvonne Bedard. The ruling upheld the membership provisions of the Indian Act which discriminate on the basis of sex. The Court ruled that the Canadian Bill of Rights cannot amend or alter the British North America Act. The ruling held that the B.N.A. Act gave Parliament the exclusive right to legislate on Indian matters and with it went the right to establish qualifications required for Indian status. For further detail, see Jamieson (1978).

14. Changes in endogamy (marriage within the group) and exogamy (marriage outside the group) among Indians between 1971 and 1976 are shown in the table below as a percentage of all marriages into which Indians entered:

| DATE | MARRIAGE PARTNERS | | |
	Indian Male, Indian Female	Indian Male, NonIndian Female	Indian Female, NonIndian- Male	Total Indian Marriages
1971	46.8%	24.2%	29.0%	100% (N = 2120)
1976	50.5%	28.5%	21.0%	100% (N = 2144)

15. Apropos our earlier discussion of the size of the Indian population, it is worth noting here that this and other changes in the number of annual enfranchisements have little effect upon the overall size of the Indian population, for their magnitude is small in comparison to the magnitude of natural increase (excess of births over deaths).

16. In the autumn of 1979, an announcement was made by the DIAND Minister that the housing subsidy would be increased to $12,500. Warden (1979a) reports, on the basis of remarks made by the Alberta Regional Director-General of IIAP, that for the entire country in fiscal year 1979-80 the forty million dollar Indian housing budget allowed for the building of 2,400 of the 24,900 new houses needed, and for renovation of 3,000 of the 33,000 existing houses in need of renovation.

17. In making this comparison it should be borne in mind that a far greater proportion of the reserve Indian population lives in remote or rural locations than is the case with the overall Canadian population.

18. For a more detailed treatment of the causes of these fires, see Sellar (1977) and the original report (Safety and Fire Prevention Services, 1977).

19. In making this comparison it should be borne in mind that most Indians make their living in rural or remote areas, while most other Canadians earn their living in urban-based occupations.

20. A more recent study (T.A.P. Associates Ltd., 1979) confined to Ontario estimated that sixteen percent of the on-reserve Indian population in that province is receiving social assistance payments. (This figure includes cheque recipients only, and calls into question the accuracy of the Ontario data in Table 2.7 where an almost identical figure (18.7%) purportedly represents both cheque recipients and their dependents.)

21. Expenditures from this trust fund can be made only by bands which have made deposits into it.

22. Inasmuch as existing studies on the occupational and economic activities of Indians and other Natives are either dated by now or plagued with methodological problems, data reported here must be treated as merely suggestive. Census data here (although not in the earlier section on migration) pertain to Natives, not merely to status Indians.

23. It should be noted that the "guestimates" and "estimates" of Indian unemployment to which we refer in this section are not directly comparable to Statistics Canada's measures of unemployment in the total Canadian population. For instance, persons who have been unable to find employment and consequently cease to look for a job are classified by Statistics Canada as no longer in the labour force and therefore not eligible to be considered among the ranks of the unemployed. Conversely, such persons are counted among the unemployed by the sources which we have used in the text. In addition, there are difficulties in applying Statistics Canada's definitional criteria in any meaningful way to those Indian people who are following a traditional Indian way of life.

24. Once again in this section the only data available are for Natives rather than for status Indians alone.

25. In particular jails, Natives sometimes constitute eighty or ninety percent (and occasionally more) of the inmates.

26. For a brief but poignant commentary on Natives' experiences in the criminal justice system, see the remarks quoted by Jefferson (1976:10).

Chapter 3

Canadians' Perceptions
of Indians

As Indians in Canada wrestle with their future and try to preserve their past, one fact is unavoidable—Indians today live within, and indeed have been almost submerged by, a vastly larger nonIndian society. Because of this, Indians lack the power to chart a future course that ignores the values of the larger society. As Indians struggle to gain control over their lives and destiny, the larger society will continue to restrict the options and opportunities open to Indian people.

In Chapter One we examined nonIndian values and perceptions as these were embedded in Indian policies of the past. In the chapters to come we will encounter them as they arise in the Department of Indian Affairs and Northern Development. Here, however, we wish to step back from public policies, politicians and bureaucrats and examine directly the perceptions of Indians and Indian issues that are held by the general Canadian public. The assumption in doing so is that the public's values and perceptions act as a nebulous but nonetheless very real source of constraint on Indians and nonIndians who are presently engaged in the renegotiation of Indian policy. The principal tool to be used will be a national public opinion survey conducted by Ponting and Gibbins in the early months of 1976. Through that survey, unique in Canada for its focus and scope, we will explore the public's knowledge of Indians and Indian issues, images of Indian peoples, and views towards land claims and other policy issues. We shall also assess the degree of public sympathy for or antagonism towards Indians' aims and aspirations, and the factors which appear to influence the degree of such sympathy expressed by individual Canadians.

Before proceeding with this endeavour, a word of caution is in order. Survey research provides an invaluable although not unflawed means of assessing public opinion at a given point in time. In effect, a well-designed survey captures opinion as a still camera freezes a single moment of action in a sports event. Yet it must be recognized that public opinions and perceptions are in a constant state of flux, that the survey snapshot is the equivalent of a single frame in a moving picture that stretches back to the first Indian-white contact and forward into the unknown future. It is for this reason that we should like to set the stage for our own survey findings by providing an overview of the social science research in this field which pre-dates our own.

RELATED RESEARCH FINDINGS

The nascent social sciences of the nineteenth century buttressed and at times championed white myths of racial superiority (Upton, 1973:52). They provided little challenge to images of Indians in the popular culture, images of an uncivilized and sometimes savage race that fought with cunning but without success against the engines of modern progress. In novels, films and comics, Indians were associated with buffalo, teepees, the massacre of white settlers, and the last minute arrival of the cavalry. Such negative historical imagery showed great tenacity in part due to its entertainment value in the mass media and in part due to its reinforcement in school textbooks. Recent studies of textbooks in both Canada and the United States (Costo and Henry, 1970; McDiarmid and Pratt, 1971; Saskatchewan Human Rights Commission, 1974) repeatedly show that textbooks not only neglect contemporary Indians, tending to draw comparisons between twentieth century whites and Indians of the seventeenth century (McDiarmid and Pratt, 1971:88), but are a source of general negative imagery. For example, in an analysis comparing pictorial treatment of Asians, Africans, white Canadians and Canadian Indians, McDiarmid and Pratt (1971:51) found that Indians were the least favoured of all groups. They were shown as primitive and unskilled, in tribal dress or only partly clothed, and frequently in an aggressive or hostile posture. None were shown in a skilled or professional occupation. Students, then, were being presented with historical imagery that failed to provide any useful handle on the contemporary Indian scene.

Apart from school texts, there have been important changes in North American society over the past few decades which have begun to reshape the cultural portrayal of Indians. The American civil rights movement, the Canadian Bill of Rights, the greater Canadian acceptance of cultural and ethnic pluralism, the post-war antipathy toward anti-semitism and myths of racial superiority, the Red Power movement, the mounting attack on gender and ethnic stereotyping in texts and the mass media, and the growing appreciation of Native art, are just some of these changes. Faced with the threats of nuclear war and environmental collapse, with urban decay, prolific crime, civil unrest, rampant materialism and a decaying social order, nonNative Canadians are now far more cautious in championing the superiority of their own civilization. As a consequence of these and other changes, older prejudicial images of Indians are beginning to disappear from films and television.

However, changes in cultural artifacts such as novels and films fail to tell us the extent to which similar changes have occurred in the views held by the general public. There is a suspicion that these views are often stripped of the dignity that embellished many historical images; that contemporary images include skidrow derelicts, prostitution, barroom fights, and destitute reserves; and that many of the negative images associated with the modern welfare state have become attached to Native peoples (Chamberlin, 1975:47).

Although public opinion towards Indians and Indian affairs has not been the topic of extensive research, a sizable body of data has been accumulating. Between 1968 and 1970, Mackie (1974) conducted survey research in the Edmonton area on public perceptions of Indians, Hutterites, and Ukrainians. The images of Indians were by far the least favourable of the three groups;

> the perception of the Indians which emerged . . . is an overwhelmingly negative image of an ostracized group that neither shares the work or success values of the surrounding society nor receives its material rewards (1974:42).

With respect to Indians, Mackie's respondents emphasized poverty, lack of education, oppression by others, lack of ambition and cleanliness, and excessive drinking (1974:43).

During the early 1970s Stymeist (1975) examined ethnic relations in the northwestern Ontario town of Sioux Lookout ("Crow Lake"). Although not a public opinion study per se, Stymeist's work sheds some useful light on the topic. The town's residents viewed Indians in an entirely different light from European and Asian immigrants. Indians were seen as racial inferiors, as being lazy and untrustworthy. More importantly, Indians were perceived as failures who would not help themselves:

> most people in Crow Lake believed that Indians suffered a humiliating social situation not because of the demands of their culture, the trauma of their history or the effects of racial prejudice, but because they somehow deserved it (1975:11).

In the mid-seventies the federal government sponsored a national survey of majority attitudes towards ethnic groups (Berry et al., 1977). Indians fell at the bottom of an ethnic prestige hierarchy that ranked public assessments of nine Canadian ethnic groups. Respondents on the

Prairies were particularly negative in their assessments of Indians, whereas French Canadian respondents were more positive than the norm.

A second national study, in which Indians played a more minor part, was conducted by sociologist Reginald Bibby in 1975. When asked how serious a problem Indian-nonIndian relations were in Canada, 15% of Bibby's respondents replied "very serious," 43% "fairly serious," and 37% "not very serious." When asked whether Indians had too much power, too little, or about the right amount of power in our nation's affairs, 9% replied "too much" compared to 54% stating "too little." The latter percentage was higher than for any other group assessed through the same question, including women, French Canadians, and English Canadians. A third question asked respondents whether they agreed or disagreed with the statement "It's too bad, but in general Canadian Indians have inferior intelligence compared to whites;" 19% agreed and 77% disagreed.

The last survey to be discussed here is a pilot study conducted by the Native Council of Canada in 1976. The study combined personal interviews with a mailed questionnaire, and the results should be considered suggestive rather than representative of the Canadian population. Respondents from across Canada exhibited little knowledge of Indian affairs, with the perceptions of the least informed being the most favourable. The federal government was attacked for giving away too much money to Natives, who themselves were criticized for laziness, the abuse of alcohol, and the lack of self-initiative. In general, the prescription for the solution of Indian problems seemed to be 'work harder, lay off the booze, and stop accepting handouts from the Government'. The conclusions of the NCC study (NCC, 1976:41) are worth quoting at length:

> . . . There often seems to be a rather optimistic faith in opportunities for social mobility within the present economic-political system. While acknowledging the special problems Native people must overcome to improve themselves, Canadian people seem to believe that any individual can lift himself out of poverty through education and hard work. This attitude tends to overlook the magnitude and efficiency of the barriers to advancement for Native people. It also overlooks the fact that in the present economic-political structure, the price of Native advancement is assimilation and thus the loss of Native culture and values.

The research discussed above presents a public image of Canadian Indians that overall is negative and harsh. The evidence, however, is at best fragmentary. In order to flesh out and clarify the character of public opinion, we turn now to a 1976 national survey that examined in detail public opinion towards Indians and Indian issues.

THE 1976 NATIONAL SURVEY

METHODOLOGY

The data upon which the subsequent sections of this chapter are based were generated by a nation-wide survey of public awareness of, and opinions towards, Native Indians and Indian issues in Canada (See also Gibbins and Ponting, 1976a, 1976b, 1977; Ponting and Gibbins, forthcoming.) The sample consisted of 1832 persons aged 18 or over, randomly selected by professionally approved methods from those living south of the 60th parallel of latitude from St. John's, Newfoundland to Victoria, British Columbia. Excluded from the sampling frame were those living in the Far North or on Indian reserves.

Successive versions of the questionnaire had been pre-tested in Calgary, Toronto, Montreal or Chicoutimi, and had been sent to Indian organizations for their comment and input. Interviewing in English Canada was conducted from January 8, 1976 to February 25, 1976, while interviewing in French Canada was conducted from February 12 to March 4. The interviews, which lasted about 45-60 minutes, were conducted in the respondent's home in the official language (English or French) of the respondent's choice.

Respondents were selected through a multi-stage sampling process whereby first the city, town or rural area within a given province was selected, then geographical areas within that city (or town or rural area), then households within those areas and finally individual respondents within the selected households. The selection process was random at every stage. Up to four calls-back were made in an effort to contact selected individuals before random, structured substitution procedures were initiated. Fifty-two percent of the initially selected respondents (before substitutions) completed interviews.

Statistically speaking, a sample of 1832 allows us to make inferences about the opinions of the larger Canadian population which it represents with very high levels of confidence—or, otherwise put, with a very low probability of error.[1] Thus, for the data that follows the reader can be confident that the sample data offer a very close reflection of the Canadian population in 1976.

The provincial subsamples making up the national sample were not proportionate to their provincial populations; Quebec and Ontario had fewer respondents than their populations warranted, whereas all the other provinces had more. This disproportionate sampling approach was adopted so that we would be able to draw accurate inferences not only about the national population but about smaller provincial populations as well. For example, while in a proportionate sense Saskatchewan was entitled to only 74 of 1832 interviews, 221 interviews were actually conducted in the province. However, for this chapter the data has been statistically weighted to bring the provincial samples into line with the provincial shares of the national population. Weighting permits the national sample to accurately represent the national Canadian population.

It should be noted that data reported on the Francophone subsample refer only to Francophones in Quebec, as Francophones outside Quebec were omitted so as to simplify the interpretation of French-English differences. However, Francophones outside Quebec are included in the national-level data and in the regional subsamples.

In drawing this methodological discussion to a close it is useful to call the reader's attention to the climate of the times during which the survey was conducted. The last half of 1975 and the early months of 1976 constituted a very active period for Indian affairs and the media carried almost daily stories relating to Indian affairs. This should be kept in mind as we now turn to an examination of the public's knowledge of Indians and Indian affairs.

KNOWLEDGE

As a first step in exploring the perceptions of Indians held by the general public, it is appropriate to examine the knowledge or informational base of these perceptions. Many of the implications that we might want to attach to public perceptions hinge in part upon the degree to which the public is informed. It is also of interest whether the relatively well-informed members of the public—the so-called "attentive public" —hold opinions that are significantly different from those held by the less informed.

One of the most basic forms of information is a familiarity with the names of people involved in Indian issues. In the survey, therefore, we determined the extent to which respondents were familiar with a number of prominent individuals in Indian affairs during the seventies. In order to minimize respondent anxiety and defensiveness, the question was worded so as to disguise the fact that respondents were being tested. The responses to this question are presented in Table 3:1 along with a brief description of the individuals at the time of the survey.

Table 3:1 makes it abundantly clear that many of the key individuals in Indian affairs were virtually unknown. For some, admittedly, the national percentages conceal a very considerable regional or provincial variability in the recognition rate. Harold Cardinal's name, for example, was familiar to two-thirds of the Alberta respondents compared to eight percent of those in Ontario and less than three percent of those in Quebec. Nevertheless, the public's overall awareness is minimal. This is

TABLE 3.1
Respondent Familiarity With Individuals Involved in Indian Issues

Name	% Familiar With Name
Jean Chrétien, former Minister of Indian Affairs, and at the time of the survey, Minister of Industry, Trade and Commerce	61.4
Dan George, B.C. Indian chief and actor	47.9
Kahn-Tineta Horn, model and Indian activist	24.9
Judd Buchanan, Minister of Indian Affairs	20.1
Harold Cardinal, author and president of the Indian Association of Alberta	13.1
Louis Cameron, radical activist	11.7
Thomas Berger, member of the B.C. Supreme Court and Commissioner of the Mackenzie Valley Pipeline Inquiry	9.2
Denis Banks, Indian activist from the United States involved in Canada	8.9
James Wah-Shee, president of the Indian Brotherhood of the Northwest Territories	7.5
Jeanette Lavell, principal figure in a legal confrontation between the Indian Act and the Canadian Bill of Rights	7.2
Gloria George, president of the Native Council of Canada	5.8
Wally Firth, Native MP from the Northwest Territories	5.4
William Wuttunee, author and early Indian activist...............	5.3
George Manuel, president of the National Indian Brotherhood	4.0
Ed Burnstick, a national director of AIM in Canada	3.5
Lloyd Barber, federal Indian Claims Commissioner	3.4
Douglas Patterson, fictitious name	4.8
Daniel Starhorn, fictitious name	4.0

demonstrated by the recognition rates for two fictitious names, "Douglas Patterson" and "Daniel Starhorn," that were included in the question to give some indication of the random error that existed in responses.

Apart from a distinct set of actors, Indian issues have their own vocabulary or terminology. For example, as noted in the Introduction, an important distinction exists between *status* and *nonstatus* Indians. Although such distinctions are central to Indian affairs in Canada, they are not ones of which most Canadians are aware or have an understanding. When respondents were asked whether they were aware of any difference between status and nonstatus Indians, a full two-thirds were not. For those who were aware of a difference, only a tiny fraction explained the difference by reference to legal registration or to the jurisdiction of the Indian Act. The most common distinctions drawn (e.g., status Indians live on reserves while nonstatus Indians do not) were related to the proper legal distinction but they did not in themselves draw an accurate line between the two groups. Indeed, many respondents described the difference by using conventional interpretations of the term status. For instance, a Maritime respondent felt that "a status Indian is someone who is more important in the tribe, someone who is a chief or who does things for the tribe, or someone with money and power." If the public debate on Indian issues employs terms like status and nonstatus, the average Canadian will be unable to follow.

For people involved in Native issues, the words *Métis, Inuit*, and *Dene* (pronounced de-nay) are basic components of their working vocabulary. Once again, however, these terms are not familiar to most Canadians. Less than one half of our respondents could state a reasonably accurate definition of Métis. Respondents outside Western Canada had particular difficulty and frequently defined the term as "the Indians of Western Canada." Only one respondent in four had a rough grasp of the word Inuit (only 14% equated the term Inuit and Eskimo), and less than one in a hundred had any idea whatsoever of the meaning of Dene, even though the Dene Declaration had been unveiled with considerable media coverage the summer before. Thus, Native leaders who talked about the Dene, or even about the Inuit or Métis, were talking past rather than to the average Canadian.

Limited public information was not restricted to the meaning and definition of terms. When respondents were asked to estimate what percentage of Canada's total population is native Indian, 47% were unable or unwilling to reply. One aspect of Indian affairs about which the Canadian public is reasonably well-informed, however, concerns the level of government having main responsibility for dealing with Indians: 56% of the respondents correctly chose the federal government while another 25% chose the federal government in conjunction with other levels of government.

To conclude this discussion we briefly illustrate five factors that are related to levels of knowledge about Indian affairs: language, gender, province of residence, formal education, and age. In order to conveniently examine the impact of these factors, we constructed a composite index to measure respondents' knowledge of Indian affairs. The *Knowledge Index* incorporated answers to six questions including those discussed above (see Appendix A). For each question a respondent could receive a score of one (little or no knowledge), two (intermediate knowledge), or three (reasonable to accurate knowledge). (See Appendix A for coding details.) Total scores on the index could potentially range from six (little if any knowledge about Indian affairs) to eighteen (a very high level of knowledge). For the sample as a whole the average index score was 9.75; the great bulk of the respondents fell below the midpoint of the index.

Using the *Knowledge Index*, Figure 3:1 illustrates the relationship between the five above-mentioned socio-demographic characteristics and

FIGURE 3.1 **Socio-Demographic Variations in Respondents'
Knowledge of Indian Matters**

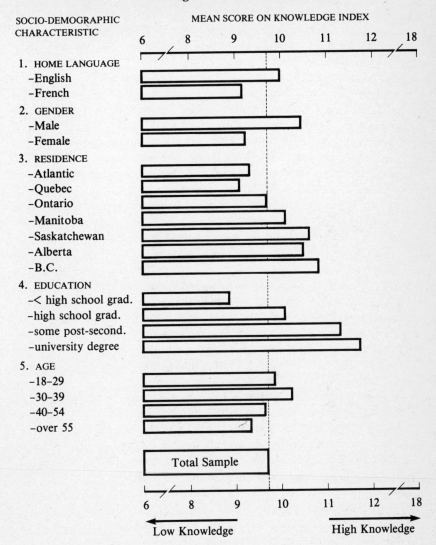

knowledge about Indian affairs by presenting the mean index scores for the various socio-demographic categories. It can be seen, for example, that there was a rough east-west gradient in levels of knowledge, with respondents living east of Ontario having low levels of knowledge and respondents living to the west having somewhat higher levels. The only weak and ambiguous relationship portrayed in the figure is that between knowledge and age.

PERCEPTIONS OF INDIAN PEOPLE

The choice of the term "perceptions" rather than the more conventional term "stereotypes" is a deliberate one that seeks to avoid a number of pitfalls addressed by Mackie (1974:39-40). For instance, a stereotype implies some consensus within the public; yet, as Mackie explains, it is very difficult to decide how much of a public consensus is necessary before a stereotype exists. Furthermore, it is often assumed that stereotypes are false simply because they are stereotypes. Mackie questions this assumption and in her own work shows that many of the stereotypes of Indians held by Edmonton respondents generally could not be considered false. While we are not in a position here to assess the veracity of public perceptions, it should be kept in mind that, true or false, they constitute an important ingredient of social reality. Indeed, their veracity is less important than is their content and distribution throughout the Canadian public.

The first question in the 1976 survey that dealt directly with Indians asked the following: *If we were to compare native Canadian Indians with other Canadians, in your opinion what would be the major differences between them? Are there any other differences?* Implicit in this question is the assumption that people do perceive differences between Indians and other Canadians. However, it is interesting to note that 16.4% of the respondents stated that there were no differences, 4.9% stated that there should be no differences, and 8.8% did not answer the question. Yet the majority of respondents (69.9%) mentioned at least one difference and many mentioned more than one.

The eleven coding categories in Table 3:2 captured the vast majority of the differences mentioned, although it must be recognized that any coding scheme can become entangled with the very complex answers that some respondents give to open-ended questions. As can be seen from the table no single difference dominated the perceptions of respondents. References to cultural differences were the most common, including references to values and attitudes, childrearing, and to rather nebulous areas such as philosophies and ways of life. The second most frequently noted difference dealt with educational disparities; perceptions of an inferior Native education are very common within the Canadian public. The third most frequently mentioned differences, which we coded as personality "deficiencies" among Indians, comes perhaps closer than any other to being prejudicial in character. No references were made to personality differences that reflected favourably on Indian peoples. Instead responses falling under this code drew attention to a putative Indian mentality that was distinguished by lack of initiative, lack of motivation, or laziness. Implicit is the belief that Indians differ from nonIndians in a racial sense independent of their socio-economic position within the

TABLE 3.2
Types of Differences Between Indians and NonIndians Mentioned by Respondents

	PERCENTAGE MENTIONING EACH TYPE*							
	REGIONAL SUBSAMPLES					LINGUISTIC SUBSAMPLES		NATIONAL SAMPLE
TYPE OF DIFFERENCE MENTIONED	Atlantic	Quebec	Ontario	Prairies	B.C.	Anglophones	Quebec Francophones	
1. Cultural Differences	22	43	25	19	21	22	44	27
2. Educational Differences	19	24	26	24	30	26	20	26
3. Personality "Deficiencies" (e.g., Laziness, Lack of Ambition)	12	7	23	32	21	25	8	21
4. Differences in Economic Opportunities, Unemployment, Job Training	22	7	23	15	15	21	3	18
5. Discrimination/Prejudice Faced by Indians	20	20	14	16	20	16	23	17
6. Poverty/Living Conditions/Standard of Living/Health	13	15	20	13	21	17	14	17
7. Government Treatment	18	6	13	13	8	13	6	12
8. Geographical or Social Remoteness of Indians	11	13	13	5	11	11	11	11
9. Difficulties in Assimilation	0	4	5	5	6	6	4	5
10. Alcohol-Related Differences	0	2	4	7	3	5	2	4
11. Indian Appreciation of, or Harmony with, the Environment	1	7	4	1	2	3	9	4
Number of Respondents	147	186	267	538	188	1130	159	1280

* Percentages based only on those respondents mentioning at least one difference. Percentages do not total to 100% due to multiple responses and "other" responses not captured by the eleven categories in this table.

Canadian society. Respondents who mentioned differences in government treatment (code 7) were almost evenly divided between those who cited preferential treatment received by Indians, principally welfare, and those who felt that Indians suffered unfavourable treatment from the Canadian government.

Following the question on the main differences between Indians and other Canadians, we asked: *What would you say are the main problems faced by Canadian Indians today? Are there any other problems you can think of?* Almost nine out of ten respondents (89.1%) mentioned at least one problem and many respondents stated more than one. Table 3:3 summarizes the problems mentioned. Perhaps the only elaboration necessary here is to note that among respondents mentioning problems with the government (code 5) the principal concern lay with the debilitating effects of welfare and government support.

Respondents were also asked what they thought was the major obstacle to improving the overall situation of Canadian Indians. In decreasing order of frequency the major obstacles mentioned were lack of education, discrimination, the need for better understanding on the part of whites, internal problems within the Indian community, the resistance of the government, government assistance, and government interference. In a somewhat related question, 17% of the national sample felt that Indian reserves help the Indian people, 33% felt they hindered Indians, 30% that they both helped and hindered, and 10% that they did neither.

A final question in this section addresses what we perceived to potentially be a source of tension within the Indian community arising from the possible conflict between aspirations for an improved standard of living and the desire to preserve traditional patterns of Indian life. Respondents were asked the following question: *Some people say that Indians have to choose between either having a higher standard of living or preserving their traditional way of life. Do you agree that they have to make that choice, or can they have both?* Nationally, 41% of the sample feel that a choice is necessary, while 53% feel that Indians can have both. Respondents who felt that a choice was necessary were also asked which choice they thought the majority of the Indian people would favour; 58% feel that the majority would choose to preserve their traditional way of life while 34% feel that the majority would choose a higher standard of living.

In summary, the perceptions of Native Canadians held by the Canadian public were seen to be complex and multifaceted. A small minority subscribes to views of Indians that are unquestionably pejorative. In this sense Indians are seen as lazy, lacking in motivation, factionalized, overly dependent upon government handouts, and facing serious problems with the use of alcohol. On the other hand a much larger proportion

TABLE 3.3
Main Problems Faced by Canadian Indians Today

TYPE OF PROBLEM MENTIONED	PERCENTAGE MENTIONING EACH TYPE*							
	REGIONAL SUBSAMPLES					LINGUISTIC SUBSAMPLES		NATIONAL SAMPLE
	Atlantic	Quebec	Ontario	Prairies	B.C.	Anglophones	Quebec Francophones	
1. Prejudice/Discrimination/Bigotry/Racism	27	51	36	31	44	35	51	39
2. Poverty/Unemployment	38	12	35	18	23	28	11	26
3. Lack of Education, Training	33	15	26	24	29	27	12	24
4. Problems of Assimilation/Reluctance to Assimilate/Forced Assimilation	10	29	16	15	15	18	28	19
5. Problems with Government/Government Assistance/Government Interference	17	18	13	20	15	16	21	17
6. Personality "Deficiencies"/Laziness, Lack of Motivation	10	5	16	18	19	18	5	14
7. Alcohol-Related Problems	7	1	13	28	12	17	0	12
8. Reservations	11	9	12	7	7	10	9	10
9. Organizational Problems Internal to Indian Movement/Leadership/Factionalism/Bickering	0	2	1	2	1	2	3	2
Number of Respondents	190	290	322	643	215	1342	249	1660

* Percentages based only upon those respondents mentioning at least one problem. Percentages do not total to 100% due to multiple response.

of the Canadian public perceives Indians to be facing problems that are not of their own creation such as a lack of economic opportunities, discrimination and prejudice, and an obstructionist government.

REACTIONS TO INDIAN LAND CLAIMS

Over the past decade land claims have received a very considerable amount of media attention. Moreover, it is through land claims that Indian aspirations impinge with the greatest potential impact upon the broader society. In one sense, however, the public reaction to land claims is difficult to measure in a national survey for the various land claims differ substantially in their scope, rationale, degree of publicity, regional focus, and potential impact upon the broader society. Our strategy was to employ a standardized set of questions which would not be especially relevant or irrelevant to particular regions within Canada, and would not be tied to specific land claims. The drawback to this approach is that we cannot predict that the outlooks expressed below in response to the general questions would necessarily apply to specific land claims.

The following question introduced the subject of land claims to respondents: *We hear a lot in the media these days about land claims being made by Indians. But since the term means different things to different people, I'd like to ask you a few questions about it and what it means to you. For instance—what percentage of Canada's land area do you get the impression that the Indians are claiming?*

In general our data suggest that the vast majority of Canadians have very little conception of the geographical extent of Indian land claims, as over two-thirds of the respondents would not even hazard an estimate as to the percentage of Canada's land area being claimed. We might add here that to the extent that Indian claims encompass large tracts of land, the absence of such public knowledge is probably tactically advantageous to Indian interests.

The second question dealt with the motivation underlying land claims: *Do you feel that when Indians lay claim to land in Canada they are mainly interested in the land for its own sake or are they mainly interested in it for the money it might bring?* The most frequent response (44%) was "land for its own sake." This response was particularly favoured by Francophones, which is consistent with the significance attached to territoriality in Québécois culture. The option "for the money it might bring" was chosen by 27% of the sample. A substantial proportion of respondents (21%) said they felt that Indians are claiming the land both for the money and for the sake of the land itself, although this option was not presented to respondents. It should be noted, by the way, that we have no evidence that the monetary motivation was any more disparaged by respondents than "land for its own sake."

The next question probed whether or not respondents were aware of the great diversity of issues involved in Indian land claims: *Do you get the impression that all Indian land claims are based on the* same *grievance, or do you feel that different land claims are based on* different *grievances?* Fifty-one percent of the national sample felt that different land claims are based on different grievances while 30% felt that all claims are based on the same grievance.

Perhaps the most politically relevant land claims question sought to establish the public's perception of the *validity* of Indian land claims. To the extent that the public perceives Indian land claims as valid, the public serves as a potential (albeit somewhat passive) source of support for such claims. Indian organizations may be able to mobilize supportive public opinion as a weapon in their political arsenal. Alternatively, if the public does not feel that Indian claims are valid, public opinion serves as a potential resource for those in the government, public service, private sector or even foreign countries (e.g., foreign investors in resource-related projects) who might, for whatever reasons, oppose Indian land claims.

The question we posed on the validity of Indian land claims is presented in Table 3:4. The data indicate that the Canadian public supports the validity of Indian land claims; 61% of the national sample replied that all or many land claims are valid. More importantly, perhaps, only 6% replied that *no* Indian land claims are valid. When assessing responses to this question, however, its generality must be kept in mind, for the question undoubtedly taps a general disposition towards Indian claims rather than a balanced assessment of all the claims personally known to the respondent.

In summary, we found the public's knowledge in the land claims area to be neither extensive nor rich. Furthermore, given the substantial differences which exist among Indian land claims, it is difficult to predict the public's reactions to specific land claims from the more general dispositions measured in this study. In general, however, the Canadian public appears more supportive than not of the general principle and strategy of Indian land claims. Public opposition to Native land claims seems to be neither broadly based nor intense.

REACTIONS TO INDIAN PROTEST AND RADICALISM

Elsewhere (Ponting and Gibbins, forthcoming) we discuss in detail the public's reaction to Indian protest and radicalism, both real and poten-

TABLE 3.4
Perceived Validity of Indian Land Claims

"Overall, do you feel that *all* Indian land claims are valid
many are valid, *few* are valid or *no* Indian land claims are valid?"

RESPONSE	REGIONAL SUBSAMPLES					LINGUISTIC SUBSAMPLES		NATIONAL SAMPLE
	Atlantic	Quebec	Ontario	Prairies	B.C.	Anglophones	Quebec Francophones	
All Claims are Valid	5%	18%	10%	6%	8%	8%	20%	11%
Many are Valid	45%	59%	50%	39%	47%	46%	57%	50%
Few are Valid	41%	13%	30%	44%	37%	36%	13%	29%
No Claims are Valid	6%	4%	7%	7%	6%	7%	4%	6%
Don't Know. No Opinion	3%	6%	4%	4%	2%	4%	5%	4%
Number of Respondents (unweighted)	220	357	354	677	224	1466	304	1832
(weighted)	174	502	663	296	197			1832

tial. To summarize that work briefly, we found that in 1976 Canadians had low levels of awareness of Indian protest; much of it went virtually unnoticed. We also found that coercive or threatening tactics received very low levels of public approval. For example, only 3% of the national respondents approved of Indians threatening violence in order to advance their interests. Finally, we concluded that there was no massive, nation-wide attitudinal backlash against Indian protest, and at the time awareness of Indian protest was unrelated to approval or disapproval of such protest. The absence of a nation-wide backlash, however, does not preclude the possibility of a more localized backlash, particularly in areas of concentrated Indian population. Nor does it necessarily preclude the possibility of a backlash in the 1980s, although the possibility here seems remote.

Backlash movements are most likely to arise when social, political or economic change causes some sector(s) of the population to experience a decline in their sense of importance, influence and power (Lipset and Raab, 1970). The affected sector of the population then seeks to preserve its status by reversing or stemming the change, often through political means. Generally speaking, the necessary conditions for such a behavioural backlash to occur are: (1) a period of profound and pervasive social change producing social strains; (2) the development of an ideology which explains what is happening to those who are bearing the brunt of this change; and (3) the designation of a target group which is defined as being responsible for the social change. While Canadians may well experience profound social change in the 1980s, change emanating from a variety of sources, the emergence of an ideology which would explain such change in racial terms seems to us unlikely. More importantly, at the *national* level Indians simply do not constitute a target which could credibly be held responsible for the types of change that we can envisage. More likely targets are readily available. Thus, a nation-wide backlash in the decade to come remains unlikely.

INDIAN SYMPATHY INDEX

Thus far we have examined a large number of specific questions relating to Indians and Indian issues in Canada. However, the very wealth and complexity of the data begs the answers to some more general questions. For example, *on balance* what is the outlook of Canadians towards Indians and Indian issues? On balance are Canadians sympathetic or antagonistic towards the Indian people, their aims and aspirations? What types of individuals are *relatively* sympathetic or *relatively* antagonistic? To answer such questions we must move beyond specific issues and construct a more general measure of respondent dispositions.

TABLE 3.5
Statements Comprising the Indian Sympathy Index

STATEMENT	% AGREEING STRONGLY OR MODERATELY							
	REGIONAL SUBSAMPLES					LINGUISTIC SUBSAMPLES		NATIONAL SAMPLE
	Atlantic	Quebec	Ontario	Prairies	B.C.	Anglo-phones	Quebec Franco-phones	
1. The Federal Department of Indian Affairs tends to be more concerned with bureaucratic red tape than seeing to the needs of the Indian people.	60	60	66	67	80	68	58	66
2. Indians deserve to be a lot better off economically than they are now.	73	77	76	56	67	70	75	72
3. If a Mackenzie Valley pipeline is imposed upon the northern Natives against their wishes, we can't blame them if they resort to violence.	25	34	28	28	33	29	35	30
4. Where Indian principles of land ownership conflict with the white man's law, Indian principles should be given priority.	26	35	30	24	31	28	34	30
5. At the present time Indians receive enough financial backing from the Federal government.	39	24	31	53	36	38	26	34

6. Since Indians feel that they were unfairly taken advantage of when treaties were originally signed, the treaties should be renegotiated.	49	60	56	46	58	53	61	55
7. On the whole, Indian leaders in Canada have demonstrated a lot of restraint in acting on their grievances.	52	41	58	58	67	60	40	54
8. Indians, as the first Canadians, should have special cultural protection that other groups don't have.	36	47	45	34	52	41	48	44
9. Most Indian leaders who criticize the Federal Department of Indian Affairs are more interested in improving their own political position than they are interested in improving the lot of their people.	35	27	27	34	24	29	27	29
10. Indian people themselves, not the provincial government, should decide what Indian children are taught in school.	31	53	31	23	23	27	54	35
Number of Respondents	220	357	354	677	244	1466	304	1832

Note: Francophone respondents had a generally higher rate of non-response to these statements, thus depressing, relative to the Anglophone subsample, the proportion of Francophones who would agree with any given statement. The comparative Anglophone/Francophone "don't know, no opinion" percentages for the ten statements are as follows: statement 1: 9/15%; statement 2: 4/16%; statement 3: 6/18%; statement 4: 8/15%; statement 5: 16/36%; statement 6: 6/16%; statement 7: 10/40%; statement 8: 4/10%; statement 9: 13/26%; and statement 10: 3/8%.

Our tool in this regard is the *Indian Sympathy Index*, a composite index of generalized sympathy, or lack of sympathy, towards Indians and Indian concerns.

A respondent's score on the Indian Sympathy Index was derived from his or her level of agreement or disagreement with the ten statements listed in Table 3:5; on each statement a respondent could agree strongly, agree moderately, neither agree nor disagree, disagree moderately, or disagree strongly. As responses to the ten statements were correlated with one another, an index score could be computed by adding together each respondent's scores for the ten statements. On each statement the respondent's score could range from five (a very sympathetic response) to one (a very unsympathetic response). Thus the total Indian Sympathy Index score could potentially range from ten (very low sympathy) to fifty (very high sympathy).

The distribution of scores on the Indian Sympathy Index approximated a normal or "bell" curve; the bulk of the respondents fell near the middle of the scale with very few respondents falling at either extreme. The distribution suggests a public disposition of neutrality or indifference towards Indian issues; there are very few extreme bigots just as there are very few extreme liberals. Figure 3:2 presents the distribution of scores on the Sympathy Index for the Anglophone and Quebec Francophone subsamples. While the shapes of the two distributions do not differ substantially, Francophones on the average received higher (more sympathetic) scores. Thus our general attitudinal measure confirms a general pattern; Francophones demonstrate a more positive outlook towards Indians and Indian issues than do Anglophones. It should be kept in mind, however, that Francophones are relatively less well-informed about Indian issues than are Anglophone respondents. The greater degree of Francophone sympathy may therefore result from a form of minority group identification with Indians rather than from a more acute grasp of the present situation of Indians in Canada.

In this light it should also be noted that, for the national sample, we found only a very weak relationship between knowledge about Indians and respondent scores on the Indian Sympathy Index. Respondents who were relatively well-informed about Indians were not, on the whole, any more sympathetic towards Indians and Indian issues than were respondents who were relatively uninformed. Knowledge per se, contrary to popular belief, does not appear to induce a more sympathetic or supportive disposition. This suggests that public relations campaigns to inform the Canadian public about the plight of contemporary Indians would show meagre returns with respect to a more supportive climate of public opinion.

An inspection of Figure 3:2 reveals a tremendous range in index

FIGURE 3.2 **Index of Sympathy Towards Indian Issues and Concerns**

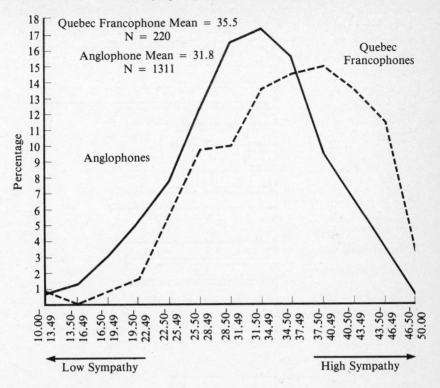

Low Sympathy   High Sympathy

scores, a range that raises some interesting questions. What are the factors that tend to propel individuals towards the sympathetic or antagonistic poles of the index? What are the socio-demographic characteristics associated with individuals on the sympathetic side of the index as opposed to those on the antagonistic side?

Figure 3:3 illustrates the impact of four potential explanatory variables. From the figure it can be seen that the provincial subsamples differed markedly in their average index scores. Respondents from Saskatchewan and Alberta were, on the average, much less sympathetic to Indian aims and aspirations than were respondents in British Columbia and Quebec. Figure 3:3 also shows that older respondents tended to be less sympathetic than did younger respondents, although a linear relationship between age and index scores was prevented by the lower-than-expected sympathy scores for respondents aged eighteen to twenty-nine. Interestingly, and somewhat surprisingly, there was no relationship between the degree of formal education and index scores; respondents with university degrees in no sense stood apart. Finally, Figure 3:3 shows that

FIGURE 3.3 **Mean Scores* on Sympathy Index by Four Respondent Characteristics**

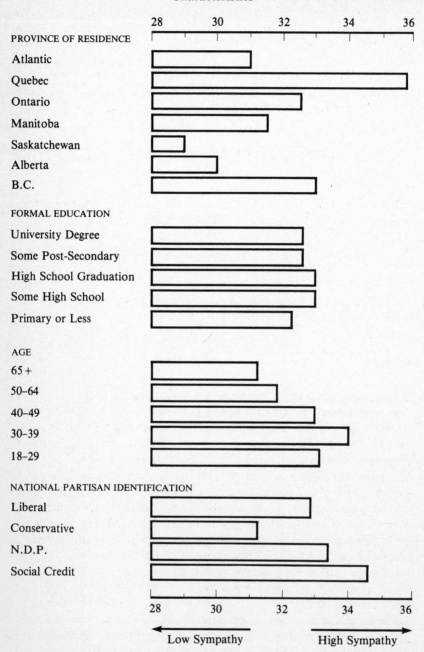

* The actual scores of individual respondents ranged from 10 to 50 on the Sympathy Index. Thus, in depicting the mean scores here we have truncated the range for ease of display.

respondents who identified with the national Conservative party were on average less sympathetic than their Liberal or New Democratic compatriots. The lower Conservative scores can partially be attributed to the prairie strength of the party just as the high Social Credit scores can in large part be accounted for by the heavy Francophone representation among the Socreds.

The discussion thus far has provided an introduction to the impact of socio-demographic factors on public opinion towards Indians and Indian issues. That discussion can now be expanded.

SOCIO-DEMOGRAPHIC DETERMINANTS OF PUBLIC OPINION

It must be stressed at the outset that it is very difficult to be precise about the impact of socio-demographic characteristics on a general and diffuse field of public opinion. For example, it is unlikely that the impact of any given factor will be in precisely the same direction and to the same degree across the hundred-odd questions in our survey that dealt with Indian issues. Thus, and due to limitations of space, the discussion below will concentrate on general effects and trends, and upon illustrative examples, rather than upon specific relationships.

REGION

The region in which respondents lived had a marked impact on their orientations towards Indians and Indian issues. Two regions in particular stood apart—Quebec, which will also be discussed in the following section on linguistic characteristics, and the Prairies. Prairie respondents were generally more knowledgeable about Indian affairs (along with B.C. respondents) but, at the same time, less sympathetic to Indian aims and aspirations (Figure 3:3) than were respondents living outside the Prairies. The reader is urged to examine the tables and figures presented in this chapter for ample evidence that orientations towards Indians and Indian affairs are clearly influenced by the regional environments within which Canadians live.

LANGUAGE

In the 1976 survey there were a substantial number of significant contrasts between Anglophone and Francophone respondents, as the tables and figures thus far have demonstrated. Francophone respondents were less knowledgeable about Indian affairs than were their Anglophone counterparts, but were, at the same time, much more sympathetic towards Indian aims and aspirations. On balance, although not consistently, Francophone respondents were also more approving of Indian protest. With respect to the major differences between Indians and nonIndians, Francophones were much more prone to mention cultural differences, while at the same time, de-emphasizing differences in personality and economic opportunity. In describing the main problems faced by contemporary Indians, Francophones were more likely to mention white prejudice and the problems associated with assimilation. Compared to Anglophones, Francophones were less prone to mention problems of poverty, unemployment, lack of education, personality deficiencies, and alcohol abuse.

In a further analysis not shown here, French-English bilinguals were generally shown to fall between unilingual Anglophone and Francophone respondents in their orientations towards Canadian Indians. For example, the mean score of English-French bilinguals on the Indian Sympathy Index was 33.9 compared to 31.4 for unilingual Anglophones and 36.7 for unilingual Francophones. English-other bilinguals, with a mean score of 30.3, were less sympathetic than the unilingual Anglophone respondents. In a second example, the proportions of respondents who felt that all or many Indian land claims were valid were as follows for the various linguistic groups: English-other bilinguals (43%), unilingual Anglophones (53%), English-French bilinguals (77%), and unilingual Francophones (81%).

EDUCATION

The impact, or lack thereof, of educational differences among respondents has already been noted in two specific cases, namely the Knowledge and Sympathy Indexes. On many of the other questions there were, at best, modest differences in the response patterns of different educational subgroups. For example, there were very few educational differences in respondent perceptions of the major differences between Indians and nonIndians, or of the major problems faced by Canadian Indians. The few significant differences that did exist were neither of sufficient strength nor consistency to support the thesis that well-educated Canadians hold generally less pejorative perceptions of Native peoples.

To the extent that education did shape opinions, the major effect was to separate respondents with less than a high school education from other respondents. It was not the respondents with the greatest amount of education who stood apart in their opinions but rather those with the least amount.

AGE

Over the past decades both the situation of Canadian Indians and the social climate of Canada have changed considerably. Because of this an individual coming of age in the 1960s or 1970s might well be expected to have a different outlook towards Indians and Indian affairs than would an individual reaching maturity during the war years. In our survey we did indeed find that the age of respondents registered an impact on perceptions, although the impact was generally modest.

As noted above, age was only weakly and inconsistently related to respondent scores on the Knowledge and Sympathy Indexes. There were also few age differences in respondent perceptions of either the differences between Indians and nonIndians or the main problems faced by Canadian Indians. We did find, however, that the proportion of respondents mentioning personality differences (laziness, lack of motivation, etc.) increased steadily with age; such differences were mentioned by only about half as many (14% vs 27%) of the respondents aged 18 to 29 compared to those aged 55 and over. With respect to the main problems faced by Canadian Indians, younger respondents were somewhat more likely to mention societal discrimination and prejudice, and somewhat less likely to mention the abuse of alcohol.

Younger respondents, reflecting perhaps their own generation's involvement in social and political protest, were consistently more willing to approve of Indian protest. A relatively sharp generational cleavage also emerged on the question dealing with the validity of Indian land claims. Older respondents were noticeably less impressed with the validity of such claims, although a majority (53.5%) nonetheless agreed that all or many Indian land claims were valid.

CONCLUSIONS

The analysis of the 1976 survey dealt with many socio-demographic determinants other than those discussed above. Across the range of issues and perceptions explored in the survey, however, none were found to have very consistent or substantial effects. For example, the gender of respondents, their location in an urban as opposed to a rural environment, and their political party identifications appeared to lack any consistent systematic impact. On particular questions, of course, significant differences were sometimes noted among respondents of different incomes, occupations, gender, and so forth. Yet, at the same time, more global generalizations, such as one pertaining to male-female differences in perceptions of Indians and Indian affairs, proved very difficult to sustain. In this respect it is interesting to note that the most marked differences were related to region and language. More individual character-istics such as age, gender, education, occupation and so forth appeared to have less impact on perceptions and opinions than did the region in which respondents lived and the language that they spoke. It seems, then, that collective differences in culture and social orientations may be more significant in this issue area than are socio-demographic differences among individuals living within a given region or linguistic community.

DISCUSSION

The major findings of the 1976 survey can be summarized as follows:

1. Indian issues were not a high priority with the Canadian public, nor was that public well-informed about Indian affairs.
2. On balance the Canadian public appeared to be more sympathetic than resistant to Indian aspirations. Of equal importance, there was no evidence of any polarization of the Canadian public into suppor-tive and hostile camps; the public seemed more characterized by in-difference and moderation.
3. While pejorative "stereotyping" of Indians was not uncommon (particularly within the Prairie provinces), it was not the norm.
4. There was no evidence of an attitudinal backlash against Indian protest.
5. There was considerable evidence that the Canadian public perceived the federal government to be an obstacle to the realization of Indian aims and aspirations. This sentiment was particularly noticeable among Francophone respondents.
6. Compared to Anglophones, Francophones displayed relatively low levels of knowledge about Indians, relatively low levels of aware-ness of Indian protest, and relatively high levels of sympathy for In-dian aims and aspirations.
7. Apart from the linguistic differences noted above, social character-istics of respondents such as their age, education, federal political partisanship, gender, and so forth bore little relationship to their at-titudes towards Indians and Indian issues. However, marked regional variations were encountered throughout the study.

It is unlikely that public opinion in Canada will be a positive force for social change in Indian affairs, in the sense that it will lead the federal government or Indian organizations. There is little parallel with the earlier civil rights movement in the United States, during which national and indeed world public opinion played a significant role in overcoming resistance to integration in the southern states and the American Con-gress. It should also be noted that, the American civil rights movement notwithstanding, generally organizations such as NIB and DIAND move the political process rather than public opinion. Finally, it must be recognized that there is no necessary correspondence between public opinion and Canadian public policy, a striking example of which is provided by the national government's abolition of capital punishment despite overwhelming public support for the retention of the death penalty.

Nevertheless, the character of public opinion is not inconsequential for the evolution of Indian affairs in Canada. Public opinion serves as a very real, if hard-to-measure, constraint on policy makers, setting limits on social change. In the face of a potentially hostile public, politicians will use public opinion as an excuse for inaction or as a rationale for the rejection of Indian demands. The sentiments of the majority cannot be readily brushed aside in the democratic political process, and minority groups must negotiate within the currents of public opinion. While in specific issues and instances public opinion may be ignored by both Indian organizations and government, over the long run such a course is perilous. It must be kept in mind, however, that the 1976 survey indicates that Canadian public opinion has at least as much potential to serve as a resource for Indian organizations as it does to serve as a resource for those seeking to block social change. On balance the Canadian public is not hostile to many and perhaps most Indian interests, and public opinion can potentially be exploited by Indian organizations in order to bring public pressure to bear upon the government.

Finally, it might be argued that in the decade to come, public opinion will gain increased importance in Indian affairs. To date most Indian issues and demands have not impinged greatly upon the lives and concerns of average Canadians. Changes in the Indian Act, the improvement of conditions on reserves, the revamping of Indian education and so forth have been of little relevance. However, issues such as Indian land claims and aboriginal rights have the potential of bringing Indians and the nonIndian Canadian majority into much more direct and visible conflict. For example, the potential clash between Indian land claims and large scale energy developments that are deemed essential to the interests of the broader Canadian society could mobilize a degree of public opposition to Indian claims far greater in magnitude than anything detected in the 1976 national survey. Thus, the future relevance of public opinion depends in large part upon the degree to which the interests of Indians and those of the larger Canadian society are compatible in the years to come.

NOTES

1. For instance, if we find on a particular question that 36% of the sample chose a particular response option, we can estimate with 99% certainty that if the

question had been posed to the total Canadian population living south of the 60th parallel of latitude, 36% plus or minus 3.3% would have chosen that response option. Stated differently, if we were to draw 100 samples of 1832 persons, in 99 samples we would find that the given response option was chosen by between 32.7% and 39.3% of the respondents. For a discussion of the principles of making estimates of population parameters from sample data, see John H. Mueller et al., *Statistical Reasoning in Sociology*, 3rd Edition, Boston: Houghton Mifflin, 1970, Chapter 13.

Part II

The Administration of Indian Affairs

Chapter 4

Fathoming the Indian Affairs Bureaucracy

Because of the complexity of the Indian situation in Canada and the broad scope of the government's involvement in the lives of Indian people, the Department of Indian Affairs and Northern Development is necessarily organized along bureaucratic lines. In this chapter and the next we attempt to unravel the complexity of the DIAND organization and to lift the shroud of mystique which cloaks large bureaucracies. Another basic purpose of this chapter is to demonstrate the lack of equivalence between the Indian/Inuit Affairs Programme (IIAP) and the Department (DIAND) as a whole.

THE OVERALL ORGANIZATION OF DIAND

Throughout most of the 1970s DIAND consisted of four main organizational subunits called "programmes," plus one small office called the Office of Native Claims. The four programmes were Indian and Inuit Affairs, Northern Development, Parks Canada, and Administration. Formally speaking, the mandate of these programmes is to implement and administer both relevant orders-in-council passed by the federal cabinet and over thirty-five statutes of the federal Parliament.[1] After the transfer of Parks Canada to the Department of the Environment in June 1979, the execution of DIAND's responsibilities involved a budget slightly in excess of one billion dollars and an authorized staff of almost 7300 persons. The size of the four programmes relative to one another is reflected in the budget figures shown in Table 4.1. There we observe that Indian/Inuit Affairs is by far the largest of the programmes and the Administration Programme is the smallest. In Figure 4.1 the programmes of the Department (plus the Office of Native Claims), along with their major subdivisions, are shown as they existed in July 1979 after the removal of Parks Canada.[2]

TABLE 4.1
Division of the DIAND Budget among the Departmental Programmes, 1965-66 to 1978-79
(x $1000)

Fiscal Year	Indian/Inuit Affairs		Administration		Northern Affairs		Parks Canada		Total	
	$	%	$	%	$	%	$	%	$	%
1978-79	678,798	55.3	26,514	2.1	327,047	26.6	194,381	15.8	1,226,740	100.0
1977-78	643,404	55.0	23,983	3.0	321,406	27.5	181,658	15.5	1,169,984	100.0
1976-77	568,404	56.3	22,750	2.3	272,315	26.9	147,002	14.5	1,010,471	100.0
1975-76	475,687	56.1	17,329	2.0	218,215	25.8	136,136	16.1	847,367	100.0
1974-75	410,183	60.8	15,658	2.3	143,359	21.2	105,925	15.7	675,125	100.0
1973-74	350,371	58.7	11,866	2.0	140,415	23.5	93,766	15.7	596,418	99.9
1972-73	306,160	58.0	11,533	2.2	129,566	24.5	80,807*	15.3	528,066	100.0
1971-72	282,221	62.3	8,059	1.8	97,112	21.4	65,559*	14.5	452,951	100.0
1970-71	242,353	66.3	6,811	1.9	78,516	21.5	38,117*	10.4	365,797	100.1
1969-70	217,759	71.5	5,872	1.9	44,836	14.7	36,166*	11.9	304,633	100.0
1968-69	165,221	62.0	5,343	2.0	55,002	20.6	41,042*	15.4	266,658	100.0
1967-68	122,517	52.9	2,349	1.0	69,592	30.1	36,717*	15.9	231,436**	99.9
1966-67	104,650	53.0	1,912	1.0	55,206	28.0	35,555*	18.0	197,415**	100.0
1965-66	81,685	52.2	1,700	1.1	44,012	28.1	28,983*	18.5	156,434**	99.9

Note: At 1969-70 fiscal year the reporting format changes.
*   Listed as "Conservation"
** Total includes a separate category ("General") not shown here.

Source: Department of Finance, *Public Accounts of Canada*, Volume I, Designated Years.

FIGURE 4.1 **Table of Organization, DIAND, July 1979**

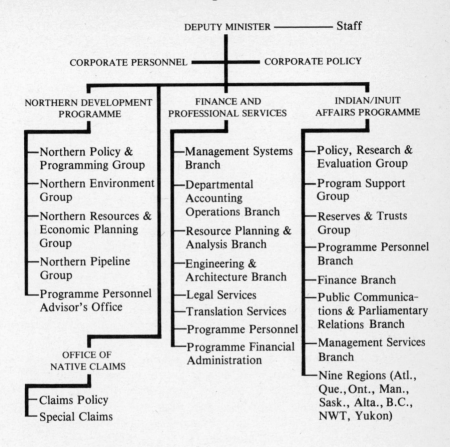

DEPUTY MINISTER ————— Staff

CORPORATE PERSONNEL ———┼——— CORPORATE POLICY

NORTHERN DEVELOPMENT PROGRAMME	FINANCE AND PROFESSIONAL SERVICES	INDIAN/INUIT AFFAIRS PROGRAMME
—Northern Policy & Programming Group	—Management Systems Branch	—Policy, Research & Evaluation Group
—Northern Environment Group	—Departmental Accounting Operations Branch	—Program Support Group
—Northern Resources & Economic Planning Group	—Resource Planning & Analysis Branch	—Reserves & Trusts Group
—Northern Pipeline Group	—Engineering & Architecture Branch	—Programme Personnel Branch
—Programme Personnel Advisor's Office	—Legal Services	—Finance Branch
	—Translation Services	—Public Communications & Parliamentary Relations Branch
OFFICE OF NATIVE CLAIMS	—Programme Personnel	—Management Services Branch
	—Programme Financial Administration	—Nine Regions (Atl., Que., Ont., Man., Sask., Alta., B.C., NWT, Yukon)
—Claims Policy		
—Special Claims		

ADMINISTRATION

The Administration Programme was authorized to employ 850 persons in 1979-80. Included here, and in budget figures for the Administration Programme, would be all of the Branches listed in Figure 4.1 under Finance and Professional Services, plus the Office of Native Claims, the Corporate Policy Group, the Corporate Personnel Group, and the Deputy Minister's office. The official function of the Administration Programme can be summarized as being the provision of overall policy direction and central advisory and administrative services to the other ("operating") programmes in the Department.

Programmes are headed by Assistant Deputy Ministers (ADMs) who report directly to the Deputy Minister. The same is true for the Corporate Policy Group. This Group is relatively small (about 43 persons), but became increasingly important throughout the 1970s. Contrary to what might be suggested by its title, this Group does not deal with policies pertaining to corporations. Rather, its main responsibilities involve: (1) policy liaison with other government departments, (2) identifying gaps and inconsistencies within and between the operating programmes of DIAND, (3) long range Departmental planning, and (4) directing policy development in areas which transcend existing programmes and in areas which do not appropriately fall within the ambit of the operating programmes (e.g., nonstatus Indians and Métis).

The Corporate Personnel Group also reports directly to the Deputy Minister. The functions performed by the seventy-six employees in its various subdivisions are much the same as would be found in most business corporations (hiring, payroll, etc.), except for added provisions for Indian and Native employment, intercultural training, and official languages (English and French) matters.

Finance and Professional Services constitutes the bulk of the Administration Programme. Finance and Professional Services is headed by an Assistant Deputy Minister whose broad responsibility areas are listed in Figure 4.1, although that chart belies the extreme structural complexity of this part of the Department.

Several of our DIAND respondents made reference to DIAND and IIAP being much more oriented towards exercising *control* over their clientele than toward generating *opportunities* for that clientele, and it is here within Finance and Professional Services that one important form of such control is exercised. This form of control, which we might call "socio-fiscal" control, is itself complex and worthy of future study.[3] However, since we shall discuss it in more detail later in this chapter we shall at this point merely describe the "damned if you do, damned if you don't" quandary which the Department faces in the financial realm.

On the one hand, the Department has been stridently criticized by the Auditor-General (Macdonnell, 1976;1978) and by some Indians (e.g., Harold Cardinal) for its inadequate financial controls that have failed to check the mismanagement of funds by some bands. On the other hand, it has been criticized by other Indians both for its lack of financial flexibility and for its failure to turn over enough funds to meet bands' needs (e.g., housing). Furthermore, the point is often made that when a people has been denied responsibility for its own affairs, as has been the case with Indians, then that people will make many mistakes and the standard rules of accountability, efficiency, and effectiveness should be relaxed. The Department appears to have tried this latter route, and then abandoned it in response to the aforementioned criticism from the Auditor-General. Under the new more rigorous mode, only modest progress has been made towards increasing Indian input in the budget-setting process and very little progress has been made towards making Indians account-able to other Indians.

NORTHERN DEVELOPMENT

The Northern Development Programme has as its official mandate the task of advancing the social, economic, and political development of the Yukon and Northwest Territories, with special emphasis on the needs of Native northerners. It is also responsible for the protection of the environment and the management of natural resources in the territories, and supports the two territorial governments in providing social and other local services. Most of the services (e.g., education) provided to registered Indians in the Territories are provided by the territorial governments and some do not appear in the budget of the territorial governments or of the Northern Programme of DIAND as expenditures on Indians (or Inuit) per se. For the same reason in the IIAP there exists only a small regional staff and a small budget for the Yukon and Northwest Territories.

The Northern Policy and Programming Group encompasses not only the regular administrative functions of a programme, but also the key functions of policy development and program evaluation. Within this Group also fall such matters as federal-territorial relations (including constitutional development), and social and cultural development for the northern Native peoples. Economic development projects in the North, including exploration and mining activities as well as economic activities outside the primary extraction sector of the economy, fall under the purview of the Northern Resources and Economic Planning Group. Environmental and pipeline matters involve yet two more Groups in the Programme.[4]

OFFICE OF NATIVE CLAIMS

The Office of Native Claims (ONC) was established in July 1974, about one year after the federal government officially reversed its earlier policy of refusing to recognize aboriginal rights to lands not surrendered by treaty (Brown, 1978). Its forty staff members receive Native claims referred to the Office by the Minister. Such claims may be ''comprehensive'' or ''specific.'' The former term refers to claims based on Natives' interest in geographic areas of Canada where the claim has not been extinguished by treaty or superseded by law. Specific claims are claims filed against the government on such matters as the government's failure to fulfill the provisions of treaties and/or of the Indian Act, as they relate to specific bands. Specific claims also involve alleged improprieties in the government's administration of Indian assets (e.g., improperly selling Indian reserve land to nonIndians).

The Office of Native Claims researches Native claims (including claims by nonstatus Indians, and Inuit), liaises with the Department of Justice, and then makes a recommendation to the DIAND Minister as to whether or not the validity of a given claim should be granted. Such advice is based mainly upon considerations of the government's *lawful obligations* and upon considerations of the policy and political implications of the claim. Once a position as to the validity of the claim has been adopted, the ONC serves as the federal government's representative during the settlement negotiations. (The government follows a policy of attempting to settle claims through negotiation rather than through the court system.) If and when a settlement is reached, ONC assists with implementing the settlement and monitors the settlement.

ONC also has other responsibilities, which include attempting to ensure consistency in the government's total approach to claims settlement, identifying policy issues (e.g., constitutional issues) related to claims, and advising on the overall strategy for dealing with Indian and Inuit claims.

Although the senior representative on each negotiating team of ONC has the authority to make certain demands and concessions during claims negotiations, the broad parameters within which he works are determined elsewhere. Crucial in the formulation of those parameters is the Claims Policy Committee. This committee comprises all the DIAND Assistant Deputy Ministers, the Executive Director (most senior official) of ONC, the Deputy Minister, and when dealing with a matter affecting the Yukon or Northwest Territories, a representative of that territorial government. In addition, representatives from other government Departments or agencies (e.g., Treasury Board, Fisheries, Prime Minister's Office) are invited as required. It is this Committee which advises the DIAND Minister on what policy proposals to take to the Prime Minister and Cabinet in respect to Native claims. There even broader parameters are set, such as the refusal of the Trudeau Cabinet to permit comprehensive claims settlements to contain provisions for the establishment of ethnically-based political jurisdictions, or the policy that comprehensive claims settlements must *extinguish* aboriginal title to the contested lands. It is, then, within the DIAND Claims Policy Committee that specific strategies and opening negotiating stances are developed for Ministerial approval, modification, or rejection; the special claims teams merely formulate more detailed bargaining tactics, scenarios, and "game plans" which they put into action during the actual conduct of negotiations.

ORGANIZATION OF THE INDIAN/INUIT AFFAIRS PROGRAMME

MANIFEST AND LATENT FUNCTIONS

The official mandate of IIAP is summarized by the government in the following terms:

> In keeping with the principles of self-development, access of opportunity, responsibility and joint participation within Canadian society, to assist and support Indians and Inuit in achieving their cultural, social and economic needs and aspirations, and to ensure that Canada's constitutional and statutory obligations and responsibilities to the Indian and Inuit peoples are fulfilled. (Department of Finance, 1979b:XII,16)

Thus, the manifest functions of IIAP include the delivery of services to Indians, the execution of certain trustee responsibilities, and the fostering of development and opportunity among Indians. However, in real life IIAP also performs another function not included in the above list—namely that of *social control.*

Social control is a very broad, rather abstract concept which we use to refer to the imposing of sanctions (positive for conformity, negative for deviance), the prevention of deviance, and more generally, the channelling of behaviour by placing restrictions upon the freedom of action of an individual or collectivity. As practiced at IIAP it is not always explicitly recognized, and even when it is, it is sometimes practiced not out of "evil motive," but rather in the belief that it is what is best for Indians. Yet this can work directly counter to the mandate to foster development and responsibility-taking on the part of Indians, as the following words of an Indian elder quoted by Cardinal (1977:37) attest:

> It's like there was a car on the reserve and Indian Affairs owned that car. At first they were afraid to even allow us in their car because we might dirty it, so we walked behind that car. Then they allowed us to ride in the back seat of that car and that was progress. Now they say we're going to have Indian control of education. They mean that now they'll let us sit behind the steering wheel—but only on the condition that they keep their hands on that steering wheel and on the gear shift, and their foot on the gas pedal. And they call that progress, too.

Inasmuch as a later section of this chapter discusses the mechanisms through which social control is exercised, at this point we shall merely specify the objectives or motivations underlying this latent function of social control. One such objective, it seems to us, is simply self-protection. That is, the greater the control which a member of an organization can exercise in his dealings with elements in the external environment, the greater his ability to avoid censure from those in authority over him. This applies equally to the cabinet minister, the senior bureaucrat, and the junior bureaucrat. The second objective, which pertains mainly to the senior levels of the bureaucracy, is to channel Indian demands and aspirations for new political structures so as to keep them within the bounds of acceptability to Cabinet, Parliament, and the Canadian electorate. This then is a further, albeit latent, function of IIAP, and is captured succinctly by IIAP's Director of Policy in his remarks to the authors about IIAP's proposals for revising the Indian Act in 1978. Said he:

> I don't see that we can make much more extensive changes than what we are now proposing. We have to take the middle of the road approach between what Indians want and what our masters—Parliament and the public—will accept.

Thus, in light of the fact that Indians are calling for new constitutional and legislative arrangements which would in some respects be tantamount to the sovereignty-association of the Parti Québécois, it is not surprising that the IIAP mandate makes reference to assisting Indians in the pursuit of their cultural, social, and economic aspirations, but not in their legislative and constitutional aspirations. In the same vein, the fact that the phrase "*within* Canadian society" (italics ours) is included in IIAP's mandate can be interpreted as an implicit recognition of the social control function of IIAP.

HEADQUARTERS ORGANIZATIONAL STRUCTURE

Turning now to the organizational structure of IIAP, we note that the Programme underwent several major structural changes in the 1970s. In fact, to properly understand IIAP we must regard it as being in an almost constant state of flux, in terms of either its structure, its operations, its policies, or its personnel. Most of these changes can be seen as part and parcel of the phenomenon which we might call *bureaupolitik*—that is, the struggle waged between different units, factions, or individuals for power, prestige, influence, and resources within a government department. In the unfolding of bureaupolitik in IIAP or elsewhere, changes in structure, operations, policy, or personnel are often closely related. That is, changes in organizational structure often reflect and embody changes in the relative power of different individuals or factions in the organization; working from a new position with new authority, those newly

FIGURE 4.2 **Realms of Responsibility of IIAP**

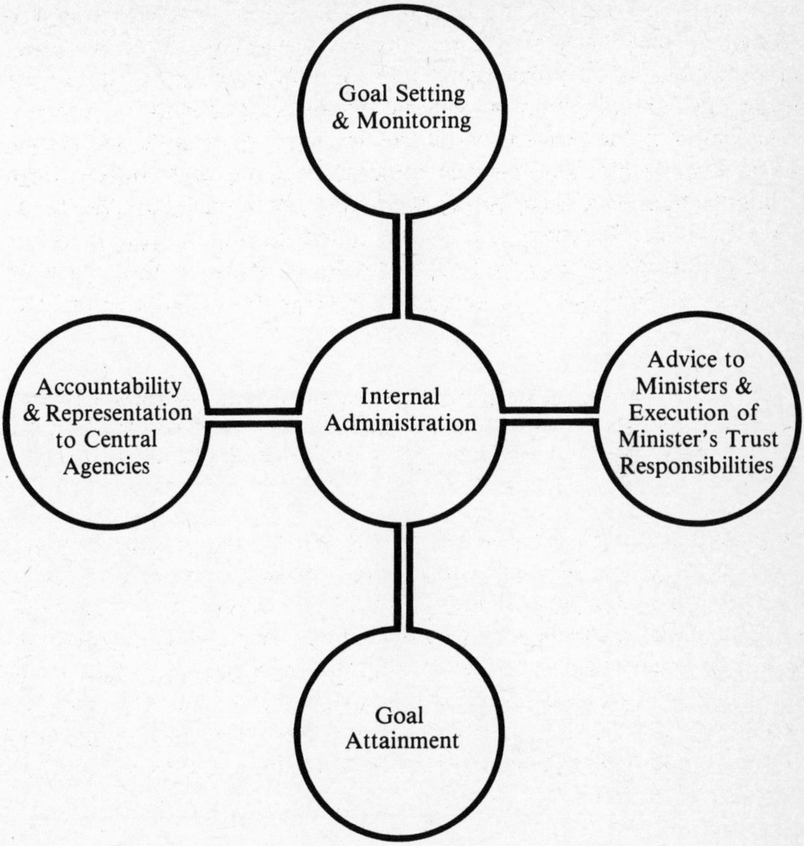

Goal Setting
& Monitoring

Accountability
& Representation
to Central
Agencies

Internal
Administration

Advice to
Ministers &
Execution of
Minister's Trust
Responsibilities

Goal
Attainment

ascendent individuals can in turn bring about changes in policy or operations. In particular, changes in the role and structure of IIAP are likely to continue on a relatively frequent basis as long as the present struggle for dominance in the Programme continues to be waged between the so-called "old guard" faction and the so-called "new guard" faction.*

---

* As if to underscore our point, after the completion of this manuscript the new Deputy Minister (Paul Tellier) announced further structural changes both in IIAP and elsewhere in DIAND. One change, which can be interpreted as a victory for the "old guard", consolidated the two Assistant Deputy Minister positions into one. ADMs Cam Mackie ("new guard") and Rod Brown ("old guard") were removed and replaced by Brown's protegé, Dave Nicholson. Another change, still unfolding in early 1980, has the Deputy Minister consolidating the policy, planning, review (e.g. program evaluation) and possibly information functions of IIAP (and perhaps also the Northern Programme) closer to him with reporting channels through the ADM-Corporate Policy.

FIGURE 4.3 Table of Organization, Indian/Inuit Programme, July 1979

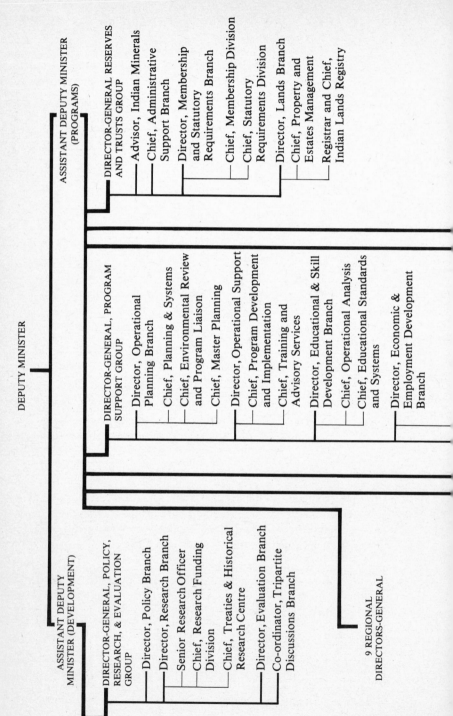

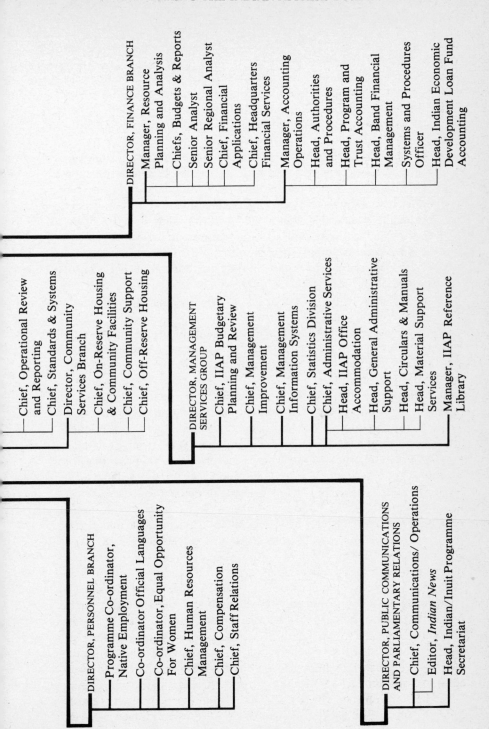

DIRECTOR, FINANCE BRANCH
- Manager, Resource Planning and Analysis
  - Chiefs, Budgets & Reports
  - Senior Analyst
  - Senior Regional Analyst
- Chief, Financial Applications
- Chief, Headquarters Financial Services
- Manager, Accounting Operations
  - Head, Authorities and Procedures
  - Head, Program and Trust Accounting
  - Head, Band Financial Management
  - Systems and Procedures Officer
  - Head, Indian Economic Development Loan Fund Accounting

- Chief, Operational Review and Reporting
- Chief, Standards & Systems
- Director, Community Services Branch
  - Chief, On-Reserve Housing & Community Facilities
  - Chief, Community Support
  - Chief, Off-Reserve Housing

DIRECTOR, MANAGEMENT SERVICES GROUP
- Chief, IIAP Budgetary Planning and Review
- Chief, Management Improvement
- Chief, Management Information Systems
- Chief, Statistics Division
- Chief, Administrative Services
  - Head, IIAP Office Accommodation
  - Head, General Administrative Support
  - Head, Circulars & Manuals
  - Head, Material Support Services
- Manager, IIAP Reference Library

DIRECTOR, PERSONNEL BRANCH
- Programme Co-ordinator, Native Employment
- Co-ordinator Official Languages
- Co-ordinator, Equal Opportunity For Women
- Chief, Human Resources Management
- Chief, Compensation
- Chief, Staff Relations

DIRECTOR, PUBLIC COMMUNICATIONS AND PARLIAMENTARY RELATIONS
- Chief, Communications/ Operations
- Editor, *Indian News*
- Head, Indian/Inuit Programme Secretariat

During periods of ascendency of the latter we can expect a decentralized organization which emphasizes developmental policies and procedures for Indians, while periods of ascendency of the former are more likely to be characterized by a thrust towards centralization (or at least putting the brakes to decentralization) and an emphasis upon structures (and processes) of accountability of Indians to IIAP. Nevertheless, in understanding the workings of IIAP, it is useful to consider its structure at the end of the 1970s.[5]

Figure 4.2 portrays the five basic functional realms of responsibility of the Programme, and Figure 4.3 provides a detailed breakdown of how the Programme was structured in June 1979 to address those responsibilities. A few caveats are in order concerning Figure 4.3. First, despite its considerable complexity, Figure 4.3 is an over-simplification of the organization of the Programme, for at many points one or even two lower levels of authority have been omitted in the interest of legibility. Yet the chart can also be misleading in the reverse sense, in that some of the subunits identified, such as those in the Management Services Branch—are actually quite small in size and flat in shape. (See also note #2 at the end of this chapter.)

Let us now consider the five functional realms of responsibility, each in turn. We begin with the responsibility of setting goals and monitoring their attainment. This is, or course, of fundamental importance to any organization. Consequently, IIAP has an Assistant Deputy Minister (ADM-Development) whose main responsibility is precisely this, and he in turn has a Policy, Research, and Evaluation Group (63 persons in 1979) to support him in this endeavour. Specific activities subsumed under the general heading in Figure 4.2 include: (1) long-range planning and the development of national goals and priorities; (2) providing for the reallocation of resources (" 'A' Base Review"[6]) in accordance with those priorities; (3) developing policy proposals and in the process engaging in consultation, negotiation, and liaison with Indian organizations, provincial governments, and other federal government Departments; (4) identifying and co-ordinating needed changes to legislation so as to be able to achieve broad policy goals; (5) conducting research upon which policy is based; and (6) evaluating programs which have been established to carry out policies, as well as assessing those policies themselves.

The mere formulation and adoption of goals and policies is, of course, no guarantee that the goals will be attained and the policies will be implemented. This, then, is a separate function in Figure 4.2, which in IIAP has been made the responsibility of a second Assistant Deputy Minister (ADM-Programs). He in turn has the Program Support Group (83 persons) to assist him and his Regional Directors-General in this endeavour. It is, then, within the Program Support Group (particularly its Operational Planning Branch) that the gap is intended to be bridged between

IIAP's field operations and its policy arm. That is to say, it is the Programme Support Group (PSG) which is supposed to ensure that the needs and realities of the field operations are taken into consideration when budgets and policies are formulated.

PSG is, however, much more than has been portrayed above. One of its main thrusts stems from the fact that the reorganization which brought it into existence had as one of its main purposes the facilitating of the process of decentralization upon which IIAP had embarked. Thus, the PSG took on the role of providing support to the nine regions in their various activities. This is done in the Operational Support Branch of PSG, and involves such things as training regional staff, equipping them to take the lead role in the development of programs to implement national policies in their region, working with them on management improvement matters, and otherwise assisting in implementing programs (e.g., by disseminating information on experiences with implementing programs in other regions). The other main thrust of PSG is one of promoting efficiency in the delivery of services to the Indian clientele. (The Regional and District offices of IIAP do the actual delivery of services; PSG does not.) This involves such activities as establishing guidelines and standards, establishing objectives to be reached on the way to meeting larger goals, developing performance indicators, and monitoring performance through the use of those indicators. These considerations of efficiency are addressed in the remaining three branches of PSG (See Figure 4.2), where the approach to the task is often highly technocratic.

The only entry in Figure 4.2, which distinguishes IIAP from a programme of most other government departments, is the trust responsibilities of the Minister. Reference here is to the fact that under the Indian Act the Minister administers certain lands, moneys, and estates for Indians, and is also responsible for keeping a central registry of who is legally an Indian. In IIAP these responsibilities are executed for the Minister by the Reserves and Trust Group (136 persons), which reports to the ADM-Programs. Specific matters falling within the purview of the Reserves and Trusts Group include leases and surrenders of Indian land; Indian minerals; band funds; adoptions, births, deaths, marriages, and enfranchisements; band elections (and protests therein); band by-laws; treaty obligations of the government; and disputes over land claimed by Indians (e.g., Anicinabe Park in Kenora, Ontario, 1974).

A fourth responsibility of any government department is to represent itself to, and be accountable to, central control agencies of government, namely, the Treasury Board, the Auditor-General, the Comptroller-General, the Public Accounts Committee of Parliament, and in this case, the House of Commons Standing Committee on Indian Affairs and Northern Development (SCIAND). For instance, the annual budget, the introduction of a new program, and sometimes even the continuation of an old program, are all dependent upon securing the negotiated approval of Treasury Board, which is a board of about five Cabinet Ministers who have responsibility for overseeing government expenditures. Such representation of the Department is always done by very senior Departmental executives.

The fifth realm of responsibility in Figure 4.2 is that of internal administration. Reference here is to responsibilities carried out by those parts of the Programme which fall towards the bottom of Figure 4.3—namely, the Finance Branch (72 persons), the Management Services Group (45 persons), the Personnel Branch (38 persons), and the Public Communications and Parliamentary Relations Branch (16 persons).

Providing advice to the Minister is the final realm of responsibility listed for IIAP in Figure 4.2. In this regard it should be kept in mind that the Minister is not the senior bureaucrat, but rather is a politician. Thus, it is his or her responsibility to make political decisions that bear upon the political acceptability of IIAP's actions and policies to the Indian population, to Cabinet, and to Parliament and the Canadian electorate as a whole. In this regard his advice comes from the Directors-General of Policy Research and Evaluation, Program Support, and Reserves and Trusts, through the Assistant Deputy Ministers and Deputy Minister. Policy advice also comes from the ADM of Corporate Policy, as well as from the Minister's own staff (particularly the Special Assistant for Indian Affairs and the Executive Assistant). Since Ministers of certain other government departments (e.g., Justice, Health and Welfare) also receive advice on some Indian-related matters from their senior executives, the DIAND Minister will sometimes have to adopt policy positions in opposition to those other Ministers or, conversely, will have to act in concert with them. The Interdepartmental Committee on Indian Affairs is designed to provide such co-ordination at the bureaucratic level, while Cabinet committees (e.g., the Clark government's Cabinet Committee on Social and Native Affairs) provide it at the political level.

In addition to those organizational units which are formally incorporated into the table of organization of the Department and the Programme, there also exist various committees and work groups which draw their members from different sectors of the organization. We have already sketched a brief overview of the Claims Policy Committee. Other examples of such working groups or committees are the Information Systems Working Group, the Indian Act Revision Committee, and the Executive Planning Committee (all of IIAP). As a standing (rather than ad hoc) committee concerned with substantive issues which directly impinge upon Indians, the Executive Planning Committee is selected for special attention below.

The basic purpose of the Executive Planning Committee is to discuss issues and problems which arise at headquarters and in the Regions, and to make recommendations concerning the future direction of IIAP. Its membership consists of the Assistant Deputy Ministers; Directors-General from headquarters and the Regions; the IIAP Directors of Finance, Management, Personnel, Public Communications and Parliamentary Relations; and the IIAP Adviser on Engineering and Architecture. The Deputy Minister is a member *ex officio* and often attends. Meetings are held about ten times per year. Two of those meetings are three day sessions which are held outside of Ottawa with a large number of Indian representatives present from bands and political associations. These two meetings are intended mainly as listening sessions at which Programme management hears directly from Indians from across the country.

The other eight meetings are each divided into two parts. In the first part there is a report on the previous meeting and on follow-up action taken in response to that meeting. Then there follows a report on the current financial and person-year status of IIAP, with projections to year's end. Then the meeting moves into a discussion of priorities, policies, and policy implementation including such matters as revisions to the Indian Act and resource allocation. The second part of these meetings is restricted to the Regional Directors-General (RDGs) and the two Assistant Deputy Ministers, and has as its basic intent, the provision of a forum where the RDGs can learn from each other's experiences and problems.

The Executive Planning Committee thus fulfills monitoring, problem solving, and planning functions for the Department. As such it has the potential to become a strategic point for the National Indian Brotherhood to gather political intelligence and to exert pressure for the rectification of various administrative irritants faced by Indians. However, it could also act as a mechanism for co-opting Indian leaders and for channelling the limited resources of Indian organizations in directions set by IIAP rather than in directions set by NIB's member organizations. Interestingly, at the time of our research IIAP was attempting to entice NIB into again participating in EPC.[7] However, in light of the pitfalls inherent in participation for NIB, and in light of NIB's preference for dealing with politicians rather than bureaucrats, it is by no means certain that IIAP's overtures will be accepted or that any such participation by NIB would be long-lived.

REGIONAL AND DISTRICT STRUCTURE

To this point we have been dealing with the organization of the Ottawa headquarters of DIAND and IIAP. However, in the mid-1970s, under Assistant Deputy Minister Peter Lesaux, IIAP began a process of decentralization of administrative authority from national headquarters to

FIGURE 4.4 Table of Organization of a Regional Headquarters (Ontario, 1978)

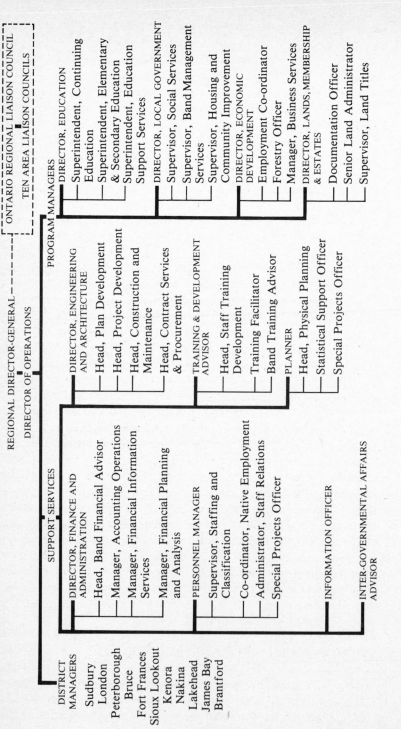

Regional headquarters, with the intent that it extend to the level of the Districts and then the bands themselves. Although that decentralization was very slow to materialize, the major reorganization of Ottawa headquarters in 1977 facilitated its coming to fruition. Thus, some important powers, such as responsibility for developing new programs, have been transferred to the Regions, and more are likely to follow as decentralization continues in the 1980s. Accordingly, in concluding our mapping of the structural-functional features of DIAND and IIAP, it is worthwhile examining briefly the nature of a Regional headquarters and a District office.

Interviews were held with one or more senior officials at the headquarters of four different regions. As the data from the Ontario Region are the most complete, and because Ontario is, in some respects, a leader in the decentralization process, we shall use it as our example.

Figure 4.4 portrays the organization of the 181 person Ontario Regional IIAP Headquarters in Toronto as it was in autumn, 1978. Several aspects of that figure merit further comment. First among these is the existence of the Ontario Regional Liaison Council (ORLC) as a formal advisory body to the Regional Director-General (RDG).

The very existence of ORLC demonstrates the rift between NIB and Ontario Indians in their strategies for dealing with government, inasmuch as ORLC represents an attempt to capture and control the bureaucracy, while NIB seeks to circumvent the bureaucracy in order to deal directly with politicians. ORLC consists of one or more representatives elected by each of the ten respective Area Liaison Councils. An Area Liaison Council consists of all of the Indian chiefs in a given IIAP District and functions in a similar capacity at the District level to the ORLC at the Regional level. As described by former DIAND Minister Hugh Faulkner, that role is "a form of 'board of directors' giving policy direction in the management of departmental business in Ontario" (ORLC Mandate, 1978). While the "board of directors" analogy overstates the actual powers of ORLC and understates the powers of the RDG, it is clear that ORLC has powers that are unprecedented in other IIAP Regions. These powers, which are to be exercised in the pursuit of the ultimate goal of achieving local government by Ontario bands, include such matters as participation in senior staffing decisions, and powers of review and approval[8] of regional resource allocations and program planning.

A second feature to note in Figure 4.4 is that the Regional headquarters staff itself can be divided into two categories—namely, support services personnel and program personnel. As in Figure 4.3, variations in the size of a unit and in the number of levels of authority under the manager of that unit are not shown in the figure. For instance, in the "Program Managers" column, under the Director of Economic Devel-

FIGURE 4.5 Table of Organization of an IIAP District Office (Sioux Lookout, Ontario, May 1979)

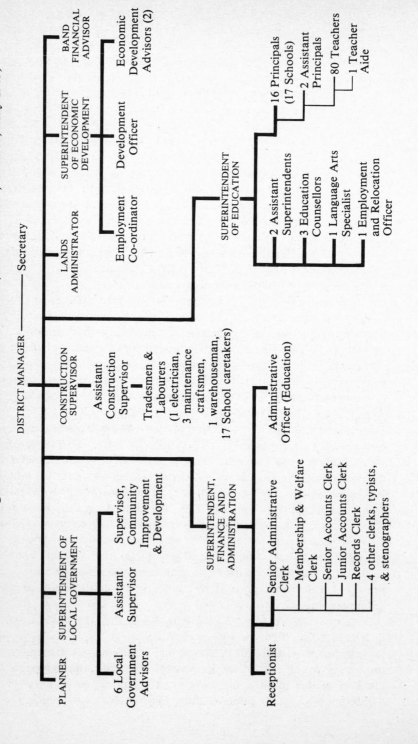

opment, the Employment Co-ordinator has reporting to him an employment services co-ordinator, an employment analyst, a youth employment administrator, and a secretary.

A third feature of Figure 4.4 is the district form of organization of the Ontario Region, whereby the region is divided into ten districts, each of which is supervised by a District Manager who reports to the Director of Operations at Regional Headquarters. This takes us to Figure 4.5 where we have portrayed the District level of organization of IIAP. We have taken, as an example, the District office at Sioux Lookout, Ontario, but the reader should bear in mind that not all district offices are identical.

With over 50 employees (not including teachers and principals), the Sioux Lookout District office stands intermediate in size among the ten Ontario District offices. The three principal program areas in which the District staff are involved are education (seventeen schools), economic development, and local government; the primary function of the latter is to help IIAP turn over to Indian bands the administration of IIAP programs. Some specific activities encompassed here for one of the six local government advisors include liaising between bands and the district office, helping bands prepare budgets, and liaising with other federal government departments on behalf of the band.

In comparing Figure 4.5 with Figure 4.4, we obtain an indication of some of the fronts on which decentralization from the regional to the district level has and has not occurred in this instance. We observe that personnel, information, engineering and architecture, and training and development have not been decentralized to the district office. Conversely, it would appear that authority for economic development, local government, lands, and planning has in significant part been transferred to the District Office. However, in other Districts and other Regions, the pattern will be different. For instance, in a conversation with the senior author, Indian leader Harold Cardinal contended that in the Alberta Region much authority has been removed from the Districts and vested in the Regional office.

THE IIAP BUDGET

As a large bureaucracy, DIAND and IIAP both have large budgets. An analysis of the nature, growth, and deployment of these moneys along with a discussion of the budget-setting process can help us to further de-mystify the Department. In addition, such a treatment can provide insights into the priorities of the Department and into some sources of power, constraint, and control therein. What it cannot do, however, is provide even an approximate answer to the highly political question of how much money actually benefits Indian individuals, for government accounting procedures simply do not permit such calculations.[9] We begin instead with a fundamental question of power—namely, the question of how the IIAP budget is set and the amount of input which Indians have in that process.

BUDGET SETTING

In response to the virtual censuring of the Department by the Auditor-General (Macdonnell, 1976:453ff; and 1978:569ff), and the concomitant wariness of the Treasury Board, DIAND and IIAP officials in the late 1970s embarked upon an effort to rationalize the budget-setting process and to control expenditures in the budget. Although in our interviews important discrepancies emerged in the accounts of various senior executives with regards to the extent to which the process had been reformed, it is clear that some reform did occur. The resultant process is a complicated one which must be launched almost two years prior to the *beginning* (April 1) of the fiscal year for which the figures are being prepared. This process is described below.

The budgetary reform involved several key features, one of which was the initiation of long-term and intermediate-term planning and the relating of budgetary expenditures to the priorities which emerged from that planning. Paradoxically, this called for an increased role in the budget-setting process for both bands and senior IIAP management. In particular, a marriage was forged between what might be termed the "roll up" procedure which bands often prefer and the "top down" procedure which central agencies like the Auditor-General had been demanding. Thus, the budget-setting process is not simply a process wherein bands and junior managers submit their budgets to the District Manager, with each more senior manager in the hierarchy gathering such budgets, making some revisions, and then passing them along to the next more senior manager. Such an approach would be highly conducive to a mushrooming in the size of the overall IIAP budget. Instead, general objectives, priorities, and Programme-wide guidelines are established by IIAP senior executives, approved or modified by the Minister, and then passed down the organizational hierarchy as a set of qualified parameters within which budget estimates must be formulated and justified by lower level managers. These lower-level managers must also seek input in one form or another from bands, then formulate the main thrusts and objectives for their unit for the fiscal year in question, and then reconcile and justify their planned expenditures in terms of both these thrusts and objectives on the one hand, and the guidelines and priorities from above on the other hand.

The next stages of the process involve the compilation of Departmental spending estimates, forwarding them to senior Departmental management for their decisions, and then sending them on to the Treasury Board. There they are scrutinized and trilateral negotiations are conducted involving the Board, the Department, and Indian organizations. After final rulings have been made by Treasury Board, the so-called "Main Estimates" are tabled by the government in Parliament and examined by the House of Commons Standing Committee on Indian Affairs and Northern Development, before which Departmental executives are sometimes called to testify. Parliament itself votes on the DIAND budget in relatively global terms, rather than line by line. Then at various times during the year, as circumstances change, budgetary revisions (usually increases) called "Supplementary Estimates" are formulated and processed with Treasury Board and in Parliament in the same manner.

INDIAN INPUT

In assessing Indian input to the budget-setting process, and degree of subsequent control over expenditures in the budget, it is important to bear in mind the distinction between discretionary and non-discretionary funds. The majority of the IIAP's funds are non-discretionary. That is, their allocation is determined by statute or by interpretation of statutes (e.g., land claims moneys, child care and social assistance payments, and tuition fees). Conversely, decisions as to the allocation of discretionary funds can be made by Indian and IIAP managers. Since this type of funds is in the minority, Indian and IIAP managers experience major constraints in planning expenditures to meet special local needs and circumstances. Even under so-called "block funding" arrangements (to be discussed below), only part of the block of funds which a band administers consists of discretionary moneys.

Indian input to budget preparation, as well as the amount of Indian control over moneys provided by Treasury Board, varies considerably from region to region and even among bands in a given district. For instance, at the time of our research in 1979, Indians in British Columbia had input into decisions concerning the allocation of the Region's seventeen million dollar capital expenditures budget (roads, buildings, and equipment) through District Chiefs' Councils. However, a senior Regional official reported that there is very little Indian participation in decisions pertaining to inter-District and intra-District allocation of funds from the seventy-seven million dollar operations and maintenance Regional budget. In comparison, in the Saskatchewan Region a representative of the chiefs from each of the seven main Districts attends all management meetings where budgets are discussed, and consultations do occur with bands for both capital budget items and operations and maintenance budget items. However, the foregoing should not leave the erroneous impression that Indians for the most part already hold broad and effective fiscal powers.

Before leaving the matter of Indian participation in IIAP budget-setting and fiscal policies, three additional points should be mentioned. First, the involvement of the National Indian Brotherhood in IIAP budget-setting was negligible until the late 1970s, for this was a matter which NIB left to the bands. This stance was reversed in 1978, when NIB fought proposed IIAP budgetary cuts. Then, in 1978, NIB obtained a commitment from the President of the Treasury Board, Robert Andras, to meet regularly with NIB to discuss the IIAP budget. Although Andras was promoted before the commitment could be implemented, this will likely be an important front for NIB's efforts in the 1980s.

Second, in some important respects the budget-setting and cutting process is not now as open as it formerly was to "power plays" by influential managers. That is, (1) budget discussions are now more open than formerly; (2) data are provided to Indians on how and where the budget is being spent; and (3) Indian leaders are sensitive to considerations of equalizing *per capita* expenditures across the Regions. Thus, it is now less common that a powerful Regional Director-General obtains a disproportionate share of IIAP's discretionary funds simply because of his power itself. However, at Ottawa headquarters the increased budgetary and person-year allocations of the Policy, Research, and Evaluation (PRE) Group in the late 1970s when the Reserves and Trust Group and the Program Support Group were experiencing budget cuts, is an accurate reflection of the increasing power of the PRE Group and of its then Director-General, Huguette Labelle.

BUDGET SIZE AND CONTENT

Turning now to the specific features of the IIAP budget, we note that the budget of this *Programme* alone is larger than that of over half of the *Departments* within the federal government. Indeed, after DIAND was formed in 1965, the IIAP share of the federal government's total budgetary expenditures increased rapidly from 1.06% to 1.74% in 1972-73. (Thereafter, it dropped as low as 1.38%, only to recover slightly and enter what appears to be a cyclic pattern.) It should also be noted that these expenditures by IIAP by no means account for all federal expenditures for status Indians. For instance, for the fiscal year 1976-77, Oliver et al. (1977:246-270) have identified approximately fifty million dollars spent by five other departments for status Indians.[10] To that figure we should add the seventy-six million dollars spent on Indian health services by the Medical Services Programme of the Department of National Health and Welfare and about four millions spent by the Northern Programme on grants, contributions, and transfer payments explicitly designated for Indians or Natives.

Within DIAND, as we observed in Table 4.1, IIAP has consistently been by far the dominant programme. At one point—the late 1960s—IIAP was experiencing yearly budgetary increases in excess of thirty percent and at the close of that decade the IIAP share of the DIAND budget peaked at 72%. These facts presumably did not go unnoticed when the federal government was formulating its 1969 White Paper calling for IIAP to be disbanded and responsibility for status Indians to be turned over to the provinces.

Government expenditures can be divided into three general types: (1) operating (also known as operations and maintenance); (2) capital; and (3) grants and contributions. Operating expenses include such items as employees' salaries and fringe benefits, consultant's services, travel and communication costs, utilities, materials and supplies, rentals, and repair

FIGURE 4.6 **Three Types of IIAP Expenditures Expressed as a percent of the Total IIAP Budget, 1970-71 to 1978-79**

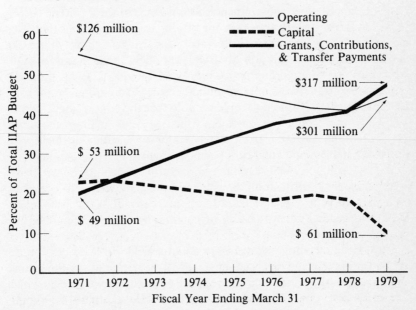

Sources: *Public Accounts of Canada* for 1971 to 1977; Budgets & Reports Section, Finance Branch, IIAP, for 1978 and 1979

and upkeep. Capital expenses include such items as road and sewer construction, acquisition of machinery and equipment, acquisition of land, and construction or acquisition of buildings. Grants and contributions include such items as payments under the James Bay Agreement, various kinds of contributions to band councils and Indian associations, payments to provincial governments for services rendered to Indians, and social assistance ("welfare") payments.

As Figure 4.6 shows, an interesting trend occurred during the decade of the 1970s. That is, while capital expenditures remained almost constant as a proportion of the IIAP budget until the inception of the fiscal restraint policy in 1978-79, grants and contributions more than doubled as a proportion of the budget, to the point where they overtook the declining proportion comprised by operating expenses. This escalation of grants and contributions is a concrete indication of the growth of Indian associations during the 1970s, and the transfer of responsibility for administering IIAP programs from IIAP to bands, associations, and provincial governments. Thus, by 1978-79, IIAP expenditures were such that out of every dollar spent by IIAP about forty-seven cents would go to Indian bands, associations, and provincial governments; a slightly lesser amount would go towards running the IIAP (operating expenses); and the remaining nine cents would go primarily to construction of such things as roads, sewers, and schools.

In addition to the above examination of IIAP expenditures by general type, we can examine those expenditures in terms of the different "activity areas" under which they fall. We do this for the decade of the 1970s in Table 4.2, where expenditures are classified as falling within the realms of: (1) administration of IIAP; (2) policy, research, and evaluation, plus consultation and negotiation with Indians; (3) education; (4) community affairs; (5) employment and economic development, or (6) a residual category. From that table we note that the largest single field of expenditure is community affairs, which at $298 million consumed almost half (44%) of the IIAP budget. Major items within this field were social assistance[11] and child care payments, which together amounted to about $147 million, while capital and operating expenditures for roads, sewers, water, electrification, housing and other physical improvements to Indian communities amounted to about $104 million. Band management and general administration of community services accounted for the remaining $47 million.

Close behind community affairs as a major field of IIAP expenditures is education—including schooling at all levels, the building and maintenance of schools, and the support of cultural expression—which consumes over one-third (39%) of the IIAP budget. In 1978-79 about half of this education budget went towards the operation of federal (22%) and non-federal (29%) schools. About one-sixth of the education

TABLE 4.2

Expenditures, Indian and Inuit Affairs Programme by Activity 1970-71 to 1978-79
(x $1000)

Year	Administration		Policy, Research and Evaluation Branch, Consultation & Negotiation		Education		Community Affairs		Economic Development		General, including Contributions to Employee Benefit Plans		Total	
	$	%	$	%	$	%	$	%	$	%	$	%	$	%
1978-79	52,240	7.7	6,427	0.9	266,034	39.1	297,981	43.8	44,889	6.6	12,019	1.8	679,590	99.9
1977-78	47,507	7.4	7,646	1.1	247,984	38.5	265,848	41.9	54,855	8.5	15,600	2.4	643,404	100.0
1976-77	40,516	7.3	11,353	2.0	226,292	40.8	230,586	41.6	44,458	8.0	1,686	0.3	554,891	100.0
1975-76	36,643	8.0	12,493	2.7	183,014	39.9	189,036	41.2	34,063	7.4	962	0.2	459,211	99.4
1974-75	32,058	8.2	4,070	1.0	164,630	41.9	163,725	41.7	27,634	7.0	902	0.2	393,019	100.0
1973-74	21,696	6.4	4,425	1.3	138,840	41.3	144,434	42.9	21,868	6.5	5,250**	1.6	336,513	100.0
1972-73	16,881	6.0	2,806	1.0	121,859	43.5	123,759	44.2	14,540	5.2	467	0.2	280,312	100.1
1971-72	15,669	6.0	1,950	0.7	120,091	45.8	109,877	41.9	13,946	5.3	394	0.2	261,927	99.9
1970-71	12,093	5.3	2,633	1.2	104,906	45.9	98,405	43.1	10,098	4.4	257	0.1	228,392	100.0

* Excluding services provided by other departments and accommodation provided by DIAND.
** Contributions to superannuation accounts is included.

Source: Department of Finance, *Public Accounts of Canada*, Volume II, Designated Years.

budget was devoted to capital costs (e.g., school construction), and the remaining one-third went to "other education" operating expenditures (e.g., post secondary tuition).

Economic development refers to the creation of business and employment opportunities for Indian people, particularly through the use of the Indian Economic Development Loan Fund (IEDLF). During the 1970s economic development doubled its share of the IIAP budget, but at less than ten percent at the end of the decade, it was surpassed by the administration costs which the IIAP incurred through its headquarters, regional, and district offices.[12] However, the IEDLF has been a source of major problems within the Programme, for as one IIAP official described it, it is "so screwed up that God and all his angels don't know how much is left in it." Until that state of affairs is rectified it is unlikely that the Treasury Board will approve major new initiatives in economic development loans in the 1980s. This could prove highly problematic in light of the major thrust towards socio-economic development which IIAP wishes to have take place during this decade.

While the foregoing shows the general areas of major expenditures of IIAP, it does not demonstrate more specific items of expenditure. These are shown in Table 4.3.[13]

In that table the residual category listed under "Grants, Contributions, and Transfer Payments" contains several separate items, two of which bear special mention here. The first is annuities owed to Indians under the treaties of the nineteenth and early twentieth centuries. These annuities now amount to only about $0.7 million or one tenth of one percent of the total IIAP budget. The second item involves payments under the modern form of treaty, in this case the James Bay Agreement. In the fiscal year in question the federal share of payments pursuant to the James Bay Agreement amounted to not quite seven million dollars.

TABLE 4.3
Itemization of Expenditures of IIAP for the Year Ending March 31, 1977

TYPE AND ITEM	MILLIONS OF DOLLARS	PERCENT
I. OPERATING		
1.1 Salaries and Wages........................ 88.7		16.0
1.2 Other Personnel Costs (e.g., pensions &		
benefits)............................... 10.3		1.9
1.3 Professional and Special Services		
(e.g., tuition @ $66.2 mil.) 82.2		14.8
Subtotal ("Personnel")	181.2	32.7
1.4 Utilities, Materials, and Supplies 27.5		5.0

1.5	Rentals (e.g., computers, buildings)	1.5		0.3
1.6	Purchased Repair and Upkeep	0.1		0.0
	Subtotal ("Facilities and Supplies")		29.1	5.3
1.7	Transportation and Communications	15.0		2.7
1.8	Information (e.g., Departmental publications) .	0.7		0.1
	Subtotal ("Communications")		15.7	2.8
1.9	Other	2.9	2.9	0.5 0.5
	Subtotal (OPERATING)		228.9	41.3
II.	**CAPITAL†**			
2.1	Housing...................................	32.7		5.9
2.2	Construction of Schools (or additions thereto) and/or Staff Units	22.5		4.1
2.3	Capital Cost of Professional and Special Services	13.4		2.4
2.4	Water and/or Sewer Systems	9.9		1.8
2.5	Construction and Acquisition of Machinery and Equipment (e.g., office furnishings, office machines)	5.8		1.0
2.6	Roads.....................................	5.7		1.0
2.7	Electrification	5.1		0.9
2.8	Other Community Facilities (e.g., community halls, band administration buildings, arenas, wharves).........................	4.6		0.8
2.9	Fire Protection	1.0		0.2
2.10	Other (e.g., community development).........	8.3		1.5
	Subtotal (CAPITAL)		109.0	19.6
III.	**GRANTS, CONTRIBUTIONS, AND TRANSFER PAYMENTS**			
3.1*	Contributions for Local Self Government and for Civic Improvement Purposes	90.6		16.3
3.2	Contributions to Band Councils and Indian Organizations ...'......................	38.8		7.0
3.3	Payments for General Assistance to Indians/ Inuit including Social Assistance Payments to nonIndians Living on Indian Reserves	31.8		5.7
3.4*	Contributions for Indian/Inuit Economic Development...........................	23.2		4.2
3.5*	Contributions for Welfare and Other Services ..	17.9		3.2
3.6*	Other (e.g., Indian Annuities, advancement of Indian/Inuit culture, research by Indian associations, payments pursuant to James Bay Agreement, etc.)	14.7		2.6
	Subtotal (GRANTS, CONTRIBUTIONS AND TRANSFERS)		217.0	39.1
	TOTAL	554.9		100.0

† Data provided by the Community Services Branch, Program Support Group, IIAP.

* Recipients of these monies are one or more of the following: band councils, Indian associations, provincial governments, or other authorities.

Source: Department of Finance, *Public Accounts of Canada, 1976-77.*

While the total payments of approximately $225 million[14] over the life of this agreement might seem very large, several factors should be borne in mind when making such an assessment. First, on the basis of cost per acre of land surrendered, the James Bay Agreement represents a tremendous bargain for the taxpayers of Canada and Quebec. According to calculations of the National Indian Brotherhood, the cost is a mere 85 cents per acre (Starblanket, 1978a:6).[15] Second, payment under the Agreement is made in many installments and usually to Indian or Native development corporations rather than to individuals. Third and finally, the payments, which will not be adjusted to keep pace with inflation, are spread over a twenty-year period and will be absorbed in part from the profits of the hydro project itself. Thus, modern treaties like the James Bay Agreement are neither the boon to Indians nor the drain on the public purse that they might at first glance seem to be.

SOCIO-FISCAL CONTROL

In concluding our discussion of the financial side of Indian affairs, we return to the matter of constraint and control over Indian people as it exists in the financial realm—what we earlier termed "socio-fiscal control." It should be noted that socio-fiscal control is merely a modern variant on a longstanding theme of government exercising power over Indians. In earlier times the social control functions of Indian administration involved physically removing Indians from the path of "progress," indoctrinating them with Eurocanadian ideology (e.g., Christianity, the Protestant work ethic) so as to prevent the "deviance" of traditional Indian practices, restricting their movement off the reserves, and keeping them dependent upon "handouts" from nonIndian administrators such as the Indian agent. In contemporary times such tactics lack legitimacy and have, for the most part, been abandoned to be replaced with socio-fiscal control.

Much socio-fiscal control is ultimately legitimated by the old adage "He who pays the piper calls the tune." That is, the provision of money is deemed to carry with it the right to specify how, for what, and by whom it will be spent. Other rights deemed to accompany the provision of money are the right to demand proof that the funds have been spent in accordance with the stipulations just cited, and the right to withdraw or terminate the funds. A primary vehicle for implementing these rights is the program "circular" which codifies the aforementioned stipulations, while the enforcers of these rules are the financial auditors and budget-setters.

In practice, socio-fiscal control takes many different forms (some of which are legitimated in the above manner, and some of which are not).

Sometimes socio-fiscal control is exercised in a deliberate and blatant fashion, particularly in an attempt to curb political deviance by Indians. One example here is IIAP's suspension of about three-quarters of one million dollars in grants to NIB's member organizations (for work on revising the Indian Act) as a direct result of NIB embarassing the government by withdrawing from the Joint NIB/Cabinet Committee. A second example is found in DIAND's withdrawal of funds from the Dene and Métis of the Mackenzie Valley until such time as they ended their political "squabbling" and came to a joint position to adopt in their land claims negotiations with DIAND. Cardinal (1977:190-1) provides yet another example.

A form of socio-fiscal control which is rooted in the discretionary powers of certain administrators is the dispensing of patronage so as to control certain factions on reserves (Dosman, 1972:57). A third form practiced by IIAP is the sowing of disunity among Indians by telling one Indian group or organization that there are insufficient funds available for it because another Indian group or organization has a disproportionately large share.

Sometimes socio-fiscal control results even when administrators' motives are not manipulative. One DIAND senior advisor remarked to the authors:

> One of the concerns of the Department is that in the future instead of the Department financially 'raping' Indians on the reserves, the Indian associations, the consultants, and the lawyers will 'rape' the Indians on the reserves.

This suggests a neo-paternalistic form of protectionism wherein Departmental members "drag their heels" on turning over greater financial responsibilities to Indians, thereby leaving Indians in a state of continued dependency. The dependency generated by lengthy periods of resort to welfare payments provides another example of socio-fiscal control occurring even when probably not intended, for prolonged welfare is fully capable of draining individuals of the initiative and sense of self-esteem that are necessary for launching any challenge to the political or administrative status quo. Another example can be found in other departments' resistance to block funding (discussed below) on the grounds that such funding arrangements would constitute preferential treatment for Indians. A final example to be cited here involves overly rigid demands from central agencies such as the Treasury Board for accountability on the part of Indians. In this regard Indian organizations have on occasion been subjected to time-consuming and belittling requirements for quarterly—rather than annual—audits of Indian expenditures of government funds.

The question arises, then, as to how to lessen the intended and unintended social control features of financial management. The answer must be multi-faceted. One facet involves augmenting the managerial skills of Indian bands and organizations so as to gain the confidence of central agencies and lessen the likelihood that they will impose special, overly rigid requirements for accountability. A second facet involves making adequate funds available for crucial programs, although the naive belief that simply making more money available is all that is required is no longer tenable. A third facet involves greater utilization of what is called "block funding"—the transfer of funds to Indians in such a manner that the number of categories of accountability is minimized and the discretionary ability of Indians to alter guidelines to suit local conditions is maximized.

By way of illustration, under block funding a band could be held accountable for attaining results from one large block of funds under the broad label of "social development," rather than having to account separately for expenditures in each of three smaller social development programs. That way the band could combine funds to make a concerted attack on the root causes of its top priority problem in the social development field, rather than having to merely tokenisticly address the symptoms of three non-priority social development problems for which the government moneys might be designated. Furthermore, if the band deems that local conditions are so severe that there is a need to take drastic measures (such as requiring all welfare recipients to work on community projects), then it would have the flexibility to impose such a rule even if it contravened the national regulations of one of the three social development programs.

A fourth facet is that the lines of accountability would have to be changed so that Indians are accountable to other Indians.[16] For instance, federal grants might be treated like many federal transfer payments to the provinces, where the provincial spenders are accountable to a provincial constituency. That is, Indian spenders could be accountable to a band electorate or to a national body of elected Indian politicians within or outside the Canadian Parliament.

A fifth facet involves the evaluation of the effectiveness of block fund expenditures by using evaluation criteria which emanate from the Indian people themselves, rather than from academic systems theory or technocratic performance indicators.

Sixth and finally, Indians can counter government socio-fiscal control by developing even a small measure of fiscal autonomy, through the diversification of funding sources. This might be accomplished through the assistance of nonIndian support organizations such as philanthropic foundations, through developing sharing mechanisms whereby the few wealthy bands assist poor bands, or through international diplomatic efforts with the United Nations or oil-rich "Third World" countries like Nigeria or Saudi Arabia.

These, then, are some directions in which fiscal aspects of Indian affairs might head in the future. We conclude the present chapter with a consideration of some of the internal problems faced by IIAP.

INTERNAL PROBLEMS OF IIAP

BACKGROUND

Our understanding of any organization can be enhanced through a consideration of its internal problems, especially since many of those internal problems have ramifications for the organization's relations with its clientele and others in its external environment. Any consideration of the internal problems of IIAP must take into account the rapidity of internal change which the organization experienced during the 1970s. As mentioned earlier in this chapter, that change involved policy, personnel, structure, and operations. More specifically, in the policy realm, the door on the 1960s closed with a resounding bang when the 1969 White Paper was so vehemently rejected by Indians. The 1970s thus opened with the Programme seemingly adrift in a policy vacuum marked by a hiatus in program development. When John Ciaccia (pronounced "See-atch-ya") arrived as the second of the six Assistant Deputy Ministers who were to head the Programme in the 1970s, the problems of the Programme were in large part seen as personnel problems, the solution to which was thought to lay in the removal of people with the "wrong" attitudes. The change in key personnel continued with the appointment in 1974 of Judd Buchanan as the second of the five Ministers which the Department was to have in the 1970s, the appointment of Arthur Kroeger as Deputy Minister (second of three in the 1970s) and the appointment of Peter Lesaux as Assistant Deputy Minister.

Under external assault from its clientele and their supporters, the new team's response was to introduce further change, by strengthening the program development capabilities of IIAP and by generating internal structural change (the third major reorganization since 1962). The dust had barely settled from these changes when, in 1976, Cam Mackie and then Warren Allmand arrived as ADM and Minister, respectively. Their leadership style constituted quite an abrupt change from that of their immediate predecessors in many respects, not the least of which was their openness to Indians and to "Indianization" of the Programme. Under them and Deputy Minister Kroeger, a renewed emphasis was placed upon policy development, especially on the policies of decentralization of administrative responsibility and devolution of authority. To accomplish this, yet another major structural reorganization of the Programme was instituted in 1977. Finally, the latter part of the decade witnessed a considerable "tightening" of operations as the management of the Programme (particularly, but not exclusively, its financial management) came under strong external attack. With Cam Mackie and new ADMs Rod Brown and Ron Fournier (Finance and Professional Services) guiding the response to these attacks, the Programme embraced a program of "rationalization" that emphasized new thrusts towards planning, accountability, and technocracy.

PERSONNEL

Thus, through much of the 1970s IIAP can be characterized as being in a state of flux, if not turmoil. That very pervasiveness of change was one important source of the morale problems which were cited by several of our interviewees as a major problem faced by IIAP. Some employees felt that change was occurring too fast, while others felt threatened by the Indianization, by the structural reorganization of the Programme, or by government cost-cutting measures. Still others were bothered early in the decade by the lack of policy direction from management, while throughout the decade the chorus of criticism from Indians and the negligible pace of accomplishment were also frustrating.

The fact that we have cited morale problems first should not be taken to mean that they are the most serious, for morale is highly variable over time and across different parts of the Programme. Furthermore, morale is merely one facet of a larger set of staff-related problems which include such matters as vestiges of racism among employees, a high rate of turnover of personnel at the level of Director-General and above, and rigid civil service regulations which encumber the hiring of Indians and prevent the dismissal of persons who are obstacles to needed changes within the Programme.

STRUCTURAL PROBLEMS

A second set of problems faced by IIAP is structural in nature. Some of these have been rectified, others were being addressed at the time of writing, and others were scarcely recognized. An example of the first type is to be found in the fact that the administrative decentralization policy of the mid-1970s faltered on the fact that the Programme was structured in a way which was incompatible with decentralization. That is, decentralization of responsibility was not accompanied by decentralization of the corresponding requisite authority. This was rectified in the second major reorganization of the 1970s. An example of the second type of structural problem is that mechanisms have, until recently, not been in place to permit IIAP managers to keep track of what is transpiring beneath them. For instance, in describing mechanisms for providing informational feedback to managers of continuing education programs, a 1977 consultant's report said:

> Several (six) manual and automated information and reporting systems now exist but give virtually no useful information. The annual cost of these information systems is likely $500,000. (Quasar, 1977:36)

At the time of writing, a new informational feedback system had been implemented for budgetary matters, while others were at various stages of consideration or development for such matters as economic development loans, post-secondary education programs, band membership registration, and social services.

The third type of structural problem involves the fundamental design of IIAP. What is not recognized by some senior executives, or what they are not yet willing to address, is the fact that IIAP is, in many respects, not structured to facilitate the attainment of one of its main objectives, the fostering of Indians assuming control over their own affairs. As we have noted, the orientation of IIAP is still one of control over Indians. The augmenting of the Policy, Research, and Evaluation Group and the negligible representation of Indians within that Group, is one example of this. Another example can be found in the realm of socio-economic development. Here, as one of our respondents suggested, Programme executives seem not to have realized that there can be no middle ground between the Department supporting and assisting Indians to achieve Indians' own objectives, on the one hand, and on the other hand, IIAP designing programs and financial structures which implicitly suggest that some ways of doing things are better than others (and that some things are more worth doing than others). Indeed, Departmental attempts in the late 1970s to find that middle ground, in the form of proposals for a charter system of Indian government, were roundly denounced by the National Indian Brotherhood as involving no more than "sand-box politics" or the handing over of tokenistic powers to Indians for them to play at municipal government, as children would play in a sandbox. Thus, it appears that yet a further major, indeed radical, structural reorganization in IIAP will be needed in the 1980s.* It may well be that senior Departmental and Programme executives believe that neither Programme employees, the Indian clientele, nor Cabinet, is yet ready to cope with such a fundamental change in structure and power. Alternatively

---

* The structural changes announced in December 1979 are not of the type to which we are referring here.

their lack of action in this regard may stem from the knowledge that those fundamental changes are going to demand a new kind of bureaucratic professionalism on their part—a professionalism which is the antithesis of that which most of them have acquired in the sense that it calls for them to be facilitators and followers more than managers and leaders.

FIELD SUBVERSION

In the interim then, the Programme is pursuing the aforementioned dual policy of decentralization and devolution. The decentralization facet of this policy stems in part from the problems which arose from a centralized administration attempting to deal with a geographically dispersed and highly diverse clientele. In such a context, headquarters tended to lose touch with the realities of the field, with the result that nationally standardized policies were sometimes actively resisted, to the point of being subverted, by officers in the field. As one Regional Director of Operations said to the authors,

> We're not mindless robots. If we think something is wrong with a policy, it is our responsibility to try to get it changed.

Said another, in the autumn of 1978,

> Subversion has been present in some areas. It's created by a lack of clear definition of goals, objectives, and responsibilities, and by a lack of a clear mandate nationally, so you get gray areas between various levels of the organization and tensions developing in these overlapping jurisdictional domains. . . . [However] in the last few months there has been far more Regional input into headquarters' directives and policy.

Yet another IIAP official with extensive field experience indicated that even as recently as the mid-1970s, subversion of national policies sometimes occurred in the regions as a self-defence mechanism by which field officers attempted to "survive in the face of ill-advised, ill-considered headquarters actions."

DECENTRALIZATION

Thus, decentralization occurred in response to internal and external problems. Although regional employees whom we interviewed spoke favourably of it (e.g., "Now we feel like more than a post office"),[17] decentralization has not been without its own problems. These include problems in finding sufficient qualified staff to fill the newly-decentralized positions, a lack of proper informational feedback and exchange mechanisms to accompany it, and a lagging in the decentralization of financial components behind program components. Furthermore, in decentralizing administrative responsibility to bands, as well as in devolving program authority to bands, problems have been encountered in that some bands have not been properly prepared beforehand.

TECHNOCRACY

A fifth problem area, which at the time of writing was more potential than actual, is that involving the increased technocratic orientation of IIAP. By "technocratic orientation" we refer to the use of principles and models of management science and systems theory in the administration of the Programme. The technocratic orientation manifests itself in such areas within IIAP as attempts to establish quantifiably measurable performance indicators, increasing computerization, the establishment of "double feedback loops," and so on. As such, it embodies the thrust towards making the operations of the Department more rational and systematic. Indeed, the fact that the Programme had in the past tended not to be systematic, but rather to base its decisions on personalities, was cited by ADM Cam Mackie as one reason for the adoption of a technocratic approach. There are, however, other reasons for its adoption.

A major impetus for adopting a technocratic approach was demands for accountability issued by the central agencies such as the Auditor-General and Treasury Board. In the face of a burgeoning IIAP budget, they came to demand that IIAP improve its efficiency, demonstrate the effectiveness of its program expenditures, and account for the vast amounts of money it was consuming. Thus, as one respondent noted, technocracy emerged as a managerial reaction to the excesses of earlier years. The problem, however, was that the central agencies had very little appreciation of the unique humanistic features of Indian affairs. Thus, the Programme was led to resort to the conventional technocratic models of public administration and accounting, but in so doing often measured and took account of the wrong things (for instance, because changes in Indian's self-sufficiency and sense of well-being were difficult to measure quantitatively they were often ignored when they should have been paramount). This source of pressure for technocracy and the potential for deleterious effects of it, is well captured by the remark of one Regional senior official who, in discussing the increased technocratic orientation of IIAP, told the authors:

> If the Auditor-General hammers us one more time, I think he'll do far more harm to Indian people than he realizes. . . . The papers I see coming out of Ottawa scare the pants off me. They're too academic. They devise systems and models that they want to apply across the country.

This respondent has captured a concern expressed by several of our senior respondents. Essentially it is a concern that standardization will once again be imposed by Ottawa. From an Indian perspective, it can be seen as another example of the analogy cited early in this chapter, whereby IIAP lets Indians sit behind the steering wheel of the car, but insists on keeping its hands on the wheel and gear shift and its foot on the gas pedal.

There are other potential dangers for IIAP in its use of technocracy. Said ADM Cam Mackie, in discussing this, "If we have a weakness, its people who either can't use the technology, or are enslaved by it." Such an enslavement can lead to yet another subtle form of neo-paternalism whereby IIAP administrators once again come to believe that they, not Indians, know what is best for Indians. Unlike the old paternalism, which was justified by a belief in the administrator's moral, cultural, and intellectual superiority over Indians, this neo-paternalism is justified by a theoretical, social scientific authority. The potential problem here is that this social scientific self-righteousness may lead Programme planners to become overly directive with regards to social change, rather than responding to initiatives from Indians.

Another potential pitfall to the technocratic orientation stems from the fact that it is more concerned with form (structures and systems) than with content. As such, we contend, it is lacking in sensitivity to Indian culture. As one Indian elder told us:

> I have grave reservations about some of the technocratic directions in which the Department is moving. It is theoretical and logical, but I don't know how practical [in the context of Indian culture.]

In particular, it does not seem to be responsive to—indeed it seems to assault—the spiritual dimensions of IIAP's Indian clients. As Ontario Indian leader Andrew Rickard said to us:

> The spiritual involvement is the key thing, the base. It's fundamental.

Yet it was also Rickard who expressed the opinion that IIAP's technocratic orientation has potential, that it "can be adapted, rather than shot down." To adapt it to the Indian clients, such that they are not left feeling that they are inanimate objects being processed by an unfeeling machine (IIAP) will, in our opinion, emerge as a major political-administrative challenge to IIAP executives.

IIAP's EXISTENCE

Finally, in considering the problems of IIAP we must cite as a problem the very fact that IIAP exists at all. That is, the contemporary IIAP is the administrative arm of a control-oriented (rather than opportunity-oriented) century-old piece of legislation—the Indian Act. As such, it has inherited, and itself contributed to, a legacy of distrust on the part of its clientele. That distrust undermines daily the very efforts of its staff to achieve the Programme mandate. We turn now, in Chapter Five, to a more detailed exploration of the people who constitute that staff.

NOTES

1. Besides the Indian Act, some examples of the statutes which DIAND administers are: the B.C. Indian Reserves Mineral Resources Act, Indian Oil and Gas Act, St. Peters Indian Reserve Act, Northern Canada Power Commission Act, and Northwest Territories Act.

2. At the time of writing some functionally minor changes were being made to that table of organization along the lines of removing some of the administrative functions (e.g., finance, personnel, and management services) from the Northern and Indian/Inuit Programmes so as to consolidate them within the Administration Programme per se. In the text when we designate the size of various units, we refer to the period prior to the implementation of these changes.

3. The very titles of some organizational units and positions in the Departmental Accounting Operations Branch (e.g., Financial Systems and Procedures Division, Financial Controls and Authorities Division, and asset control officer) themselves suggest an emphasis upon systematization, codification, and control. An interesting research project would focus upon the extent to which these appearances are accurate and upon the exercise of any discretionary authority held by officials in such units.

4. One interesting feature of the structure of the Northern Programme is the manner in which it deals with potential conflicts between economic development activities, on the one hand, and the environment of the Native peoples, on the other hand. Such conflicts are able to be addressed between Groups within the Programme first, and then must be resolved to some degree before leaving the desk of the Programme Assistant Deputy Minister. That resolution will also be subject to scrutiny by the ADM of the Indian/Inuit Programme and by the Corporate Policy Group before the Deputy Minister makes any final recommendation to the Minister.

5. The reader will note that the structure of IIAP at the end of the 1970s represented an accomodation between the "new guard" and "old guard" factions, in that a separate Assistant Deputy Minister position was created at the summit of the Programme for each faction.

6. At the time of our interviewing, the Programme was in the midst of a lengthy three-stage budgetary and management exercise. Stage 'A', The

Base Review Stage, involved the identification of all existing basic activities of IIAP and the allocation of resources to them, as well as the establishment of the Programme's priorities and the articulation of objectives for all units of the Programme. Stage 'B' involved the identification of needed new programmes and activities. The third ('X') stage involves the cutting and reallocating of resources between units within the Programme.

7. The NIB did participate in the Executive Planning Committee for over a year, but then withdrew.

8. According to correspondence to the senior author from the ADM-Programs, the revised (November 1979) ORLC mandate refers to a joint management, consultative, and advisory role, but makes no specific reference to any authority on the part of ORLC to reject budgetary allocations.

9. Stinging criticisms by the Auditor-General and others have forced IIAP officials to recognize and admit the existence of major deficiencies and inefficiencies in the treatment of funds within the Programme. This having been conceded by them, the question of how much money gets to individual Indians is probably best regarded by us as a rhetorical one. There is, for instance, no way of measuring how much of the salary and expenses of a local government advisor actually benefits the bands. Furthermore, there is not necessarily a strong correlation between the amount of money spent and the benefits derived from it. Also, the example of social assistance ("welfare") payments demonstrates that even when money goes directly to Indians, its effects may be largely negative (in the sense of generating an economy and psychology of dependence). And finally, even as bands and other Indian organizations take on greater program responsibilities from IIAP, the question remains as to what proportion of the budget will penetrate beyond Indian bureaucrats and political leaders to reach the grass roots clientele.

10. The fifty million dollars spent on status Indians by other departments are distributed among the respective departments as follows (in millions of dollars): Regional and Economic Expansion (6.9), Justice (0.5), Secretary of State (5.3), Central Mortgage and Housing Corporation (7.7 in loans), Manpower and Immigration (30).

11. In 1978-79 social assistance payments amounted to about four-fifths of the $147 million "social services" budget, while child care payments accounted for the other fifth. Social assistance payments amount to about one-fifth to one-sixth of the entire IIAP budget. This is of major concern to Indian leaders due to economic and psychological dependency which such "welfare" tends to produce.

12. The administration item within the IIAP budget is separate from, and in addition to, the Administration Programme of the Department. Administration costs within IIAP are, of course, predominantly operating (rather than capital) in nature. During the mid-1970s IIAP administration costs peaked at 18% of the total operating costs of IIAP, compared to 8% at the beginning of the decade and 15% at the end.

13. For yet two other ways of disaggregating IIAP's budget data, see Oliver et al. (1977:167-168) and Department of Finance, (1979b). The latter is particularly useful for breaking down "Grants, Contributions, and Transfer Payments," although it lacks much of the data on capital expenditures which our Table 4.3 provides.

14. The arrangements for payment to the Indian and Native signatories to the Agreement are rather complex. The maximum amount which could be paid by the federal government is $65.5 million. Half of this would be paid in ten unequal installments between 1976 and 1985.

15. According to NIB's calculations, the 1978 COPE agreement to settle Inuit land claims in the Western Arctic represents only forty-one cents per acre.

16. Making Indians accountable to Indians can itself produce difficulties if the accountability is of a bureaucratic nature, as events demonstrated in Alberta when an Indian was made Regional Director-General.

17. Other advantages to decentralization, as cited by interviewees who had experienced it in the regions, included the ability to respond more rapidly to Indians' needs and the ability to adapt to local situations.

Chapter 5

Peopling the Bureaucracy

Historically, the predecessors of the contemporary Indian/Inuit Affairs Programme tended to attract to their staff a disproportionately large number of people with a career background in the clergy, military, or to a lesser extent, the Royal Canadian Mounted Police. This should not be surprising, given the role of the missionaries among the Indians and given the fact that the Programme (Branch) at one time fell under the jurisdiction of the commander of the British colonial military forces and at another time was attached to the Department of the Interior. In addition, upon the cessation of World War II the government's guidelines giving preference in hiring to military veterans resulted in many so-called "return men" joining the staff of the then Indian Affairs Branch. Yet although most of this so-called "old guard" who entered the Branch around that time are now retiring, their legacy will remain in the form of those whom they recruited and trained, and in the form of a conviction in some quarters that the Department, not Indians, knows what is best for Indians.

This latter conviction came under serious and sustained attack in the 1960s, not only by Indians, but also by social workers trained in the "community development" school. Indeed, in 1964 when IIAP launched the community development program (See Chapter One) in an attempt to reduce Indian welfare costs, it simultaneously and unwittingly launched a new dynamic force which continues as a source of major tension in IIAP to this day. This tension, which stems from a fundamental conflict in values and in philosophies (See our concluding chapter), is in large part a conflict between the developmental and the social control orientations, between an autonomous self-development of Indians and a directive, overseeing role for IIAP. One consequence of it is a continual jockeying for position by the new and old guards as they compete for budgetary and staff allocations, and more generally, for the power to determine IIAP policy.

Historically, an enormous amount of power was concentrated in the Indian Agent (or, correctly, the Agency Superintendent) who resided right on the reserve with the Indians. However, around 1956, Indian agents were moved off reserves into offices in nearby towns. A few years later they were joined by specialists in education, housing, architecture, engineering, etc. Thus was born the district structure of IIAP's field operations, wherein each District Manager would have several reserves fall within his jurisdiction. This district format characterizes all provinces or regions except Manitoba, where it has for the most part been replaced by a service centre concept. Thus, it is now mainly just teachers and health personnel who actually live on the reserves with Indians.

IIAP is clearly a bureaucracy when assessed in terms of the usual sociological criteria mentioned in the Introduction to this book. However, because of the sweeping mandate which the Indian Act and the Treaties have bestowed upon it, the IIAP bureaucracy is uncharacteristically diverse in its occupational composition. A suggestion of this is contained in Table 5.1.

When we think of the term "bureaucracy" most of us probably think of the so-called "paper-pushers" and the people behind the counter who deal with the public—the "Administrative" and "Administrative Support" categories in Table 5.1. Yet these two types of occupation are held by less than half (47%) of all IIAP employees. Indeed, the largest single category of workers is that labelled "Scientific, Professional, and Related Technical" which constitutes 40% of the Programme. Most of these people are involved in education, although their numbers will likely shrink considerably in the 1980s as Indian bands take control of on-reserve education and teachers come to be employed by the bands rather than by IIAP.

Table 5.1 also reveals the small army of almost three hundred accountants and other commercial and financial officers,* and of over four hundred welfare workers employed by IIAP. The duties of the former would involve such work as helping to prepare budgets, assisting with the planning of economic development projects, advising bands, and enforcing the socio-fiscal control to which we referred in the previous chapter. Welfare program workers exercise considerable power over the lives of many Indians; they make the field decisions as to who is qualified and disqualified for the different types of social assistance payments. Their duties also involve advising bands with regard to social development programs in housing, employment, and local government.

By the very fact of classifying employees into general categories and sub-categories, Table 5.1 necessarily masks some of the occupational

---

* With the consolidation of Programme financial services into the Administration Programme of DIAND, most of these commercial and financial offices (and their support staff in Category IV of Table 5.1) will, strictly speaking, no longer be a part of IIAP.

TABLE 5.1
Regional and Occupational Distribution of Full-time, Indeterminate Employees in Northern & Indian/Inuit Affairs Programmes, February 1979

OCCUPATIONAL CATEGORY	NORTHERN DEVELOPMENT PROGRAMME		TOTAL INDIAN & INUIT AFFAIRS PROGRAMME		IIAP REGIONS								
					Ottawa Head-quarters	Atlantic	Quebec	Ontario	Manitoba	Saskatchewan	Alberta	B.C.	Yukon
	n	%	n	%	n	n	n	n	n	n	n	n	n
I. *Senior Executive*	16	2	18	<1/2	9	1	3	1	0	1	1	2	0
II. *Scientific, Professional, & Related Technical*													
— Education*	7	1	1699	36	19	81	174	394	362	330	250	88	1
— Soc. sci. & social work	44	5	106	2	32	3	9	14	1	10	14	21	2
— Engineers, architects, physical sci. & sci. support	114	14	117	2	18	5	17	11	12	11	16	27	0
III. *Administrative*													
— Commerce & financial	15	2	294	6	40	21	42	45	34	35	33	41	3
— Programmes & personnel; admin. services & information services	157	19	517	11	157	29	47	82	35	40	51	70	6
— Welfare programmes	1	<1/2	435	9	1	18	49	41	62	116	58	72	18
IV. *Administrative Support*													
— Clerical and regulatory	175	21	726	15	102	28	87	136	59	91	91	122	10
— Secretarial & stenographic	57	7	264	6	50	16	36	33	28	38	30	32	1
V. *Operational*													
— general services, general labour, trades & stationary plant	170	20	577	12	0	8	75	72	84	166	71	77	22
VI. *Other*	84	10	29	1	3	1	8	3	3	2	4	4	0
Total	840	101	4782	100	431	211	547	832	680	840	619	556	63

* Includes teachers, teachers' aides, and education services (e.g., curriculum development).

Source: Corporate Personnel Group, DIAND.

diversity which we wish to portray. Those occupations cover a broad spectrum ranging from the numerous blue collar workers (e.g., food services and laundry workers at residential schools, hospital workers, and even three ships' deckhands) to skilled professionals such as statisticians, economists, demographers, engineers, physical scientists, and senior executive managers.

Before leaving Table 5.1, a further comment is in order with regards to the aforementioned senior executives of the Programme. This category includes persons at the level of Director-General and above. In 1979, people falling in this category could earn from $31,000 (minimum for Directors-General) to $55,000 (maximum for Assistant Deputy Ministers). These people (and the Deputy Minister) are the elite of the Programme; they and the Deputy must answer to the Minister, to the Standing Committee on Indian Affairs, and to other control agencies such as Treasury Board and the Public Accounts Committee. It is within the ranks of these senior executives that broad directions and strategies are formulated for the Programme, and, in concert with the Minister, that decisions are made on policy options.

However interesting Table 5.1 may be, it does not provide any information on the extent to which this broad spectrum of occupational opportunities within IIAP embraces Indians and other Native people. We do know, however, that historically, status Indians and other Natives have been virtually "ghettoized" within DIAND and the federal Public Service in general. That is, they have been concentrated in the lowest level of the bureaucracy (Categories IV and V in Table 5.1) in menial jobs where their knowledge of, and sensitivity to, their people had no bearing on the actions of decision-makers. That this situation in IIAP had not changed greatly by the end of the 1970s is well demonstrated in Table 5.2. There we observe that although those in non-menial ("officer-level") positions constitute a slight majority (676/1263 = 54%) of all Native employees in IIAP, Natives still make up a far larger proportion of IIAP employees in the menial positions (38.1%) than of IIAP employees in officer-level positions (18.8%). Indeed, of over three hundred officer-level employees at IIAP's Ottawa headquarters, less than three dozen were Natives. In the next section we shall examine DIAND's efforts to improve this whole situation through the recruitment of more Indian and other Natives and the more strategic deployment of those already in the Department.

PARTICIPATION OF INDIANS AND OTHER NATIVES

By the 1970s the federal government had responded to the astronomically high levels of unemployment among Natives with several

TABLE 5.2
Native Employment in DIAND, by Level, April 1, 1979†

PROGRAM	LOCATION	OFFICER LEVEL* POSITIONS			NON-OFFICER* LEVEL POSITIONS			TOTAL POSITIONS		
		Total Employees	Native Employees	Percent Native	Total Employees	Native Employees	Percent Native	Total Employees	Native Employees	Percent Native
Indian and Inuit Affairs	Headquarters	304	32	10.5	170	21	12.4	474	53	11.2
	Regions	3286	644	19.6	1369	566	41.3	4655	1210	26.0
	Sub-total	3590	676	18.8	1539	587	38.1	5129	1263	24.6
Northern Development	Headquarters	303	13	4.3	109	7	6.4	412	20	4.9
	Regions	202	10	5.0	323	52	16.1	525	62	11.8
	Sub-total	505	23	4.6	432	59	13.7	937	82	8.8
Administration	Headquarters	456	13	2.9	328	10	3.0	784	23	2.9
Total (excluding Parks Canada)	—	4551	712	15.6	2299	656	28.5	6850	1368	20.0

† Totals do not correspond exactly with figures cited in the text or in Table 5.1. This is due in part to staffing changes between the dates shown and in part to the fact that some of the data supplied by DIAND/IIAP included term, casual, seasonal, and part-time employees, while some did not. About fifteen percent of the Native employees of IIAP shown in this table would be of the former types.

* "Non-officer level positions" are Categories IV (Administrative Support) and V (Operational) in Table 5.1. "Officer level positions" are all other categories in that table.

Source: Corporate Personnel Group, *Action Plans for Increased Native Employment in DIAND*, Ottawa: DIAND, Executive Summary Appendix 'B'.

programs aimed at increasing Indian and Native employment in government, in non-profit organizations, and in private industry. Two examples of such programs outside of DIAND are the RCMP's Indian Police Program to train Indians as peace officers on reserves, and the Manpower Services to Natives Program of the Canada Employment and Immigration Commission, in which employment counsellors of Native origin were hired to serve communities where the majority of clients were Natives. Other programs were offered by such government agencies as the Departments of National Health and Welfare and Justice, the Central Mortgage and Housing Corporation, and the Public Service Commission.

By the end of 1976 the three main Programmes of DIAND itself had seven recruitment or development programs directed exclusively at Indians and other Natives (Dept. of Indian and Northern Affairs, 1977: Appendix 'B').

One of these, the Indian and Inuit Recruitment and Development Program (IIRDP), was established in 1969[1] exclusively for Inuit and status Indians. That it did not exactly constitute a frontal assault on the problems of Indian participation in the Department can be seen from the fact that it originally had a mere twenty-five staff positions ("person years"). These trainee positions were distributed among the Regions and were predominantly at the lower levels of the bureaucracy. They permitted the hiring of individuals who were trained for one year and then replaced by a different twenty-five trainees the next year. After a few years the program was doubled in size and re-oriented so as to train participants for predominantly junior-level management positions. As of 1977, approximately 205 persons had received training in this managerial stream. While many Indians who now hold middle management positions came through the IIRDP, in other respects the program was clearly a disappointment. According to a Departmental memo, only slightly more than half (56%) of the managerial trainees had apparently secured related full-time employment in IIAP or anywhere else.

Indian and Native organizations appear to have been somewhat ambivalent about their people participating in the Public Service. Some leaders worried about the assimilative effects of such employment, while others saw it as strategically important that their people get to know the government from the inside. Despite their reservations, five Indian and Native national organizations pressured the federal government into launching a major initiative to increase the participation of status and nonstatus Indians, Inuit, and Metis in the federal Public Service. This venture was backed by the prestigious and powerful Treasury Board, and was formulated through the co-operative efforts of the Native associations, the Public Service Commission, the Treasury Board Secretariat, and several government departments (including DIAND). The government policy which resulted from this was originally announced by Treasury Board President Robert Andras, a former Minister Without Portfolio with responsibilities for part of DIAND, in July 1977. However, it was not set forth as official policy until over a year later, in November 1978 (Treasury Board and Public Service Commission Circular 1978-79).

The new policy, which for the sake of convenience we shall call the Native participation policy, has three specific objectives. These are to ensure that:

1. Indian, Metis, nonstatus Indian, and Inuit people participate fully in the Public Service, with particular emphasis on middle and senior management and advisory roles;

2. the Public Service is sensitive and responsive to the training and developmental needs of indigenous employees;

3. indigenous people are effectively involved in the conception, design, development, and implementation of socio-economic and cultural programs where Indian, Metis, nonstatus Indian, and Inuit people constitute a significant portion of the client population.

Under the policy, government departments are required to develop detailed action plans which are reviewed by the Treasury Board Secretariat, the Public Service Commission, and the national associations of the Indian and Native peoples. These action plans specify precisely how the above objectives are to be met and identify yearly targets. Examples of specific actions taken by Departments include: (1) the elimination of practices which discriminate against and/or present barriers to indigenous people; (2) the development of training and information (e.g., cultural awareness) programs for all employees; (3) the identification of Indians and other Natives already in their employ with good potential for promotion or training; (4) the rewriting of job descriptions and statements of required qualifications in job advertisements to ensure that relevant qualifications other than academic ones are also considered and that these statements realistically reflect the needs of Indian and Native clients; and (5) the monitoring and reporting of results. In addition, members of the national Indian and Native organizations were brought onto the Public Service Commission selection boards in order to have input into the hiring of key personnel whose jobs bear directly on Indians and other Native people (e.g., the Director of Indian Economic Development at IIAP and the Director of the Native Citizens Secretariat at Secretary of State).

At DIAND the Native participation policy had a mixed reception. The policy did receive the official endorsement of senior executives, and since no new financial resources were made available by Treasury Board, the

Department diverted one percent of its "operations and maintenance" person-year allocation for hiring under the Native participation policy. After the application of government hiring restraints, this was translated into the intended hiring of about thirty people at the "officer" level in IIAP during the 1979-80 fiscal year. One of our respondents, who was well-informed on IIAP's actions under the Native participation policy, reported that he had experienced "foot-dragging" at the senior executive levels on the implementation of the policy. This resistance, he felt, was in part rooted in a concern that implementation of the policy depletes the not overly-large pool of Indian leaders and, in so doing, conflicts with IIAP's own professed policy of augmenting local control by bands and district tribal associations. It may also be that resistance by senior executives was based in part on a concern over the possibility of a "white backlash" among departmental employees, particularly in the aftermath of the disruptions which occurred in the Alberta Regional headquarters when Indian leader Harold Cardinal assumed the Regional Director-Generalship in April 1977.

MORALE AMONG NATIVE EMPLOYEES OF IIAP

With regard to the IIAP's efforts to recruit Natives under the Native participation policy, it should be noted that IIAP is not an easy place for an Indian to work. In the first instance, Indians have historically felt a deep antagonism towards IIAP and its predecessors. The day has not yet fully passed when an Indian joining IIAP raises suspicions among other Indians that (s)he has "sold out." Second, Natives already in IIAP report (Dept. of Indian and Northern Affairs, 1977: Appendix "A") that among IIAP employees there is a vast ignorance with regards to such basic features of the Programme's environment as Indian history, values, legal and cultural distinctions, family and kinship structures, and concepts of time and work. NonNatives were also seen as overlooking the positive features of Indians while stressing the negative, and of being poor listeners when Native people speak. Clearly, it would be difficult for an Indian or other Native to not feel estranged when working in an environment where such characteristics prevail. Such estrangement would likely be particularly acute for those Indians and other Natives who enter IIAP needing assertiveness training or needing familiarity in nonNative styles of problem-solving, scheduling, work-ordering, and decision-making. Although as a result of the Native participation policy IIAP employees are required to participate in cultural sensitivity training sessions, much remains to be done (if, indeed, it is even realistic to imagine that it can be) before the worst of the alienating and demoralizing aspects of the IIAP work environment disappear for Native employees.

Confident, assertive, aggressive Natives who, in bureaucratic parlance, have "done their homework" (i.e., "properly" prepared themselves for the position or task at hand) tend to meet with high acceptance on the part of their nonNative colleagues who are well aware of the effort, under the Native participation policy, to "Indianize" the Department. However, those nonNative employees are also aware that, due to government spending constraints, the jobs of many of their colleagues are officially being declared redundant and some colleagues are being laid off. Thus, where a new Native employee is not self-evidently meritorious, and fails to convey the impression of self-confidence and competence, he can easily be defined by these nonNative employees as having been "parachuted in" as a tokenistic gesture. The result is often a reaction of resentment and condescension on the part of the nonNatives, and an undermining of whatever self-confidence the Native employee did have.

According to the Departmental Co-ordinator of Indian, Metis, Nonstatus Indian, and Inuit Employment, morale among Native employees in the Department has always been low, and continues in like manner. In the past, morale problems reportedly focused on individual personalities (e.g., feelings that one is not trusted by his/her supervisor, or perceptions of discriminatory treatment at the hands of a nonNative). Now, as expectations are raised, Native morale problems are much more heterogeneous in origin. They tend to derive from the conditions cited earlier, low salaries, the halting pace of progress in hiring Natives, and the realization that the funds for attacking one's particular concerns are quite limited.

Government announcements of fiscal "belt-tightening" seldom bode well for Native employees. For instance, hiring "freezes," the elimination of jobs, and spending cuts may affect Native applicants or employees directly; or the impact may be indirect, in that when nonNative employees are being laid off or having their jobs declared redundant, the atmosphere is not conducive to a program of "Indianization." Indeed, in October 1978 a newly-formed Native Employees Action Team expressed the concern that there was a subtle racist backlash developing against the Native participation policy in DIAND and other departments (Canadian Press, 1978b).

For some Natives low morale also stems from the frustration of not being able to bring about changes quickly enough, or from the frustration of having to do the paperwork of a bureaucracy, rather than being in the field where the results of one's work can be seen. Further fuel is added to the morale fire by symbolically important events within the Department, such as the lay-off or dismissal of fellow Natives (prominent or not), the adoption of unilateral or uncompromising stances by the Minister (e.g., on land claims or Indian Act revisions), or the apparent appeasing of Francophones at the expense of Indians (e.g., hiring competent people and then sending them on English or French language training leave rather than deploying them in the field where they are acutely needed).

Information about such symbolically charged events, be they public or private in nature, travels quickly in the Indian and Native communities through what is sometimes called "the moccasin telegraph." This is an active and far-reaching informal communication network which transcends distinctions of legal status and cultural background. It links Indians and other Natives employed by the Department with those employed in the political associations and elsewhere around the country. On occasion it even reaches into the Minister's office. Through this "underground" network, information of various sorts is passed, including notification of job vacancies and policy changes, assessments of new personnel, character assassinations, complaints to senior executives, and stories of insensitivity, insincerity, or wrong-doing by Departmental officials. Inasmuch as the history of antagonism and distrust towards the Department would likely predispose most Indian recipients of these latter stories to believe them, the stories themselves are probably subjected to very little critical scrutiny. Clearly, then, as such an active and powerful mechanism, the moccasin telegraph has an important impact on the morale of Natives in DIAND.

Low morale among Native employees, and the various factors generating it, constitute a potentially serious obstacle to the success of affirmative action programs such as those initiated under the Native participation policy. Another factor which undermines such programs is the tremendous problem of personal adjustment faced by Natives who must commute long distances or totally leave their rural communities (and sometimes their families) to go to work in the unfamiliar, impersonal world of the urban bureaucracy. For some, the culture shock is overwhelming, with the result that absenteeism is a noteworthy problem. However, when asked in 1979 about this and other forms of Native withdrawal, officials involved in the Department's Native employment efforts reported to the authors that neither absenteeism, alcoholism, nor drug abuse had reached major proportions among Native employees. Indeed, it should be noted here that although this section of the chapter has dwelled upon the problematic aspects of working for DIAND, there are many Native employees in the Department who have been able to surmount or otherwise avoid those problems and have made highly constructive Native input into the work of the Department.

SENIOR LEVEL INDIAN PERSONNEL

The Indian/Inuit Affairs Programme, and DIAND itself, have long been criticized for failing to bring significant numbers of Indians into

middle level and senior positions in the Programme. With the advent of
Cam Mackie as Assistant Deputy Minister of IIAP, in 1976, the former
state of affairs began to change. Of the sixteen such appointments made
during his early tenure as ADM, four were Indians, including Indian ac-
tivitist Harold Cardinal. All four took on the most senior position in
their respective regions.

These appointments were not intended to be the only form of Indian
input to the Programme's senior management levels. Later in this section
we shall discuss other mechanisms, such as the hiring of policy advisers
by the ADMs. However, before doing so, it is worth considering briefly
the controversial and complicated case of Harold Cardinal's appointment as Alberta Regional Director-General and subsequent dismissal,
both because of Cardinal's fame as an Indian leader, and because his
case offers some insights into Indian affairs.

Harold Cardinal is a Cree Indian from the Sucker Creek reserve in
Northern Alberta. After attending residential school and high school, he
studied sociology at Carleton University, where he became active in an
official capacity in Indian politics. As a leader of the vociferous Indian
attack on the government's 1969 White Paper, author of two books (*The
Unjust Society* and *The Rebirth of Canada's Indians*), and elected President of the Indian Association of Alberta (IAA) for nine years, he had
long been a thorn in the side of IIAP. Nevertheless, and despite being
labelled as a radical by the press, he was regarded in senior DIAND ranks
as being less doctrinaire than many Indians, and in many respects, a
moderate. He was also highly respected in those same quarters as being
one of the most intelligent and sophisticated Indian leaders in the
country.

As President of IAA, Cardinal participated on the Public Service
Commission selection panel choosing the new Alberta Regional Director-
General. He was not a candidate, although the then Director of Operations for the Alberta Region, Robin Dodson, was a candidate. When no
candidates were found to be satisfactory by the selection panel, the panel
eventually offered Cardinal the position. After consultations with Indian
elders and with Deputy Minister Arthur Kroeger and ADM Cam Mackie,
Cardinal, at the age of thirty-two agreed to accept the position for a maximum period of five years.

The goals which Cardinal discussed with the Deputy and ADM were
four in number. One involved instituting a system in which band leaders
would be more accountable to band members—a move which, it was
recognized, was bound to generate political dissent amongst bands and
bureaucratic dissent in the Programme, inasmuch as it would necessitate
a re-distribution of power on the reserves and in the Programme. A second goal involved revamping existing programs so as to capitalize upon
Alberta's economic boom and in turn alleviate the economic hardships

of Alberta Indians. A third goal involved enhancing the educational achievements of Indians to provide skills needed for managing local government. The fourth and final goal involved a reorganization of the staff and structure of the Alberta region.

At this point the story becomes so entangled that it would literally take another book to properly research it and portray it. The following paraphrasing provides but one example of the inconsistencies in the accounts of the events as told by the different parties:

> Cardinal: Kroeger and Mackie said they'd support me [in these goals] and make funds available for manpower.
>
> Mackie [reacting to an earlier draft of this manuscript]: We found no areas of disagreement and on several occasions indicated to him the appropriate steps that he might take to resolve what we agreed were some personnel problems. As a senior civil servant in the Department reporting to an ADM and DM, it would have been and would still be unthinkable for there to have been an agreement on the part of . . . myself to 'support Cardinal in his job'.
>
> Kroeger: He told us he would go slowly; yet he relieved his six senior officers of their responsibilities on the very first day. . . . He inherited one of the best staffed Regional offices in the country and took a sledge hammer to it.
>
> Cardinal: [reacting to statements above by Kroeger and Mackie]: Kroeger and Mackie did promise to support me. There was no misunderstanding. . . . Kroeger's statement gives the impression that I fired the six, which I did not. It also gives the appearance that I made a commitment to go slow in the staffing area; but any commitment I made to go slow was in the policy area with regards to getting Indian leaders to be accountable to band members. With regards to economic development and program changes I stressed the need to go quickly so as not to lose opportunities.

Cardinal's eventual downfall was related to three sets of problems. The first was personnel-related. Cardinal hired a number of Indian consultants over whom it appears he did not have full control, such that they sometimes came between him and the rest of his staff. For instance, it is alleged that on his first day in office two of these consultants who had recently been active in the American Indian Movement (in Canada), proceeded around the office identifying themselves as "Special Assistants to the RDG" and ordered employees to stand against the wall to have their picture taken "for our records." Cardinal reportedly put a stop to this as soon as he learned about it. On his first day in office, Cardinal also temporarily removed his six senior managers to research new directions for the programme to pursue in the region. These managers were temporarily relocated to basement offices in another building, a move which appears to have been insignificant to him and (according to Dodson) to them, but which became a cause celebre in the hands of the local Edmonton newspaper. Although Mackie did initially provide support to Cardinal, after intense phone calls between the two men the six were restored to their high-rise offices. However, according to Dodson, within a few days of Cardinal taking over, the organization was totally demoralized and becoming increasingly alienated from Cardinal.

Various personnel-related measures taken by the Cardinal team prompted the intervention of John McGilp, which marked the beginning of Cardinal's second set of problems. McGilp, a long-standing member of the Department (the "old guard") and Director of Operations from Ottawa headquarters, was also a fairly close advisor to the Deputy Minister. McGilp's involvement proved to be a problem for Cardinal, in that McGilp and certain others were reportedly already involved in an internal dispute with Mackie (old guard versus new guard). With Mackie having been identified with Cardinal's appointment and having supported Cardinal in the early days of his term, the McGilp faction, according to Cardinal, pounced on the issue.[2] The Deputy Minister became involved, and after he and Cardinal clashed at a subsequent Executive Planning Committee meeting in Jasper in front of the ADMs and the other RDGs, it appeared that Cardinal's fate was sealed, if it had not already been beforehand. Cardinal was certainly left without a base of supporters in the senior ranks of the programme and of the department.

Cardinal's third set of problems, and that which provided the final impetus for his dismissal, involved his relationship with the Alberta Chiefs and the Indian Association of Alberta. Cardinal reports that early in his term in office he was confronted with an auditor's report alleging fraudulent activity on the part of bands at Morley, Alberta. Cardinal withheld funds from those bands and some others, and although he contends that the chiefs involved initially agreed to the corrective measures he stipulated, very shortly thereafter they came out publicly in strong opposition to him. One of the most vocal of these critics was Chief John Snow of Morley, whose band administration offices some months before had been the scene of an armed occupation led by one of the consultants whom Cardinal subsequently hired.

Cardinal antagonized the chiefs of the province in at least three ways—by publicly referring to some as "village tyrants," by withholding the funds of some bands, and by not consulting directly with them or the Indian Association of Alberta on his steps to reorganize the Programme in the Region. The chiefs eventually acted through the vehicle of the IAA, under its President Joe Dion, by obtaining the signatures of twenty-seven of the forty-two provincial chiefs on a petition to the Department calling for Cardinal's dismissal. The support of the National Indian Brotherhood, which Cardinal helped found and of which IAA is a member, was also enlisted against Cardinal in the form of lobbying for his dismissal. In November of 1977 the tensions came to a head with the presentation of the petition. The outcome of several months of intense departmental infighting, involving allegations of the use of such tactics as anonymous letters by one side and the tampering with a letter on the other side, was that Cardinal was dismissed when he refused to accept a transfer to a job in economic development which the Minister (Hugh Faulkner) offered him.

Cardinal left office issuing a barrage of allegations pertaining to a financial "kick-back" system (between band leaders and IIAP officials) and improper and/or non-existent accounting practices involving millions of dollars from the Indian Economic Development Loan Fund (IEDLF). A report by Ministerial appointee, Jack Beaver, did find serious financial mismanagement of the IEDLF but did not substantiate Cardinal's other allegations. However, the very day after the release of the Beaver report, the RCMP announced that four charges of theft were being pressed against the former supervisor of the IEDLF in the Calgary District. Subsequently seven Indians from Morley (not band leaders) and a nonIndian construction contractor were charged with fraud or bribery in two other unrelated incidents. At the time of writing this chapter, the charge against the IIAP official and the three fraud charges were still before the courts. One charge in the bribery case was dismissed and the three related bribery charges were therefore dropped.

What does the Cardinal case tell us about Indian affairs in general, and about the involvement of Indians at intermediate or senior levels of IIAP in particular? With regard to the former, it can at least be said that the Cardinal case revealed that the cleavage in the IIAP between the "old guard" and the "new" is not just a matter of differences in age or attitudes and orientations, but rather is a fundamental feature of the bureaupolitik of DIAND/IIAP which is capable of acting as a dynamic force which shapes events in the department.[3] Second, it highlighted a mismanagement of IIAP funds. Third, as a result of the Cardinal episode it has become more widely recognized that corruption does exist in certain parts of IIAP, for once Cardinal levelled his allegations, reporters started cataloguing other instances involving court convictions against band officials and IIAP personnel. (See White, 1978 for examples from Saskatchewan.) Furthermore, the Cardinal episode suggests that achieving major changes in Indian affairs may take a long time, since such change will disrupt power structures on the reserves (See Dosman, 1972:57) and in DIAND, and the incumbents of those power structures will likely fight back.

The Cardinal episode also suggests how very difficult it is for Indians (or nonIndians) to hold senior positions in the regions or at Ottawa headquarters. Cultural sensitivity, although an asset, is insufficient to see a person through these difficulties, especially in the case of Indians who were formerly political leaders and who are therefore bound to have made enemies during their climb to the political top. The Cardinal episode suggests that the RDG must be a political fence mender and must skillfully nurture his political relationships with all his constituencies (i.e., his Minister, senior departmental personnel in Ottawa, his own staff, leaders of the provincial Indian organization(s), and at least the band chiefs and councils, if not the actual band members themselves). He must not get too far ahead of them in the changes he makes and the policies he adopts.

The Cardinal episode was a learning experience also for senior Programme and Departmental managers. They received a first hand look at the potential vulnerability of Indian RDGs to both Indian and nonIndian resistance to an Indian manager, and some seem to have been strengthened in their earlier reluctance to appoint Indians to that position. While hastening to add that they feel that Indians Phil Fontaine and Fred Kelly did very well in their respective RDG positions, the interesting fact remains that six of the nine RDG (or Regional Director) positions became vacant within a year of Cardinal's appointment and none were filled by an Indian.

The further lesson from the Cardinal case was that other means of procuring Indian input to the upper echelons of the Department and the Programme must also be used. While some of these had been in existence prior to the Cardinal episode, their importance was highlighted by it. There are now many such mechanisms which have been used, including district-level advisory councils to the RDGs (e.g., Manitoba and British Columbia), Regional level councils (e.g., the Ontario Regional Liaison Council), individual Indian advisors to the RDG or the ADM (e.g., Ahab Spence and Anthony Francis), and—outside the Department—the Joint NIB/Cabinet Committee and special Indian assistants to the Minister. To conclude this section on senior level Indians, we present a brief profile of the background and duties of one of the special Indian advisors to the ADMs.

Ahab Spence joined IIAP on contract in 1976, at the age of sixty-five, as the first Indian Special Advisor to an ADM. He brought with him a wealth of experience with Indians as a result of a lengthy and variegated career. A product of a Manitoba residential school, where he entered grade 1 at the age of ten, he eventually went on to receive a theology degree from Emmanuel (Anglican) College in Saskatoon in 1937. From then until 1965, he taught at different day and residential schools in Saskatchewan and northwestern Ontario. He also kept a rigorous preaching schedule which at one point encompassed a nonIndian parish. In 1965 he joined the public service as a liaison officer for Saskatchewan in IIAP's Community Development Program, after which he served as head of the Cultural Development Division of IIAP at Ottawa headquarters. In 1970 he left to join the Manitoba Indian Brotherhood, first as a researcher, then as Executive Director, and finally as President for two and one-half years, during which time he participated as a member of the Executive Council of the National Indian Brotherhood. Two weeks after he retired from the Manitoba Indian Brotherhood, he was approached by Cam Mackie to serve as Mackie's special advisor. Already restless with retirement, he accepted the offer, and with it the reprobation of some of his friends.

In describing for the authors the role which Spence plays from his office beside Mackie's, Mackie referred to him as "my personal elder and senior advisor who tells me biblical stories that I have to interpret in terms of Indian Act revisions, or tells me stories of his childhood days." By mutual agreement, Spence has no administrative responsibilities. Instead, drawing mainly from his own experience and his two weeks of travel per month, he advises Mackie concerning general directions being proposed for change, and how Indians would perceive them. He also attends all meetings of SCIAND and, at Mackie's invitation, sometimes accompanies him to meetings (e.g., with the Minister or with Indian people) inside or outside Ottawa. Knowing that he is strategically positioned at Ottawa headquarters, chiefs, Indian organizations, and even Indian IIAP employees frequently seek his intercession in a "troubleshooting" capacity. (However, having no authority in the Programme himself, he usually turns over such requests to Mackie.)

Spence has been strongly attacked in the moccasin telegraph as being tokenistic "window dressing," in response to which he told the authors: "I have so far seen no signs that I am being used that way." While this perception of Spence's was supported in another interview by an Indian who served as Mackie's Executive Assistant, it is nevertheless clear that the position of Special Advisor is very circumscribed in the scope of its influence. Spence, it appears, has not been aggressive in seeking to expand that scope, for he told the authors:

> I don't push myself on them. I figure if they need advice they know I'm next door. . . . I try to confine my remarks to Mackie and I feel I should not be that vocal in meetings, although he encourages me to speak out at larger meetings, which I now tend to do more and more.

Despite Spence's manifestations of reticence, the "window-dressing" charge would seem to the authors to be somewhat over-drawn. For instance, although Mackie clearly does derive benefit to his own personal image by having Spence (and other Indians) on his staff, he also benefits from advice which Spence provides. Second, although Spence does appear to be selectively utilized by Mackie, such selectivity is to be expected with a man of Spence's age, and he does use Spence in important matters. This is illustrated in the case of the proposed revisions to the Indian Act. Having been involved in the Indian Act revision process as early as 1947 and again in the mid-1970s (with the Joint NIB/Cabinet Committee), Spence was assigned by Mackie to sit on the IIAP Indian Act Revision Committee, although he seldom participated in its discussions. He did provide formal feedback to Mackie on various drafts of that committee's discussion paper on Indian government—perhaps its most important discussion paper—but not on its other papers on education, band membership, etc. Finally, the independence provided by Spence being on a contract rather than a member of the Public Service, does permit him to speak forthrightly when he deems it appropriate. He has, for instance, challenged the Minister on the value of tribal councils—a mechanism which the Minister had previously endorsed publicly (Bernard, 1978).

In concluding this discussion of Indian input to the senior echelons of the Department and the Programme, it should be noted that it is sometimes difficult to disentangle the characteristics of a position from the characteristics of the incumbent of that position, especially when historically there has only been one incumbent. Thus, in the case of the Special Advisor to the ADM-Development, some of the strength and weaknesses exhibited by Ahab Spence as the incumbent are attributable to his own background and personality, while others are inherent in the nature of the advisor position.

Clearly, there are significant deficiencies in DIAND's attempts to systematically obtain Indian input. These deficiencies can be seen in terms of the virtual absence of Indians in the Policy Branch (one policy advisor among twelve is an Indian), the apparent shying away from Indians as Regional Directors-General since the Cardinal case, and the circumscribed role of special advisors and special assistants. While those who have been hired in such positions have brought with them keen intellects and/or a wealth of personal experience, their participation is only a beginning step, and not necessarily in a direction which will be sustained. However, we turn now to a consideration of those individuals who hold executive positions in the bureaucracy and who, despite policies of administrative decentralization and devolution of authority, still exercise much power over the lives of Indians today.

PROFILES OF THE POWERFUL

Most Indians on reserves or in the city probably seldom give any thought to senior officials in the Department and Programme. On those rare occasions when they do, they probably think of those officials as remote and anonymous bureaucrats—in the pejorative sense of the term. But to Indian band administrators and to Indian political leaders, these senior officials are very real and the consequences of their decisions or non-decisions impinge upon them daily. Similarly, it is these senior officials who determine the conditions and circumstances under which other IIAP personnel will relate in their jobs to each other and to the Indian on the reserve. Through their actions these senior officials can raise hopes and dash them, open doors or erect obstacles. Overall, they are in many ways more powerful than their superior, the Minister. We devote this section of the chapter to the sketching of profiles of some of the most influential of these people who shaped Indian-government relations in the decade of the 1970s. Although some have already left DIAND and further turnover will undoubtedly occur, it is worthwhile describing these people for historical purposes. Furthermore, collectively speaking, they are likely to be replaced by others of the same ilk.

ARTHUR KROEGER (DEPUTY MINISTER)

Born in 1932, Arthur Kroeger is a Rhodes Scholar with a graduate degree (1958) in philosophy, politics, and economics. After a thirteen-year career with the Department of External Affairs, he moved to the Treasury Board at a rank equivalent to Assistant Deputy Minister. There he gained a close familiarity with DIAND and established contacts with Cabinet Ministers of various departments. In January 1975 by Prime Ministerial appointment, he was promoted to succeed Basil Robinson (who also had a background in foreign affairs) as Deputy Minister (DM) of DIAND.

Kroeger appears to be well connected in influential Liberal circles. Among his close external advisors he lists Gordon Robertson who, as former Clerk of the Privy Council was the most senior civil servant in Canada, and Lloyd Barber, the former Indian Claims Commissioner who not only has good rapport with Indians but also had access to senior government officials (including Pierre Trudeau). Within the Department he had a particularly close working relationship with his "right hand man," the ADM responsible for departmental policy, Geoff Murray, whom he described as "my alter ego" and "a wise uncle to all of us."

As Deputy Minister the frequency of his interaction with the various Ministers under whom he served varied considerably. With Warren Allmand he had a very strained relationship and interaction was rare, whereas interaction with Hugh Faulkner was so frequent that it was not uncommon that the two would talk six times per day.

Kroeger did get involved in policy making in the department, although this involvement tended to be restricted to major policy issues (e.g., Indian Act revision, Alaska Highway pipeline decision, negotiations with the provinces, budgetary review).

Kroeger is highly respected by his subordinates, especially for his intelligence. Although viewed by NIB officials as an obstacle to change, he at least brought many changes to IIAP, including an increased policy making capability, some new policy thrusts, a formal recognition of the "new guard," a professionalization of administration, and increased technocracy.

GEOFFREY MURRAY (ADM—CORPORATE POLICY)

Born in 1918, Geoff Murray came to DIAND at a late stage in his career. A veteran of the Canadian Army (World War II) with degrees in history and law, he held many senior positions in the Department of External Affairs and joined DIAND in 1971 at the request of Basil Robinson, with whom he had formed a friendship when both were at External Affairs.

There can be no doubt as to either the power he held within the Department or the legacy he left when he semi-retired at the end of 1978. Inspection of the list of his main areas of involvement reveals every one of them to have been a high priority of the department. These include forming the Corporate Policy Group (1972-73), developing a comprehensive land claims policy for Cabinet, writing a new policy governing government-Indian relations (1976), and serving as the principal participant for DIAND (and briefer of other Cabinet Ministers) in the Joint NIB/Cabinet Committee of 1974-78. He was also closely involved in the Indian Act revision process and in the writing of many speeches for the Minister.

Murray's stature with his subordinates was very high, probably due to his wealth of experience, respected judgement and pronounced influence. He is reputed to change the whole tenor of a meeting with subordinates by his mere presence, for he rarely speaks. When he does speak his words are carefully measured, and weighted heavily by those in attendance.

After his official retirement, Murray continued to be involved in the department as a private consultant on a contract basis. However, the fact that he was not present in the Department daily provided new latitude for the realignment of the Departmental power structure in the senior echelons. One person who came to play a prominent role, both because of her abilities and her position, was Murray's successor, Huguette Labelle.

HUGUETTE LABELLE (ADM—CORPORATE POLICY)

Huguette Labelle is a fluently bilingual francophone with a string of university degrees in Nursing and Psychology and an almost completed Ph. D. in Educational Administration. Her special interest in Indians resulted from her participation in a 1972 Department of National Health and Welfare study of Indian health in the North. In 1973 she joined Health and Welfare where she had many senior-level assignments including Ministerial speech writing, policy development, and participation in federal-provincial relations and in the negotiation of bilateral health agreements with several foreign countries (e.g., USSR and China).

In 1976, at the age of thirty-seven she was "hand picked" by Kroeger to join DIAND as Director-General of the Policy, Research, and Evaluation Group (PRE). After turning PRE into what in some ways was the most influential Group in the Programme, she was promoted to replace Murray in January 1979 and embarked upon a major expansion of the Corporate Policy Group. At the time of her appointment she was one of perhaps only half a dozen women in the entire federal government to reach the ADM level or its equivalent.[4] Giving every appearance of being a skilled practitioner of bureaupolitik, she has since taken the position of ADM—Corporate Policy well along the road to becoming the senior ADM position in the Department.

It would appear that several new thrusts can be expected under her direction, including the establishment of a long range planning capability, the use of socio-economic development as a keystone around which would be assembled many other aspects (e.g. housing, Indian Act revisions) of IIAP, and significantly, the integration of the government's policy towards Indians with its policy towards other Natives.

CAMPBELL MACKIE (ADM—DEVELOPMENT, IIAP)

As Assistant Deputy Minister responsible for development in IIAP, Mackie is considered to be the leader of the "new guard." After graduating from the University of Manitoba in 1960 with a specialization in the group work and community development aspects of Social Work he worked for five years in north Winnipeg, during which time he developed strong negative feelings towards IIAP due to IIAP, in his words, "making Indians patsies for welfare." His career in the federal government has been a variegated one, at every stage of which he has had much involvement with Indians. His career has spanned several departments and agencies but in each he has held a senior position and either developed or managed innovative programs. For instance, he served as Director of Domestic Programs for the Company of Young Canadians, established the Opportunities For Youth (OFY) program at Secretary of State, was a Regional Co-ordinator of the Local Initiatives Program of the Department of Manpower and Immigration, and eventually became Director-General of the Job Creation Branch in that Department. In January 1976 he joined DIAND as ADM responsible for IIAP (a position which was subsequently split in two).

Mackie describes himself as bringing to the Indian scene "a fairly strong sense of moral indignation at what I have seen and continue to see." He views himself as a man who is progressive, committed to change, and accessible to Indians. He sees a constructive potential in conflict, and does not shy away from it. As he told the authors: "There are times when a little shouting and screaming is very helpful to us at DIAND and lets us get things done. . . . When I came, the Department was scared of Indians shouting at them, which suggests to me that they weren't listening well." He sees himself as having a knowledge of how the bureaucracy can be used and must be changed to facilitate Indians attaining their objectives. A strong believer, also, in the notion that some of the skills which Indians need to acquire can come from Indians working within the federal bureaucracy, he was initially a strong supporter of the idea of bringing Indians into the Programme in management positions, even in the face of hesitation from above. He also believes in what he calls, "the notion of some form of Indian sovereignty as a structural requisite for Indians to take their special place in a pluralistic Canadian society."

Mackie is certainly no stranger to conflict or controversy. Indeed, he has been involved in disputes with the National Indian Brotherhood on such fundamental matters as what constitutes consultation (versus informal discussion) and his alleged deliberate interference in Indian politics. He also incurred the ire of a senior Opposition member of SCIAND for his allegedly less than forthright testimony before the committee on the matter of procedures surrounding the appointment of Harold Cardinal as Alberta RDG. (He denied the latter two allegations.)

As ADM responsible for such crucial matters as policy and developmental aspects of government-Indian relationships, Indian Act revisions, evaluation of program effectiveness, budgetary review, and the promotion of Indian self-government and socio-economic development, Mackie potentially wields much power. However, in the exercise of that power to implement his ideas and philosophy, he faces several constraints. These include politically cautious superiors, an often-resistant field staff, Indian leaders who increasingly wish to circumvent not only bureaucrats, but the Minister of DIAND as well, and fiscal restraint by the government. While the ADM of Programs for IIAP, Rod Brown, may or may not be a constraint in the negative sense of the term, he is a constraining influence in the sense that he and Mackie share power at the top of the Programme. It is to a consideration of Brown that we now turn.

ROD BROWN (ADM—PROGRAMS, IIAP)

Rod Brown joined the department in 1948 at the age of twenty-one as a teacher of industrial arts and later of academic subjects. In 1964 he became an assistant superintendent, and subsequently superintendent of the Indian agency located at Prince Edward Island. After he had spent two more years as an employment and relocation supervisor in the Atlantic Region, the government introduced the 1969 White Paper. Partly as a result of that policy, he decided to resign from the department, but was asked by Indian leaders to remain and did, as senior liaison officer in the Atlantic Region. In 1971 he took over the senior IIAP post in the Maritimes, that of Regional Director-General, a post which he held for about three years before being transferred to the identical position in the Manitoba Region. Then in the summer of 1977 he was appointed Assistant Deputy Minister (Programs) in IIAP.

As ADM, his main administrative goal has been that of upgrading the management capability of IIAP. Cognizant also of the deteriorating stature of IIAP in the eyes of Treasury Board officials, and of the difficulties that posed for securing Treasury Board approval of new programs for Indians, he worked with the ADM of Finance, Ron Fournier, to establish a budgetary control system within IIAP. His responsibilities also involve him in liaising with Cam Mackie, in an attempt to ensure that policy proposals are operational.

Overall, Brown has a reputation as a tough and capable administrator who, in the words of one official "likes to put the boots to people." His approach to management is conservative, in the sense of preferring to work through prescribed organizational channels, rather than manipulating the organization by circumventing those channels. Despite his reputation as being a member of the "old guard," he and Mackie appear to share a commitment to at least a certain degree of social change in the realm of Indian affairs. However, the sharing of certain principles by these two men does not mean that they are always in agreement. Contrary to Mackie's contention that there was no strain in the relationship, Brown reports that he and Mackie "had a couple of blow-ups before we sat down and talked them out." Although most of our Regional respondents could not (or would not) cite any specific negative consequences arising in their daily operations as a result of the strain in the Mackie-Brown relationship, one such respondent expressed the view that policy development in the Programme (e.g., in the realm of economic development) has suffered under the weight of the constant tension in the relations between the old guard and the new guard.

Power and influence are matters of degree. Accordingly, the preceding does not exhaust the list of people in DIAND who had a significant impact in shaping IIAP in the 1970s. The individuals discussed, however, are the persons with the broadest scope of influence (excepting the ADM of Finance and Professional Services, who refused to be interviewed). Our main purpose in presenting their profiles was to introduce, as human beings, these heretofore largely anonymous individuals who have exercised a significant influence over the lives of status Indians, rather than to develop descriptive generalizations about them. Nevertheless, to conclude this section we can formulate certain generalizations which characterize both these persons and other senior persons whom we interviewed.

These individuals do not at all fit the stereotype of the narrow-minded bureaucrat of mediocre ability who rises to the top by a process of default rather than through merit. Rather, most of them are intelligent, professional executives who seem self-confident that they finally have IIAP heading in the right direction. Although that self-confidence may not be as far removed as some of them like to think from the "old guard" conviction, "We know what is best for Indians," they reluctantly accept the political necessity of proceeding slowly so as to avoid a repeat of the 1969 White Paper fiasco. However, they do seem frustrated at that slow pace of change and at having, in the current political climate, to curb the leadership abilities which propelled them to these senior positions in the first instance.

Also as part of their professional orientation they are becoming increasingly technocratic, in the sense that they are putting much faith in the principles of systems theory and management science. Yet, as we have suggested, despite the apparent promise of the technocratic approach and the receptivity to it on the part of control agencies like the Auditor General, they may well find that it puts distance between them and their Indian clientele.

The element of challenge seems to be an important attraction of their jobs and one gets the impression that they view Indian affairs almost as a complex chess game. However, some of the challenges they face prove to be insurmountable, such as the challenge of winning the confidence of national Indian leaders for themselves and their ideas. The environment of government-Indian political conflict in which they operate almost daily also proves frustrating, at times exasperating, and (we suspect) highly fatiguing. That conflict environment also leaves them somewhat defensive, notwithstanding their self-confidence.

For the most part, the picture which emerges of these persons is complimentary. Yet individually, almost all are held in very low regard by political leaders at the National Indian Brotherhood. The explanation for this discrepancy lies partly in stereotyping (each side does stereotype the other) and partly in the cultural and political chasm that separates the two sides. Notwithstanding their intelligence, the DIAND executives often simply do not understand the nuances of Indian cultures and politics which underlie many Indian actions and aspirations.[5] Furthermore, and more importantly, the two sides have fundamentally different goals for the manner in which Indians should be incorporated into Canadian society, as we shall discuss in our concluding chapter. Thus, simply by virtue of the fact that DIAND executives are pursuing goals which are incompatable with those of Indians, their actions are experienced by Indians as obstructionism. In trying to convince Indians of the merit of the government's goals, DIAND executives strike Indians as being paternalistic and sometimes condescending. Such assessments carry with them at the very least a diminished regard, and sometimes an outright condemnation of those DIAND executives.

Returning to this chapter's main concern with personnel matters, we noted earlier that most of the senior DIAND executives are in midcareer. They thus have the capability of further career mobility if they so choose. Indeed, there was a high rate of turnover in some of these positions during the 1970s. This takes us to the concerns of the final section of this chapter.

PROBLEMS IN RECRUITING SENIOR NONINDIANS

The aforementioned high rates of turnover in some of the senior positions in DIAND and IIAP permit us to state with considerable assurance that the policies and programs of the 1980s will also reflect the input of several new executives and managers who had not yet moved into positions of prominence in the department at the time of writing. If past recruitment patterns persist, these new faces will come primarily from outside the department, rather than coming up through the ranks from the "old guard" within the department. We conclude this chapter with a brief discussion of some important factors which will stand in the way of efforts to recruit these new high calibre senior personnel to the department. Having already discussed at length the recruitment of Natives, we shall confine out attention here to nonNatives.

Let us assume, in accordance with Maslow's (1965) classic theory of motivation, that human beings possess several sets of needs which they seek to gratify, consciously or unconsciously. These are: (1) physiological needs; (2) safety and security needs; (3) affiliative or love needs; (4) esteem needs; (5) cognitive and aesthetic needs; and finally, (6) a need for self-actualization or for utilizing one's capacities to their fullest extent. While these needs will vary in strength from individual to individual, or within any given individual over time, some of them are presumably very relevant sources of motivation for persons who are considering the major step of making a change in their career.

Let us further assume that senior management and executive personnel in large government departments are committed to norms of administrative professionalism which place a high value upon service to the client. To the extent that this assumption is valid, it follows that such professionals do not really need to work for DIAND. Unless they are liberals seeking to establish their credentials as liberals by working with a disadvantaged sector of society, their commitment to the value of serving the client can be met by working for any one of numerous other government departments, for there is, otherwise, nothing inherently compelling about working for and with Indians as a client group. Furthermore, if working for DIAND is likely to do little to gratify their personal needs, or if it is likely to actually frustrate those needs, then they are likely to avoid the department. The question arises then as to how working for the Department or for IIAP in fact relates to those personal needs.

While working for any large bureaucracy can be rather frustrating for some of the needs listed above, working for DIAND is often particularly frustrating. The contemporary IIAP has inherited, and indeed sometimes contributed significantly to, a legacy of distrust on the part of its clientele. As a result, initiatives taken by senior personnel often meet with suspicion and attack from the Indian clientele. Indeed, from the perspective of the National Indian Brotherhood, the very legitimacy of senior departmental personnel taking initiatives has been severely eroded, especially in the policy field, where the NIB position is that NIB, and not the department, should be making policy for Indians. Thus, a certain defensiveness is necessary in the face of attacks from Native organizations, and this defensiveness can hardly be said to contribute to a realization of personal needs (particularly the sixth listed above).

Presumably, occupying a senior position in a prestigious department would be a source of gratification of the need for self-esteem. However, in the past, DIAND has tended not to have a high prestige rating among civil servants in Ottawa. The departmental budget was not among the largest, the Cabinet members appointed to the portfolio were often not themselves highly prestigious at the time, and the clientele itself was very low in prestige. Furthermore, as has already been noted, IIAP included within its ranks many former military or RCMP personnel who often tended to harbour more traditional, paternalistic attitudes towards Indians, rather than having a modern professional orientation to their clientele. In the late 1960s and early 1970s these problems were compounded by the Indians' outspoken rejection of the infamous 1969 White Paper, and by a rash of other Indian public protest which gave IIAP a reputation as a "firefighter" rather than a "doer." Then, in the late 1970s the department was embarrassed by budget over-expenditures and by the laying of criminal charges against some of its junior members in conjunction with their work. While many of these circumstances have since changed, reputations are slower to change; thus, a person contemplating a career change might be reluctant to join a department with such a reputation.

Being mobile in one's career—moving on to conquer new challenges—is one way of realizing the need for self-actualization. However, as a ministerial assistant reported to the authors, IIAP has had a reputation of isolating its employees from other departments, rather than exposing them to inter-departmental committees where they have the opportunity to show their skills and intelligence to a broader range of potential government employers. Thus, the belief was that people working for IIAP had little opportunity to move in the types of circles that would enhance their careers. They also had the reputation of being "Indian specialists," with skills which were not readily adaptable to the needs of other departments. As of the late 1970s, however, the process of revising the Indian Act and the phenomenon of Indians relating to other government departments have reduced the isolation of IIAP personnel within the government. Similarly, the diversity in the career backgrounds of such people as Cam Mackie, and Huguette Labelle should challenge the notion that senior IIAP personnel lack generalizable skills.

Three further problems involved in recruiting nonIndian executive and senior management personnel should be mentioned. The first is the existence of a demanding, articulate, and politicized clientele which subjects every IIAP move to critical and public scrutiny. While this is related to the previously mentioned phenomenon of distrust, it also goes beyond it. A consequence is that life in the department can take on certain features of living in a fish bowl. Any attempt by senior personnel to cope with this by means of secrecy only compounds the problem when, as is the case for IIAP (but not for, say, the Department of External Affairs), one is working within an ideological climate of participatory democracy. These and other constraints—such as the Indian Act itself, disagreements among Indian organizations, the slow pace of Indian decision making, the cultural gap between Indians and nonIndians and the apathy of the Canadian public—all mean that it is often an extremely difficult and frustrating task to achieve any visible accomplishments. Finally, a question which has already been raised, but which will likely be pressed with greater forcefulness in the 1980s, is that of the legitimacy of these senior management positions being filled at all by nonIndians. Such challenges to legitimacy might turn away some potential applicants and can scarcely contribute to the fulfillment of the affiliative needs of nonIndians who do assume such positions.

Thus, it can be said that while the Department will probably continue to succeed in attracting some very high calibre people to fill these senior positions, because of its special features which assault some of the basic needs of healthy psychological functioning, it will probably lose or fail to attract more than its proportionate share of such people. For the same reasons it may also be prone to attracting people who are concerned mainly with their own career upward mobility, and wish to use DIAND as a stepping stone in their career progression. We can hope, but not assume, that actions taken in the interests of career mobility will also be in the best interests of the Indians themselves.

NOTES

1. The original name was Indian and Eskimo Recruitment and Development Program (IERDP).

2. Cardinal's view of events here is buttressed by another departmental official who was involved. According to him, there clearly were people at Ottawa headquarters who saw Cardinal's actions and Mackie's apparent unwillingness to "curb" him as an opportunity to pursue their grievances over Mackie, and consequently the events in Alberta attracted more attention than might otherwise have been the case.

3. McGilp was eventually transferred out of IIAP to the position of Director of Policy and Programming in the Northern Development side of the Department.

4. This estimate is based upon Shorter's (1978:25) statement that in the federal civil service there are only thirty-eight women with executive status ("SX-1" and higher), including at that time, three SX-3s and no SX-4s. Labelle's position is an SX-3.

5. We hasten to add that we do not profess to have any greater understanding than do the executives; we probably have less. We should also emphasize that increased understanding of Indians on the part of these senior DIAND officials will by no means necessarily lead to agreement between the two sides and resolution of problems.

Chapter 6

External Relationships of the Indian/Inuit Programme

INTRODUCTION

The Indian/Inuit Affairs Programme of DIAND is not an island unto itself. Rather, it is embedded in a complex web of relationships with other organizations, governments, departments, communities, and individuals, some of which have goals, values, or cultures which stand in opposition to those of IIAP. All organizations are influenced in one way or another by such an "external environment." Most organizations, including IIAP, themselves attempt to influence their environment by cultivating some parts of it and neutralizing other parts. This is usually done to ensure their own survival (or that of some larger organization of which they are a part) or to make it easier for the organization to achieve its goals. Indeed, this is crucial to IIAP, which must influence numerous other organizations or agencies such as Treasury Board, Cabinet, band councils, etc.

One dimension of an organization's external environment is its *complexity*, which can be further refined to take into account both the number of organizations in its "organizational set,"[1] and the degree of heterogeneity of those elements. IIAP's external environment would receive a high score on both of these aspects of complexity. For instance, with regard to the number of organizations in its set, one must consider not just the 573 bands, but also: (1) numerous other Indian organizations and associations at various levels;[2] (2) about a dozen other federal government departments or agencies; (3) ten provincial and two territorial governments; and (4) several nonIndian lobby groups (for and against Indians). This list also attests to the extreme heterogeneity of IIAP's external environment. One noteworthy consequence of this heterogeneity is that the issues and decision making processes in which the senior personnel of IIAP are involved are likely to be very complex.

A second dimension of an organization's external environment is its *degree of change*. Since our research was not intended to systematically address environmental change, our comments here are necessarily impressionistic. It is our impression that overall, the rate of change in IIAP's external environment at the end of the 1970s was moderately high,[3] although it must be recognized that that rate varied from one sector of its environment to another. In Table 6.1 we have listed changes and other major events which transpired in IIAP's external environment during an eighteen month period prior to the writing of this chapter. Using a highly subjective and perhaps not readily replicable approach in composing that table, we find that about thirty major changes or events occurred during those eighteen months—an average of one major change or event every two and one-half weeks. Significantly, some of these changes constituted complete reversals of earlier changes, for instance, prospects for the completion of the Alaska Highway gas pipeline through parts of Canada oscillated almost wildly during this period. With respect to the degree of difference involved in any given change, it should be mentioned that several of our IIAP respondents, on their own initiative, expressed to the authors the belief[4] that the grass-roots Indian community is fundamentally conservative and prefers a very cautious, incrementalist approach to change. Said the Deputy Minister:

> I think it's reasonable to say that the Indians have so often seen the status quo altered to their disadvantage over the past 100 to 150 years that they're very circumspect about *any* proposal to alter the status quo.[5]

A third dimension of a focal organization's external environment pertains to the degree of *certainty* with which senior personnel in the organization can make decisions concerning future courses of action. Thus, by environmental uncertainty we refer to both the predictability of the behaviour of members of the external environment and the nature, amount, and reliability of information which the decision-makers have at their disposal concerning that environment. In Table 6.1 the items cited in categories I and V were generally low in predictability,[6] while most of the remaining items were more predictable. With regard to obtaining other more bureaucratic information from the field, IIAP's information gathering system for most of the 1970s could accurately be characterized as grossly deficient, as we observed in Chapter Four. The efforts of the late 1970s to redress this problem and thereby to reduce environmental uncertainty, will likely continue through at least the first half of the 1980s.

A fourth and final dimension of a focal organization's external environment is the amount of *autonomy* the environment permits, or conversely *dependency* it imposes upon, the organization in question. Paradoxically, despite the wide ranging control which IIAP has histori-

TABLE 6.1
Major Changes and Events in the External Environment of IIAP During the 18 Month Period Beginning January 1, 1978

I   *Among Indian Political Associations*

1 — NIB withdrawal from Joint NIB/Cabinet Committee
2 — Land claims settlement with COPE and Indian criticisms thereof
3 — NIB rejection of IIAP's conception of Indian government
4 — NIB emphasis on Constitution, not Indian Act
5 — NIB chiefs' trip to England
6 — Change in leadership of certain associations, including twice at Federation of Saskatchewan Indians

II   *In Federal Government*

1 — Change in governments
2 — Change in Minister of DIAND
3 — Issuing of proposals for constitutional revision (BNA Act)
4 — Indians as official observers at First Ministers' Constitutional Conference
5 — Report of Task Force on National Unity recommends Indian involvement in constitutional talks
6 — Proclamation of Native participation policy by Treasury Board

III   *Among Provincial Governments*

1 — Launching of tripartite discussions in Ontario
2 — Hearings on Alberta tar sands developments affecting Indians
3 — Hearings of Ontario Royal Commission on the Northern Environment

IV   *Among Bands*

1 — Bands' assertion and enforcement of aspects of Indian sovereignty
2 — Various bands taking over various programs from IIAP
3 — Various band elections

V   *Disputes, Controversies, and Protests*

1 — Peigan band blockade of irrigation project
2 — St. Mary's band blockade of CP rail line
3 — Protests in Quebec re provisions of Bill 101
4 — Controversy over cuts in medical services to Indians
5 — Controversy in Ontario over excavation of Indian burial sites
6 — Fishing and wildlife court disputes
7 — Fluoride (etc.) pollution at St. Regis reserve
8 — Protest March of Native Women concerning Indian Act sex discrimination

VI   *Other*

1 — Changing prospects for Alaska Highway natural gas pipeline
2 — Political changes among Dene and Metis of Mackenzie Valley re land claim
3 — Launching of various lands and aboriginal rights claims (e.g., Baker Lake)

cally held over its Indian clients as individuals, and despite the persistence of many aspects of that control today, the contemporary IIAP is also characterized by high degrees of dependence in its relations with certain members of its organizational set. This is particularly true with respect to its suppliers of resources. IIAP as a branch of government is totally dependent upon external agencies—Parliament and the Treasury Board—for one of its main "raw materials," money. That dependence is accentuated by the fact that the Parliamentarians are in turn dependent upon the electorate to get returned to office. Accordingly, politicians are inclined either to be hostile to IIAP (the Opposition), or (in the case of the governing party) to be responsive to those—such as the Comptroller-General and the Auditor-General—who themselves wish to decrease IIAP's autonomy and increase its accountability. Another main raw material for which IIAP is dependent upon an external body (the Cabinet) is the ratification of its major policies. Not only is IIAP not self-sufficient in regard to policy ratification, but it must also enter into a competitive arena with other departments and agencies in seeking the attention and priority of Cabinet in order to get its policy recommendations ratified.

The dependency of an organization upon its external environment is not only created by the aforementioned lack of alternative sources of resource inputs; dependence may also stem from the fact that the suppliers of an organization's raw materials are influenced by the consumers of that organization's output. The attempts of NIB to gain direct access to the Treasury Board for purposes of influencing the IIAP budget constitute an example of such supplier-client integration. Furthermore the influence of the NIB with the Opposition members (particularly those from the New Democratic Party) of SCIAND, while of a slightly different nature, should not be overlooked here, particularly if the parliamentary committee system is reformed in such a way that a parliamentary committee can block passage of a departmental budget.

In summary, the external environment of IIAP can be said to be characterized by considerable complexity, turbulence, and uncertainty, and to place IIAP in a highly dependent position in certain important respects. In response to this, and consistent with Pfeffer's (1976) observation that administrators manage environments as well as their own organization, IIAP engages in attempts to manipulate its environment, as we shall describe later.

IDENTIFICATION OF THE SPECIFIC COMPONENTS OF IIAP'S EXTERNAL ENVIRONMENT

The members of IIAP's external environment can be arranged, as we have done in Figure 6.1, in a concentric circles model. Because different

FIGURE 6.1 **The Components of the External Environments of IIAP Headquarters (Senior Echelons)**

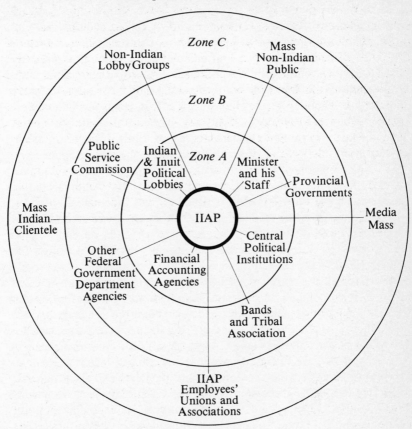

subunits of IIAP themselves have different external environments, we have chosen in Figure 6.1 to depict only the external environment of the senior echelons of IIAP's Ottawa headquarters. Thus, the concentric zones in that figure represent the salience and/or frequency of interaction which IIAP senior headquarters staff have with members of the external environment—the closer the zone is to the centre, the more salient or more frequent the interaction between headquarters executives and occupants of that zone.[7]

Within Zone A, the zone closest to IIAP, the most important and most immediate interaction is with the Minister and his staff. It is the Minister who makes the final departmental decisions on major policy matters and who represents the Programme in Cabinet and in Parliament. The most important among the central political institutions would be the Cabinet, the Privy Council Office (PCO), and the Prime Minister's Office.

Although the frequency of interaction with most of these central political institutions is not great, the salience of that contact is extremely high.

Similarly, interaction with the financial accounting agencies is of a high enough salience to include them in Zone A. These financial accounting agencies, elsewhere designated as "central control agencies," include the Treasury Board and its Secretariat, the Public Accounts Committee of the House of Commons, the Auditor-General's office, and the Comptroller-General's office. The frequency of IIAP's contact with these agencies varies among them. High on the list, in terms of both salience and frequency, is the Treasury Board and its Secretariat. Its power over the budget of government departments makes it one of the most crucial interaction partners of any government department or programme.

The final component of Zone A consists of the various lobby groups which Indians and Inuit have formed, such as the National Indian Brotherhood, the Inuit Tapirisat of Canada, and Indian Rights for Indian Women. Of these, the National Indian Brotherhood scores highest in terms of both saliency and frequency. However, as we shall discuss below, contact with NIB's leaders is usually mediated through the Minister, due to the conviction in NIB that the appropriate interaction partners for NIB's political leaders are the government's *politicians* rather than its *bureaucrats*. Nevertheless, interaction between NIB senior staff members (rather than its elected leaders) and IIAP managers at the level of Director and Director-General is not uncommon, particularly insofar as it involves IIAP's Policy, Research, and Evaluation Group.

In Zone B we have four types of members, one of which is the provincial governments. At the time of our writing DIAND was involved in multi-level tripartite discussions with certain provincial governments (e.g., Ontario, Alberta) and the corresponding status Indian political organization(s) of those provinces. A major purpose of these discussions was to make arrangements for the federal government to transfer to the provinces the responsibility for delivering (but not financing) certain services, such as child care, to status Indians. The importance of these tripartite relationships to IIAP is illustrated by the fact that the Deputy Minister himself was involved. Also involved, of course, was the Federal-Provincial Relations Office (FPRO) of the Privy Council.

FPRO is but one of many federal government Departments or agencies with which our senior IIAP respondents reported important interactions. Others include the Departments of Justice, Environment, Fisheries, Employment and Immigration, Secretary of State, National Health and Welfare, Regional Economic Expansion, and the Central Mortgage and Housing Corporation.

Also found in Zone B is the Public Service Commission, whose rules and procedures governing the hiring, firing, promotion, and demotion of civil servants are analogous to the rules of accountability enforced in the financial realm by the Auditor-General.

Bands and tribal associations constitute the final type of occupant of Zone B, although along with provincial-level status Indian organizations, their contact is mainly with the IIAP Regional headquarters. Tribal associations, which reappeared in increasingly large numbers in the 1970s and will likely continue to do so in the 1980s, often involve bands from one or more IIAP Districts in innovative efforts pertaining to such matters as administration, tribal government, and economic development. Because these activities are innovative or because they may involve departures from past practices of accountability they sometimes capture or require the special attention of senior personnel at national headquarters. The same applies to bands. Another important arena of interaction between bands and Ottawa headquarters is land claims. Overall, however, especially as a result of decentralization, contact between bands and tribal associations on the one hand, and the senior echelons of Ottawa headquarters on the other hand, is not of a high frequency. This, of course, poses dangers in terms of a gap possibly arising between policy formulated in Ottawa and conditions in the field.

In Zone C we find individuals as well as organizations. Included here is the grass roots mass Indian clientele of the Programme, although opportunities for interaction between this clientele (as distinct from its leaders) and headquarters senior personnel are relatively rare.

The interactions which headquarters senior personnel have with the mass nonIndian public on matters directly pertaining to Indian affairs tend to be mediated through other parties, namely the mass media or public opinion pollsters. DIAND does conduct a comprehensive monitoring of the mass media and summarizes its findings in a twice daily briefing memo to headquarters executives. However, prior to the authors' survey described in Chapter Three, results of which were made available to IIAP and to Indian organizations, no comprehensive national survey of public opinion on Indian issues had ever been conducted by the Programme. Subsequently, a more systematic monitoring of public opinion was commenced, as the department either commissioned or had access to three national surveys between 1976 and 1979. The continued use of such surveys should help to balance the weight of such traditional inputs as letters to the Minister and letters, articles, or editorials in *The Globe and Mail*.[8]

Notwithstanding the foregoing, the reader should bear in mind that public opinion can only be important to these officials at the level of broad policy directions and limits. Most issues in Indian affairs are enormously complex, and the opinion of the *mass* public, virtually by definition, cannot be expected to be of any assistance in formulating the specific implementing mechanisms for, say, the self-determination of the Dene. Rather, as we have noted elsewhere in this book, Indian affairs executives must be aware of the broad contours of public opinion mainly in order to keep the government's relationship with the Indian clientele from venturing too far beyond the bounds of acceptability to the electorate (e.g., on the Indian sovereignty issue). This becomes a particularly important role for IIAP when, as was the case in the 1970s, nonIndian public opinion was not treated as a major constraint by Indian organizations such as the NIB.

In Zone C, we also find nonIndian lobby groups. Examples here include women's rights groups lobbying for legislative changes to end sex discrimination in the Indian Act, and wildlife and sport fishermen's associations which lobbied to put an end to Indian privileges with respect to certain hunting and fishing laws and regulations. While contact with such lobby groups is infrequent and often mediated through the Minister of DIAND (or of another Department such as Fisheries), when properly orchestrated it can become highly salient, as it did in both of the examples cited above. During its existence the Canadian Association in Support of the Native Peoples, a pro-Indian lobby group which we examine later in the book, did not attempt to enter this zone by exerting systematic influence on IIAP. Indeed, its contacts with the Minister were rare and with IIAP almost non-existent.

Finally in Zone C we have several unions and associations representing IIAP employees. Examples here are the Native Employees Action Team (NEAT), the Public Service Alliance of Canada, and the Economists, Sociologists, and Statisticians Association. Interactions with these organizations is infrequent and tends to focus upon grievances or appeals with regards to working conditions, positions being declared surplus, and layoffs or dismissals. (IIAP does not become involved in contract negotiations, as this is handled on its behalf by the Treasury Board.) Of these types of associations, NEAT is the most salient, due to its ability to bring embarrassing publicity to IIAP on the sensitive issue of Native employment in the programme and department.

IIAP'S RELATIONS WITH SELECTED MEMBERS OF ITS EXTERNAL ENVIRONMENT

THE MINISTER AND HIS STAFF

In discussing the relationship between the Minister's office and the programme, we should keep in mind the Minister's role. During the decade of the 1970s, five different Ministers presided over DIAND and IIAP. There was much variation among these Ministers with respect to the degree to which they became involved in the daily activities of the department. However, as a general rule it can be said that all Ministers will define their role as relating to politics, policy, and strategy. With respect to policy, Ministers tend to be more involved in policy relating to legislation than in policy relating to the administration of the department. Ministers are also likely to be involved in decision making pertaining to the allocation of scarce resources, due to the need for political sensitivity to clients' reactions to such cuts and allocations. While the Minister will have advisors and strategists on his own staff, he will also seek such political input from the senior executives on the departmental bureaucracy.

To bring to life the notion of "the Minister's office" as an organization, let us briefly describe that of Hugh Faulkner, who held the DIAND portfolio from September 1977 until the defeat of the Liberals in the general election of May 1979.

Faulkner had previously been the Minister of State for Science and Technology and then Secretary of State. He therefore brought with him to DIAND certain of his existing staff members, such as Peter Lyman who, as Faulkner's executive assistant, was his most senior staff member. Altogether his staff at DIAND numbered twenty-one persons. In addition to his executive assistant, his key staff members included his constituency assistant, a special consultant on Indian affairs (Ken Marchant), and one special assistant for each of the three operating Programmes of DIAND (including Judith Moses for Indian Affairs). There was also a special assistant for public relations and a special assistant to Faulkner's Parliamentary Secretary. (The Parliamentary Secretary is a member of Parliament, not a clerical helper.) To round out the staff there were various clerical and administrative persons.

With such a large team, Faulkner adopted a quite different approach from that of his predecessors. One respect in which he differed markedly from his immediate predecessor, Warren Allmand, was in his degree of control over the department, and as part of that, in his degree of penetration of the department.[9] Allmand, who had been deliberately misled by senior RCMP bureaucrats when he was their Minister (Solicitor General), was widely reported to have harbored a strong dislike for and suspicion of bureaucrats—sentiments which he reportedly made little effort to conceal. Whereas Allmand travelled a great deal and operated rather independently of the departmental bureaucracy, Faulkner kept in close touch with the department's senior officers. With his large staff Faulkner penetrated the bureaucracy in unprecedented ways. For instance, Marchant and Moses became actively involved in such areas as the IIAP Management Committee, the Claims Policy Committee, and the Indian Act Revision Committee. They were actively involved in policy development and in gathering intelligence for the Minister's use in his meetings with departmental personnel, for the relationship between the Minister's staff and the senior bureaucrats was, especially at first, one of rivalry.

In our interviews, two executive assistants to DIAND Ministers made direct or implicit reference to the element of strain in the relationship between the Minister and the Department. As Faulkner's executive assistant noted, on some issues the matter is defined by the senior bureaucrats as simply a technical one on which there need be no debate about their recommendation, whereas the Minister's staff feels that political considerations should be taken into account. Another executive assistant to a Minister described instances where the recommendations of senior bureaucrats had been rejected by one Minister, but were placed before the Minister's successor for perfunctory ratification before that new Minister had an opportunity to come to know the full scope of the issues. These, then, are but two of several ways in which the senior public servants attempt to manipulate crucial elements in their external environment.

Under Faulkner the Minister's staff was used by him to counter the senior departmental officials and ensure that they did not overwhelm him. As one Assistant Deputy Minister noted to the authors,

> This caused a certain amount of eyebrow raising at first, because we weren't used to it. We didn't doubt for a minute that the Minister got advice from his staff, and it might even be counter advice. But the staffs of other Ministers didn't normally sit down and have, in a sense, arguments in front of the Minister with them taking one line and officials from the Department taking another. . . . There are two problem areas. First, Mr. Faulkner has a very large staff. So it means that there are a lot of people who have lots of time to spend on things on which the Assistant Deputy Ministers certainly don't have the same amount of time to spend. So I think some of the ADMs tend to regard this as a bit unfair that they should be, in a sense, badgered by people who've got more time for free thinking, detached from responsibility. The other thing, though, that causes more trouble is that there's a tendency for the Minister's staff to get themselves involved in operations in that they try to trouble-shoot things and in a sense to second-guess what the Programme people are doing in the way of operations. There's a certain amount of looking over the shoulder and checking out things and going to talk to staff well-down in the echelon. . . .

The relationship between Faulkner's office and the senior echelons of the department thus involved a competitive rivalry. In contrast, the department's relationship with Allmand involved outright alienation, indicated by the almost complete breakdown in communications between the Minister and the Deputy Minister near the end of Allmand's tenure in office. It appears that a primary reason for the deterioration in Allmand's relationship with the department was that his style of operation made life very difficult for senior executives in the bureaucracy. For instance, he reportedly made appointments and commitments (including financial commitments) to interest groups without consulting with departmental officials, and occasionally without informing them. He also tended to be slow in dealing with the paperwork aspects of his job (e.g., signing his approval to documents), thereby creating a fundamental problem for the bureaucracy. Furthermore, he reportedly devoted very little attention to the Northern Development aspects of his portfolio. That it was Allmand, and not Deputy Minister Kroeger, who was replaced by the Prime Minister is noteworthy.

In concluding this discussion of relations with the Minister's office, it should be noted that even when there is a close rapport between a Minister and the senior echelons of the department, it is not always possible for the Minister to have much of an impact on policy matters. Although Faulkner was able to attain that impact through the vehicle of an unusually large staff and the active involvement of his Parliamentary Secretary in operational aspects of the department, for Judd Buchanan the situation was different. Buchanan sat on three Cabinet committees that would meet for three hours each per week. Each committee had to deal with up to twenty-five agenda items at any given meeting. Consequently, with little time available for discussing the details of policy recommendations, the recommendations of the Privy Council Office often prevailed in those committees. (Note the importance here of a Deputy Minister cultivating contacts within the Privy Council Office.) Furthermore, if a Minister takes a policy initiative in his Department that infringes upon another department (which is frequently the case), then it must be processed through an interdepartmental committee, the workings of which are often elaborate and time-consuming. Finally, there is not only the aforementioned "contest" to be won with senior departmental bureaucrats (who, even if over-ruled, can blunt or neutralize a policy through unenthusiastic implementation), but also the possibility of strong opposition from client lobby groups. Thus, significant change in the realm of Indian affairs is likely to be of an incremental, rather than dramatic, nature.

INDIAN POLITICAL LOBBIES

The primary Indian political lobby group with which IIAP headquarters interacts is the National Indian Brotherhood, although (as we shall describe in Part III) NIB is more than a lobby group. Two features dominate this relationship: (1) a lack of trust, and (2) a crisis in legitimacy.

The suspiciousness and lack of trust with which NIB leaders view departmental and programme personnel is a product not only of the historical legacy which they have inherited, but also of the contemporary actions of government officials in IIAP and elsewhere. Historically, Indians have observed as the government repeatedly violated the spirit and letter of the treaties, failed to conscientiously execute its legal trust responsibilities to Indians, sold off Indian lands, and let Indians sink from a position of pride and autonomy to a position of poverty and dependence. Then, in 1969, after a year of putative consultative hearings, Indians saw the federal government develop on its own a policy of termination and assimilation which, under the guise of equality, would abrogate its legal obligations and lead to the first Canadians becoming "merely an ethnic group like the others."

At the time it was made public, that 1969 White Paper was not known to have been authored by the Privy Council Office rather than by DIAND (Weaver, forthcoming). As a result, the furore it generated was focused squarely upon DIAND. If history had sown the seeds for the growth of distrust of DIAND among contemporary Indians, then that White Paper provided a flood of germinating moisture. In its wake, that flood left a residue of suspicion and negativism that would permeate Indian-government relations for at least a decade and perhaps much longer. It also had the consequence of galvanizing Indians across the country into unprecedented united political action. Furthermore, it spawned a number of Indian political organizations, some of which had opposition to it as their primary raison d'être. Consequently, in the years that followed the government's repudiation of the White Paper in 1971, many organizations had a vested interest in seeing the spectre of the hated White Paper behind a wide variety of government moves.

Often those Indian organizations did not have to look too hard to discern the elements of the White Paper, such as in the "Nature of Government-Indian Relations" paper and the earlier-mentioned cabinet document on Native policy, both of which appeared in 1976 and both of which we shall discuss in more detail below. However, sometimes DIAND was attacked by Indian organizations for trying to implement the White Paper "by the back door," when in actual fact it was not involved in, nor consulted about, the issue in question (e.g., the 1978 cuts in certain free medical services to Indians by the Department of National Health and Welfare). Furthermore, certain changes (e.g., transferring to the provinces responsibility for the delivery of child care services), which had considerable merit in and of themselves and might have been accepted by Indians if there had been no 1969 White Paper, were opposed by Indians because they were consistent with, and appeared to be an implementation of, the White Paper's proposal to shift responsibility for Indians to the provinces.

The Nature of Government-Indian Relations paper was developed at Cabinet request by DIAND's ADM of Corporate Policy, Geoff Murray. It was designed to provide guidance as the government attempted to pick up the pieces after the aborted 1969 White Paper. It sought to reassure Indians that "Indian status will continue as long as the Government and the Indian people feel there is a need for it" (p.1) and that the preservation of Indian identity would be a central thrust of government policy. It also sought to institutionalize various consultative mechanisms—namely, the Joint NIB/Cabinet Committee at the national level and the tripartite format at the provincial level—and to institutionalize the continued transferral of programs and resources from the federal government to the band.

The paper was endorsed by Cabinet, but denounced by resolution of the NIB General Assembly. It is not difficult to understand why Indian organizations opposed it. In the first instance, it was formulated entirely without consultation with Indian leaders. Second, it held open the possibility of the termination of Indian legal status and seemed to rule out the possibility of Indian sovereignty. Third, by advocating consultation with the Indian group directly affected, it held open the possibility that NIB and its provincial-level member organizations could be circumvented by the government and that "divide and rule" tactics would then be used by the government. The paper's endorsement of the tripartite (federal government, provincial government, provincial Indian association) negotiation format and the policy of devolution of programs to bands also excluded NIB and left open the divide and rule option for the government. Fourth, the document contained an implied acceptance of the government policy of recognizing aboriginal title to land but extinguishing that title in land claims settlements. Fifth, it explicitly did not call for any major new expenditures in programs affecting status Indians. Sixth, it suggested the exploration of the potential of various funding sources that were fraught with potential difficulties for Indians. For instance, it directed Indians to other federal and provincial government departments that would have no legal and constitutional obligations to Indians. It suggested cost-sharing agreements; yet the federal government has been known to withdraw from such agreements when they became too expensive. Furthermore, merely by including proceeds from claims settlements in this list of other potential sources of funds, it led some Indian leaders to fear that large claims settlements might be followed by reduced levels of regular funding from the federal government. Seventh, and of no small importance, the paper called for a co-operative relationship between Indians and the government, whereas some Indian associations felt that they could secure a better deal for their people in an adversary relationship in which they would press for the acceptance of certain special Indian rights. Finally, the paper failed to recognize any paramount role for Indians in the policy formulation arena.

The second document, dealing with an overall policy towards Native people, was prepared for Cabinet by an inter-departmental group. However, as a representative of the government, DIAND became the lightening rod which absorbed most of the energy contained in status Indian leaders' vehement rejection of the paper. Although primarily addressing the situation of Métis, nonstatus Indians, and urban Indians and containing many promising passages for them, this widely leaked Cabinet document also contained several alarming passages for status Indians. Among these was a reference to the Indian Act as being in some ways arbitrary, anachronistic, and harsh in excluding certain classes of individuals from eligibility for special federal government programs. Other controversial sections of the document sought to ensure Cabinet control of federal policy initiatives, suggested that trade-offs might be reached whereby government programs would be reduced after large claims settlements had been awarded, and in general suggested a blurring of the legal distinction between status Indians and nonstatus Indians and Métis.

In our interviews DIAND's Geoff Murray attempted to disassociate DIAND from this document (which bore the name of DIAND and several other government organizations as authors) and contended that Cabinet "totally put it aside" except for: (1) establishing a Joint Committee of Cabinet and the Native Council of Canada; and (2) granting funding for claims research by Métis and nonstatus Indians. However, such reassurances of the irrelevance of the document were greeted with initial skepticism by the National Indian Brotherhood and were later rejected outright as various events unfolded which were either consistent with the paper, or outright fulfillment of its recommendations. Such events included, to cite but a few examples: (1) the announcement by Treasury Board of an "Indian, Métis, Nonstatus Indian, and Inuit Participation Policy," as recommended in the 1976 leaked document, (2) the undermining of the special position of status Indians in Bill C-60, the Trudeau government's 1978 proposed Act to Amend the Constitution of Canada (see National Indian Brotherhood, 1978); (3) the new-found concern of the Corporate Policy Group of DIAND with matters relating to Métis and nonstatus Indians; and (4) what one IIAP executive called "an almost explicit proposal" from the Socio-Economic Development Sub-Committee of the Métis and Nonstatus Indian Consultative Committee (which reported to Deputy Prime Minister MacEachen) to the effect that socio-economic affairs of all Native people (status and nonstatus) be placed in a new and separate federal department.

That Murray's inclination to protect his Minister and the Cabinet might have led him to somewhat of an overstatement (in describing the document as having been "totally put aside") is suggested not only by the above events, but also by the comment of another respondent. This person, who was very close to Cabinet, remarked to the authors:

NIB's opposition to the use of the term "Native peoples" in legislation [e.g., Bill C-60] is well-founded in terms of what's up.

A surprisingly blunt statement indeed from so highly placed an official!

There is, then, a well-founded and fundamental lack of trust on the part of Indians in their relationship with IIAP. Interestingly, several IIAP respondents indicated to the authors that this lack of trust is not totally unreciprocated. Although they did not elaborate, we suspect that any such sentiments would be related at least to feelings that NIB was not totally honest in some of its dealings with the press and perhaps also to feelings that NIB sometimes did not enter into joint ventures in good faith.

We mentioned above that in addition to the lack of trust, IIAP's relationship with NIB was characterized by a lack of legitimacy. Once again, this feeling is held by key persons on both sides of the relationship. For instance, our interviews with senior departmental officials clearly indicate that near the end of the Joint NIB/Cabinet Committee (JNCC), they came to hold the view that despite relevant resolutions passed by the NIB General Assembly, NIB had no mandate to negotiate anything with the government. (We shall take this up again when we discuss the JNCC.) For their part, NIB leaders view DIAND and IIAP's policy initiatives as quite illegitimate. To them, Indian policy should be formulated by Indians, especially by the NIB's Indian Policy Development Secretariat. Furthermore, they view IIAP as obstructionist and tokenistic in its actions, especially its actions bearing upon Indian government. In effect, on behalf of Indian bands they were competing with IIAP for the authority to govern Indian communities, and IIAP's efforts to devolve responsibilities to bands without what NIB believed to be commensurate authority, only served to further undermine the legitimacy of IIAP in the eyes of NIB.

With the IIAP-NIB relationship in such a state, it is not surprising to find that an indirect and inefficient structure of formal communication characterizes the relationship. That structure takes the form of an inverted letter "u". That is, rather than a direct horizontal (↔) communicative linkage existing between corresponding levels of each organization, an official communication from NIB to IIAP must first go up the NIB hierarchy to the NIB President, then go to the DIAND Minister, and then be directed downwards to the appropriate level of IIAP. Informally, other communication does sometimes occur in a more direct, less roundabout, manner. Clearly, though, there is a major communications chasm which exists between IIAP and NIB, so much so that the situation sometimes resembles the "two solitudes" of which Hugh MacLennan so powerfully wrote in describing English-French relations in Quebec.

Evidence of that communications chasm was found not only in our initial field interviews, but also in our respondents' reactions to our early research findings and in their reactions to the first draft of this manuscript. A striking example involves the assessment of departmental personnel by their departmental colleagues on the one hand, and by NIB officials on the other hand. Usually agreement extends no farther than an assessment of the individual's level of intelligence, if that far. For instance one senior DIAND official was widely held in very high regard by his colleagues and was even described by our senior NIB respondents as intelligent, a skillful negotiator, and a formidable opponent. Thereafter, however, he was assessed in such strikingly harsh terms by those NIB officials as to easily lead the listener to think that they and the DIAND respondents were describing two different individuals. Interestingly, when shown NIB's assessments of him this official dismissed them as rhetoric—as part of a negotiating stance in a larger adversarial strategy. Admittedly the NIB respondents had proven themselves to be colourful rhetoricians. However we believe these to have been genuinely-held views, in part because they were conveyed in a non-rhetorical manner and context. While the respondent's dismissal of the NIB's assessment of him is certainly understandable in terms of basic psychological needs and in terms of not undermining the work of IIAP, his apparent denial of the existence of the communications gap does nothing to bridge that gap. Ironically, in a totally different context[10] that same respondent had earlier given the author the impression that he recognized the existence of the communications gap when he said in an interview:

> The more I hear what you say about NIB the more I'm convinced that that is a continuing problem to which we have to find an answer.

While we have focused our attention in this section on IIAP's relationship with the NIB lobby group, it should be stressed that there are other Indian lobby groups, particularly at the provincial level (e.g., ORLC), who do not take an adversary approach to IIAP. Since their relationship with IIAP is not conducted across a communicative chasm, we should be surprised to find them holding such a harsh assessment of their main interaction partners in IIAP, for as social psychologists have noted, the social context does influence persons' perceptions of others.

In alluding above to the decision by some provincial Indian associations not to adopt an adversary stance, we raise the matter of a fundamental strategic dilemma which Indian political lobbies face in dealing with IIAP. Among IIAP bureaucrats it is referred to as the Indians' dilemma of whether or not to "get into bed" with government. In some respects it is reminiscent of the ages-old dilemma of subordinated groups as to whether they should fight the dominant group or "work the system" by exploiting it for what it has to offer; for, in agreeing to work in co-operation with IIAP they must agree to "play the game" largely by IIAP's rules. From IIAP's perspective this is ideal for several reasons, not the least of which is that such an arrangement permits it to maintain some degree of control over a crucial component of its external environment without having to resort to coercion or other potentially embarrassing tactics. However, as we noted in Chapter Four, there are situations when IIAP does resort to rather blatant use of power to manipulate or control Indian bands or Indian lobby groups in its external environment. Several examples could be cited, among which would be its withdrawal or withholding of funds, its entry into Indian internal politics, and, particularly at the lower levels of the programme, the playing off of one group of Indians against another (e.g., telling northern Manitoba bands that there is insufficient money available for them because southern Manitoba bands received more than their proportionate share, which was a specific complaint registered with the authors by several Manitoba band leaders). In Chapter Nine we shall encounter Indian allegations, which are also relevant here, of a DIAND conspiracy to manipulate both Indian and Cabinet participants in JNCC. While we could not ascertain the validity of those allegations, if true it would constitute a further illustration of IIAP attempting to manage and manipulate its external environment.

In closing the discussion of this component of IIAP's environment, we should stress a point which is easy to overlook in the midst of the above lengthy discussion of IIAP's conflict relationship with Indian lobbies. The point is simply that IIAP *needs* those lobby groups to perform for it what political scientists call "demand aggregation" and "interest articulation" functions. That is, IIAP is, to a degree, dependent upon Indian lobby groups to bring together, priorize, explain, and suggest directions for the solution of, problems facing IIAP's Indian clientele. By saying that it is responding to concerns raised by NIB, along general directional lines approved by NIB (e.g., in JNCC), IIAP ironically can and does derive a certain degree of legitimacy for its actions. Thus, viewed from IIAP, NIB is a component of the external environment which is to be controlled but not eliminated.

BANDS AND TRIBAL ASSOCIATIONS

There were five hundred and seventy-three Indian bands in Canada at the time of writing. As Frideres (1974:12) has noted, a band is an aggregate of Indians grouped together for administrative purposes by IIAP. This grouping may or may not cut across traditional cultural differences (e.g., Indians from matrilineal tribes who trace their descent through their mother, being combined with Indians from patrilineal tribes who trace their descent through their father). Although, sociologically speaking, some bands were thus rather fragile and artificial entities when they were created, over the years bands have come to be a focus of a major component of the identity of many status Indians. Furthermore, and partly because of that, bands have taken up a place beside the family and the clan as the fundamental units of social organization in the registered Indian population. Consequently, a conscious policy decision was taken by IIAP to make the band the cornerstone of government policy towards status Indians. In light of their importance, we have selected the bands—and the tribal associations they form—to be the third and final component of IIAP's external environment to be discussed in detail in this chapter.

IIAP's Services to Bands and Band Members

The reader will recall from Chapter Two that almost half (48%) of all Indian bands have less than three hundred members and 17% have less than one hundred members. In addition, over a quarter (28%) of the entire Indian population, while still retaining band membership, does live off-reserve. Thus, as we stressed before, the population pool from which to recruit talent on the reserve is often small, and economies of scale in the delivery of services to that population can seldom be realized. Furthermore, the delivery of services is complicated by the fact that over a quarter (29%) of the bands are located in geographically isolated areas not serviced by road, and by the fact that one band is sometimes spread over more than one such reserve. Thus, the delivery of services by IIAP to the band population is sometimes a major problem from a sheer logistical-demographic viewpoint.

The list of programs and services offered by IIAP is extensive. Table 6.2 is merely illustrative of the wide range of programs and program areas in which IIAP has involved itself. Indeed, the scope of its involvement is so wide that in many ways IIAP resembles a government within a government, at least insofar as the provisions of services is concerned.

Under Section 91.24 of the British North America Act, the federal government has the right to legislate on Indians and lands reserved for Indians. This right the provinces recognize. Beyond that, however, the responsibilities of the two levels of government are in dispute—a dispute in which band members suffer. Some provincial governments (e.g., Saskatchewan), in concert with the provincial Indian association, contend that the phraseology of Section 91.24 places full responsibility on federal shoulders for the delivery of services to *all* status Indians. However, the federal government's position, as explained to us by DIAND Deputy Minister Kroeger, is that although the federal government has the constitutional right to legislate on (and provide services to) Indians, where it chooses not to exercise that right the normal division of powers in the constitution prevails. The federal government has chosen

TABLE 6.2
Illustrative List of Programs and Program Areas in which IIAP Delivers or Finances Services to Status Indians

I. Education
1.1 Operation of federal schools on-reserve
1.2 Funding of band schools on-reserve
1.3 Tuition and capital support for Indian students in provincial schools
1.4 Counselling and referral
1.5 Maintenance of students away from home
1.6 Transportation (daily and seasonal)
1.7 Adult education
1.8 University tuition and maintenance
1.9 Cultural education

II. Community Infrastructure
2.1 Loans and subsidies for repair and construction of housing (on and off reserve)
2.2 Capital support for the construction of roads, bridges, sewers, electrification, etc.
2.3 Recreation
2.4 Engineering services

III. Reserves and Trusts
3.1 Management of land, minerals, and other resources
3.2 Keeping of membership register
3.3 Overseeing band administration

IV. Protective Services
4.1 Support for band policing
4.2 Fire protection

V. Economic & Employment Development
5.1 Direct and guaranteed loans
5.2 Non-repayable equity support
5.3 Assistance to Indian-run development corporations
5.4 Counselling and advisory services
5.5 Summer employment activities

VI. Band Government
6.1 Administrative ("core") funding, including overhead
6.2 Planning
6.3 Support for band training
6.4 Advisory services

VII. Social Services
7.1 Social Assistance
7.2 Child care
7.3 Adult care
7.4 Rehabilitation
7.5 Day care
7.6 Preventative Counselling and Referral

VIII. Other
8.1 Financial administration
8.2 Program evaluation
8.3 Grants for claims research by Indians
8.4 Grants to Indian political associations
8.5 Indian Act Revision Consultative Study

Source: Program Support Group, IIAP.

to exercise its right on reserves, but essentially not in urban areas. Therefore, in opposition to those provincial governments the federal government argues that the responsibility for providing services to the approximately 80,000 Indians who live off-reserve lies with provincial governments. However, the complexity of the whole matter is exacerbated when we consider the case of on-reserve Indians. While provincial governments take the position that the *financing* of all services to on-reserve Indians is a federal responsibility, some provincial governments nevertheless object to the *delivery* of certain of those services (e.g., post-secondary education) by the federal government on the grounds that federal delivery of those services would be an incursion into what is a provincial jurisdictional domain under the BNA Act. Thus, provincial recognition of federal legislative jurisdiction over Indians and lands reserved for Indians is not always accompanied by a recognition of the right to deliver services under that legislation.

One consequence of this entire constitutional wrangle is that when band members migrate from the reserve to an urban area, even though they are still members of the band they are denied many (but not all) services offered by IIAP to reserve residents. Furthermore, they are often denied the corresponding provincial services. Thus, a status Indian band member seeking social assistance in the city will usually be referred by DIAND to the provincial social services department. In some provinces the band member will be told by provincial public servants that because he has not resided off-reserve for one full year, he is ineligible for provincial welfare.[11] Our band member will thus be referred by the provincial agency either to municipal agencies or back to IIAP. The municipal agency will often refer him back to the provincial agency or to IIAP. From the applicant's perspective, it is a classic case of "getting the runaround." The experience generates mounting frustrations on the part of the applicant and Indian leaders who attempt to redress the problem. Indeed, it was precisely those frustrations, exacerbated by stalling and backtracking by IIAP officials in Ottawa, which led to the occupation of the IIAP district offices in Calgary in 1975, as Ryan (1978) has described.

Thus, the matter of delivery of services to bands and band members is beset by demographic, geographic, political, and constitutional problems that render the matter extremely complex and not amenable to easy solutions, although attempts are nevertheless being made through tripartite discussions.

Band Membership

The aforementioned jurisdictional questions are not the only realms in which the individual is caught in a cross-fire between the federal government (represented by IIAP) and the provincial Indian associations. A second major area of dispute involves the question of who should have the right, under a revised Indian Act, to determine who qualifies to be included as a member of a band. Band councils and provincial associations argue that the band itself should have that right. For instance, in cases where a female band member marries a nonIndian, bands wish to have the right to permit or not permit the woman to retain her membership in the band, whereas under the Indian Act as it existed at the time of our writing, such women automatically lose their registered Indian status and band membership. The government, however, has stated its intention of amending the Act, and a key discussion paper which it has circulated only partly accepts the principle of bands determining band membership. At the crux of the issue are three major concerns. The first involves the matter of sharing of band revenues. Existing bands are not anxious to see changes in the Indian Act such that large numbers of persons (e.g., children born of an Indian woman married to a nonIndian man) who would formerly not have had the right to Indian status and band membership, would now have that right and the accompanying right to their proportionate share of band wealth. Bands argue, however, that if their ranks are to be swelled by government fiat, then they should be allotted more lands and the IIAP budget should be increased as well. The federal government, of course, is not at all anxious to undertake such commitments. Finally, the issue of who is and who is not entitled to be a band member is of major concern not only in negotiating land claims settlements and the subsequent distribution of benefits, but also with respect to who is and who is not to fall within the jurisdiction of Indian governments.

Under the Trudeau government the IIAP proposal (Anonymous, 1978) to deal with the issue involved elimination of the Indian Act's discrimination on the basis of sex. Thus, Indian women marrying non-Indian men would retain their registered Indian status and nonIndians, be they men or women, would not gain registered Indian status. Children of first generation mixed marriages would be entitled to registered Indian status,[12] but in the case of children of second generation mixed marriages, band bylaws governing a new category, called "band beneficiaries," would determine the person's legal rights. Band bylaws could also contain provisions for accepting nonIndian spouses as band beneficiaries. Those band bylaws, which IIAP proposed be adopted or changed only through a referendum and two-thirds majority, would also specify precisely which benefits would accrue to which type of band beneficiary (e.g., right of residency on reserve, inheritance, participation in band government, participation in IIAP programs). Contrary to the demands of Indian women's rights activists, IIAP initially appeared to rule out the possibility that any of these changes would be applied retroactively to enable involuntarily enfranchised women to be reinstated as registered Indians. However, under the Clark government IIAP backed off this position and left it as a matter to be decided by the politicians.

Tribal Associations

Whereas the decade of the 1970s opened with a major thrust by Indians in the direction of a "pan-Indianism" which transcends tribal distinctions, the decade closed with a pronounced revival of tribal and local geographic bonds. That revival took the form of the establishing of district level associations of bands, such as those in northeastern Alberta, coastal British Columbia, and southwestern Manitoba, to name but three. Emerging at a level between the bands and IIAP, these associations often came to take on some of the responsibilities of both. In this section we shall present a brief case study of one such tribal association, the Dakota-Ojibway Tribal Council (DOTC) of southwestern Manitoba, in order to elucidate somewhat this new form of organization and IIAP's relations with it. The reader should bear in mind that although the DOTC concept has served as a model or point of departure for various tribal associations in most other provinces, it constitutes only one approach among several which will likely emerge in the 1980s.

The DOTC was formed in 1974, with the active backing of the then RDG Rod Brown, as a federation of ten bands oriented towards attaining the goals of local government, and eventual self-determination and independence. DOTC's constitution identifies its general purpose as being to "unify and maintain and expand the interests, lives, and identity of the Band."

DOTC's main thrust is programmatic, not political, for the political realm of government-Indian relations is left to the provincial Indian association, The Manitoba Indian Brotherhood. Working from the principle that there is strength in unity, DOTC acts on behalf of the bands in negotiations with government designed to enhance the program services received by the on-reserve band population. It by no means supplants the bands; rather the bands remain pre-eminent, as DOTC acts only on authority delegated to it by the bands. From the standpoint of IIAP, DOTC is a vehicle for transferring to the bands the responsibility for the delivery of services, and in this respect it does supplant IIAP. To a lesser extent DOTC serves as a vehicle for IIAP to also devolve to Indians authority and accountability for certain of those transferred responsibilities.

Although the members of DOTC are the 5,500 individual members of the ten bands, the decision making body, which is known as the Council of the Tribal Council, consists of the elected Chief from each of the bands. This body in turn elects the Executive Committee and hires from outside its ranks the senior staff member, called the Tribal Administrator. The staff itself numbers about forty-five people.

A major activity in which DOTC engages is the monitoring of the financial and managerial aspects of bands' own administration, and the recommending of corrective measures if and when necessary. Other important activities include the provision of direction and assistance to the bands in planning and budgeting for their needs, and negotiating with IIAP for the receipt of funds, of program responsibilities (especially responsibility for the delivery of program services), and of authority.

One such authority which the Council of the Tribal Council holds under experimental block funding arrangements is the authority to freeze the funds of a band. However, the overall subservient role which DOTC plays to the bands is illustrated by the facts that the financial agreements are between IIAP and the individual bands (not DOTC), and the funds do not come through DOTC.

As general rules of thumb, DOTC never duplicates services which a band can provide itself and never takes on programs unless at least two of the bands will be participating. In accordance with those rules, DOTC administered about a dozen IIAP programs at the time of our interview in December 1978. These program areas included culture, housing, economic development, alcohol, education, policing, fire prevention and others, with still others under negotiation. The policing program was a source of particular pride to DOTC members, since it was designed by them rather than having an existing policing program of IIAP or RCMP simply handed over intact for them to administer.

It should be noted, though, that the administrative authority of DOTC is by no means absolute. DOTC must follow IIAP general financial guidelines and priorities, but does have flexibility with regard to the specific content and staffing of programs. To cite but one example used in Chapter Four, in the welfare program which it administers DOTC requires able-bodied recipients to work for their payments.

In taking over administrative responsibilities from IIAP, DOTC has developed a table of organization which in some respects is not unlike that of an IIAP District office. Indeed, in its formative stages it absorbed some IIAP employees whose positions had also been absorbed. One distinct difference from IIAP, however, is that DOTC often forms working committees comprised of community volunteers rather than hiring more paid staff. The DOTC approach here has the advantage of generating a sense of involvement, responsibility, and accomplishment in the participating band members.

In reaching a final assessment of DOTC, we note that the DOTC concept of Indian administration might be criticized by some observers as a form of indirect or "puppet" rule by IIAP. Although DOTC's actual authority is circumscribed and not commensurate with its responsibilities, we feel that such a criticism is somewhat over-drawn. The DOTC approach, we argue, has the advantage of giving Indian people experience in managing aspects of their own affairs. To our knowledge there is nothing inherent in the DOTC concept which precludes its expansion to include more authority. Whether that expansion occurs or not is in many respects dependent upon pressure in its favour being applied by political associations such as the MIB and NIB. What seems obvious, though, is that IIAP would not likely respond positively to that pressure if the Indians most directly affected had not already acquired some degree of experience and skill in managing their own affairs; DOTC provides precisely that kind of experience, without which the assumption of new authority might actually be counter-productive. Thus, as a transitional measure, DOTC in our view does have a useful role to play. There is no question that those most directly involved in it are convinced of its value.

Notwithstanding the above, the DOTC concept is vulnerable to criticism on other grounds. One criticism made by Indian leader Harold Cardinal is that it increases the interdependency between the government bureaucracy and the council and does not come to terms with the long-term economic development of Indian people; that is, making Indians themselves able to finance the institutions which their leaders are creating for them. While this criticism appears to be valid, it is also perhaps somewhat unfair in that DOTC never had economic development as its primary purpose. Another criticism of Cardinal's which is not easily dismissed is that the DOTC mechanism fails to address the need to make band councils more accountable to band members. Finally, it is worth noting that the DOTC mechanism and others similar to it have no legislative or statutory basis and therefore for their continued existence they are almost completely dependent upon individual bureaucrats and politicians remaining in power and remaining favourably disposed towards them.

IIAP's Policy of Devolution of Authority

The contemporary policy of "devolution" being pursued by IIAP is markedly different from a policy of the same name which was inaugurated in 1964 (Weaver, 1978). Under the first policy IIAP attempted to shift responsibility for Indians onto the provinces. However, provincial resistance doomed it to failure, although that did not prevent it from reappearing in the 1969 White Paper. As a result of Indians' resounding rejection of the White Paper, and strident calls for self-determination, IIAP responded with proposals for a new devolution policy. That policy was to be accompanied by policies of Indianization, decentralization, and transfer of responsibility. A brief word of explanation of each is in order.

Indianization and decentralization are policies of internal applicability. *Indianization* is essentially identical to what we in Chapter Five called the "Native participation policy" of Treasury Board, insofar as it applies to IIAP. *Decentralization* is the process of removing authority and administrative responsibilities from Ottawa headquarters and placing them in the Regional headquarters or District Offices. *Transfer of responsibility* involves handing over to Indian bands the responsibility for administering their own affairs. However, under this policy accountability requirements may or may not still be rigid, and accountability is still largely to IIAP employees. Also, under this policy bands usually administer programs designed by employees of IIAP or other government agencies. Another form of the transfer of responsibility policy has IIAP transferring to provincial governments the responsibility for the delivery of certain services to status Indians (on or off reserve), although those services are financed by IIAP by means of transfer payments to the provinces. Finally, the *devolution* policy presently being proposed would hand over to bands not merely administrative obligations, but also authority that is (in IIAP's view) commensurate with those administrative responsibilities. Under this policy, band administrators are not accountable to IIAP bureaucrats, but rather directly to the DIAND Minister, to Treasury Board, or to some elected Indian body, while band councils are to be more accountable to their band members. Administrative accountability would be much less rigid in format and the freedom would exist to develop new programs and priorities, rather than having to adhere to those of outsiders.

In a rare exhibition of unanimity, planners at IIAP, NIB, and in the provincial-level associations agree that an integral part of devolution (or to use the Indian term, Indian government) is increased autonomy for band or tribal governments. In concluding this chapter we offer a brief description of one form which that increased autonomy could take. It is the form being advanced for discussion by IIAP and, we should note at the outset, it has been denounced by NIB as "sandbox politics" in which Indians are expected to play at governing themselves while the Minister retains the important powers.[13] Depite NIB's objections to it, we present it here for two reasons: (1) Indians' own concepts of Indian government are still in the formative stages[14] and are therefore not readily summarized here; and (2) the mechanism, in revised form, may eventually become part of a form of Indian government which Indians do adopt.

There are two keystones to the mechanism which IIAP has advanced. The first is that the band must be the basis of authority in Indian government. District, tribal, regional, or national associations and groupings of bands should derive their authority from a decision making system at the band level, and Indian government should be responsible and accountable to band members.[15] The second is the principle of flexibility. That is, individual bands should have the opportunity to "opt in" to the type of Indian government best suited to them. They should also have the option of remaining under the provisions of the present Indian Act.

The specific mechanism originally proposed in 1978 was called by IIAP a "charter system of tribal government" (Anonymous, 1978), but this term was replaced in 1979 by the phrase "band constitutions" system when the scattered feedback received from Indian bands revealed Indian uneasiness with the term "charter." The charter system was developed by IIAP on the basis of (but going beyond) certain concepts which emerged in deliberations of the Joint NIB/Cabinet Committee, and then was modified in 1979 on the basis of the aforementioned feedback from bands. To become effective in its fullest sense a band constitution would require legislative revisions to the Indian Act by Parliament. Under the terms of its constitution, which would have the force of law, a band would be empowered to exercise local government authority in certain jurisdictional realms, such as one or more of: education; housing; hunting, fishing and trapping; public health and social services; socioeconomic development; etc. Specific powers accruing to the band within those jurisdictional realms would also be clearly identified, as would be IIAP's funding obligations. The band would be empowered to make bylaws in these realms and those bylaws would themselves have the force of law. Bands would also be empowered to enter into agreements with other legal entities or to form a constitution with other bands as partners (along the lines of DOTC).

If the band constitution system were to be adopted, those constitutions would likely vary considerably from one band to the next, as some bands took on only one or two realms of authority (leaving the others to IIAP) while others took on several realms.

Through revisions to the Indian Act a band constitution commission would be established with powers greatly reduced from those initially proposed for its counterpart the "Charters Commission." The commission's main role, rather than being one of negotiating the content of band constitutions, would mainly be that of an appeals and ombudsman mechanism (e.g., concerning disputes arising out of the constitution or disputes over band elections.) The second level of appeal would be the courts, not the DIAND Minister. The commission would also have the responsibility for making recommendations to the DIAND Minister on the suspension or cancellation of a band's constitution. The Minister would not be able to unilaterally change the terms of a band's constitution but would still maintain the special ministerial responsibilities for Indians including (at least in the short term) responsibilities to Parliament and to Treasury Board for funds that are allocated to IIAP.

Whereas the charters system proposed in 1978 could be faulted for its tremendous complexity and for the relatively large bureaucracy which the Commission itself would have required to carry out its functions, these criticisms do not pertain to the band constitution system. However, despite its innovativeness in Canada, the band constitutions system is still very much a gradualist approach which falls far short of the revisions to the Canadian constitution (BNA Act) which NIB is seeking. However, this is certainly to be expected, for as the IIAP Director of Policy said in remarks which we quoted in Chapter Four, IIAP must take the middle of the road between what Indians want and what Parliament and the public will accept.

NOTES

1. The "organizational set" of an organization consists of those organizations in its external environment with which it most frequently interacts—that is, organizations from which it receives input and to which it directs its own output (Zey-Ferrell, 1979:74-5).

2. Some provinces, like British Columbia and Ontario, have two or more organizations representing status Indians. In British Columbia, unlike Ontario, the several associations are still quite divided.

3. Interestingly, many of the responses of IIAP to this relatively high rate of change in its external environment in the 1970s were identical to some of those predicted by Zey-Ferrell (1979:91). One example among several here is the diversion of energy from the task of pursuing goals to the task of restructuring the organization internally.

4. We observed, and indeed had a few respondents comment upon, a considerable degree of homogeneity of beliefs among our IIAP respondents. This homogeneity encompassed ethnic ideology (as discussed in our concluding chapter), interpretations of key events (e.g., the withdrawal of NIB from the Joint NIB/Cabinet Committee), and sometimes even extended to shared metaphors and phraseology (e.g., Indians "getting into bed with government").

5. Another belief which had some currency at various senior levels within IIAP held that when an Indian project experiences success, it is particularly likely to collapse, for it is then most vulnerable to being undermined by Indian leaders who are jealous of its success. How accurate or inaccurate this belief is, we do not know.

6. Where the behaviour of members of an external environment is low in predictability, pressures often arise to co-opt those members into the organization so as to increase the predictability of their behaviour.

7. The collapsing of the salience and frequency dimensions into one is recognized as a distortion created by the model. Another distortion arises due to the fact that some members of the environment are likely to occupy different zones at different times.

8. One knowledgeable DIAND respondent reported to us that in his opinion people in government place inordinate weight on what appears in the media, and in particular, on what appears in the Toronto *Globe and Mail*. Said he: "The *Globe* seems to mesmerize senior bureaucrats, not just in our Department, but in others." He also indicated that the Montreal *Gazette* and the Montreal *Star* (now defunct) were becoming influential, although they still ranked behind the *Globe and Mail*.

9. For a description of how Faulkner related to senior DIAND officials, as seen from the perspective of his executive assistant, see Lyman (1979).

10. The context in which this remark was made was the concluding part of an interview in which, among other things, the author had conveyed to the respondent certain statements by NIB officials and asked for his response to those statements.

11. The federal government contends that this is illegal under federal-provincial agreements which prohibit provinces from establishing residency requirements for welfare recipients.

12. Since publication of the Trudeau government's proposals, government thinking on this issue has changed, such that this particular provision is now being offered as merely one among several possibilities for dealing with the case of children of first generation mixed marriages. IIAP thinking on the other aspects of membership has changed very little with the exception of granting a somewhat greater role for bands in the determination of band membership.

13. IIAP's devolution policy has also been denounced by Indian leaders on the grounds that, in their view, the principle commitment of IIAP is still to its social control function; so long as this commitment remains unchanged there can be no real and meaningful granting of powers to Indians, they argue. Thus, they see the much publicized notion of devolution as a cosmetic change introduced for public relations purposes.

14. On the basis of the report on NIB's Indian Government Development Conference in 1979, it can be said that Indians are in agreement that no one single form of Indian government can be applied uniformly across the country. There are, however, some basic principles which appear to be common to all notions of Indian government. Those are: the presence of a land base, a spiritual base, an exercise of jurisdiction, and an appreciation of human rights and freedoms (Jamieson, 1979).

15. Our discussion of NIB's internal constitutional arrangements in Chapter Eight will reveal that NIB does not meet these criteria.

Part III

The Politicization of Indian Affairs—The National Indian Brotherhood (NIB)

Chapter 7

History of the National Indian Brotherhood

INTRODUCTION

We now shift our focus from IIAP as a government organization to the National Indian Brotherhood (NIB) as the organized, federal-level political voice of status Indians. After detailing NIB's history in this chapter we proceed in the subsequent two chapters to discuss aspects of its internal and external environments, respectively.

At the outset several points should be made clear. First and foremost, NIB should not be mistaken for a mere lobby group or for the voice of but one among Canada's many ethnic groups, seeking mainly to enhance the identity of its followers. While it may have approximated those models during its early days, even then the fit was only approximate. In the 1980s those models scarcely fit at all. This is because the NIB is now *seeking power* more than it is seeking to exert influence or to extract concessions. It is seeking the enhancement and entrenchment of Indian treaty and other aboriginal rights in the Canadian constitution, and the authority, resources, and structures necessary to implement and enjoy those rights. This takes us to our second major point, which is that NIB is engaged in a *conflict* relationship against the government.

The primary object of the conflict between NIB and the government is the *right to Indian self-determination*, which is to say the authority to govern and service Indian people on Indian territory. This is the single factor which is at the root of numerous other disputes involving such diverse matters as land claims, governmental obligations, IIAP policy, and IIAP procedures. Thus, although Indians avoid the term, the main goal of the contemporary NIB is to achieve a form of sovereignty-association which in many ways is quite similar to that enunciated by René Lévesque for Quebec, particularly insofar as it seeks to wrest authority away from the Canadian Parliament and expand the scope of another level of government (e.g., Indian band councils). The conflict stems from a fact which we noted in Part II, namely, that IIAP has taken on the function of containing the social and political changes demanded by Indians within the bounds of acceptability to Cabinet, Parliament, and ultimately the electorate.

A final point which needs to be stressed is that despite the conflict relationship between NIB and IIAP, IIAP has a definite need for NIB. That need revolves around the functions which NIB fulfills for IIAP, one of which is the provision of a certain amount of order, predictability, and manageability to the IIAP's conflict with Indians. Without NIB that conflict would at best have to be conducted on several different provincial fronts at once, and at worst would have to be simultaneously waged with all 573 bands across the country. NIB also provides feedback—usually in rather unequivocal terms—on IIAP's endeavours, helps establish some of IIAP's priorities, and provides legitimation and political support for some changes which IIAP senior personnel wish to implement within the programme.

FORERUNNERS OF THE NIB[1]

Throughout most of the first half of the twentieth century, numerous factors militated against the establishment of Indian organizations at any level above that of the band (Hawthorn et al., 1967a:364-5; Frideres, 1974:112). Those factors included Indian poverty and adult illiteracy, interference by the Indian agent or the RCMP, a requirement of the Indian Affairs Branch that all grievances be routed through the local Indian agent, and a section in the Indian Act (1927) prohibiting political organizing. Other factors made it particularly difficult to form national-level Indian organizations. These included the lack of the federal franchise; the geographic dispersal and, in many cases, isolation of Indian communities; the linguistic diversity of Indians and lack of a shared second language; parochial identifications with a particular tribe or treaty; and the lack of explicitly articulated common objectives.

Despite these obstacles, various attempts were made, with varying degrees of success, to organize Indians at the district, provincial, and national level. According to Frideres (1974:112), the first such national effort was the League of Indians of Canada, which was formed in Eastern Canada around the time of the formation of the League of Nations in 1919. The League of Indians of Western Canada was formed the next year. Both of these ventures faltered, the former apparently due to government suppression, while the latter collapsed into separate provincial organizations due to a schism in 1930 between its Alberta and Saskatchewan delegations. The next attempt at organizing Indians nationally was the North American Indian Brotherhood. Like its predecessors, the Brotherhood emerged in an atmosphere of co-operation and optimism after a World War; in this case at a meeting in Ottawa in June 1944. Led by Andrew Paull, an organizationally experienced Squamish Indian from North Vancouver, the Brotherhood adopted a watchdog and lobbying role in Indian affairs (Patterson, 1978). Despite some successes, the Brotherhood apparently dissolved after 1950 due both to Paull's inability to expand it beyond its original British Columbia and Quebec non-treaty base, and to interference by such governments as that of the CCF in Saskatchewan.

In 1954 the foundations for another interprovincial organization were laid when the Community Welfare Planning Council of Greater Winnipeg sponsored the first of a series of annual conferences for Indians and Metis (Sealey and Lussier, 1975:164-5). The purposes of these meetings were to focus attention on Natives' needs and to provide Natives with a platform from which to offer solutions to their social and economic problems. These annual meetings were reportedly quite successful and soon delegates from other provinces began attending. As an off-shoot of this, the National Indian Council (NIC) was founded at an August 1961 meeting at Saskatchewan House in Regina. The prime mover of this effort was Bill Wuttunee, a Cree of mixed ancestry from the Red Pheasant reserve in Saskatchewan. Having studied philosophy at McGill and graduated with a law degree from the University of Saskatchewan (1952), Wuttunee worked with the high-ranking Saskatchewan Provincial Committee on Minorities (namely Hutterites and Indians) and in the course of those duties had interviewed almost every Indian chief in Saskatchewan. In 1958 he had brought Saskatchewan Indian leaders together to found the Federation of Saskatchewan Indians, which today is regarded by IIAP as the most militant of provincial Indian organizations and as the member organization having the most influence on the NIB.

In an interview with the authors, Wuttunee described those early organizational efforts. A major obstacle was simple lack of interest on the part of people he approached to join. Says Wuttunee, "Trying to get them interested was like trying to get people interested today in the constitution of Afghanistan." Travel on behalf of NIC was extensive, and usually at one's own expense. Contrary to the assimilationist, anti-special-status ideology which he later expounded in his book *Ruffled Feathers* (Wuttunee, 1972), in his early career Wuttunee was a staunch Indian nationalist who advocated the establishment of a separate Indian state.

The purposes of the NIC were "to promote unity among Indian people, the betterment of people of Indian ancestry in Canada, and to create a better understanding of [the] Indian and non-Indian relationship" (Patterson, 1972:177). In pursuing these aims, Wuttunee tried to encompass treaty and non-treaty Indians, as well as Metis and nonstatus Indians. (Under the Indian Act Wuttunee himself had been automatically enfranchised in 1943 when his father was.) He also tried to involve Indian women and to encourage their leadership. Indeed, Marion Meadmore, of Winnipeg played an important organizing role in the Council.

The activities and programs of NIC included such events as travelling exhibitions of Indian art, Indian Princess pageants, the planning of the Indian Pavillion at the Expo '67 World's Fair (a symbolically very important event for Indians which brought national and international attention), exchange visits between Indian students in eastern and western Canada, and Indian dances and singalongs which awakened interest in Indian cultural expression. Political lobbying was not absent, but appears to have been subordinated to these cultural activities.

The membership of NIC consisted mainly of middle class, urban, and nonstatus Indians. This was one of several contributing factors which led status Indians to the decision to form a national organization of their own. Another factor was the practical consideration that Metis and nonstatus Indians fell under provincial jurisdiction while status Indians fell under federal jurisdiction. Other important differences, some of which were highlighted by the 1968 Indian Act consultation meetings, also emerged. For instance, lacking treaties, Metis and nonstatus Indians were more concerned with aboriginal rights than with treaty rights. In addition while Metis and nonstatus Indians sought equality with non-Natives, registered Indians sought special status as "Citizens Plus." In light of such differences in goals and interests, the 1968 NIC membership meeting in Toronto decided to amicably split into two organizations —the National Indian Brotherhood and the Canadian Metis Society.[2]

In the remainder of this chapter we shall trace the evolution of the National Indian Brotherhood. In so doing we find it to be convenient and generally faithful to the facts to break the NIB's history into three main eras, each one corresponding with the NIB president at that time. As we shall observe, the three presidents were very different in their leadership styles and in the main thrusts which they gave to the organization.

THE FOUNDING PERIOD:
THE WALTER DEITER INTERLUDE

The impetus for establishing NIB as a separate entity from NIC came from the three Prairie provincial associations—the Federation of Saskatchewan Indians (FSI) under Walter Deiter, the Manitoba Indian Brotherhood under Dave Courchene, and the Indian Association of Alberta under Harold Cardinal. Accordingly, one of the Prairie presidents, Walter Deiter, was made the first president of the new National Indian Brotherhood.

Deiter faced a less than enviable task since the new organization not only lacked resources, but also contained within it strong personalities from across the country. Those personalities proved to be only too ready to challenge Deiter, who himself lacked a strong national political base.

The aims and objectives of the NIB were enunciated in very general terms, which we have paraphrased below:

a. To *assist* the Provincial and Territorial Organizations (PTOs) and to *work towards a solution* of problems facing the Indian people;

b. To operate as a national body to *represent* the PTOs and to *disseminate information* to them;

c. To *study*, in conjunction with Indian representatives from various parts of Canada, the problems confronting Indians and to *make representations* to the government and other organizations on behalf of the PTOs;

d. To *assist in retaining Indian culture* and values;

e. To act as a *national spokesman* for the PTOs throughout Canada; and

f. To *secure* the enforcement and fulfillment of all Indian *treaties* and of the *aboriginal rights* of Indians.

(N.I.B. Constitution and General Bylaws; italics not in original.)

Inspection of these goals reveals them, for the most part, to be an identification of the functions and activity areas (e.g., rendering of assistance, representation, lobbying, problem solving, research) in which the Brotherhood would engage. This stands in contrast to many other organizational charters which specify end states (e.g., change of the Indian Act, Indian self-government) towards which the organization seeks to move. This lack of clear specification of goals was perhaps necessary, in light of the wide differences within the status Indian population, for aims expressed in such general terms can easily accommodate many different factions.

The activities of NIB under Deiter consisted mainly of laying the groundwork for the organization, including such tasks as formulating a constitution to which all PTOs could agree, establishing relations with the PTOs, co-ordinating the efforts of PTOs so that they would not undermine each other, and raising funds. Although Deiter was skilled at fund-raising, the needs were great and he himself had to shore up the organization with personal loans that reportedly resulted in his own bankruptcy.

As Deiter's term in office progressed, behind the scenes preparations were being made to replace him as president. In the East, Andrew Delisle was mounting a challenge for the presidency from his springboard as

Chairman of the National Council on Indian Rights and Treaties. In the West, prairie leaders were formulating a strategy to keep the presidency in their camp. They wanted to counter what they saw as the progressive weakening of the NIB under Deiter, the paucity of consultation with them, and the undesirably close linkage emerging between NIB and DIAND. These Western preparations came to a climax at a three day long closed-door meeting in Drumheller, Alberta in early June of 1970. At that meeting—attended by Dave Courchene, Dave Ahenakew, Harold Cardinal, and George Manuel—Manuel was urged to contest the NIB leadership.

THE GEORGE MANUEL ERA

THE COUP

George Manuel is a Shuswap Indian who was born in 1921 and raised on the Neskainlith reserve about fifty-five kilometers east of Kamloops, B.C. A self-educated man, he served his political apprenticeship at the age of sixteen under the experienced Indian leader Andrew Paull in British Columbia. Intelligent and articulate, he worked for three years as a researcher in a law office, which is where he received his first sustained exposure to nonIndians. A skilled politician and tactician, he held many political offices, including chief of his band and founding vice-president of NIC. He also served on several government committees and commissions, including a term as chairman of the National Indian Advisory Board. In 1968 he was enticed by Harold Cardinal to go to Alberta to help develop the Indian Association of Alberta.

Reminiscing for the authors, Manuel recalled that he did not take seriously the overtures made to him at the Drumheller meeting since 1970 was not supposed to be an election year for NIB and he was not interested in the job. However, at that meeting the three Prairie leaders prevailed upon him and over-rode his protestations that it was not an NIB election year, with the response that he should not worry about that, for they would take care of it. They said that he had to agree to run and that then and there he had to give them his commitment, which he did.

At the 1970 General Assembly at the Hotel Vancouver, Deiter was overthrown on an ingeneous technicality. The Prairie cabal pointed out that the NIB constitution under which Deiter was operating was not valid since it had not been officially registered and incorporated with the Department of Consumer and Corporate Affairs. With Courchene arguing legal points and Cardinal and Ahenakew rounding up delegate support, the day was carried by the argument that the NIB had not officially existed previously, that this 1970 General Assembly was actually the founding meeting, and that a presidential election would now have to be held. Opposed by Deiter and Noel Doucette, but not by Delisle, Manuel entered the election and won on the first ballot. Re-elected by acclamation in 1972, he held the presidency until he decided to step down in September 1976.

MANUEL'S LEADERSHIP STYLE

To properly understand the Manuel era at NIB it is important that we understand Manuel's leadership style. Thus, we shall now jump ahead of ourselves somewhat in order to describe the approach which Manuel brought to NIB.

As described for the authors by those who worked for him, Manuel's approach to the task of being leader of NIB seems to have combined the skills of an astute politician with those of a sensitive social worker trained in the community development field of social work. Indeed, Manuel did work as a community development officer in British Columbia for IIAP in the 1960s. Manuel was always very conscious of being representative of his people and of consulting closely with them. Thus, whereas outsiders might look to particular victories over government as indicators of NIB's progress, Manuel was inclined to look for success indicators in terms of such accomplishments of the *internal development* of NIB as the building of a relationship of trust between himself and the executive council members.

Manuel's emphasis upon the internal development of NIB and of the broader Indian community could be seen in other ways as well. He stressed participation and a non-hierarchical orientation, and sought to involve as many people as possible in NIB's work by delegating authority to them. Thus, he used NIB as a vehicle for educating the rank and file and for developing leadership skills in them. To quote his executive assistant Marie Marule, "People got the impression that they were working for themselves and their people, not for him."

Manuel was very conscious of Indians' dependency on government and of the implications of NIB going into debt. He was very strict about money and, in the words of Marule, "believed in getting everything we could out of every cent, which had quite an impact on provincial and community leaders and lent much credibility to the organization."

Several sources commented upon Manuel's tactical prowess. With government he insulated himself from most bureaucrats, to avoid being sidetracked by them. However, he was careful to identify and cultivate contacts with selected influential persons who were not necessarily always at the top of the bureaucratic hierarchy (e.g., the special assistant to the Director of Housing). With the Indian community he tried to get the PTOs which were strong in a given field to work with those which were weak in that field, so as to bring the latter along developmentally. As we shall note below, he sought to involve the "technicians" (i.e., policy advisors and other non-elected professionals) at the early stages of the policy process so that they would not balk later when the Indian politicians took over. Finally, his strategy within the Indian community was one of building a consensus, rather than operating by majority rule. This, and a sensitivity to Indians' wariness of change, often resulted in him soft-pedalling his ideas; rather than pushing them aggressively on the Indian people, he would air his ideas and then let them rest until the Indian community came to share those views.

Thus, while our concern with Indian-government relations below has led us to select and discuss events in terms of their significance at the level of NIB's relationships with government and IIAP, the reader should be aware that for some of these events (e.g., the Joint NIB/Cabinet Committee), Manuel's NIB was also pursuing a hidden agenda on a quite different plane—namely, the plane of the internal development of the Indian community.

QUEST FOR STABILITY AND LEGITIMACY

Manuel took over an NIB which had already been overshadowed by Delisle's Ottawa-based National Committee on Indian Rights and Treaties, even though that committee was officially a part of NIB. The NIB office was located not in Ottawa, but rather, in a cramped corner of the Manitoba Indian Brotherhood's offices in Winnipeg. Files were reportedly in a state of disarray, and finances were meager. Of the four staff members, Manuel laid off two, including young Noel Starblanket, who was later to become president himself.

As part of the deal with Cardinal, it was arranged that the IAA would continue to pay Manuel's salary as well as his travel expenses. However, an indication of how precarious the overall NIB financial picture was can be seen in the decision by Manuel, once he had moved the NIB offices in with the NCIRT in Ottawa, to declare NIB bankrupt and to fold the organization.

This decision was overruled by the NIB Executive Council and intensive efforts began to put NIB on its feet again. According to Manuel, the key role here was played by the large Alberta delegation with its so-called "technicians." After helping to draft the budget, this delegation remained in Ottawa and successfully lobbied the Privy Council Office and the Department of The Secretary of State to obtain funds to meet most of the budget, thereby ushering NIB through its crisis and launching it on a relatively stable financial course.

Having temporarily secured a base, Manuel, vice-president Omer Peters, and Marule, all set out to build the organization administratively and politically. Administratively, the staff was increased to eleven persons in the first year. Politically, Manuel, Peters and Marule embarked upon a program of extensive travel designed to promote Indian unity, to establish the legitimacy of the NIB at the reserve level, and to obtain input from Indians across the country. Manuel alone travelled over 180,000 kilometers by car, train, plane and bus during his first year, including a 55,000 kilometer trip with the DIAND Minister to learn about the situation of the Australian aborigines and New Zealand Maoris. By his second year in office, Manuel reported spending at least half his working days away from Ottawa.

Although Manuel's international travels as NIB president sometimes aroused controversy within the organization, these trips had important consequences both for him personally and for NIB. They led not only to new insights into strategies of colonization and decolonization, but also to the development of a Fourth World consciousness on the part of NIB and Manuel himself (Manuel and Posluns, 1974).

Two particularly influential trips were his visits to Tanzania in 1971 and to Europe in 1972. The Tanzanian trip, which was in conjunction with the celebrations of Tanzania's tenth anniversary of independence, was seized by him as a perfect occasion to attract international attention for Canadian Indians and to gain international legitimacy for NIB. By means of the trip he also sought to embarrass the Canadian government over its insensitivity in sending its Minister of Indian Affairs to represent it at a celebration of the independence of Native people. Manuel received VIP red-carpet treatment, including an audience with Tanzanian President Julius Nyerere. Nyerere had a strong influence on him, for in many aspects of his style and work as leader (e.g., his cutting back of his own salary, his strategy of economic development), Nyerere embodied the teachings of Manuel's grandfather and proved those teachings to be viable.

The June 1972 visit to Europe was officially in Manuel's capacity as an advisor (representing NIB) to the Canadian delegation to the United Nations' Conference on Human Environment in Stockholm, Sweden. At the conference itself Manuel cultivated contacts with other nations, such as China, Brazil, Germany, Australia, and East African countries. He also gained valuable experience in international politics and political diplomacy. During a break in the conference he toured isolated Sami (Lapp) communities inside the Arctic Circle in Sweden and learned about the erosion of their aboriginal rights. This tour was important in convincing him of the need and feasibility of establishing an international council of indigenous people. Such a body was eventually organized in 1975 in the form of the World Council of Indigenous Peoples (WCIP) of which Manuel was the founding president.

Manuel's experience at the 1972 Stockholm conference led him to conclude that Canadian Indians are in direct competition with developing countries for funds and other support from the Canadian government. He also concluded that for Canadian Indians in general, and NIB in particular, to achieve their goals, they must achieve international recognition and aid. He subsequently lobbied for this strategy at NIB and in this regard in February 1974 he appeared before the Non-Governmental Organizations (NGO) Status Committee of The United Nations Economic and Social Council. In the face of reportedly strong opposition from certain developed countries (e.g., USA, UK, France) he successfully presented NIB's application for membership in the United Nations as an NGO. In 1978 this highly prestigious NGO seat was turned over to WCIP.

While the early 1970s were thus important years for NIB on the international scene, those same years witnessed important developments on the dometic scene as well. Once the problems of the organization and administration of the NIB office had been addressed, NIB was able, in 1972, to embark upon the second phase in its development. In this phase an attempt was made to overcome the bickering and distrust which arose after the initial closing of the ranks in opposition to the 1969 White Paper. Thus, in 1972 Indian national unity was identified both as a goal and as a means to the larger (albeit inherently defensive) goal of protecting Indian rights. A three-pronged approach, similar in many respects to government procedures, was also developed for the pursuit of this larger goal and is still in place today. The first prong to this approach involves the identification of priorities and definition of problem areas by Indian political leaders. The second facet calls for the technicians of NIB and its member organizations to meet, and organize information and research findings into draft position papers. Then, as the third facet of this approach, the Indian politicians first use this data to formulate final positions and then make decisions on strategies and tactics for pressing these positions upon the government. Aboriginal rights and Indian control of Indian education are two NIB policies which were developed in this way in the early seventies.

EARLY DOMESTIC ACCOMPLISHMENTS

Several important developments in NIB's relationship with IIAP and the larger government bureaucracy also occurred during the early seventies, as Manuel sought to provide to his constituents some tangible evidence of NIB's success. Included here are such events as the aforementioned procurement of core-funding from the Department of the Secretary of State; the procurement of funds for Indian treaty and aboriginal rights research (and the channelling of this through IIAP rather than through the Privy Council Office); and the placement of an NIB representative on the selection board which hired national and senior regional staff for IIAP. It was also during this period that NIB distributed to all Members of Parliament and all other embassies copies of Dee Brown's powerful book *Bury My Heart At Wounded Knee* (just two weeks prior to the much publicized confrontation at Wounded Knee, S.D.) and Harold Cardinal's book *The Unjust Society: The Tragedy of Canada's Indians*. A former member of the Privy Council staff has reported to us that Brown's book had quite an impact on the Prime Minister and became recommended reading in the Privy Council Office.

The adoption in August 1972 by NIB, and endorsation by DIAND Minister Chrétien, of the Indian Control of Indian Education national policy paper was one of the milestones in the history of NIB. Recognizing the crucial importance of education to Indians if they are to deal with the larger nonIndian society on equal terms, the leaders of NIB and its PTOs set out to devise an approach to Indian education that would end the prevailing situation of education as an alienating and often counterproductive experience for Indians. The path they chose involved such features as enormous changes in school curricula, greater involvement of parents and elders, the hiring of teachers who understand Indian culture, a reversal of "one-way" off-reserve school integration, and band administration of Indian education on reserves. The specifics of the content, trials, and tribulations of this policy are detailed in Cardinal (1977) and will not be repeated here. Suffice it to say that this was a very important accomplishment symbolically, but in practical terms it was marred by the fact that the agreement reached with the Minister contained no provisions for implementation. On that flaw it faltered badly for several years.

During 1973 the pace of NIB's accomplishments eased in what was to become the lull before the storm of nation-wide protest in 1974. Externally, important events were transpiring in the courts in cases of vital interest to NIB and its PTOs. We refer here to Supreme Court of Canada decisions on the Nishga land claim (which led the Prime Minister to reverse his previous policy and grant the legitimacy of Indians' claims to aboriginal rights) and on sex discrimination in the Indian Act. Important also were favourable decisions by other courts on such matters as the James Bay hydroelectric project injunction and Dene land claims in the Northwest Territories.[3]

Not all of the action was in the courts, though. In its dealings with IIAP, NIB became more strident, as evidenced by the issuance of demands that the DIAND Task Force on Housing be disbanded (which it was), that Assistant Deputy Minister John Ciaccia resign (which he did, but months later, and for purposes of entering Quebec provincial politics), and that the Assistant Deputy Minister appear before the NIB Executive Council (which he did). The summer of 1974 found Indian protest at local levels reaching a feverish pitch and IIAP in a state of virtual seige. A cross country bus caravan, styled after the Poor Peoples March on Washington in the USA, was also organized. It travelled from the west coast to Ottawa, stopping at various communities along the way to hold press conferences and recruit participants. When the caravan reached Ottawa and protested at the opening of Parliament on September 30, 1974 a bloody clash with RCMP guards occurred. (See Ticoll and Persky, 1975.) Consequently, NIB vice-president Clive Linklater, in the absence of president George Manuel who was in Washington, worked through Cabinet Minister John Turner to revive a moribund Cabinet/NIB consultative mechanism from the early 1970s. Thus was born the Joint NIB/Cabinet Committee (JNCC, 1974-78), and the opportunity for status Indians to have a unique form of access to the highest levels of government. That opportunity, however, soon lost its glitter, as we shall observe later.

THE END OF THE MANUEL ERA

Although the establishment of JNCC was a singular accomplishment and was to have the lasting effect of greatly increasing Indians' access to Cabinet Ministers, it was by no means greeted with unbridled enthusiasm at NIB. Admittedly, some PTOs welcomed JNCC as a vehicle for overcoming the DIAND Minister's gatekeeping role vis-à-vis other Cabinet Ministers. Manuel, however, was very wary of it because Indians had not yet formulated clear policy positions in certain key areas and therefore in this respect were not yet ready for JNCC. In addition his priorities revolved around the internal development of Indian communities and organizations, rather than around relations with government. Thus, although JNCC was quick to convene (with the Prime Minister briefly in attendance) within ten days of the clash on Parliament Hill, NIB under Manuel did not press for frequent meetings. Indeed, JNCC met only twice in 1975 (April 14 and December 12) and then not again for nineteen months.

Towards the end of his third and final term in office, Manuel pulled back noticeably from NIB and the organization began to drift. However, it remained active throughout. For instance, in 1975 it reached internal agreement on a statement of principles on economic development (as formulated by a working group of JNCC) and intensified its efforts against mercury pollution. It extended its full support for the Dene Declaration and, in response to the signing of the James Bay Agreement, announced its rejection of the federal government's policy of extinguishing Indian rights, titles, and interests as a condition of land claims settlements. The following year Manuel, himself, intervened in the Yukon land claims negotiations and succeeded in preventing the adoption there of an agreement patterned after the James Bay settlement.

Manuel's final year in office (1975-76) saw NIB closely involved with the government bureaucracy on many fronts. Under the auspices of JNCC, a co-operative mechanism was established for revising the Indian Act and consultative work began on the revisions themselves. In addition, NIB participated in various federal government review, advisory, and liaison activities, clearly emerging as more than just a lobby group. Vice-President Clive Linklater, for instance, reported close involvements with the Privy Council Office, the Public Service Commission, JNCC, and the Departments of Manpower, National Revenue, Health and Welfare, Justice, Solicitor General, and Secretary of State.[4] Thus, NIB was not merely standing outside government, sniping in a wholly negativistic way at objectionable features of government programs. Instead it had achieved a penetration—of considerable scope and depth—right into government itself.

This penetration into government and incorporation of NIB into the early stages of government advice-gathering efforts (and sometimes in actual decision making bodies themselves) was, to a significant extent, engineered by Clive Linklater. In an interview with the authors, Manuel reported that he disagreed with Linklater's close involvement with the government bureaucracy and put the brakes to it when he found out about it. More consistent with Manuel's philosophy of detachment from the bureaucracy was NIB's rejection of two important initiatives from the government just prior to his stepping down. These initiatives were the Government-Indian Relations paper discussed in Chapter Six,[5] and an invitation to hold a joint meeting between NIB's Executive Council and IIAP's Executive Planning Committee. Consistent with Manuel's concern to establish NIB's presence and legitimacy at the international level, the final term of Manuel's presidency was also marked by the holding of the founding conference of WCIP in Canada and by NIB's participation as an NGO in the 1976 United Nations Conference on Human Settlements ("Habitat").

Manuel, however, was becoming increasingly frustrated and fatigued after six years of combat. In failing health, and apparently finding it more and more difficult to muster the intense motivational commitment which had marked his earlier years in office, Manuel heeded the advice of his doctor, advisors, and friends and stepped aside as president of NIB. In contrast to the organization he had inherited, he left his successor an organization which was financially secure, and relatively strong and united. Important practical and symbolic victories had been won, Indian self-confidence was climbing, and international prestige and contacts had been acquired. In sum, an important start had been made in paving the way for the next major stage in Indian development—namely, the assumption of greater authority and self-determination by Indians in Canada.

NOEL STARBLANKET AND THE INDIAN GOVERNMENT ERA

THE MAN AND HIS STYLE

George Manuel was succeeded (by acclamation) by Noel Starblanket, a twenty-nine year old Cree from the Starblanket reserve in Saskatchewan. Starblanket came to the NIB presidency with a remarkable record of political and organizational involvement for such a young man. The great great grandson of one of the signatories to Treaty 4, Starblanket attended residential school in Lebret, Saskatchewan and high school in Regina. He represented Saskatchewan on the board of the Canadian Indian Youth Council and then did short stints as a film maker with the National Film Board and as a liaison officer for the National Indian Brotherhood before being laid off as part of Manuel's austerity measures in 1970. The next year he was elected Chief of his band at the age of twenty-four. In 1973 he was elected vice-president of the Federation of Saskatchewan Indians. There his connections with the Company of Young Canadians helped earn him a reputation as a radical and he and the organization parted company as he enrolled in a Bachelor of Laws program at the University of Saskatchewan. Ever interested in Indian politics, he became the vice-president of the Native Law Students' Association of Canada. In 1975 he was re-elected vice-president of FSI where he directed the Indian Rights and Treaties Research Program.

As president, Starblanket brought a new leadership approach to NIB. In contrast to Manuel's emphasis upon the internal development of the Indian community in Canada, Starblanket brought with him an emphasis upon the development of a technically proficient Indian staff—youthful, energetic, and possessing a high degree of formal education—which would make NIB a strong and effective Indian lobby on Parliament Hill. However, this emphasis upon a professionalized Eurocanadian approach, which differed so radically from traditional Indian ways, carried with it the risk that it would put a distance between NIB's leaders and their local Indian constituents. Thus, unlike Manuel, Starblanket appeared to not be reluctant to move out well ahead of the Indian community.

Other contrasts between the two leaders, as noted by the authors and by those who have worked for one or both of them, are to be found in Manuel's greater political experience, his stronger commitment to involving NIB at the international level, and perhaps a greater ability on his part to step back and adopt a more holistic view of an issue. For his part, Starblanket seems to have a stronger sense of personal ambition, to be more adept at certain important administrative and organizational tasks, and to have a greater commitment to developing and politicizing Indian youth. Although both men are conscious of their image as a leader, Manuel's emphasis upon the internal development of the Indian community made him very concerned with leadership-through-example, while Starblanket's initial concern with building an effective lobby in Ottawa required him to be quite conscious of image projection in white men's terms. However, lest the foregoing convey the impression that these two leaders of NIB were totally dissimilar, it should also be noted that both were intelligent, committed, diligent, politicized, and very much oriented to the future of their people.

THE FIRST YEAR

Starblanket's first year in office began in September 1976, within a week of Warren Allmand being installed as Minister of DIAND. At that time Indian affairs were still riding the crest of public attention associated with two events which had transpired but a few months earlier —namely, the highly publicized southern Canada hearings of Thomas Berger's Mackenzie Valley Pipeline Inquiry, and the shocking act of protest-by-suicide of Nelson Small Legs Jr., a twenty-three year old leader of the American Indian Movement in southern Alberta.[6] Starblanket's tenure got off to a fast start with the adoption (by the NIB General Assembly) of several important policy stances, and with the establishment of a positive relationship with Allmand.

On the policy front NIB called for the splitting off of IIAP as a department separate from Parks and Northern Development. Keynotes to what were to become some of the central themes of the Starblanket era were found in three other moves made by NIB at that time: (1) the issuing of the demand that Indians be involved, to their satisfaction, in developing policy for Indians; (2) the decision to change the priority of the Indian Act Consultative Study to the advancement of Indian band government; and (3) the emergence of a new concern with the Canadian constitution as it relates to Indian rights.

As a result of both the deliberations of a sub-group of JNCC and the new positive relationship between NIB and Allmand, agreement was

reached on an Indian housing program. Despite the financial emascula-
tion (i.e., a 40% reduction) of this program by Cabinet, it stands as a
significant accomplishment of the NIB and its highlights are worthy of
mention here.

The basic principles upon which the agreement is based included: (1)
assigning priority to people in the "no-income" category; (2) the
maintenance of DIAND's (rather than CMHC's) lead role in the provision of Indian housing; (3) direct input of Indian people at every level of
housing policy development and program management, including Bands
designing their own houses and managing their own housing activities;
(4) loan and subsidy amounts geared to income; (5) the personal involvement of the resident through cash or contributed labour, (6) the co-
ordinated use of housing resources (e.g., training and employment programmes) of other federal departments (e.g., DREE) and provincial
agencies; and (7) preservation of the special status of reserve lands.
Modification of these principles the next year due to dissent from Bands,
resulted in the elimination of financial "means tests" by IIAP and the
delegation of responsibility to Bands for establishing subsidies. Specific
provisions flowing from these principles included such features as subsidies of $15,000 per house for new house construction (reduced to
$12,000 by Cabinet in September 1977) and $6,000 for renovations; job
creation grants; the elimination of the compulsory loan requirements;
and a six-year program for providing the basic infrastructure of water,
sewage, electrification, roads, and fire protection, without which
deterioration could be expected.

STRUCTURAL CHANGES

Starblanket had not been in office long when he began to apply his
organizational and administrative talents to the task of better adapting
NIB to its new thrusts. In addition to recruiting new young advisors (See
Chapter Eight) he implemented several structural changes in the
organization. Foremost among these was the establishment of an Indian
Policy Development Secretariat (IPDS) to further the aim of meaningful
Indian involvement in the development of policy affecting Indians.
While consensus on this aim was easily attained, agreement on the IPDS
as the vehicle was not, as some of the older Indian politicians were wary
that NIB would develop policy in isolation from the bands and PTOs,
(which was one of their main criticisms of IIAP).

Originally directed to give top priority to the formulation of policy
dealing with Indian sovereignty and with the government-Indian trustee
relationship, the IPDS, in the words of one NIB respondent "fell out of
the nest fairly often while finding its wings." That same respondent

described the IPDS as being handicapped by a lack of a clear definition of "policy," a lack of political acumen, a failure to take a holistic approach which would integrate various policy areas, and even a fear of the word "policy." After several months of faltering attempts, mounting frustration and depression, and staff turnover, the NIB Executive assumed a more prominent and more directive role in the IPDS.

The concern that NIB would lose touch with its roots was addressed through other structural modifications. The first of these was the restructuring of all NIB committees (e.g., housing, education, health) to include representatives from all member organizations, rather than from just those member organizations who had developed a particular interest or expertise in that area. The second structural change involved the addition of a new unit to the organization—the Council of Elders. Its purpose is to advise the Executive and Executive Council on all policy and program matters, so that NIB actions are, to the fullest extent possible, consistent with Indian cultures and philosophies. As an extension of this, the position of resident elder was also created.

To further his aim of making NIB a highly effective lobby organization, Starblanket created the Parliamentary Liaison Unit, which we shall discuss in Chapter Nine. Other new units which were created, sometimes on a "task force" basis, reflected either Starblanket's own interests or developing directions and priorities in Indian thinking. For instance, the new Sports and Recreation Advisory Committee reflected Starblanket's interest in attracting and politicizing Indian youth, while the new National Commission of Inquiry on Indian Health reflected Indian concerns over Indian health rights. Similarly, Starblanket's establishment of a Canadian Indian Constitutional Commission to consolidate Indian views on the constitution reflected the growing conviction that Indian rights should be enshrined in any patriated or revised Canadian constitution. Although not of a task force nature, the formation of the Indian Government Development Secretariat (consisting of IPDS, the Indian Act Consultative Study, and Indian Rights and Treaties Research) was also very much a response to a new priority, specifically the priority attached to Indian sovereignty.

EXTERNAL RELATIONS

Consistent with Starblanket's goals for NIB, the organization engaged in numerous and intensive lobbying efforts during his term in office. Inasmuch as this will be treated in Chapter Nine, a few examples should suffice here. On the less successful side of the ledger we include NIB's lobbying on such issues as the Northern gas pipeline, gun control legislation, and (after 1977) housing. On the more successful side of the ledger would be lobby efforts pertaining to post-secondary education ("E-12") funding guidelines, health services cuts, and Indian involvement in constitutional revision talks.

NIB's external relations were, however, by no means restricted to lobbying efforts. For instance, early in 1977 NIB signalled its rejection of what it considered to be a calculated government attempt to erode the special status of registered Indians by withdrawing from all government committees whose titles included the word "Native." Yet this did not signal the beginning of an isolationist era for NIB, for the same year also witnessed NIB participating in new ventures with IIAP's Executive Planning Committee, with the Treasury Board (concerning Native employment in the public service), with the WCIP, and with the National Congress of American Indians in the U.S.A. NIB also publicly expressed its willingness to form alliances with any group interested in protecting Indian land from environmental degradation.

Although the main committee of JNCC remained inactive well into Starblanket's first term, NIB did continue to interact during that period with government representatives at the subcommittee or joint working group level. NIB brought a policy consensus to these working groups on several issues, such as the policy position that the determination of band or tribal membership is an aboriginal right reserved for Indian governments. Then, in the summer of 1977 the main committee of JNCC became active once more. However, in a dramatic move which precipitated a major crisis within NIB, NIB announced on April 13, 1978 that its Executive Council had voted to withdraw from the entire JNCC mechanism.

Although divisions within the NIB ranks apparently emerged almost immediately, the major crunch came when the government flexed its muscles and showed itself to be not averse to using a measure of fiscal coercion in responding to this attempt to embarrass it with an election apparently imminent. The government cut off funds to the PTOs for the Indian Act Revision Consultative Study. The predictable result of withholding this approximately one million dollars was that the NIB national executive was caught in a squeeze play as PTOs and bands started clamouring for the suspended funds. As the unpopularity of the withdrawal from the Committee became apparent at the band level, certain PTOs which had supported the withdrawal turned on the national executive. The national executive was blamed for the withdrawal and a serious challenge to both NIB and Starblanket's leadership of it was launched in Ontario. The crisis did not begin to subside until late August (a few days before the General Assembly) when funding was restored under an arrangement that allowed both the government and the NIB to save face.

The JNCC and the subsequent withholding of Indian Act Revision

Study funds from the PTOs were but two of several arenas in which NIB clashed head-on with DIAND in 1978. A third arena was departmental budgetary cuts, which NIB vehemently denounced and partially succeeded in countering. A fourth arena was the agreement in principle announced in the western Arctic land claim of C.O.P.E. Dissatisfied with that Agreement, and concerned with the Minister's declaration that other claimants should not expect a better deal from the government, the NIB roundly denounced the Agreement.[7]

In the closing years of the 1970s, NIB was active on still other fronts, a few examples of which can be cited here. In the realm of education it monitored the implementation of the Indian control of Indian education policy and conducted a preliminary evaluation of that policy. NIB also participated in evaluation studies of some IIAP programs and intervened with the Council of Yukon Indians (a body established by DIAND to negotiate Yukon land claims) on behalf of the Yukon Native Brotherhood in a successful effort to force the CYI to include Yukon chiefs in its organization. In the nonIndian private sector, NIB established working and/or political relations with at least one foreign government (Libya) and with several other domestic and foreign pressure groups. Examples of the latter are the U.S. Native American Rights Fund, the Canadian Labour Congress, the Ontario Federation of Labour, the United Steel Workers of America, and several U.S. environmental agencies.

CONSTITUTIONALISM AND INDIAN GOVERNMENT

The notions of Indian sovereignty and of entrenchment of Indian rights in the Canadian constitution were not novel to the Starblanket regime; however, it was during the Starblanket era that they came into prominence. Rather than seeking to negotiate concessions from the federal government on these dimensions, Indians began *asserting* and enforcing their sovereignty in certain domains. Fishing and taxing (road tolls) rights are two such domains in which NIB was involved in formulating the strategy of assertion of Indian sovereignty. A somewhat similar strategy was followed by NIB with regards to the revision of the Canadian constitution, as NIB informed the Prime Minister that NIB intended to attend the 1978 First Ministers' Conference on the constitution. (An invitation to attend as an observer was subsequently issued and accepted, while the February 1979 conference was boycotted by NIB because participant status had not been granted.)

NIB became very heavily involved in matters pertaining to the revision of the Canadian constitution after Prime Minister Trudeau stated his government's intention of unilaterally patriating and revising certain federal parts of the constitution by July 1979 if the provinces had not reached agreement on patriation (and an amending formula) by then. Specific proposals for revision (Bill C-60) advanced by Trudeau led Indians to fear that the special status accorded to Indians in the British North America Act, and the federal responsibility for "Indians and lands reserved for Indians," would both be eroded in any constitutional revisions. Thus, NIB initially lobbied Parliament and the government's constitutional review committee to safeguard Indian rights and to preserve the separate designation of status Indian. This was followed by a decision to lobby the British government not to permit the BNA Act to be patriated to Canada until Indian rights had been guaranteed and entrenched in the constitution.

The decision to lobby in England was predicated upon the realizations that: (1) the basic issue in the constitutional talks was the *redistribution of power*; and (2) that if Indians did not get involved they would be bypassed and would not be able to acquire the new powers they sought for Indian governments. NIB noted that all the First Ministers, except René Lévesque of Quebec, agreed that the constitution should be patriated to Canada. Assuming that Lévesque's opposition stance would soon prove untenable, the NIB strategists were of the opinion that NIB could gain leverage with the government if NIB could delay or block patriation.

NIB's plan called for a trip to England by three hundred Indian chiefs, elders, and band councillors to lobby the British Parliament, Prime Minister, Foreign Secretary, and Queen. In Canada, the Liberal government sought to avoid the embarrassment of such an event and instead, offered to have the Cabinet and Governor-General hold a two-day meeting with a delegation of Indian chiefs. NIB rejected this and adopted the position, with the new Progressive Conservative government of Joe Clark, that the trip would be cancelled if the government guaranteed that Indians would be involved as participants in constitutional conferences and that Indian rights would be enshrined in the constitution. When the government refused, the lobbying trip went ahead as planned in July 1979.

The lobbying efforts in England, per se, seem to have yielded little by way of tangible results. However, the threat of the trip, combined with the legitimacy accorded to the Indians' position by a recommendation of the Pepin-Robarts Task Force on National Unity that Indians be included in constitutional negotiations, did produce results. In May of 1979, Federal-Provincial Relations Minister Marc Lalonde guaranteed NIB a limited *participatory* role (as opposed to observer status) in the First Ministers' Conference scheduled for fall 1979, and assured NIB of representation on the Continuing Committee of (federal and provincial) Ministers on the Constitution (CCMC). The very day on which the chiefs were scheduled to depart for England, William Jarvis, Lalonde's successor in the new government, stated his intention of honouring Lalonde's commitment on CCMC. Then, shortly after the trip a meeting involving NIB, the Prime Minister, and certain cabinet members did result in the new government granting NIB a participatory role at constitutional talks on matters directly pertaining to Indians. Even though those matters were not precisely identified, the extraction of such a commitment from the government is of major significance. In marked contrast to but five years earlier when NIB had difficulty procuring a meeting with even the DIAND Minister, NIB had been accepted as a participant in constitutional negotiations at the First Ministers level. It is not unrealistic to expect that the next five years will witness an expansion of the areas defined as directly pertaining to Indians and the inclusion of NIB in the "closed door" sessions of constitutional negotiations.

One of the objectives of NIB's involvement in revising both the Canadian constitution and the Indian Act is to pave the way for the assumption of greater authority by Indian governments, whether at the local level or at some higher level (e.g., an elected representative Indian assembly at the national level). Although this thrust towards greater powers for Indian governments might be said to have begun with Manuel's policy of Indian control of Indian education, under Starblanket and the new Executive Council it became a major preoccupation of NIB.

In some respects the development of Indian demands concerning Indian government is as remarkable as the developments described above in the constitutional realm. From an original concern primarily with Indian education, Indian thinking has come to view numerous other institutional realms as properly falling within the purview of Indian governments. The following quotation from the 1978-79 annual report of NIB's Indian Government Development Program illustrates some of the breadth of these claims:

In a discussion paper entitled *The Principles of Indian Government* it is stated that Indian Governments have exclusive, legislative, executive and administrative jurisdiction over Indian lands, resources, and people within its territory. Indian territory includes: (i) territory as presently recognized; (ii) territory to which there is a claim; and (iii) hunting, fishing and gathering tracts. Under sections of a paper entitled *Areas of Jurisdiction*, Wildlife and Fisheries are mentioned as areas of jurisdiction that an Indian Government may want to legislate for.

Other NIB documents include other jurisdictional domains, notably health and justice.

At the close of the 1970s Indian thinking on Indian government was, with the exception of a few organizations, very much in the formative stages. Thus, the identification, refinement, and implementation of

alternative models of Indian government stands as one of the main
challenges facing NIB and other Indian organizations in the 1980s.

SUMMARY

In their attempts to describe the evolution of social movements, social
scientists have formulated various models, all of which are necessarily
somewhat selective, distortive, and over-simplified vis-à-vis the actual
events in the history of the social movement. One such model is Guy
Swanson's (1971:79-81) problem-sequential model, which despite its
limitations serves us well in summarizing the development of NIB to the
end of the 1970s.

The critical assumption of the problem-sequential model is that each
stage in the history of a social movement can be seen both as the solution
to a problem posed by the stage that preceded it, and as itself the source
of the problems that force the social movement to move on to the subsequent stage. So, prior solutions contain problems for the future,
although those prior solutions are not the only source of such problems.
(Furthermore, to Swanson's formulation we should add the caveat that
the problems of earlier stages are sometimes not fully resolved, with the
result that they may recur in later stages and affect the dynamics of those
later stages.) In Figure 7.1 we have portrayed the evolution of NIB in
terms of such a problem-sequential model.

To illustrate the specifics to which the model refers, let us consider
stages five and six. With the failure of the co-optative mechanism embodied in JNCC, NIB took its distance from the government by
withdrawing from JNCC, harshly criticizing the government in the process. Starblanket's handling of the JNCC, including the withdrawal, led
to a challenge to his leadership from within Ontario. Having abandoned
the co-optative relationship, NIB now stood in need of some source of
leverage against the federal government if it were to be successful
in advancing the cause of Indian rights. That leverage was created
through a multifaceted approach in which NIB tried to take more initiatives rather than responding in reactive fashion to initiatives taken by
the government. It not only helped plot lobbying and protest strategies
which would attract much media attention and embarrass the government (e.g., the trip to England, collecting tolls on roads passing through
Indian reserves to raise money to off-set cuts in government expenditures
on Indian health), but also began unilaterally asserting Indian rights
(e.g., fishing). Simultaneously new coalition partners (and new sources
of revenue) were sought so as to increase Indians' autonomy from the
federal government.

As part of its new assertiveness, NIB succeeded in injecting itself into

FIGURE 7.1 A Problem-Sequential Model of the Evolution of the National Indian Brotherhood

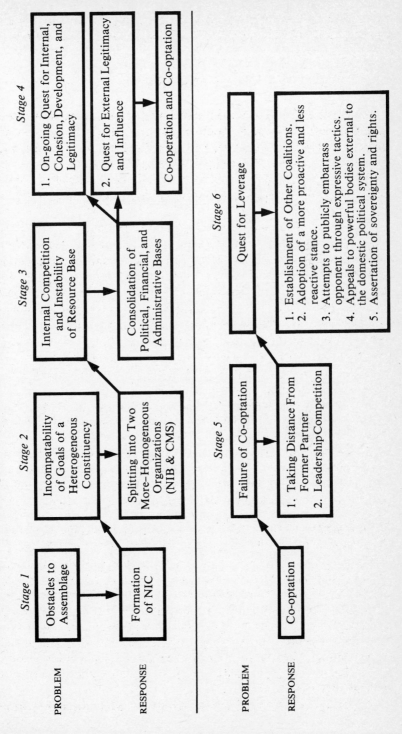

the process of revising the Canadian constitution. There, in the 1980s, as it attempts to enshrine and enhance Indian rights and to arrange a transfer of powers to Indian governments, it will encounter new problems which will demand new responses and the model shown in Figure 7.1 will continue to unfold.

NOTES

1. The history of organized political efforts by Indians to improve their lot in life is a complex one which has been described and analyzed by various authors (e.g., Patterson, 1972:145-197; Hawthorn et al., 1967a: Chapt. 17; Sealey and Lussier, 1975: Chapt. 11; and Frideres, 1974: Chapts. 5-6).

2. According to one of the principals involved, the Alberta Métis leader Stan Daniels was largely responsible for ensuring that the split was an amicable one. Sealey and Lussier (1965:165) point out that while the split pleased the Métis and registered Indians, it left the enfranchised (nonstatus) Indians out in the cold. In the authors' words ". . . the nonstatus Indians turned, with a degree of reluctance, to the Métis Society and were, with equal reluctance, accepted as members." For a useful discussion of the tensions between Métis and nonstatus Indian members of the Canadian Métis Society and its successor, the Native Council of Canada, see Sealey and Lussier (1975:168-173).

3. These latter two victories were reversed by higher courts.

4. Some examples of the specific topics of forums in which NIB became involved with these agencies are: Native employment in the public service; the Manpower Task Force Advisory Board which advises the Department of Manpower on employment opportunities for Indians; funding of NIB and its programs; and advisory councils dealing with Native peoples' involvement in alcohol and drug abuse and in the criminal justice system.

5. At the same time (summer 1976) the NIB Executive Council also vehemently rejected the content of the leaked cabinet document outlining aspects of a Native policy for Canada.

6. Two days after appearing before the Berger hearings in Calgary, Small Legs returned to his home reserve, donned full ceremonial regalia, and took his life by gunfire. In his suicide notes he said: "I give my life in protest to the present conditions concerning the Indian people of southern Alberta. I also give my life in the hope of a full-scale investigation into the Department of Indian Affairs' corruption and also the resignation of Judd Buchanan, Minister of Indian Affairs and Northern Development, and the divide and conquer tactics present on each reservation. For 100 years Indians have suffered. Must they suffer another 100 years? My suicide should open up the eyes of non-Indians into how much we have suffered."

7. NIB opposed the COPE agreement on the grounds that it: (1) contradicts NIB's objective of developing Indian self-government and Indian governmental control over Indian lands and resources; (2) extinguishes aboriginal land title; and (3) provides insufficient financial compensation.

The Internal Environment of NIB

INTERNAL POLITICAL ENVIRONMENT

A central feature of the internal environment of NIB, and a trait which differentiates it from most other "interest groups," is the high politicization of the internal environment. In an interest group such as the Canadian Manufacturers Association or the Canadian Medical Association, the leaders are usually selected because they possess particular interpersonal skills or contacts that would be useful in Ottawa, or because they epitomize the best of the profession. Although formal elections may be held, leadership positions are rarely seriously contested. In short, the internal environment of interest groups is usually apolitical and the organizational control held by the executive is seldom challenged. NIB leaders, in contrast, face a very politically-charged internal environment and far more demanding electoral hurdles to winning office and staying in office.

The president and vice-president of the NIB are elected biannually by a General Assembly to which each provincial or territorial member organization (PTO)[1] sends delegates. Although in the NIB constitution each adult registered Indian is considered to be an NIB member ex officio, the politically relevant membership category is the "national member" or voting delegate. These voting delegates are elected or appointed by their respective PTOs, and together they constitute the members of the General Assembly. Each PTO (or in the case of Ontario, group of PTOs) is entitled to elect or appoint two voting delegates plus an additional one for each five thousand (or portion thereof) Indians residing within its jurisdiction. The resultant PTO delegations to the General Assembly usually consist of the PTO president and/or another member of the executive, along with representatives from different tribes or regions within the province or territory.

The Assembly is divided into eleven regions consisting of the Yukon, the Northwest Territories, and all provinces except Newfoundland. The head of each regional delegation—normally the president of the PTO—sits on the Executive Council, along with the president and vice-president of the NIB. Whereas the Assembly meets once yearly, the Executive Council meets about six to eight times per year. The Executive Council can also take on strong political overtones, as it did in 1978, inasmuch as each PTO president must periodically face an election campaign among his own constituents back in his province or territory.

The president and vice-president are both elected for two-year terms by the Assembly. The politicking which goes into these elections is extremely intense. Reflecting on this intensity, one defeated candidate observed that embarking upon Indian political office is not just a job, but rather a commitment to a way of life and almost a religious experience. Indian political leaders, he pointed out, eventually have to go back to live in the results of their actions, which is not true to nearly the same extent for nonIndian politicians. In addition, veteran Indian politician George Manuel suggested to us that Indian politicians have traditionally been more ruthless to each other than to nonIndians and, when pressed by the authors, he confirmed the use of "dirty tricks" among Indian politicians as illustration of his point.[2] Harold Cardinal, who himself has first-hand experience with the vicissitudes of Indian politics expressed yet another view, and one with which Manuel fully agreed. Cardinal suggested that the intensity of Indian politics can be traced in large part to the vulnerability of leaders to counter-moves from outside their organization. These counter-moves might come from leadership challengers or from a government department offering legitimacy and funding for programs. Existing leadership in Indian political organizations usually does not control sufficient political "plumbs" which it can dispense as patronage to its constituents to ensure their allegiance through ties of obligation. Thus, if leadership challengers can plausibly offer greater rewards in the short term, they can often create an abrupt swing by convincing constituents that their best interests lie with the challengers. Of course, government departments can wittingly (as part of their efforts at social control through the divide and conquer strategy) or unwittingly become entangled in such a situation in the course of making program funds available to some Indian organizations but not to others. Finally, the lingering intertribal rivalries among Indians should not be overlooked in any attempt to explain the intensity of Indian politics.

As with nonIndian politics, much of the political manoeuvering for NIB presidential and vice-presidential elections is carried on behind the scenes, rather than on the floor of the Assembly itself. For instance, in a fashion similar to leadership conventions of nonIndian political parties, George Manuel reports that he no sooner arrived at the hotel for the 1978 General Assembly than he was whisked away to Starblanket's campaign headquarters and "wined and dined" by Starblanket supporters seeking to line up the bloc of votes which he controlled as president of the Union of British Columbia Indian Chiefs. Then, immediately upon leaving that meeting he was led away by a group of supporters of Starblanket's opponent, Fred Kelly, who sought Manuel's support for their candidate. Indeed, so much of the political action takes place off the floor of the General Assembly that it was suggested to us that a nonIndian outside observer attending a General Assembly meeting where a president and vice-president are being elected would undoubtedly be perplexed by the political complexity of events and by the frequent lack of correspondence between appearance and actuality.

The presidential and vice-presidential election of 1978 was very interesting in that the candidate was returned by vote rather than by acclamation, as had been the case in the previous three presidential elections. The challenger faced by incumbent Noel Starblanket was Fred Kelly, one of three politically active Ojibway brothers who have been prominent in elected office in the Grand Council Treaty No. 3 organization in northwestern Ontario. Kelly had recently resigned from the position of Director-General for the Ontario Region of IIAP, where he received much credit for laying the foundation to the Ontario Regional Liaison Council mechanism. With opposition (especially in Ontario) to the NIB's withdrawal from the Joint NIB/Cabinet Committee as fuel, and Kelly's charismatic oratorical skills as lubricant, the Ontario "machine," acting with uncharacteristic unity, forced the presidential contest to a close vote. Although no one is certain of the exact distribution of all votes, it appears that it fell somewhat along the following lines. First, Kelly undoubtedly capitalized upon an undercurrent of resentment of Saskatchewan[3] to carry the large Ontario delegation. Personality attractions and clashes are important in Indian politics and undoubtedly played a significant role in some or all of the Manitoba and Nova Scotia delegations lining up against Starblanket and in the Quebec delegation under Andrew Delisle lining up against Kelly. Starblanket could count on the support of Saskatchewan and probably most or all of Alberta and the two Territories. Prince Edward Island's allegiance was unclear. The deciding bloc of votes was held by former NIB president George Manuel, with his eleven member delegation from British Columbia. Manuel swung that bloc behind Starblanket when he agreed to be his formal nominator, with the result that Starblanket polled a close 39-29 victory in the sixty-eight member Assembly.

From the foregoing it should be clear that the successful Indian political leader is one who can first and foremost handle the internal political situation within the Indian polity; success vis-à-vis the external political environment is necessarily secondary. Thus, the leaders of NIB face a very different and much more demanding leadership task than that confronting most interest group leaders whose constituencies are usually less heterogeneous or diffuse, less fragmented, and less politicized. The task of aggregating and articulating the demands of such a constituency, while still surviving politically one's self, is not an easy one.

The presidential and vice-presidential elections are not the only stage upon which the drama of NIB's internal politics unfolds. Two other such forums have been the National Committee on Indian Rights and Treaties (NCIRT) and the NIB Negotiating Council. The NCIRT was formed in the early days of NIB, at its initiative, partly as a means of heading off a leadership crisis in the organization. With NIB facing the possibility of a public split on the basis of a challenge to the leadership of Walter Deiter by Andrew Delisle of the Caughnawaga reserve in Quebec, the NCIRT was created. The prestigious chairmanship of the committee was awarded to Delisle, whose reputed ties with IIAP and the federal Liberal Party were viewed by some NIB members as grounds not only for concern, but also for keeping him out of the NIB presidency. As Delisle's political strength eroded in Quebec, the NIB leadership moved to "defang" the NCIRT by transferring its moneys to the PTOs and eventually dissolving the Committee itself.

The NIB Negotiating Council was the forerunner to the Joint NIB/Cabinet Committee of 1974-78. Spearheaded by the Prairie provinces' representatives on the NIB Executive Council throughout the early 1970s, this Council pitted those Prairie representatives against Quebec, the Guy Williams (now Senator Guy Williams) faction in British Columbia, and certain factions in Ontario, in a struggle to determine whether DIAND should be the sole disburser of funds and programs to registered Indians. The prairie contingent sought to dilute the monopolistic power of DIAND by having programs and funds for registered Indians come from a variety of federal departments. This can be seen as Indians' own version of the divide and conquer approach. However the efforts of the pro-diversification contingent in this struggle faltered within NIB in the face of counter-pressures from DIAND. Through parliamentary techniques in the Executive Council, the Negotiating Council mechanism and its philosophy of dispersal of authority was effectively stalled by the Quebec-led faction,[4] such that the Negotiating Council never did develop to the point of entering into broad-level policy discussions with Cabinet. However, before the idea of the Council could be "pronounced dead," it was revived as the Joint NIB/Cabinet Committee in response to the September 30, 1974 demonstrations on Parliament Hill.

The story of the Negotiating Council brings to light a fundamental parameter of Indian politics of the late sixties and early seventies. We refer here to belief on the part of certain Indian politicians that certain other Indian organizations were, in essence, controlled by DIAND. For instance, commenting upon the Indians of Quebec Association (IQA), led by Andrew Delisle, one Indian leader told the authors: "We felt the IQA was mainly a paper organization funded by DIAND to counterbalance prairie organizations, and I think events subsequently confirmed that."

Indications are that IIAP definitely did play more than a passive or indirect role in Indian politics, although it would be difficult to prove that this role was based on any manipulative intent. For instance, while the Union of Ontario Indians was receiving funds from the Department of the Secretary of State, IIAP intervened to fund three other provincial level organizations. Then, the next year, IIAP withdrew its funding from these three and told them to get funds from Secretary of State, where they would, of course, have to compete with the Union of Ontario Indians. Similarly, Cardinal (1977:187-188) describes a situation wherein the Indian Association of Alberta (IAA) obtained a commitment from Cabinet for Secretary of State to provide forty-two million dollars over five years to build and operate a program for cultural learning centres. IIAP responded by successfully encouraging the submission of similar proposals from other NIB member organizations which competed with Alberta for the forty-two million dollars, thereby diluting the impact of the available money. Of course, one result was that relations between IAA and other NIB member organizations became strained, as IAA saw others as riding on its coat-tails and others saw it as being pushy, selfish, and arrogant.[5] IAA itself walked out of NIB meetings in protest, on different occasions.

INTERNAL OPERATIONAL ENVIRONMENT

In addition to the political aspect, a second aspect of NIB's internal environment can be analytically distinguished.[6] We refer here to the operational dimension—the day-to-day work of the organization by its paid staff employees. Included here are such matters as the organizational structure within which that work takes place, the procurement and deployment of financial resources, the key staff members, and operational problems.

As part of the process of becoming institutionalized, social movement organizations, like NIB, usually become more structured. In the first ten years of its existence the NIB experienced remarkable structural growth to the point where certain Indian leaders, such as former National Indian Council president Bill Wuttunee, have accused the Brotherhood of being more interested in "empire building," or building a "brown bureaucracy," than in helping Indian people. While NIB leaders, of course, deny such allegations, or contend that a bureaucracy is needed to counter that of IIAP, the fact remains that in comparison with other

Canadian social movements and many other lobby groups in Ottawa, NIB has a large organizational core relative to the size of its membership or constituency base. Just as with DIAND, so too with NIB, no proper understanding can exist without an understanding of how the organization is structured, and we therefore consider it first.

Figure 8.1 is a slight modification of a table of organization which NIB provided to the authors in 1978, with a cautionary note that "things don't really work that way," which can probably also be said of the organizational chart of most other organizations. Examples come readily to mind within NIB of such departures from the formal patterning of relations. For instance, the special assistant to the president, Arnold Goodleaf, temporarily served also as director of the IPDS; the executive director, Dan Brant, also served simultaneously as Director of Housing and as a member of the president's inner circle of advisors, which is not formally delineated on the organizational chart.

The full size of the NIB staff is not apparent from Figure 8.1, for in simplifying the chart we have omitted various researchers, secretaries, administrative assistants, and other support staff. The inclusion of all such persons would reveal the NIB to have a core staff of fifty-four persons, who during the summer months are supplemented by various students (21 in 1978) who are hired under government student employment grants. One consequence of having this large a staff size is that NIB necessarily becomes an important competitor in the contest between itself, DIAND, PTOs, bands, and others for educated and skilled Indian individuals.

Apart from its size, to what extent and in what ways is the contemporary NIB really a "brown bureaucracy?" Returning to the characteristics of a bureaucracy which we listed in our Introduction, we note that the very nature of NIB's activities is so political and highly variable as to virtually preclude the first characteristic—namely, standardization. Another characteristic of bureaucracies is that they are hierarchically organized and that career progression is possible by means of promotion through the ranks. In contrast, NIB has a relatively flat organizational structure with only three levels of authority below the elected vice-president. Career progression through these few ranks seems highly unlikely. Another characteristic is that job candidates are hired on the basis of their technical qualifications. Although this has become more pronounced under Noel Starblanket's regime, there are other considerations than purely technical ones which enter into employee selection. The most obvious is race, which is used not only for obvious political reasons, but also for reasons of cultural sensitivity (an important, but non-technical qualification). A related criterion for bureaucracy is the specialization of roles and tasks. NIB would receive an intermediate score on this dimension, for although many specific func-

FIGURE 8.1 Simplified Table of Organization of the National Indian Brotherhood, July 1978

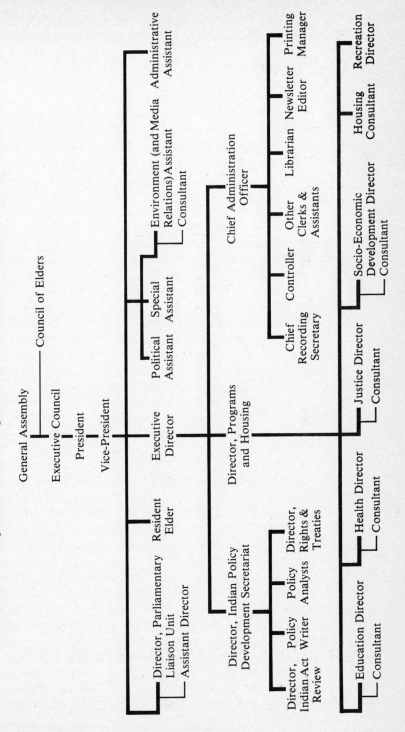

tional areas have been formally designated (e.g., housing, education, socio-economic development) those working in each of these areas tend to be generalists within that area.

Yet another criterion of bureaucracy is the formalization of acts, decisions, and rules in writing. On this NIB would receive a relatively high score, as illustrated by its extremely detailed and lengthy annual reports or the "contact cards" which the Parliamentary Liaison Unit asks to have completed each time an NIB member meets with a parliamentarian. Conversely, on the criterion that a bureaucratic organization is oriented toward the efficient and rational attainment of specific goals, NIB would receive a low to moderate score. In this respect we have already referred in Chapter Seven to the generality of its goals; to this we should add that NIB is first and foremost a political organization and that strict rationality must sometimes be sacrificed to political considerations. Also militating against the assignment of a high score on this dimension is the NIB resident elder and council of elders, whose respective mandates are more spiritual than rational. Finally, on other criteria the contemporary NIB clearly is of a bureaucratic nature. We refer here to such criteria as the separation of the property of the organization from the property of the individual, the absence of any appropriation of a position by its incumbent, and remuneration being made by fixed salaries paid in money. Overall, though, NIB emerges as being a "mixed" organization. That is to say, although it possesses some characteristics of a bureaucracy, these are generally not highly developed and are found in conjunction with other off-setting, non-bureaucratic characteristics.

Another feature of an organization which is often considered as part of its structure is its budget. With an annual budget of about two and one-half million dollars[7] in the late 1970s, the NIB had come a long way from the late 1960s when Walter Deiter reportedly secured a personal bank loan to run the organization. Indeed, with its current budget it is one of the very largest social movements/lobby groups in Ottawa, and holds the remarkable position of receiving large amounts of money from the government in order to change and influence that very government. However, despite these seemingly large amounts of government support, the NIB finds itself in an unenviable financial position in several ways. First, the Brotherhood has to invest much time and energy in the procurement and allocation of funds (which often arrive in insufficient amounts) and in justification of expenditures. Second, the Brotherhood is financially dependent upon government, from whence came 98% of its funds in 1978. Consequently, it is vulnerable to the kind of fiscal coercion which it faced from the DIAND Minister after NIB withdrew from JNCC, for DIAND/IIAP alone supplies about 70% of NIB's total budget.

In Tables 8.1 and 8.2 we depict the fiscal history of the Brotherhood, in terms of revenues and expenditures for the period 1971 to 1979. On the revenue side of the ledger, we note again the key role played by the core funding grant from the Department of the Secretary of State. It is these moneys from the Secretary of State, totalling over one-half of a million dollars in 1979, which provide that essential stability, continuity, and predictability of financial base around which the organization erects a superstructure of programs. However, the procurement of these core funds was not an easy matter. Cardinal (1977:175), in what he calls the "dance of the bureaucrats," has described the intense jockeying between federal government departments for control over money and programs for Indians so as to enhance the prestige and influence of their own department.[8] In Table 8.1 we observe the initial, but short-lived success of DIAND in this core funding struggle, its displacement by Secretary of State, and then the gradual re-entry of DIAND into the field in 1975 to take on an ever-expanding and increasingly significant role in core funding by 1978.[9]

The lower panel of Table 8.1 dealing with special projects also reflects some of the aforementioned political struggles. On the top line we observe the success of George Manuel in subordinating the "upstart" National Committee on Indian Rights and Treaties to the point where, by 1973, it had been completely absorbed within NIB and no longer had a separate identity.[10] We also observe the resurgence of DIAND over Secretary of State in this "special projects" realm of the interdepartmental competition. By 1978, for instance, even excluding the DIAND $720,135 special projects moneys which NIB merely passed along to its PTOs, DIAND still accounted for four-fifths of NIB's special projects budget (and 63% of its total budget). The Department of National Health and Welfare, which was handed responsibility for Indian Medical Services in 1945 and now has a one hundred million dollar budget for that, is also becoming an increasingly important player in the interdepartmental contest. As the only federal department, other than DIAND and Secretary of State, which is providing on-going funding to NIB, it is beginning to rival Secretary of State in this special projects field.

The notes at the bottom of Table 8.1 are interesting in that they, too, suggest the existence of an interdepartmental competition upon which NIB capitalizes. For instance, DIAND and Secretary of State both fund NIB's summer student, departmental liaison, and library programs. Similarly, while Secretary of State funds provincial all-chiefs conferences, DIAND funds band council liaison. While Secretary of State funded the Annual General Assembly, DIAND funded Executive Council Meetings and then, in a move that does not appear in the notes to Table 8.1, it also entered into the funding of the Annual General Assembly.

TABLE 8.1

Statement of Revenue, National Indian Brotherhood, 1971-79 (thousands of dollars)

FISCAL YEAR ENDING MARCH 31	1971	1972	1973	1974	1975	1976	1977	1978	1979
I. Core Funding									
— Secretary of State	—	292.0	292.0	297.0	321.2	340.5	300.5	367.5	508.2
— DIAND	181.0	—	—	—	2.7	4.3	31.0	75.0	*
— Administration Charges	—	—	—	—	—	—	55.5	45.8	—
— Deferred Revenue	—	—	—	—	—	—	(6.3)	8.0	—
— Donations and Miscellaneous	14.9	2.6	12.8	32.9	14.2	5.8	7.7	4.1	1.0
Sub-total	195.9	294.6	304.8	329.9	338.1	350.6	428.4	500.4	509.2
II. Special Projects*									
— Nat'l. Cte. on Indian Rights & Treaties**	550.9	500.0	230.3	—	—	—	—	—	—
— Accountable Grants and Contributions from:									
Secretary of State	—	24.0	145.8	—	133.9	142.8	133.6	143.9	47.1
DIAND	81.2	31.6	34.3	147.9	257.6	157.5	1,056.0	1,832.8	1,752.6†
Nat. Health & Welfare	—	—	—	2.3	51.0	103.9	83.5	114.5	182.4

Central Mortgage & Housing Corp.	—	—	—	—	31.3	—	—	—	—
Solicitor General	—	—	—	—	—	9.6	—	—	—
Manpower & Immigration (CEIC)	—	—	—	—	—	—	40.0	—	—
Deferred Revenue	—	—	—	—	—	—	(116.7)	—	—
Donations & Miscellaneous	—	—	—	8.1	54.4	21.1	4.9	—	—
Sub-total	632.1	555.6	410.5	189.7	506.5	425.4	1,201.2	2,091.1	1,982.1
Total Revenue	828.0	850.2	715.2	519.6	844.6	776.0	1,629.6	2,591.5	2,491.3

* Special projects grants are designated for various activities. Examples of these are indicated below, by granting agency.

  a. *Secretary of State*: (i) summer students; (ii) departmental liaison; (iii) library and research; (iv) provincial all-chiefs conferences; (v) Annual General Assembly

  b. *DIAND*: (i) through (iii) above; (iv) education workshops; (v) housing study; (vi) Indian Act Revision Project; (vii) information services; (viii) Executive Council Meetings; (ix) band council liaison; (x) newsletter; and (xi) IPDS

  c. *DNHW*: (i) mercury pollution study; (ii) health liaison; (iii) drug and alcohol symposium; and (iv) dietary study

  d. *Central Mortgage and Housing Corp.*: (i) Housing study

  e. *Solicitor General*: (i) National Conference on Native Peoples and The Criminal Justice System.

** The National Committee on Indian Rights and Treaties ceased to exist as of July 31, 1972.

† See text, Note 9.

Source: Annual Reports of the National Indian Brotherhood.

TABLE 8.2
Statement of Expenditures, National Indian Brotherhood, 1971-79 (thousands of dollars)

FISCAL YEAR ENDING MARCH 31	1971	1972	1973	1974	1975	1976	1977	1978	1979
I. *Core Funding*									
Salaries & Benefits	56.8	123.4	192.9	170.2	162.8	159.5	176.1	181.0	541.0
Office and Administration									
— Rent	n.a.	29.3	34.4	36.2	38.9	25.6	43.8	9.6	86.0
— Telephone & Telex	n.a.	17.8	24.9	13.3	13.1	17.8	30.2	23.9	71.5
— Office Supplies & Postage	n.a.	16.5	4.1	6.2	13.9	11.1	15.5	11.8	24.3
— Printing & Publications	n.a.	11.1	19.4	48.1	14.8	8.2	11.2	14.3	10.9
— Promotion	n.a.		3.4	2.1	5.8	5.2	7.9	12.1	17.3
— Other (e.g., insurance, bank charges, interest)	n.a.	26.8	12.8	.7	2.5	12.5	19.3	151.5**	31.4
Sub-total: Office & Administration	28.1	101.4	99.1	106.5	89.1	80.4	127.9	403.2	241.3
Meetings (e.g., General Assembly, Exec. Council)	114.9	75.8	62.6	32.4	48.4	45.6	73.4	80.6	18.0
Staff Travel (Other than meetings above)	25.6	31.5	37.2		21.8	24.4	52.5	102.6	73.9
Advisory Services	32.6	40.3	27.6	3.8	17.7	13.4	14.3	24.4	12.1
Sub-total	258.1	372.5	419.4	313.0	339.7	323.3	444.1	610.7	886.3

II. *Special Projects**

Grants transferred to PTOs	354.9	443.9	175.3	—	—	—	401.7	720.1	692.4
Salaries & Benefits	46.9	86.0	52.3	74.5	196.1	185.2	262.1	415.8	500.1
Office & Administration	17.2	14.0	19.5	48.2	77.0	79.3	182.3	404.8	70.7
Meetings & Related Expenses	17.6	13.5	nil	nil	68.4	91.5	121.2	135.0	141.1
Advisory Services	43.2	27.2	12.9	25.5	60.0	43.2	155.1	215.8	121.0
Staff Travel other than meetings	34.3	4.1	2.7	52.8	140.9	40.6	109.0	161.9	83.5
Unclassified.................	4.0	—	14.3	—	—	—	—	6.0	1.7
Sub-total	518.0	588.6	277.0	201.0	542.4	439.7	1,231.3	2,059.2	1,610.3
Gross Expenditures	776.0	961.1	696.4	514.0	882.1	763.0	1,675.4	2,669.9	2,496.6
Excess of Revenues Over Expenses (or Expenditures Over Revenue)	52.0	(110.9)	18.9	5.6	(37.5)	12.9	(45.8)	(78.4)	(5.3)

n.a.   denotes "not available."
—   denotes "nil."
* Prior to April 1, 1974, expenditures are not clearly designated as core or special projects. As a result of our so classifying them, distortions arise in year to year line-item comparisons, although gross expenditures for those years are accurate.
** This figure includes $137,517 in salary and administration overhead costs for special projects but not recovered from special projects.

Source: Annual Reports of the National Indian Brotherhood.

TABLE 8.3

Programs and Selected Examples of Sub-areas of Involvement, National Indian Brotherhood, 1977-78 Fiscal Year

I. Education

1.1 Provision of technical assistance and political support to reinforce education rights of Indians.

1.2 In collaboration with PTOs, assist bands in the areas of education policy, the implications and responsibilities of local control, and government procedures pertaining to education.

1.3 Specific activities include study and research; development of techniques for implementing Indian control of Indian education; discussion, evaluation, and feedback (e.g., workshops); monitoring the implementing of Indian control of Indian education; and making recommendations.

II. Environment

2.1 Legal research into environmental issues.

2.2 Development of relations with labour and other organizations whose constituents are adversely affected by environmental pollution.

2.3 Commissioning, organizing, conducting, or monitoring research designed to establish the levels or impact of pollutants in particular communities.

2.4 Preparation and presentation of briefs (on behalf of an Ontario PTO) to the Hartt Inquiry on the Northern Ontario environment.

III. Newsletter

3.1 Monthly publication of *The National Indian* newsletter of NIB activities (circulation 3700).

VI. Indian Act Revision

6.1 Activities curtailed when Minister withheld funds in response to NIB's withdrawal from Joint NIB/Cabinet Committee.

6.2 Worked on tribal government, education, land surrenders, and discrimination on the basis of sex.

VII. Indian Policy Development Secretariat

7.1 Development of a position paper on the Government/Indian Trust Relationship.

7.2 Coordination of the NIB Task Force on the Canadian Constitution and development of a position paper in response to the government's Bill C-60 (on the constitution).

7.3 Participation in the Joint NIB/Cabinet Committee.

7.4 Monitoring the IIAP Management Information Study.

7.5 Fighting "brush fires" for PTOs, NIB Executive, or other NIB Programs.

VIII. Socio-Economic Development

8.1 Participation in evaluation of the Indian Economic Development Loan Fund of IIAP.

8.2 Convened national meeting on topic of bands taxing nonIndian leasees on reserve land.

8.3 Liaison with IIAP on behalf of bands involved in socio-economic development programs.

8.4 Provided advice on needed changes in Indian Act for facilitation of socio-economic development.

IV. *Health*
4.1 Establishment of a National Health Policy Committee.
4.2 Assisting Yukon Native Brotherhood in attempting to negotiate the transfer of the provision of health services from the federal to the territorial government.
4.3 Sitting on the National Native Alcohol Abuse Board.
4.4 Participating in research on reserves relating nutrition to the learning and behavioural problems of Indian children.
4.5 Examined Indian health education and service programs in the United States southwest, including traditional Indian health measures.
4.6 Approached thirty private foundations for further funds for NIB's National Health Policy Committee.

V. *Housing*
5.1 Updating of the National Housing Survey.
5.2 Negotiation, with DIAND Minister, of major changes in the Joint NIB/DIAND Housing Agreement for Cabinet endorsement.
5.3 Lobbying Minister of Employment and Immigration to release more labour funds for Indian housing construction, so as to use housing construction to help alleviate on-reserve unemployment.

IX. *Resource Centre*
9.1 To provide library resources to the NIB Executive and staff.

X. *Rights and Treaties Research*
10.1 General research of current issues for bands, PTOs, or NIB Executive, especially to buttress land claims and other claims.
10.2 Analysis of Government Bills and Agreements (e.g., COPE Agreement).
10.3 Consultation and Liaison with IIAP's Policy, Research, and Evaluation Group.

XI. *Sports and Recreation*
11.1 Establishment of a National Indian Sports and Recreation Advisory Committee to:
— develop leadership, good health, pride, and personal growth among Indians.
— promote participation by Indian people and recognition of Indian accomplishments in sports, recreation, cultural, and youth activities.
— help increase the political awareness of Indian youth.
11.2 Develop a five-year plan for recreation and sports in Indian communities.
11.3 Preparations for negotiations with government for funding of sports and recreation.
11.4 Organized an Indian demonstration of lacrosse at Commonwealth Games in Edmonton.

The overall size of the NIB budget has increased three-fold over the decade of the seventies, from eight hundred thousand dollars in 1971 to two and one-half million dollars in 1979. However, as we have just observed, the vast majority of that income derives from just two sources, both of which are within the federal government. A diversification of funding sources to include such additional sources as Indian bands themselves, private foundations, private industry, and perhaps even the United Nations (through the WCIP) would certainly be in order if the vulnerability of NIB to government funding cuts or controls is to be lessened. By 1978 there was some evidence that this was beginning to happen, especially with regards to approaching foundations.

On the expenditures side of the ledger, Table 8.2 provides a detailed breakdown of expenditures for both core operations and special projects. Several features of that table are worthy of further comment. First, the largest single expenditure item in recent years consists of the aforementioned money ($720,135 in 1978) transferred to NIB's member organizations as part of the Indian Act Revision Consultative Study. Second, communications costs are a major item in the NIB budget. This can be attributed not only to the wide geographic expanse of Canda, but also to the large number of bands in the country and the internal political needs for NIB to keep in close touch with its constituency. Thus, in 1978, for instance, if we exclude from the budget the $151,502 unrecovered and unspecified administration charges from special projects, we find that telephone and telex charges accounted for 5% of the core budget, meetings consumed another 18%, and staff travel accounted for a further 22%, for a total of 45%.

A third noteworthy feature of Table 8.2 is the institutionalization of NIB which it reflects. With over $800,000 spent in 1978 on office and administration expenses (excluding salaries and benefits), there can be no doubt that NIB has become entrenched—that it has carved out a functional niche for itself and has gone about establishing itself in that niche to such an extent that it would be difficult for government or for Indian competitors to dislodge it. In short, NIB has become part of an establishment.

A fourth and final feature of Table 8.2 which we wish to mention is the substantial sum ($133 thousand in 1979 and $240 thousand the previous year) which NIB spends on "advisory services" or consultants' fees. These fees are paid to Indian and nonIndian consultants alike for special expertise which they contribute to NIB. Lawyers have stood out here as one type of outside professional of whom Indians have made great use. However, even in the early 1970s a backlash was starting to develop against lawyers, for some appeared more interested in their fees than in their clients' interests.[11] By the end of the decade there was also an adverse reaction against what some considered to be an overly legalistic orientation which stemmed from the heavy reliance upon lawyers (Little

Bear, 1979). However, lawyers were not the only consultants used, as the bottom line of Figure 8.1 suggests. The overall list of consultants used by NIB encompasses a broad range of expertise representing the fields of nutrition, environmental studies, chemistry, journalism, medicine, business, education, and others.

To focus on the raw budgetary figures of an organization, as we have done above, without reference to the programs and projects to which those moneys are applied, is to present an incomplete picture of the organization. That bias is countered somewhat in the preceding chapter where our discussion of the historical development of NIB cited some of the accomplishments of these programs and projects. In order to provide a less fragmented picture of the programmatic side of NIB, we list in Table 8.3 the main programs and projects of an illustrative year (1977-78), along with a brief description of the purposes and/or activities of each.

PERSONNEL

Although our research stopped short of enabling us to fully map out the informal power structure of NIB, we were able to identify some of the most influential persons on the staff during the 1970s. In this section we shall identify those persons and provide a profile of each, with the exception of the two presidents, Manuel and Starblanket, who were discussed in the previous chapter.

OMER PETERS

During the 1970s NIB had three vice-presidents, the first of whom was Omer Peters. A Seneca Indian from the Moraviantown reserve near London, Ontario, Peters served in the Royal Canadian Air Force during World War II. He also served his own band for seventeen years as chief, councillor, and administrator before helping to organize the Union of Ontario Indians. He served as president and executive director there prior to being elected vice-president of NIB in 1970. Those who worked with him described him as "a natural diplomat . . . congenial . . . a raconteur who was always laughing and joking and was well liked and respected by both Indians and nonIndians." Since his personality disinclined him towards difficult executive and administrative level decisions that might hurt someone else's feelings, he was used by Manuel mainly as an ambassador and an advisor. In that capacity he attended many meetings with bands, and PTOs, and in the words of his successor, "came to know the people at the grass roots level from one end of the country to the other." His friendly demeanor and ability to "read" Indian people made him highly successful at winning the co-operation of Indians who had formerly been hostile to NIB, which proved to be a valuable contribution at a time when NIB was seeking to build its legitimacy. In 1974 Peters was succeeded as vice-president by Clive Linklater. After retiring from elected political life he served briefly as chairman of NIB's Council of Elders prior to his death in 1978.

CLIVE LINKLATER

The other vice-president during NIB's formative years was Clive Linklater, a Saultaux from the Couchiching reserve near Fort Francis, Ontario. After completing residential school Linklater graduated from teacher's college in Moose Jaw, Saskatchewan in 1955. His teaching career involved him with Indian students in the remote reaches of three provinces, after which he worked for the Alberta government as a community development officer (CDO) in Indian and Métis communities. From 1969 to 1972, while still a CDO, he worked as a lecturer, organizer, and resource person with the University of Alberta's Intercultural Education Program for university students who were to become teachers in Native communities. At the same time he served as an education consultant for the Indian Association of Alberta. In 1972, at the age of thirty-eight he accepted George Manuel's invitation to join NIB as executive assistant to the president. He subsequently became executive director and then in 1974 was elected vice-president. While at NIB he was active in the international arena, including liaison work with national Indian organizations in the U.S.A., organizational and fund-raising efforts surrounding the founding of the World Council of Indigenous Peoples, and the bringing of victims of Minimata disease from Japan to Canada. A shrewd tactician with a firm belief in the constructive potential of confrontation, Linklater was also heavily involved at home in NIB's dealing with the government and its bureaucracy. A partial list of his areas of activity here would include the James Bay case, the development of a housing policy and of a strategy for Indian economic development, funding negotiations, and programs to combat alcoholism and drug abuse among Indians. In 1976 he stepped down from office to pursue a consulting career in human relations and group dynamics, although he rejoined NIB on a part-time contract basis in order to take charge of the organizing and strategizing behind the 1979 Chiefs' trip to England.

MARIE SMALLFACE MARULE

Another influential person in the early years of NIB was Marie Smallface Marule (pronounced Maroolay), a Blood Indian from southern Alberta. After studying sociology and anthropology at the University of Alberta, Marule spent four years with Canadian University Students Overseas (CUSO) in Zambia. For three of those years she worked with the Department of Community Development of the Government of Zambia popularizing the concepts of self-help and community development. There she applied skills which dove-tailed nicely with George Manuel's orientation to NIB and she joined NIB in early 1971 at the age of twenty-seven. She was soon made executive director, after which she served as special assistant to the president and subsequently executive assistant to the president. In addition to administrative matters, her work at NIB involved her in writing for Manuel (e.g., position papers, press releases, critiques of government papers), building legitimacy for NIB through frequent public speaking engagements before bands and other organizations across the country, organizing the World Council of Indigenous People, and formulating strategies for NIB. She was also instrumental in the behind-the-scenes manoeuvering which led to Manuel's important trip to Tanzania. Exhausted after five years with NIB, she returned home to become a faculty member in the Native American Studies Program at the University of Lethbridge, from which base she remained active in the Secretariat of the WCIP.

ARNOLD GOODLEAF

Two key advisors to Noel Starblanket during his presidency were Arnold Goodleaf and Dave Monture. Goodleaf is a young Mohawk from the Caughnawaga reserve near Montreal. A high school graduate at the age of fifteen, he contends that his efforts to enter computer science at the university level were blocked by IIAP. In the Mohawk tradition he held jobs as a high level iron worker and bridge painter. In 1973 he joined the staff of the Indians of Quebec Association (IQA) and subsequently held many senior positions there, including that of political advisor to the president. In July 1977, at the age of twenty-seven, he left to join NIB. Describing himself to the authors, he said "I like to be near power." As special assistant to the president he has succeeded in that desire. His responsibilities at NIB have been wide-ranging, involving him in the land claims area, Indian Act Revision, the Indian Policy Development Secretariat, and especially, the Canadian Constitution review process.

DAVE MONTURE

Dave Monture is a Mohawk from the Six Nations reserve near Brantford, Ontario. After working as a labourer, he joined DIAND Information Services in Ottawa in 1969. Within a year he had become Editor of *Indian News* and had gained first-hand exposure to the new Indian advocacy when interviewing Indian leaders concerning their reactions to the government's White Paper and the Indians' Red Paper. He was eventually seconded to the IQA where he informally served as a strategy advisor in the James Bay controversy. The James Bay experience angered him and drove him to return to university (University of Western Ontario) in the fall of 1972 to develop his skills. While there he exposed himself to a wide variety of subjects, including philosophy and political science. After graduating in 1974 he became the Native Employment Coordinator for the Ontario Region of the Public Service Commission of Canada. Then accepting a promotion to Ottawa in late 1975, he became involved in the preparation of the cabinet document outlining the Trudeau government's Native employment policy, an endeavour in which he involved NIB closely. His friendship with George Manuel and involvement with Manuel in the World Council of Indigenous Peoples had a considerable politicizing effect upon him and in August 1977 he joined NIB as a political advisor to the president. In that capacity he is involved in speech writing, the preparation of sensitive correspondence at the Ministerial level, in strategy advising, and in liaison with the Minister's assistants, as well as with the PCO, the Federal-Provincial Relations Office, and DIAND. His other responsibilities at NIB have involved him in such areas as Indian employment in the public service, Quebec's Bill 101, relations with the PTOs, and attempts at tightening political discipline among the PTOs.

DAN BRANT

Dan Brant is another young advisor recruited by Starblanket. Brant is from the Mohawks of the Bay of Quinte band in eastern Ontario. A high school dropout in 1966, he too worked on construction, only to renew his academic career two years later. He graduated in architecture from Ryerson Institute and went on to earn a graduate degree in management and civil engineering from the University of Waterloo. His graduate thesis was an analysis of the structure controlling community development on Indian reserves, while his undergraduate thesis focused on Indian housing. Upon graduating he went to work in July 1975 for the Housing Branch of IIAP, but within six months he was assigned to the minister's office as special assistant to the minister for IIAP. He held that position under three ministers, with an interlude back in the department as Director of the Management Systems Group of IIAP. His duties in the minister's office provided much opportunity to get to know the NIB leaders and he moved directly to NIB from that office. He joined NIB in

December 1977, officially as Director of Housing, although his actual responsibilities were broader. He subsequently put his managerial skills to use as executive director, while remaining an informal advisor to the president.

LLOYD TATARYN

While NIB has employed many nonIndian consultants who have left a mark on the organization or its policies (e.g., Jacqueline Weitz on education, Douglas Sanders on legal aspects, Walter Rudnicki on housing and other areas), journalist Lloyd Tataryn appears to have been closer to the presidents than have most nonIndians. Raised in Sudbury, Ontario, he comes honestly by his intense concern for environmental degradation. A former producer for the CBC Radio program "As It Happens," Tataryn is an author himself and the holder of journalism, history, and political science degrees from Carleton and Waterloo Universities. He first joined NIB as a consultant in 1974 (at the age of twenty-seven) during George Manuel's presidency and his subsequent contributions to the organization have been varied. He served as an advisor and writer of speeches and briefs for both Manuel and Starblanket, and is sometimes used as a "trouble-shooter" on sensitive matters. He has been a driving force behind the NIB's environmental program and was instrumental in forging alliances between NIB and labour and environmental organizations. As a relative outsider who is not embroiled in Indian internal politics, he is sometimes sought out to provide an opinion on different proposed courses of action, and as a journalist he plans or advises on much of NIB's media strategy. Politically astute, he adopts the low profile appropriate to a white in an Indian organization. His influence has nevertheless been felt in several important NIB decisions and activities outside his formal responsibilities as media and environmental consultant (e.g., the chiefs' 1979 trip to England).

PROBLEMS

To round out our description of the internal environment of the Brotherhood, it is useful to identify some of the problems with which NIB, as an organization, must grapple on an almost daily basis. These problems are numerous, but for our purposes can be reduced to the following general types pertaining to: (1) its charter; (2) its relationship to, and control over, its beneficiary base; (3) personal costs borne by its leadership; (4) staff relations; and (5) goal setting and resource procurement.

CHARTER

NIB's problems pertaining to its charter are largely constitutional ones. The NIB is a federation of its PTOs, and as such its president has very limited authority to take initiatives; usually he can only take action when mandated to do so by resolution of either the Executive Council or the General Assembly. This was a major complaint of George Manuel, who found that the constitution encumbers the president in his ability to provide leadership or to represent the organization in situations where time is of the essence and there is no opportunity to consult with the Executive Council. Both Manuel and Starblanket found themselves in such situations on different occasions and sometimes found themselves being sharply criticized for not having consulted Executive Council. Other times their hands were effectively tied, either by the lack of such a mandate or by a weak mandate from Executive Council. Manuel cites an example involving the 1978-79 crisis over reductions in Indian health care services. According to him, the only mandate which NIB president Starblanket had been given by Executive Council to take to his meeting with the Minister of National Health and Welfare (Monique Begin) was to demand of her that each PTO be given the opportunity to state to her its own position on the issue.

Another problem which stems from NIB's charter is a representational one. NIB's original constitution (Article IV.a.2) provided for *regional* representation on the Executive Council—that is, the entire Prairie region had only one seat, as did the entire Maritimes region. Ever since that arrangement broke down and was replaced by a system allotting one representative on Executive Council to each province or territory, there has been internal bickering to expand the Executive Council to allow for representation of various member organizations. Thus, at the time of our writing, all four Ontario organizations wished to be on the Executive Council simultaneously which, if implemented, could exacerbate the Brotherhood's already difficult task of developing a consensus on the Executive Council. Conversely, there are some bands or aggregations of bands who are not even indirectly represented on NIB, and do not wish to be. As one IIAP official said to the authors, "If those bands find out you're talking to NIB, then they don't even want to talk to you." This does not appear to be a serious problem yet, and NIB denies that it is a problem at all. However, if a significant number of bands do come to fall in this category it will constitute a significant undermining of NIB's claims to speak on behalf of all Indians. The failure to accommodate "splinter" groups such as those in Ontario could also lead to the formation of a second national association competing with NIB to represent status Indians.*

---

* Indeed, after this was written we became aware of an unsuccessful attempt which was made in Ontario to launch just such a competitive venture.

A further representational problem revolves around the fact that there is no representation in NIB from the Chiefs and Band Councils, as such. Thus, the NIB is left in the awkward position of trying to win gains for a grass roots beneficiary base, while the voting membership consists of an intermediate layer of autonomous politicians from the provincial-level and territorial-level organizations (PTOs). While the establishment of direct linkages at the band level appears to be in the best interests of NIB if NIB is to ensure its relevance and its future, the by-passing of the PTOs which that might entail could well be perceived as threatening by the PTO leaders, particularly by those without such direct linkages themselves. The solution to this dilemma will require imagination and diplomacy, while the failure to reach such a solution leaves NIB dangerously prone to drifting away from the real concerns of its intended beneficiary base, and therefore vulnerable to attack from within the Indian community. A case in point may be the NIB's thrust towards greater Indian sovereignty. One IIAP official reported to the authors that on the basis of the feedback which IIAP received from bands on its proposals for a charter system of tribal government, he felt there is little support for NIB's Indian sovereignty position outside of Saskatchewan and Alberta.[12] Indeed, he reported that even the IIAP proposals were seen as being too radical by some bands and were therefore looked upon with some trepidation by those bands. This moves us squarely into the second problem area—that of NIB's relationship to its members and to those who are intended to benefit from NIB's efforts (its beneficiary base).

RELATIONSHIP TO BENEFICIARY BASE

Professionalized social movement organizations (McCarthy and Zald, 1973) like NIB not only have difficulty keeping attuned to the grass roots in whose interests they are supposed to be acting, but also often find themselves working on a plane that is not well understood at the grass roots level. Thus, as an NIB official pointed out, just as you and I do not understand the intricacies of consumer protection legislation, despite our status as consumers and the daily impact of that legislation upon our lives, so too most Indians on reserves (and some of their chiefs and councillors) do not understand the Indian Act. Consequently, even the most rudimentary progress is often painfully slow. Moreover, the need for proceeding slowly is particularly acute due to the atmosphere of guarded trust or outright mistrust which sometimes prevails.

Another facet of this second problem is the extreme diversity of NIB's beneficiary base. Given this great variability of life conditions and of priorities among Canadian Indians, NIB experiences difficulty in moving beyond the level of consensus on general principles to achieve consensus on the details or specifics of particular programs or demands to government.[13] This is illustrated by the case of the housing agreement it reached in 1977 with IIAP, for certain bands objected to certain provisions and demanded that they be changed. Indian wariness of possible divide and conquer tactics by government militates against decentralization as a solution to this problem of diversity. Consequently, reliance must in large part be placed upon the creative ability of negotiators to develop specific yet flexible mechanisms and arrangements, often where precedents are lacking. Such creativity is not always forthcoming, and when it comes from the government side of the negotiating table it may be greeted on the Indian side with the skepticism and extreme caution which the history of Indian-nonIndian relations counsels.

Another consequence of the diversity of the NIB's beneficiary base is the existence of factions within the organization. Indeed, NIB leaders report that it is only in recent years that Executive Council meetings have been able to focus on issues and subordinate factional disputes and personality clashes. Such a lack of discipline or ability of the NIB to exert control over its PTOs, has also been observed in the case of the NIB withdrawal from the Joint NIB/Cabinet Committee. In that case the PTOs apparently initially agreed unanimously to the withdrawal. However, when the effects of the IIAP's retaliatory withholding of funds and other budget cuts began to be felt at the local level and PTO leaders came under heavy local criticism for the NIB withdrawal, those PTO leaders reportedly repudiated the NIB move and blamed the withdrawal on the national leadership, weakening the NIB politically in the process.

TOLL ON LEADERS

A third type of problem faced by NIB consists of the personal toll which national leadership can exact. The constant immersion in internal or external conflict relationships can itself be a very fatiguing experience. (See Coles, 1964, on social movement fatigue.) In addition to the strain on marital and family relationships which stems from the long hours and rigorous travel schedule, national Indian leaders who must work out of Ottawa as a base find that the urban experience cuts them off from their rural, reserve-based culture. Such cultural isolation can be not only personally discomforting, but also politically dangerous.

STAFF RELATIONS

A fourth type of problem faced by NIB involves staff relations. Much has been written (e.g., Levy, 1968) about the problems of staff race relations which arise within a subordinate group movement when dominant group members also participate in the movement, and it is not our intention to review that literature here. Rather, we merely wish to indicate that interracial strains have not been absent from the NIB staff. These strains came to a head in October 1978 at a staff retreat after a nonIndian NIB secretary was overlooked for promotion in favour of an Indian employee. If NIB follows a similar path to that of many United States black civil rights organizations, a diminished role is in store for nonIndian staff members and nonIndian full-time consultants/advisors.

GOAL SETTING AND RESOURCE PROCUREMENT

Two final problems to be discussed here involve NIB goal setting and resource procurement. With regard to the former, the Brotherhood throughout much of the 1970s was hampered by the fact that it usually found itself in a reactive, rather than a proactive, position. Numerous examples of this could be cited, but one will suffice. In 1971 the government sought to transfer authority for Indian housing from IIAP to the Central Mortgage and Housing Corporation (CMHC). NIB opposed that move[14] and instead of being able to channel staff energies towards, say, the development of a new approach to funding housing or a new housing policy to combat the deplorable housing conditions on reserves, those staff energies instead had to be directed towards the secondary issue of which government department was to administer the woefully inadequate funds available. In fact, ever since the 1969 White Paper, NIB has mounted a vigilant guard against government actions or proposals which might threaten Indian rights. Although NIB officials became aware of the strategic disadvantage which such reactive stances entailed for them in their struggle with government, they often have no choice but to respond. Indeed, even as late as 1978 the director of the Indian Policy Development Secretariat—a body deliberately designed to be proactive rather than reactive—complained to the authors about how the need to fight "brush fires" detracted from the ability of the IPDS staff to pursue its actual mandate. That being the time when the Trudeau government had come forth with proposals to change the Canadian constitution within a year, one could readily understand the director's problem.

The other problem, that of obtaining the resources necessary to run the large scale operation which the NIB has become, is perhaps the most serious of all. As one NIB staff member expressed it, "As an organization, way too much energy is spent on getting money, justifying it, and lobbying for more." Again, this diverts staff energies from the actual goals of the organization. But equally important, as we indicated earlier, NIB is virtually totally dependent upon government for its revenues, and consequently is vulnerable to the kind of socio-fiscal control to which government sometimes resorts. In addition, George Manuel, when asked by the authors about the future of Canadian Indians, expressed deep concern about the role of money, from a different perspective. Said Manuel,

> Money may be our downfall in the sense that we'll have too much of it. When Indian people were poor we were able to retain our Indian identity. But the more money we get, the more we seek, and the more we get entangled in economic and political institutions of the white man and lose track of our Indian cultural identity and values.

In the next chapter we shall examine NIB's involvement in those nonIndian political institutions of which Manuel spoke.

NOTES

1. The provincial or territorial member organizations (PTOs) of NIB are: The Union of British Columbia Indian Chiefs, The Indian Association of Alberta, The Federation of Saskatchewan Indians, The Manitoba Indian Brotherhood, The Chiefs of Ontario (representing Grand Council Treaty #9, Grand Council Treaty #3, Union of Ontario Indians, and The Association of Iroquois and Allied Indians), The Confederation of Indians of Quebec (formerly the Indians of Quebec Association), The Union of New Brunswick Indians, The Union of Nova Scotia Indians, The Lennox Island and Abegweit Bands of Prince Edward Island, The Yukon Native Brotherhood, and The Dene Nation (formerly the Indian Brotherhood of the Northwest Territories).

2. Manuel went on to say that the new breed of "academic" Indian politicians has changed Indian politics. He sees this new breed as being less ruthless and less likely than traditional Indian politicians to use silence as a political tactic. Of the traditional style he said, "Only an Indian can tell when an Indian is saying 'No' when he appears to be saying 'Yes'.

3. The Federation of Saskatchewan Indians (FSI) is regarded by some as the most "militant" Indian political organization, excluding AIM, in southern Canada. It has developed many position papers, some of which have been asserted nationally. This aggressive stance has generated resentment in some Indian quarters, particularly Ontario. Coming from Saskatchewan and supported by the FSI leadership, Noel Starblanket has borne the brunt of some of that resentment and has been criticized by Indian leaders, and by IIAP officials, as being too heavily influenced by FSI.

4. The implication is that at least part of the motivation of the anti-diversification forces was based upon a desire not to undermine Delisle's relationship with DIAND. However, the stance of Delisle's faction was also based upon the belief that the lobbying task of the fledgling NIB could be more efficiently conducted if it were focused upon one governmental department rather than scattered among several.

5. Funds controlled by IIAP and designated for cultural education are still a divisive force among Indians today.

6. Although we are treating the internal political realm and the internal operational realm as separate, it should be remembered that in practice they are closely linked in at least two ways. First, the president is accountable annually to the General Assembly for the work of the operational staff. Second, the directions to be pursued by the operational staff are largely determined by mandates issued to the president by the General Assembly or by the Executive Council.

7. This figure includes about three-quarters of a million dollars distributed directly to the PTOs through NIB.

8. In times of funding restraint and criticism of bureaucratic "empire building," it is quite possible that interdepartmental competition will be supplanted or at least tempered by a "pass the buck" approach in which departments try to pass off some new funding responsibilities to other departments.

9. In fiscal 1979 NIB entered a new funding arrangement whereby it received $680,000 from IIAP as "global funding for projects." This global funding included moneys for expenditures previously funded by IIAP under the label "core funding" (e.g., General Assembly), plus moneys for other program areas (e.g., education). In essence it appears to be core funding in all but its name and perhaps its accountability requirements.

10. Although it is not shown in this table, the strategy behind this absorption involved getting the source of the funds changed from the PMO to DIAND where they were more susceptible to NIB's influence. The strategy also involved getting the recipient of the funds changed from NCIRT to NIB itself, so as to undermine NCIRT's independence of existence.

11. A popular cliché of the 1970s held that the party who benefits the most from Native land claims is the lawyers. That lawyers fees can mount to significant proportions of land claims settlements is demonstrated by the dispute between the Inuit of Northern Quebec and their attorneys for part of the James Bay settlement proceedings. The bill from a team of six lawyers who were replaced part way through the proceedings amounted to $454,000 (Canadian Press, 1979b).

12. NIB officials are quick to point out that it is very much in IIAP's interests to disseminate views such as this.

13. This problem, which is sometimes expressed as a criticism that Indians cannot "get their act together," is one to which Indians are very sensitive. Some brand it as a racist criticism; they see it stemming from the racist colonial view that established the term "Indian" to lump together people who sociologically, politically, economically, and identificationally were quite separate. They see this criticism as being particularly hypocritical, in light of the federal-provincial and interprovincial dissensus which characterizes nonIndian political life in Canada.

14. The main reason for NIB's opposition to the transfer was that the basis upon which Indians would receive housing money from the federal government might in the process change from non-repayable subsidies to repayable mortgage loans.

Chapter 9

External Relations of NIB

PARLIAMENTARY RELATIONS

Historically, Indian contact with the national government in Ottawa was limited almost exclusively to the Department of Indian Affairs. More recently, Indians have sought to broaden their base of contact with the government, in part to circumvent the IIAP bureaucracy and in part to move closer to the centre of the decision making process. Rejecting, as had the government, the Hawthorn report recommendation that DIAND act as an advocate of Indian interests within the political process, Indian organizations set out to strengthen their own advocacy. In so doing they encountered a political and institutional environment that was multi-faceted and extremely complex.

As we indicated in Chapter Six, policy decisions affecting Indian interests are influenced by a number of powerful agencies quite apart from IIAP, such as the Prime Minister's Office (PMO), the Privy Council Office (PCO), the Treasury Board, other federal departments, the staff of the DIAND Minister, the cabinet and the Prime Minister. In addition to the above-mentioned actors, Indians attempting to negotiate the political environment in Ottawa must also deal with parliamentary institutions. Of particular concern here are the House of Commons and the Standing Committee on Indian Affairs and Northern Development (SCIAND). Although both the House and the Committee are ultimately controlled by the party in power—the same party that dominates the agencies cited above—they, nevertheless, serve as alternative points of Indian access to the political process and, less frequently, as actors in the policy process. To set the stage for a discussion of the character of contemporary relations between NIB and parliament, we shall first describe the nature of the committee system in the Canadian House of Commons.

The committee system in the Canadian House of Commons was substantially reworked in 1968 in the hope that the committees could examine legislative proposals in more detail than would be possible on the floor of the House and could do so in a less partisan environment

(Special Committee on Procedure, 1968). It was also hoped that the revitalized committees would provide a greater sense of legislative and policy participation for government backbenchers and opposition MPs. At the heart of the reform, then, lay the expectation that the quality of both legislation and the legislative experience of MPs would be improved.

The House committees in Canada should not be confused with American Congressional committees, which are both more independent of the executive and more powerful actors within the legislative process. In Canada the political executive—the cabinet—ultimately controls committee decisions by means of its party's majority on the committee. In Canada a committee can only act on matters referred to it by the House through an order of reference, which in effect means that the government also controls the committee agenda. While committees may challenge the details of legislative proposals or spending plans, they are not at liberty to challenge the basic parameters of government policy. Significantly, committees are free to adopt a stance contrary to that of the government only when such a stance poses no significant threat to the government's legislative program. When that program is at stake, party lines and party discipline will prevail in the committees as they prevail in the House.

THE STANDING COMMITTEE ON INDIAN AFFAIRS (SCIAND)

Indian interests are affected by many departments other than DIAND, and as a result, Indian spokesman have appeared before a number of Senate and House committees. In 1978, for example, the NIB made presentations to six Senate or House Committees other than SCIAND. The principal point of NIB contact with the committee system, however, comes through SCIAND.

SCIAND, as noted above, acts on matters referred to it by the House. At times, the scope of the referred business can be very broad; the Annual Reports of DIAND, for example, would provide the committee with the opportunity to probe into virtually any aspect of Indian administration and policy. However, neither Warren Allmand nor Hugh Faulkner, when serving as the Minister of DIAND, referred the Annual Reports to the committee and the bulk of committee activity was thus taken up with more circumscribed discussions. The committee's principal task was to scrutinize departmental spending estimates when these were made available to the committee in the early spring. During the discussion of spending estimates the committee meets for approximately three two-hour sessions a week, with at least fifteen meetings usually being held. It should be noted, though, that the committee does not have the power to hold up the passage of estimates; the government's "guillotine" terminates the committee hearings at the end of May regardless of whether or not committee members feel that the hearings were complete.

Although the committee is empowered to summon witnesses and documents, so far no individual has been forced to appear before SCIAND. Generally, the committee hears from group spokesmen who have requested a hearing. During the examination of spending estimates, IIAP is represented by a delegation selected by the department rather than by the committee, although committee requests to specific officials are difficult to refuse. Faced with a barrage of departmental reports and experts, the committee is in constant peril of being "snowed-under" by the department which it is supposedly scrutinizing. The committee has no research capacity of its own through which to evaluate information originating from IIAP, although some limited research support is available from the House of Commons Library. If substantive criticism of IIAP is to emerge in committee hearings, it is more likely to come from committee witnesses, such as those representing NIB, than from the parliamentary committee members themselves.

At the time of our field research in 1978-79 SCIAND was chaired by Ian Watson (Liberal, Laprairie). Watson, whose interest in Indian affairs can be traced to the location of the large Caughnawaga reserve within his constituency near Montreal, was appointed to SCIAND when he was first elected to the House in 1963. In 1966 he became chairman, a post that he held until the defeat of the Liberal government in 1979. When interviewed, Watson estimated that when the committee is active he devotes about ten hours a week to its business. When SCIAND is inactive or the House is adjourned, committee-related business amounted to little more than a few letters a week. Watson estimated that he sees the Minister of Indian Affairs about six to ten times a year (apart from committee hearings), but that these meetings deal primarily with constituency concerns rather than with committee matters. He found little at fault with a *Globe and Mail* article (Simpson, 1978) that described the chairman's role as follows:

> A chairman's job is to keep the committee running smoothly, to prevent members from breaking the rules and to stop the opposition from hatching procedural plots embarrassing for the Government. The chairman does not probe or develop expertise he can use to defend the taxpayers' money, or change departmental thinking. His job is to keep order—the Government's order.

As mentioned above, SCIAND lacks any research capacity that is independent of DIAND. Nor is this void filled by the political parties; for example, the Conservative committee members (then in opposition) shared the time of a single party researcher with two other committees.

As a consequence NIB has assumed an important role as an alternate source of information and policy perspectives. In effect, NIB functions as an informal research arm for the committee, and particularly for the opposition members of the committee. At times this can result in a paper war between DIAND and NIB, with the committee members being buried in the middle. Witness the comment of Frank Oberle (P.C., Prince George) a new committee member, on a committee presentation by NIB president Noel Starblanket:

> Quite frankly, this Committee has no power to do anything the way we are sitting here right now, and if you are talking about paper shifters and shovellers, it concerns me that you people are getting to be real masters of it. You shovelled more paper there this morning than I did all week. And quite frankly, between you and me, I will not read all that stuff. I do not have the time, nor would it mean much to me. (SCIAND, 1978:30)

NIB witnesses are frequently heard before the committee. In 1978, for example, the committee hearings on DIAND estimates heard from Starblanket and from seven band and regional representatives in a single morning's session. The committee hearings are published as part of Hansard and thereby provide a permanent, public record of Indian presentations. Unfortunately, though, committee hearings receive very little coverage from the press (Franks, 1971:471). Thus while SCIAND may present Indian leaders with a parliamentary forum, it is a forum possessing very little public visibility. It cannot be used effectively to communicate with NIB's Indian constituency or with the broader Canadian public. This in itself would be of less significance if SCIAND played a major role in the policy process. As we shall see shortly, this is not the case.

SCIAND has engendered a fair degree of informal contact between parliamentarians and NIB. NIB's director of parliamentary liaison holds separate luncheon meetings with the party delegations to the committee. Conservative members of the committee appeared to serve as a useful conduit between NIB and the Progressive Conservative party; the NIB position on policy issues was frequently sought out by the party and a Conservative policy paper on Indian affairs, *Indian People*, was circulated within NIB for comments and re-write suggestions. The general working relationship between NIB and the committee members seems to be relaxed, open and positive; it is, in short, quite different from that between NIB and DIAND.

Because the great bulk of NIB's activity in Ottawa is directed towards governmental agencies (IIAP, PMO, PCO, etc.), SCIAND is important as the principal link between NIB and the opposition parties. The opposition critic on SCIAND at the time of our research was J. R. Holmes, Conservative MP from Lambton-Kent (near London, Ontario). Holmes was first elected to the House in 1972 and was appointed to SCIAND late in 1974. He estimated for us that the committee's business takes up more than half of his time in Ottawa. He would receive three to five Indian delegations a week while the House was sitting and spent a considerable amount of time on the telephone and travelling in an attempt to establish contacts within the Indian community. The Conservative members of SCIAND, led by Holmes, have been the most active members of the committee. Except for votes, it was not uncommon for chairman Watson to be the only Liberal member present at committee hearings.

Compared to the Conservatives, who had three committee members with specialized areas of interest, the NDP had only a single position on the committee, a position that rotated among three party members. As a consequence the NDP developed neither continuity nor specialization in its committee participation.

Interestingly, both Watson and Holmes stressed in their interview with us that partisan divisions within the committee have seldom emerged and have not been problematic. However, in part this has been due to the fact that committee members tended to focus more on constituency concerns than on general policy matters where partisan divisions would be more likely to occur. Both Holmes and Watson felt that there were few partisan points to be scored in the Indian field; in the jockeying for position within the national electorate, party policies and records on Indian affairs carry little weight.

To bring this decision of SCIAND to a close it is useful to examine the committee's role in the policy process. The committee does have some accomplishments to its credit, the most notable being its 1971 review of Indian education, a review that helped reverse the trend of turning Indian education over to provincial governments. The committee had also had some significant impact on the Indian Economic Development Fund, the controversy over mercury poisoning, the James Bay settlement, and the policies governing the Anik B Satellite system. At times, moreover, the committee has adopted a public position divergent from that of the government, such as when it endorsed NIB's demand for the recognition of aboriginal claims. Yet, overall, the committee cannot be described as a powerful actor in the policy process. Its members have not developed a sufficiently high level of competence and expertise for the committee to stand apart as an authority and as a policy actor independent of IIAP. The committee is hampered by high rates of turnover (March, 1974:115) and by high rates of absenteeism. For instance, during Simpson's examination of SCIAND's 1978 hearings on departmental estimates, only eight of the twenty members attended at least half of the eleven meetings.

SCIAND is handicapped by the lack of any significant research or investigative capacity. It is also limited by the paucity of Indian-related legislation that has passed through the federal government over the past decade. Without legislation to consider, the committee is stripped of much of its opportunity for policy impact. If legislative revisions of the *Indian Act* are advanced by the government, then the role of the committee could be considerably enhanced, particularly if the committee travelled across Canada to hold public meetings in Indian communities.

Despite these handicaps, SCIAND does hold considerable potential for NIB. The parliamentary liaison director for NIB described the committee as the "best thing we have going," a remark that may reflect both on the potential of SCIAND and on the somewhat precarious political position of NIB within the nation's capital. In testimony before the committee (SCIAND, 1978:10), NIB president Starblanket commented that ". . . we have more confidence in this committee operating in public than we have in the government which prefers secrecy and fears the public." Given increased press coverage, the committee could serve as an important public forum where, if policy decisions are not made, Indian viewpoints could nevertheless be advanced. Yet in conclusion it must be stressed that the importance of the committee remains one of potential rather than of actuality. As chairman Watson remarked, "Indians like to go as close to the top as possible. If they think we're at the top, they're wrong."

LOBBYING PARLIAMENT

In 1976 as part of an effort to extend its lines of political communication beyond DIAND and the Cabinet to parliamentary committees, opposition MPs, and parliamentarians generally, NIB hired a full-time director of parliamentary liaison. In doing so, NIB launched a major lobbying undertaking that has interesting implications for the evolution of NIB as a political interest group.

The impetus for a more vigorous and systematic form of liaison between NIB and parliament came from Noel Starblanket and Michael Posluns. A writer by trade, Posluns had worked in the past with the Company of Young Canadians and the Canadian Civil Liberties Association, and had been involved in radio and press coverage of Indian affairs. By avocation he had been for twenty years an avid follower of activities on Parliament Hill. In 1976, while working under contract with NIB, he proposed that a parliamentary liaison unit be established as a support group within NIB; when the proposal was accepted he became the new unit's director.

At the time of our field research the parliamentary liaison unit employed three persons apart from Posluns and commanded a yearly budget of approximately $100,000.[1] The unit is designed to generate a two-way flow of information between NIB and parliament. On the one hand it functions as a conventional political lobby, channelling NIB information and positions to individual parliamentarians and parliamentary committees. (Contact with cabinet ministers and government leaders is handled by the NIB president and his special assistants, not by Posluns.) On the other hand, the unit gathers political intelligence from "the Hill" and disseminates it within NIB and its PTOs. Intelligence in this sense would include information on legislative scheduling, information on the activities of various departments relating to Indian interests, and the attitudinal dispositions of MPs on both the government and opposition sides of the House and the Senate.

These general functions entail a host of more specific activities. Parliamentary debates and committee hearings are monitored, and the highlights are circulated to appropriate policy units and political leaders within NIB. The progress of legislative bills and departmental spending estimates is watched in order to enable NIB input to be made at the most opportune time. A major internal effort is being made to educate the staff and leadership of NIB about the vocabulary, norms and processes of parliamentary government. Points of political access are sought and contacts with individual parliamentarians in both the House and the Senate are nurtured. As part of this last activity, the parliamentary liaison unit has been compiling detailed profiles of key Senators and MPs including members of the Treasury Board, other cabinet ministers involved with Indian interests, members of SCIAND, and members of other parliamentary committees that might deal with legislation affecting Indian interests. Among other information, the profiles include the individual's basic biographical background, positions taken on issues of concern to NIB, and the individual's relationship, if any, to the Indian electoral constituency. The profile also includes ratings of the individual by Indians who have had some personal contact with the parliamentarian. The parliamentary liaison unit also arranges appointments for chiefs and councillors visiting Ottawa.

The scope of the unit's parliamentary activity is extensive. In 1978 lobbying was carried out relating to bills dealing with Northern gas pipelines, gun control, the Yukon Health Transfer Agreement, British Columbia agriculture, DIAND and health care spending cuts, humane trapping, and constitutional reform. The most massive lobbying effort was undertaken with respect to the Bill C-25 legislation dealing with the proposed Yukon natural gas pipeline. Posluns calculated that, in total, 311 person-hours were put into the endeavour, one in which the NIB was generally unsuccessful in the legislative changes that it sought.

It should also be mentioned that on some occasions the parliamentary liaison unit may be involved not in lobbying the government but in selling agreements between NIB and the government to the broader

254 PART III — THE NATIONAL INDIAN BROTHERHOOD (NIB)

parliamentary community. As an internal document drafted by Posluns points out, "even when there is complete agreement between the NIB and cabinet, cabinet may, in turn, look to us to sell the matters with which we are concerned to the rest of parliament." Beyond political agreement, then, NIB may have to create the impetus for legislative action.

The creation of a lobbying capacity offers certain advantages to NIB. In particular, it provides a base of political input that extends beyond the government and the government party. It also provides a mechanism through which parliamentarians can be sensitized to the concerns of status Indians, a mechanism through which they can hopefully be brought to understand and even support the position of NIB.

One of the problems that NIB lobbying encounters is the poor background parliamentarians possess on Indian affairs. It appears that the basic ignorance of the Canadian public concerning Indian history and Indian affairs (see Chapter Three) is shared by parliamentarians, making a meaningful dialogue between NIB lobbyists and their parliamentary targets difficult. As Posluns explained in an internal NIB memo,

> we should understand that even the most sympathetic parliamentarians have very little background in Indian history, and even less in Indian attitudes and concerns; we are largely involved in running a kindergarten for graduate students, providing the most elementary perspectives for people who feel themselves to be quite learned.

Given this situation, lobbying payoffs, in terms of a better informed and more empathetic parliamentary community, may be long-term indeed. There is a lot of ground to be made up, and the high rate of turnover among Canadian MPs means that the process of basic education must be continuous.

In assessing the NIB lobbying effort, it must be recognized that NIB incurs some very real costs which must be weighed against offsetting gains that may be both long-term and ephemeral. The financial cost of the parliamentary liaison unit is already substantial, but given the monumental task of effectively monitoring events on Parliament Hill, it may not be sufficient. The NIB must keep track not only of the affairs of SCIAND, but of a number of other committees, departments and legislative acts that may impinge upon Indian interests. For example, NIB has had to be increasingly vigilant against the rather loose use of the term "native" in government legislation. As Noel Starblanket (1978:2-3) argued in an NIB brief to the Special Senate Committee on the Northern Gas Pipeline, Bill C-25:

> Our objection to the increasing use of the term "Native" in place of the historic and well understood term "Indian," is that we believe this term to be

an example of government double talk designed to avoid fundamental constitutional responsibility . . . when the government introduces a concern for "native rights" as in this Bill, we are left with the firm conviction that the real thrust of their concern is to avoid the protection of the rights they should be protecting under the BNA Act.

Similar problems arose for NIB in the Trudeau government's constitutional revision bill (C-60) and in its 1978 gun control legislation. In the latter case, former justice minister Ron Basford argued that he did not want to treat nonstatus Indians any differently from Indians. The response of NIB was that nonstatus Indians legally are not Indians, and that Basford was therefore undermining Indian rights by treating the two groups alike.

In any competition for scarce resources within NIB, the parliamentary liaison unit may find itself in a weak position because the payoffs it generates are both long-term and difficult to document. Yet there is a pressing need for the unit to expand its present scope of activities, to move beyond a fire-fighting or crisis-response role. As Posluns argued in his 1977 year-end report to the NIB executive:

> . . . our goal must be to communicate the Brotherhood's position thoroughly, systematically, and before hard and definite positions are formulated within government and within the several political parties. Only when we reach that stage of development where we avert crises rather than fighting brush fires will we start to be truly effective. The hunter who knows where his deer will be at sunrise also knows he needs to be on the move well before dawn if he is going to feed his family.

The organizational endurance needed for a sustained and multipronged lobbying effort is considerable and it remains to be seen, given the other demands on the staff and resources of NIB, whether the endurance will be forthcoming. The parliamentary liaison unit has been very much the creation of one individual, Michael Posluns. If Poslun's involvement in the unit is to be gradually phased out, as was his plan when we interviewed him in the fall of 1978, then the future of the unit is difficult to forecast.

CONCLUSIONS

In a major analysis of Canadian interest groups, Paul Pross (1975) drew a contrast between "institutionalized" and "issue-oriented" interest groups. The former are those which possess organizational continuity and cohesion, a stable membership, concrete and immediate operational objectives, and an extensive knowledge of the governmental process. The latter are more intently focused on the pursuit of a particular political issue, and both the organizational health of the group and the long-standing ties between the group and the governmental process are of secondary importance. The NIB, it appears, may be in a transitional stage between issue-orientation and institutionalization, and the steps in this transition are apparent in the parliamentary liaison activities of status Indians.

The NIB is clearly seeking to establish a more thorough and informed grasp of the governmental process. It is endeavouring, moreover, to establish contacts with both the government and the parliamentary sector which will be long-lasting. In short, the NIB is digging in as a permanent part of the Ottawa political scene; it is an organization consulted by the government and by opposition parties, and one with extensive and long-standing ties to bureaucrats and parliamentarians.

This evolution towards institutionalization suggests an increasing degree of political sophistication, and undoubtedly of political power. There are, however, some problems inherent in this transformation. As Pross (1975:10) points out, institutionalized interest groups tend to place more importance on their own survival and status within the political process than on any particular issue objective. This means that actions are avoided that might damage the organization's status and credibility even if such actions might offer short-term benefits. It also means that institutionalized interest groups are prepared to lose gracefully on one issue so that the group's long-standing contacts and goodwill within the political process are not damaged. Group leaders become attuned to the norms and folkways of the Ottawa environment, recognizing that in the long run overly expressive, uncompromising or assertive behaviour may work to the detriment of the group's interests. While public posturing is acceptable when kept within the limits of convention, less-public negotiating and bargaining is ultimately more productive. Thus, less-public channels of contact and influence must be protected at all costs. Such channels are strengthened if interest group representatives have a class, educational and social background similar to that of the politicians and bureaucrats with whom they interact. Here it should be noted that NIB shares a liability with organized labour, in that its leaders do not move in the same social circles as does the Ottawa establishment. Hence, both lack important opportunities for informal lobbying and both suffer from reduced legitimacy within the political process (Presthus, 1974:81).

For NIB, the above model poses some serious problems. The internal organizational environment of NIB is much more politicized than is that of most interest groups, and the leaders of NIB must first and foremost be able to cope with that environment. Unfortunately, the skills required to do so may be antithetical to those which interest group leaders must have to be successful within the bureaucratic environment of Ottawa. At times, internal political considerations may force NIB to adopt a publicly aggressive and indeed antagonistic stance towards the government that may impair more productive non-public interest group relations (e.g., the pullout from JNCC). Admittedly, to a degree, the government will accept the necessity of an aggressive public stance by NIB, for the government has a stake in the continued ability of NIB to aggregate and articulate Indian perspectives. Nevertheless, NIB leaders may find an increased tension between the public posture they adopt for their clientele and their more practical interface with the Canadian political system. While this is not to predict that NIB leaders will be forced by necessity into a hypocritical position, it is to suggest that a degree of hypocrisy may be a necesssary ingredient of interest group success.

A second aspect of the dilemma is even more problematic. If there is an essence to interest group politicking, it is that of bargaining, compromise and negotiation. One is prepared to lose today for what can be won in exchange tomorrow; one is prepared to dismiss the possibility of total victory for the satisfaction of modest but real gains. However, the leaders of NIB are constrained here because they are representing fundamental group rights rather than more general group interests that can be partially protected through partial sacrifice. If the notion of compromise on Indian rights is repugnant to Indian leaders, then the road ahead may be rocky. Interest groups lacking the flexibility and the pragmatism to wheel and deal, to bargain, to lose today so that they can win tomorrow, are severely handicapped within the political process.

THE JOINT NIB/CABINET COMMITTEE (JNCC)

The story of the Joint NIB/Cabinet Committee (JNCC) is a tangled and fascinating one. We shall probe into it in considerable detail here for two reasons. First, it is a historical milestone, in the sense that it marked the winning of unprecedented special status for Canadian Indians. That is, in having a special ad hoc sub-committee of Cabinet formed to deal specifically and exclusively with Indian matters, NIB had attained a form of direct access to Cabinet which had been enjoyed by no other ethnic lobby or ethnic special interest group. NIB had seemingly reached the inner circle of power, the political "promised land," where it could carry on the less-public, and potentially highly efficacious, lobbying to which we referred in the preceding section. To see what really happens in the promised land is, we feel, valuable to our understanding of Indian-government relations. In particular, and this is the second reason for our in-depth treatment of the subject, the JNCC captures in a nutshell certain features, such as the communications gap, which characterize so much of contemporary government-Indian relations.

ORIGIN AND PURPOSES

The formation of JNCC in 1974 was a direct result of the violent confrontation on Parliament Hill between the RCMP and the Native
People's Caravan.[2] In a sense NIB was caught in the middle of the
dispute between the Caravan and the government, for, to paraphrase the
remarks of NIB vice-president Clive Linklater,

> . . . the Caravan leaders were demanding support from Indian organizations
> and the civil servants were saying "Haven't you got control over Indians?"
> NIB was looking bad. We're supposed to be the Indian spokesman, but we
> were not taking a side. Several times I went down to the old mill that they
> were holding, but they were just fiddling around and cancelling meetings.
> For me the question was "What is NIB going to get out of this?" Finally I
> said that we agree with their issues, housing, unemployment, etc.

With NIB president George Manuel out of town, Linklater handled
NIB's response. He attempted to reach Judd Buchanan, who had been
DIAND Minister for about six weeks, but Buchanan reportedly would
not co-operate. Linklater also tried to meet with the Prime Minister, but
in Linklater's words, "I could not penetrate his Haldeman-Erlichman
curtain." Then, said Linklater,

> It suddenly dawned on me that John Turner was my MP in Carleton
> East. . . . He finally agreed to talk to me for 15 minutes, but only because I
> was a constituent of his. But we talked for two or three hours.

Through the influence of John Turner and former DIAND Minister Jean
Chrétien, it was arranged that Buchanan would talk to Linklater.
However, that telephone conversation proved unproductive, as
Buchanan was reportedly hostile and not receptive to NIB's desire for a
meeting with Cabinet. Linklater then went out on a limb and called a
press conference. There, despite having no commitment from either the
government or from NIB's Executive Council, he announced that there
would be a meeting between Cabinet and the Executive Council. The
government acquiesced in this bluff and the first meeting of what was to
become a new and on-going sub-committee of Cabinet was held October
9, 1974 with the Prime Minister briefly in attendance.

Thus was born the Joint NIB/Cabinet Committee, as a conflict
regulating mechanism or safety valve to relieve pressure in the midst of a
crisis situation. The fact that it later faltered was due to many factors,
but should come as no surprise considering that after a short while the
pressure had been released and the parties no longer had the same incen-
tives to achieve visible results.

A fundamental feature of JNCC was that it began without a clear mutual understanding as to its purpose. According to its terms of reference, the committee was established

> to provide Ministers and Indian leaders with an opportunity to discuss problems and issues of concern to both; the scope of the Joint Commitee to be broad and focussed essentially on questions of principle and policy (Rich, 1978).

Such a vague statement provided little guidance as to what the mechanism was really expected to accomplish and equally little on whether it was to entail actual negotiations or merely consultations.

The NIB participants apparently envisaged the JNCC as a forum in which they could extract commitments from the government which the ministers could then impose on the civil service and the latter would be obliged to deliver. Such an orientation reflects both Indians' basic lack of trust of the bureaucracy (particularly IIAP) and Indians' lack of appreciation of the fact that individual ministers vary considerably in the amount of control which they are able to exercise over their department. As NIB was to discover with its agreement with Minister Chrétien on Indian control of Indian education, an agreement with a minister is worth little unless the details of implementation are also included within it.

The Cabinet's view of the JNCC appears to have been quite different. The Prime Minister indicated that the JNCC would neither have the same status as other Cabinet sub-committees nor be empowered to make commitments which would be binding upon Cabinet as a whole. Rather, JNCC was to be a mechanism for policy consultation at the highest level before matters reached the full Cabinet.

STRUCTURE AND OPERATIONS

The structure which was eventually developed for JNCC consisted of three levels. The upper level was the Joint Committee, which consisted of the NIB Executive Council and Cabinet Ministers drawn from the Social Planning Committee of Cabinet.[3] This Joint Committee was first chaired by Mitchell Sharp and then by Marc Lalonde, who was Chairman of the Cabinet Social Planning Committee. Later Deputy Prime Minister Allen MacEachen took over as Chairman of the Joint Committee. The so-called "core Ministers" of the Joint Committee were the Ministers of DIAND, Secretary of State, National Health and Welfare, and Justice. Provisions also existed for non-core ministers to attend if an item of particular relevance to their portfolio were to appear on the agenda (e.g., the Minister of National Revenue for taxation).

The second level was the Joint Sub-Committee (JSC) level, where a committee of three Cabinet members (Lalonde, Justice Minister Ron Basford, and Buchanan) and three members of the NIB Executive Council (the president, Harold Cardinal, and Fred Kelly) would meet to prepare agendas and to discuss issues within more narrowly defined areas between meetings of the Joint Committee. The third level was the Joint Working-Group level where still more narrowly defined and more specific issues were discussed by government bureaucrats (mainly from IIAP) and NIB "technicians" (non-elected leaders). The Joint Working Groups (JWGs) numbered four in total. These were the JWG on Indian Rights and Claims, the JWG on Indian Act Review, JWG on Housing, and the JWG on Education.

The DIAND Assistant Deputy Minister of Corporate Policy (Geoff Murray) and the Department of Justice Assistant Deputy Minister (Barry Strayer) were the central non-politicians on the government side. It was Murray who briefed the Cabinet Ministers and led the government delegation at the JWG level. Also involved was Anne Midgely (Executive Assistant to the Deputy Minister of DIAND) and then in the later stages Huguette Labelle (then Director-General of the Policy, Research, and Evauation Group of IIAP) and Peter Gillespie (then Director of Policy for IIAP).

On the Indian side there were numerous participants in the JWGs. One of the more actively involved persons was Vicki Santanna, a lawyer and American Indian who was part of a staff exchange between NIB and its American counterpart, the National Congress of American Indians. Although bright and reportedly quite efficacious, she eventually became the focus of some dissent within NIB, as she came to play a larger and larger role that was not always in tune with the thinking of the rest of the NIB delegation.

Before discussing the actual operations of JNCC, two other aspects of its structure should be mentioned. First, it had never been attached to a permanent, full-time secretariat, which could have provided continuity over time and which might have been able to relieve NIB of some of the paperwork burdening the comparatively small staff. Second, there was another structural component to the JNCC called the Canadian Indian Rights Commission (CIRC), whose major objective was to be the categorizing and inventorying of Indian claims. It was chaired by Brian Pratt who had been Lloyd Barber's assistant as Indian Claims Commissioner. However, the CIRC never really got off the ground, except for Pratt's effective work chairing the Joint Working Groups with the assistance of Roberta Jamieson, a lawyer and former executive assistant to NIB president Noel Starblanket. A major factor in the overall failure of the CIRC was that there was a prolonged and major disagreement between Indians and government (Harold Cardinal versus Ron Basford) on the matter of whether or not the CIRC commissioners would have the power to subpoena witnesses and documents under the Inquiries Act.[4]

Altogether there were only five meetings of the Joint Committee in its three and one-half year life, although there were many more meetings at the JGW level, and to a lesser extent, the JSC level. Meetings of the Joint Committee took place in the Cabinet Room in Parliament. It is symptomatic of the gulf that exists between Indians and government that one Indian official complained to the authors that the environment and layout of that meeting room were themselves not conducive to productive discussion.

The specific content of the meetings is difficult to ascertain, for neither side saw fit to comply with the authors' request for agendas, and the proceedings themselves were protected by Cabinet rules of secrecy. However, inspection of NIB executive council minutes revealed the proposed or actual agendas for two JNCC meetings and these can be treated as suggestive of the others. These are reproduced below:

Proposed Agenda for Joint Committee April 14, 1975	*Actual Agenda for Joint Committee July 11, 1977*
1. Indian Act 2. Aboriginal Land Claims 3. Strategy of Education and Economic Development	1. Introductory Remarks (Those by NIB dealt with IPDS, Mackenzie Valley Pipeline, and British North America Act) 2. Canadian Indian Rights Commission 3. Education Revisions to Indian Act 4. Economic Development Revisions to Indian Act 5. Taxation

Reports of the substance of the Joint Committee meetings, as provided by the two sides, are different to reconcile. On the one hand, officials on the government side complained to the authors that the Indian side tended to speak in eloquently rhetorical terms about general rights rather than specifics. On the other hand, one NIB official described the meetings as ''complaining sessions.'' Another NIB participant alleged to the authors that the senior-most policy strategists in DIAND and in the DIAND Minister's Office were deliberately attempting to subvert the Joint Committee by getting Indians to focus on specific details. His reasoning is interesting and plausible. According to this reasoning, cabinet ministers cannot afford, and are unaccustomed, to getting immersed in details. Indeed, they wish to discuss general directional thrusts and to have problems identified in crisp terms. However, Indians' relationship with IIAP had always focused on details, so the Indian side had difficulty adapting to the Cabinet's plane of discussion. This tendency, the argument continues, was reinforced both by DIAND and by the grass roots political pressure upon Indian leaders to have rectified certain local problems such as housing. The allegation was that DIAND hoped to sow frustration on each side over the inability to communicate with the other side, so that the Joint Committee would disband or be rendered impotent. The result of that would be that DIAND and its Minister would once again have a monopoly in Cabinet on status Indian matters, rather than having the JNCC as a counterweight to their influence. This, of course, is the crux of the matter, for a fundamental assumption of this line of argument is that the DIAND bureaucracy is very jealous of its direct relationship to Cabinet through the DIAND Minister. Another assumption is that when outside organizations (e.g., NIB) get direct access to Cabinet without having to use the offices of the minister, it reflects unfavourably upon that department's relative position in the Ottawa bureaucracy.

In attempting to reconcile the divergent views of the government and the Indian sides, we find it useful to distinguish between three levels of discussion in the Joint Committee meetings. The first, and most general level, is that of Indian rights (e.g., treaty and aboriginal rights). The second, or intermediate level, involves problem definition and the defining of broad policy directions. The third, and most concrete level, involves specific administrative details. If the views identified above as held by government and Indians, respectively, are both to be accepted, it would appear that much of the Joint Committee discussion was conducted at levels one and three, with very little being conducted at what was probably the preferred level of each side, level two. Once again, there appears to have been a failure to bridge the chasm.

The validity of the Indian argument of subversion[5] of the Joint Committee by DIAND officials is difficult to assess. It may well be that future, more detailed research (Weaver, forthcoming) will at least partly substantiate the subversion thesis, but will also call into question how conscious or clearly articulated the intent was in the minds of these officials. However, the important point is, as the famous American sociologist W. I. Thomas once said, that situations are real if they have real consequences. It is clear that in these terms the situation, as defined above by the Indians, was real, for certain actions of the Indian side were predicated upon that definition of the situation. Thus, perceiving the successive DIAND Ministers as "stonewalling it" or attempting to act as a "gate-keeper" for Indians vis-à-vis the other Cabinet Ministers, the Indian side (especially Harold Cardinal) responded by attempting to isolate the DIAND Minister from his Cabinet colleagues during the meetings.

Frustrations did mount on each side, with both Indian leaders and senior DIAND officials coming to feel that little was being accomplished and that the Cabinet might accordingly withdraw. One indication of the lack of progress was the nineteen month (December 1975 to July 1977) hiatus when the Joint Committee did not meet at all, although the Joint Sub-Committee and Joint Working Groups did meet during that period. Several factors contributed to this interlude. The aforementioned disagreement over subpoena powers for CIRC was one important factor, as was the poisoning of the atmosphere created by the release of the Government-Indian Relations paper and the leak of the Cabinet document on Native Policy. In addition, outgoing NIB president George Manuel was clearly losing interest in JNCC, although during this period he did consult with Canadian Labour Congress president Joe Morris about the NIB's whole approach to JNCC. Finally, with September 1976 witnessing both a new Minister (Allmand) at DIAND and a new leadership (Starblanket et al.) at NIB, the interlude continued as each side became acquainted with the other.

PERCEPTIONS OF THE JOINT COMMITTEE

Some of the participants' perceptions of the Joint Committee have already been mentioned above and will not be treated again here. Others not yet treated are also quite revealing.

On the government side, the change in the NIB leadership was definitely seen as problematic. For instance, a senior DIAND official expressed the opinion that the new NIB leadership had little interest in JNCC, did not understand the purpose of JNCC, and did not provide for sufficient continuity of personnel on the Indian side. The comment about lack of interest is itself interesting, in that it squarely conflicts with comments from one NIB official who portrayed Starblanket as committed to JNCC and as having worked hard to resurrect it after the nineteen month hiatus. The comment about the new NIB leadership allegedly not understanding the purpose of the JNCC brings to mind our earlier statement about the lack of a shared understanding as to the purpose of the whole endeavour. In this regard the following quotation from Geoff Murray, the DIAND ADM of Corporate Policy, is useful. Although it focuses upon operational procedures, unmet expectations concerning those procedures are indicative of divergent purposes. Said Murray:

[We expected the] Indians to develop policy papers the same way that we, in this department, work up policy papers, both internally and with other departments. In other words, we get the views of various people and get them assembled in some order and develop some recommendations and we may develop some alternatives. Then we get the issues sorted out and we present the stuff to the Ministers and they make up their minds whether they like it or don't like it or suggest some variation. I mean, that's the way it's done and that's what I had in mind and certainly the Deputy [Minister] had in mind and other people had in mind. But we never really got to that kind of thing in the Joint Working Groups.

Once again we observe that the game was being played by the two sides under different sets of rules.

Another perception held by some government officials was that Indians approached JNCC with enormous wariness bordering on paranoia. Elaborating on this, one senior DIAND official expressed to us the view that if a minister showed an inclination to move on an issue, that inclination would be met by a tendency on the Indian side to draw back and say "wait a minute; what's up?" Here we see a concrete manifestation of the colonial legacy of distrust which is a major component of the atmosphere that fills the chasm between Indians and government.

Another important view which formed on the government side was that the Indian side was adopting absolutist positions. Cabinet Ministers being politicians, and politics being "the art of compromise," the government side had considerable difficulty dealing with this. Such was especially the case on various Indian rights. This unwillingness to deal in terms of special status for Indians was probably largely responsible for Indian participants characterizing the Cabinet side as "unwilling to negotiate," which, or course, was precisely the government's accusation against the Indians.

The matter of Indian rights was definitely a focal point of the problems of the JNCC. Said one Indian participant:

> There can be no doubt that P.R.E. [the Policy, Research, and Evaluation Group of IIAP] must take major responsibility for the breakdown of the Joint NIB/Cabinet Committee. Their function was to stall, to make unclear, and to delay commitment on fundamental Indian rights like education and taxation. Everything we talked about as a right they talked about as a privilege.

The issue of rights poignantly arose at the final meeting of the Joint Committee on December 12, 1977. From the Indian side we were told that NIB entered the meeting "prepared to make deals and trade-offs and to state policy." The government side, according to the Indians, "wanted to philosophize and justify its actions, but not to compromise."

According to sources on both sides, Minister Marc Lalonde, in speaking for the Cabinet side, said "You have not convinced us that these specific areas [e.g., education] are properly areas of special rights for Indians over and above the larger population." Added another Minister, "If you can find additional arguments, come back to us." Ministers also pressed for specifics as to how the Indian side defined education rights, in terms of practical application. It was decided that the matter would be referred back to the JWG for further work on specifics, and the JWG did meet in January, February, and March 1978.

NIB respondents report that the "intransigence" of the government on this issue and the referral back to the JWG left NIB feeling frustrated and without hope. They are quick to refer to the "repeated referral of items up to the Joint Committee and back down to the Joint Working Groups" as stalling tactics. The government side, now in control of the situation (temporarily), viewed the meeting quite differently. DIAND Deputy Minister Kroeger, admitting but downplaying the fact that an impasse had been reached, described the meeting to the authors as a productive one, as "one of the best discussions," and one in which "both sides really came clean." We think it fair to say that notwithstanding the impasse, the government side viewed the meeting as one in which progress was starting to be made; issues were, in some cases, being well defined and the Indian side was expressing a willingness to talk in specifics. In light of this and the subsequent meetings of the JWG, most government participants were surprised when NIB withdrew before the next scheduled meeting of the Joint Committee.

THE FAILURE OF JNCC

The first question which must be raised in discussing the failure of JNCC must be, "Why did NIB withdraw?"

The reasons stated publicly by NIB at the time of its withdrawal on April 13, 1978 were that: (1) the JNCC was not making any progress, in that not one major decision had been made by the Joint Committee in the three and one half years since its inception; (2) the government, rather than treating the committee meetings seriously, was cynically using the NIB as window dressing in an attempt to avoid criticisms over its lack of Indian policy; and (3) the government was purposefully eroding Indian rights and attempting to implement its 1969 White Paper which proposed to wipe out special Indian Status (Rich, 1978; Canadian Press, 1978a).

However, in addition to these public reasons there were other reasons which NIB leaders subsequently explained to the authors. One of these was the severe frustration which the Indian side felt as its members observed agenda items being referred back and forth between the different levels of JNCC. This frustration was exacerbated by government announcements of cuts in funding to bands and by the prospects of band staff consequently being laid off. Also extremely frustrating were government refusals to make funds available in "meaningful" quantities for some of the highest Indian priorities, such as housing. Said one Indian leader, in reflecting on this, "Housing is absolutely fundamental. To deny it is almost genocide."

Another important reason for the NIB's withdrawal is that political pressure was mounting on NIB for the committee to demonstrate some tangible and meaningful progress, and the prospects of being able to deliver were not encouraging. These political pressures apparently became manifest in the NIB Executive Council. Said one NIB official in an interview with the government's own *Indian News*, "There had always been a faction in favour of withdrawing from the Joint Committee process, but it was only at the [April 12, 1978] meeting that everybody agreed the process was useless." On this matter, one DIAND senior official claimed to have information that one faction of the Executive Council was very dissatisfied at Noel Starblanket's handling of JNCC. He contends that rather than air its "dirty linen" in public, the Executive Council decided to eliminate the problem by deflecting the issue by withdrawing from JNCC. Such a manoeuvre would enable NIB to score some public relations points at the government's expense, rather than undermining NIB's own position by allowing its lack of internal unity to become public. While this is at least partly consistent with the above quotation, our repeated efforts to substantiate or refute it proved unsuccessful.

The timing of the NIB withdrawal appears to have been governed primarily by the timing of the federal general election which a wide variety of federal political observers anticipated would be called in May 1978. The belief in the Executive Council was that an NIB withdrawal from JNCC just before the election campaign would embarrass the government, make Indians an issue in the election campaign, and strengthen Indians' bargaining position with government after the election.

The nature of the actual decision to withdraw is unclear. Yet it is important due to its impact upon NIB's credibility with government. NIB steadfastly maintains that the withdrawal decision by Executive Council was a unanimous one. DIAND officials, on the other hand, report that they have reliable information that the decision was reached by the narrowest of margins, five votes to four, and that the losing side was extremely dissatisfied with the outcome of the vote. Regardless of the margin of victory at the time of the vote, it is clear that any front of unity on the matter began to disintegrate almost immediately after the vote and deteriorated further in the months after the vote. The result, rather than being a political victory for NIB, was a serious political setback for NIB in the eyes of the government, and a near defeat for Starblanket in the subsequent NIB presidential election. The irony of the withdrawal was that it appears to have been what DIAND and Cabinet also wanted.

The factors leading to the failure of the JNCC can be classified as either fundamental or merely ancillary. The list of ancillary factors would probably include such logistical problems as the lack of a permanent Secretariat and of sufficient support staff for the Indian side to properly prepare itself for some of the meetings. Second, one NIB participant suggested that due to a lack of trust of each other, all of NIB's PTOs demanded to be represented on the Joint Committee, with the result that the size of the Indian delegation and the length of the agenda became unwieldy. Another NIB participant suggested that some of the Indian delegates were afraid of dealing on the same plane with Cabinet. This observation is buttressed by that of yet another NIB official whose experience with the Indian Policy Development Secretariat led him to conclude that some NIB staff and politicians were intimidated by the very word "policy" and did not really understand the meaning of the word.

All of these factors, however, are of secondary importance. The fundamental causes of the failure of JNCC were, in our view, organizational, structural, historical, and political. We shall consider each in turn.

The organizational flaw in JNCC was its lack of a clearly defined mandate. As we noted, this led not only to the two sides addressing themselves to problems at different levels, but to conflicting expectations over whether the Joint Committee would be a negotiating or merely a consultative body.

The structural flaw of JNCC was that it involved NIB in a co-optative relationship. Co-optation has been defined as "the process of absorbing new elements into the leadership or policy-determining structure of an organization as a means of averting threats to its stability of existence." (Gamson, 1968:135) This led to the conflict within the NIB Executive Council between those who preferred to adopt an adversary role and pursue a confrontational strategy from outside governmental structures, and those who preferred to join government (and capture its bureaucracy). As one NIB Executive Council member reportedly said to a DIAND official, "There are those who want to get into bed with government and those who don't. I'm one who wants to." The problem, however, with this co-optative approach is that NIB did not retain the broad scope of options which a lobby group not so co-opted does possess.

Historically, the JNCC might have been the right mechanism at the wrong time. We refer here to the incumbent of the Prime Minister's office, to the parliamentary majority enjoyed by the government, and to the obvious implications which granting special status to Indians would have for the Quebec situation. Pierre Trudeau's staunch opposition to collective rights and his firm belief in individual equality is well known.

The political problems surrounding JNCC were numerous. We have already cited some of these, such as the difficulties faced by NIB in aggregating the demands of such a heterogeneous constituency, the subsiding of the political crisis which had led to the formation of JNCC and the consequent easing of the pressure to negotiate, and the fact that by its very existence the JNCC placed the DIAND Minister and bureaucracy in an awkward position vis-à-vis their respective peers. Another political problem faced by JNCC was the seemingly unitary or indivisible nature of NIB's key demand of special status for Indians ("Indian rights"). It appears that both sides adopted the view that special status, like pregnancy, is a binary phenomenon. That is, it was felt that just as a woman cannot be slightly pregnant, a group cannot be designated as slightly special, for that very designation would ipso facto make it very special. That this definition of the situation prevailed for so long in JNCC unquestionably contributed to JNCC's inefficacy.

The JNCC also appears to have been seriously undermined by the fact that neither side ascribed a very high priority to it. We have already discussed the mixed feelings about it which existed in the NIB Executive Council, as well as George Manuel's own orientation to it. On the government side, as DIAND Deputy Minister Kroeger pointed out, only two or three ministers can be considered to have much knowledge of Indian matters. Ministers' attention to JNCC was infrequent, their schedules were busy, and they would sometimes leave a JNCC meeting while it was still in progress, in order to attend some other meeting. As one NIB respondent suggested to us, JNCC became a forum which each side used in order to be able to tell its constituents that it was talking with the other side.

A final political problem which we wish to cite here is a very important one that reappeared periodically after the expiration of JNCC. We refer here to a crisis of legitimacy for NIB in the minds of senior DIAND officials. One influential official expressed the view that toward the end of the life of JNCC the government side concluded that NIB did not have any mandate (from the PTOs, the bands, or the Indian people as a whole) to negotiate about anything. While a mandate from the NIB Executive Council was recognized, such a mandate carried very little weight.[6] The same can be said of a mandate from the General Assembly. That same official spelled out some of the background to this view:

> There was no consensus behind anything, even though they emerged from the Annual General Assembly every once in a while with either sets of priorities or some basic principles. My feeling is that even if something gets through the General Assembly, there's no sustained life to it. It may only last for the next week or so before something else happens and they get on a different kick. And certainly with shifts in leaders.

Thus, the NIB allegation that the government side was not taking the NIB participants seriously seems to be not totally unfounded.

To conclude this discussion of the failure of JNCC, it is useful to identify in passing some of the features of Indian affairs which appear in JNCC. First and foremost is the highly politicized, and crisis-like atmosphere which surrounded its birth and its death. Second is the communications chasm that separated the two sides. Part of that chasm can be attributed to Indian distrust of government in general and IIAP/DIAND in particular (e.g., the subversion theory), although the distrust which exists among Indians also surfaced with JNCC. A further feature of the ongoing Indian-government relationship which emerged in this instance is the high level of Indian frustration juxtaposed against a wariness of any change to the status quo.

RELATIONS WITH NON-GOVERNMENTAL ORGANIZATIONS

Our purpose in this section of the chapter is to provide a brief sketch characterizing certain relationships which NIB has in the non-governmental sphere, and demonstrating the breadth and variety of those relations. Our approach will be illustrative rather than exhaustive.

In Chapter Ten we describe relations between NIB and the Indian-Eskimo Association (IEA) which later took on the name Canadian Association in Support of the Native Peoples (CASNP). Little more need be said here about that, except to reiterate the crucial role played by George Manuel in setting the terms of the relationship. The two specific events which soured Manuel were IEA's competion with NIB for funds, particularly during NIB's 1970 fiscal crisis, and Manuel's firm conviction that the IEA President lied outright to him on this matter. Manuel's assessment of IEA/CASNP comes through clearly in various remarks he made to the authors:

> They needed us more than we needed them. . . . If we can't do that [sensitizing nonIndian people to the situation of the Indian people] ourselves, then we shouldn't exist. . . . Their board members were "do-gooders" of the worst kind. They should be fund-raisers. . . . They're fulfilling their needs, not ours.

Manuel's lingering influence and CASNP's inability to deliver political resources (e.g., funds, support) in sufficient, tangible quantities both suggest that although the NIB door was set slightly ajar for CASNP in 1978, the demise of CASNP is unlikely to have been greeted with sorrow at NIB.

Throughout the 1970s, NIB relations with the various Christian churches revolved mainly around the mustering of support for the World Council of Indigenous Peoples (WCIP). There was no systematic effort by NIB to enter even loose liaisons with the churches in the similar manner that was possible with environmentalist organizations. The prime reason for this would seem to be the history of paternalism which long characterized Indian-church relations. However, the guilt feelings engendered by that very history now constitute a potentially exploitable resource for NIB. As one NIB official said to the authors, "The churches owe us one! They f--- up a whole generation of Indians." While church leaders are unlikely to describe the situation in precisely those terms, our interviews with national leaders of three churches revealed an awareness and concern over past injustices perpetrated by the churches and a demonstrated commitment to a more constructive, supportive role in contemporary times. While one of the Indian advisors to the NIB president expressed a desire to capitalize upon that commitment, it is our expectation that, for various reasons, the cultivation of this relationship will not be high on the list of priorities of NIB. Similarly, if the recent history of church involvement in Indian and Native affairs is any indication, we should anticipate that in the 1980s the churches will support mainly localized, innovative projects, rather than the national-level and more institutionalized efforts of NIB. Church support for NIB, we suspect, will consist mainly of two types—limited financial support for WCIP, and second, moral support at home for stands taken by NIB or its PTOs, particularly in matters related to land claims and frontier industrial development.

The relationship between NIB and charitable foundations can best be described as underdeveloped. It appears that only towards the end of the decade of the seventies did NIB seek to tap the foundations' resources in a concerted manner. Yet even then the approach was not as professionally systematic as it could have been. For instance, there was no evidence of any attempt to cultivate an informal relationship of mutual familiarity with either the largest foundations or with any of the several foundations identifying Native peoples as one of their main areas of interest. Indeed, some of the PTOs, such as The Union of British Columbia Indian Chiefs, demonstrated more sophistication than NIB in the finer points of raising funds from foundations. Assuming that the trend towards professionalization of NIB continues in the 1980s, we anticipate a greater systemization of NIB's efforts to obtain grants, and perhaps even reduced interest loans, from foundations.

To date, NIB's relations with the corporate sector have been virtually non-existent. One of the few exceptions to this is the relationship with the Bank of Nova Scotia, which has assigned a senior staff member to the task of developing a business relationship with various Indian organizations, including NIB. The Bank seeks to attract Indian banking business, presumably including the administration of some sizable land claim settlement moneys. The only other corporate relationships which NIB had launched as of mid-1979 consisted of an attempt to obtain funding from the Hudsons Bay Company for a world-wide music festival of aboriginal peoples, and a working relationship with the Cadillac-Fairview corporation on the matter of Indian housing.

One other set of relationships in the nonNative sector should also be mentioned, namely, that between NIB and labour and environmentalist groups. As indicated earlier, a deliberate strategy decision was taken for the NIB Environmental Secretariat to develop co-operative relations with other groups concerned with environmental degradation and its effects upon workers or upon the larger population. Given the fact that the diets and livelihoods of many Indians (e.g., fishermen) are dependent upon an unspoiled environment, this has been the focus of concerted effort by NIB. Thus, relations have been established with a long list of organizations, including the following: Canadian Labour Congress, the Ontario Federation of Labour, the United Steel Workers of America, the Canadian Association of Smelters and Allied Workers, United States environmental agencies such as the National Institute of Occupational Safety and Health and the federal Environmental Protection Agency, the Ontario Public Interest Research Group, the Sierra Club, and biology or environmental sciences departments in certain Canadian and American universities. From these contacts comes a sharing of information which NIB and its PTOs use in attacking various scientific and legal problems. The resultant accumulation of scientific expertise, both in-house and contracted, enables NIB to approach government and industry at a level of sophistication which commands respect and makes it unlikely that NIB will "have the wool pulled over its eyes" by government or industry experts.

Of the several national-level Indian and Native organizations, the most politically prominent, after NIB itself, are the Inuit Tapirisat of Canada (ITC) and the Native Council of Canada (NCC). The significant differences in the life situations of Inuit and status Indians, the small numbers of Inuit (approximately 20,000), the later political evolution of ITC, and NIB's resistance to being treated as "merely" Native people (rather than as status Indians with special rights) have been prominent among the many factors which have militated against the establishment of on-going, close relations with ITC. So far, relations have tended to pertain mainly to WCIP and to the federal government's constitutional initiatives of 1978. Some sharing of strategies has occurred on an informal basis and this may evolve to include the sharing of technical information as well. However, each organization is likely to continue operating relatively independently of the other as NIB's attitude towards ITC seems to be one of "get what you can, but don't drag us down."

Relations with NCC through the 1970s were somewhat more frequent, but not much closer. At the time when NIB broke away from the National Indian Council, in 1968, relations remained positive. However, the tension which has long characterized Metis and treaty Indian relations on the Prairies eventually broke through to the surface. Thus, one respondent who was active in NIB until 1976 described relations with NCC as "testy at the best of times". Much of that testiness stemmed from personalilty clashes between the leaders of the two organizations, but much was also grounded in specific events and in positions taken by each side on specific issues. For instances, the less-than-oblique support which NCC provided to the Indian Rights for Indian Women organization on the issue of sex discrimination in the membership provisions of the Indian Act was a significant irritant within NIB. Similarly, Indian-Metis tensions over land claims settlements in British Columbia and the Mackenzie Valley had ramifications for the relationship between the two national organizations. However, by the end of the 1970s there had emerged a new political will to foster a closer and more co-operative relationship with NCC. Very real differences do exist between status Indians on the one hand, and Metis and nonstatus Indians on the other hand, particularly on such issues as the desirability of industrial development, reserves, and large-scale monetary settlements to land claims. However, in the face of governmental inclinations and outright pressures to subsume status, non status, Metis, and Inuit under the rubric "Native," and to treat them uniformly, it seems that closer relations between NIB and NCC are inevitable, even if only to develop strategies for more forcefully articulating to government these differences which divide them.

Whereas NIB's relations with NCC have been cool, its relations with the Canadian branch of the American Indian Movement (AIM) have been characterized by outright hostility, even to the point where AIM has threatened the personal safety of one of the senior advisors to the NIB president. Our casual conversations with AIM leaders and their supporters on different occasions have yielded a rather undifferentiated condemnation by AIM of established Indian political organizations such as NIB and its PTOs. They are seen as having lost touch with the "grass roots" Indian community and having been co-opted by the government. However, whereas AIM takes pride in its closeness to the grass roots, NIB leaders take pride in the fact that unlike AIM's leaders, who are self-appointed, NIB's political leaders are democratically elected and have to endure the trial of the political electoral struggle before they can take their place as leaders.

AIM also constitutes a threat to NIB, in two ways which NCC does not. First, AIM is competing with NIB to represent status Indians. Second, AIM's use of militant protest tactics involving blatant coercion and threats of violence permits nonIndian politicians to profess concern about a nonIndian backlash and to accordingly move slowly on NIB's demands. Yet, as we have already observed in the circumstances surrounding the creation of the Joint NIB/Cabinet Committee, under certain conditions the AIM-NIB relationship can take on a symbiotic character. NIB benefits by arguing to government that if it does not deal seriously with "reasonable" men from NIB, it will have to deal with "hot-headed radicals" from AIM. AIM benefits by being able to point to its tactics as being the ones that bring immediate results. Thus, the AIM-NIB relationship is a complex one involving elements of symbiosis, competition, and conflict. However, the complexity of the relationship should not be allowed to overshadow the fact that the frequency of interaction is quite low and the relationship is of quite secondary importance to both parties.

The Indian Rights for Indian Women (IRIW) organization is another with which NIB has had contact over the years. When George Manuel was NIB president there was a concerted effort by IRIW to get NIB's support for the goal of ending sex discrimination in the Indian Act (especially Sec. 12.1.b). However, NIB resisted out of a concern that Parliament would proceed to open other sections of the Act to revisions before NIB was ready. Whereas the interests of IRIW tended to be focused upon education, housing, health and the aforementioned sex discrimination, Manuel attempted to enlist IRIW's support in a broader range of issues, particularly Indian hunting, fishing, trapping, and gathering rights. However, his efforts appear to have met with little success. Although NIB does send delegates to IRIW's conferences and workshops and did support IRIW's request for funds to pursue its interests in Section 12.1.B, there otherwise appears to be very little substance to the relationship.

Finally, a few words are in order on the topic of NIB's relations with individual Indian bands. These relations can be most succinctly described as uneven. The majority of the 573 bands in the country do not have any direct dealings with NIB, apart from receiving NIB's newsletter, *The National Indian*. Some bands, however, do use NIB in a "trouble-shooting" or expediting capacity when they encounter a problem with IIAP or some other governmental department and are unable to resolve it themselves. A handful of bands receive direct and intensive assistance from NIB. This assistance may be in the form of lobbying with the Minister or other senior governmental officials to block or implement some planned change or project (e.g., the building of a school on a reserve). Alternatively, the assistance rendered may take the form of providing specialized legal, scientific, or other technical expertise to aid in the development of a particular program, study, law suit, or protest. Since the size of the NIB staff precludes the offering of this intensive assistance to all bands, the cases taken on are selected with a keen eye directed towards both their national ramifications and the political leverage that they can provide NIB in its relations with government.

Overall, though, NIB has a very low profile on reserves, just as the federal government has a low profile with municipalities.

THE FUTURE OF NIB

During the period of Walter Deiter's presidency (1968-70), the main accomplishments of NIB were the establishment of NIB's presence on the federal scene, the establishment of a constitution with which all PTOs could agree, and the reduction of the longstanding isolation of status Indians from one another. Accomplishments during the George Manuel era (1970-76) were more numerous. Internally, these consisted of the financial, administrative, and political consolidation of the organization, including the establishment of the legitimacy of NIB at the local, regional, and provincial levels across the country. Also of considerable importance internally was the making of progress towards certain developmental goals which Manuel held for Indians, such as the development of Indian self-confidence and a willingness to take on responsibility and make decisions that would have ramifications for succeeding generations. Externally one of the most significant and more enduring accomplishments (notwithstanding the eventual failure of the JNCC) was the gaining of direct access to Cabinet Ministers other than the DIAND Minister. Another important accomplishment, for which the Supreme Court, the Nishaga, and the NCC also share credit, was the reversal of the federal government's refusal to recognize aboriginal rights. Other noteworthy successes on the domestic scene during the Manuel years were the agreements reached with the government on Indian control of Indian education, housing, and socio-economic development strategy, and the establishment of a skilled and forceful environmental secretariat. On the international scene the crowning achievements of the Manuel regime were the formation of the World Council of Indigenous Peoples and the bestowal of international recognition on NIB as a Non-Governmental Organization member of the United Nations.

At the time of writing the Starblanket regime was only about halfway through its second two-year term. Accordingly, some of its accomplishments are more difficult to assess. Clearly, though, the Starblanket period should be seen as one of increasing professionalization and systemization of NIB's efforts through the recruitment of highly educated staff and the development of such mechanisms as the Indian Policy Development Secretariat and the Parliamentary Liaison Unit. Externally NIB's achievements during this period include the securing of representation at federal-provincial First Ministers' Conferences on the Canadian constitution, the assertion and actual enforcement of certain Indian rights, and the broadening of external liaisons.

To balance these various accomplishments, mention should be made of the main weaknesses or failures which characterized these respective regimes. In Deiter's case the main failures could be said to be the failure to recognize and control the divisive forces within the organization and the failure to establish financial and administrative stability within the organization. Any list of the shortcomings of Manuel's regime must include near the top its failure to better exploit the potential of the JNCC and to obtain an agreement with Jean Chrétien on the implementation of the Indian control of Indian education policy. The JNCC criticism can also be levelled at the Starblanket regime. Some observers have also expressed concern over an erosion of NIB's legitimacy with the bands and the federal government. While legitimacy with government is likely to fluctuate, if history should prove the concern about NIB's legitimacy with and sensitivity to the bands to be valid, this would have to rank as a major failure of the Starblanket regime.

The future of the NIB will be shaped by many factors, one of which is the composition of the Executive Council. The late 1970s witnessed a significant change in the membership of the Executive Council, whereby some of the older hands were replaced by younger men such as George Erasmus. This new order tended to have higher levels of formal education and to be more militantly politicized. Whereas the old order has been characterized as knowing more what it did not want than what it did want, the new order seems to operate in a less reactive and more proactive fashion. It has been characterized by the political assistant to the president as holding "a carefully considered ideology of Indian self-determination."

Indications are that this new, more aggressive leadership can be expected to develop NIB in certain directions in the 1980s. First, Indian sovereignty will likely be vigorously pursued, and simultaneously from three directions, namely land claims settlements, Indian Act revisions pertaining to band self-government, and entrenchment of special rights for Indians in a new Canadian constitution. The rhetorical and substantive forcefulness with which these demands are likely to be pursued is suggested by NIB's submission to the parliamentary committee considering the Trudeau government's 1978 proposals for constitutional revision. Said NIB president Starblanket:

> We, the elected representatives of Indian nations of Canada, are considering the possible terms on which we may negotiate the development of a relationship between Canada and the Indian nations. (Starblanket, 1978b:7)

In the 1980s the new Executive Council can also be expected to push NIB towards a much greater emphasis upon the development of policy. Rather than attempting to develop a bureaucracy parallelling that of

IIAP, with all its adminstrative responsibilities, NIB will attempt to appropriate the policy development role from IIAP. Here it will collide head-on with government's views on its own responsibilities. As former ADM of Corporate Policy in DIAND, Geoff Murray, points out, policy development will probably never be a case of "this is what Indians want, so this shall be the policy." Rather, the adopted policy in Indian affairs must be government policy as well, in the sense that government must be able to "float" that policy with government's broader constituency. Thus, government must take into account its responsibilities not just to Indians, but also to Parliament, to taxpayers, and to its own supporters. Therefore, unless vastly different mechanisms of political and fiscal accountability are put in place, NIB's efforts to control policy making in the Indian field are likely to meet with limited success, although opportunities for input to IIAP policy making will likely remain available.

Another important factor which will influence the future developmental path of NIB is the IIAP's twin policy of decentralization and devolution. To the extent that the 1980s witness any sustained and meaningful devolution of powers to bands and decentralization of administrative responsibilities away from Ottawa, the role of NIB could change. Specifically, provincial-level organizations could well assume many of the current activities of NIB, leaving NIB to act as a national information clearinghouse and as a lobbyist on an increasingly narrow range of policy issues which are of national scope.

Similarly, we have already observed a number of consultative, administrative, governmental, and negotiating mechanisms (such as the Ontario Regional Liaison Council, the Dakota-Ojibway Tribal Council, regional governments established under the James Bay Agreement, and the tripartite negotiating process), all of which function quite independently of NIB. These, and Indian Act revision proposals for band government, all point in the direction of a diminution in some of NIB's traditional roles. However, while NIB will likely be the cutting edge in fewer areas, it may be able to carve out a new role for itself as a central advisory body and as a body which monitors the implementation of agreements reached by other parties.

If the revision of the band government provisions of the Indian Act is not achieved by the early 1980s, government could lose patience. In that event, government proposals for such special status for registered Indians could be eclipsed by de facto, although probably not de jure, moves to subsume registered Indians and other Canadian aboriginal peoples under the common rubric of "Native people." In that event NIB would be forced to divert resources to countering the threat, and accordingly would likely make slower headway on other policy and programmatic fronts, especially if it were placed in the position of having to compete with other Native organizations for funds from the same government department.

If NIB does experience a prolonged period of minimal visible accomplishments, whether due to the reason just stated or some other reason, it will nevertheless have to create the appearance of accomplishment. In particular, if it cannot deliver programatic and policy victories, it will be expected by its membership to at least deliver what might be called "status victories." Status victories often come from contests where Indians encounter government and in the process exhibit superior cunning, rectitude, or ability to embarrass the government or its officials (e.g., the 1979 chiefs' visit to England). The quest for such victories, however, carries with it the danger of what sociologists call an "ends-means" inversion, which is to say that the ability to, say, stage a good demonstration can become an end in itself, rather than a means to some policy or program goal. Thus, tactics could come to be adopted for the psychological gratifications which they provide to the membership rather than for their strategic value. The danger of this happening will be all the more acute if NIB is unable to resolve its internal constitutional problems and PTOs, such as those from Ontario, break away to form a rival organization, for leadership competition tends to foster such expressive tendencies (McWorter and Crain, 1967).

With the winning of representation at First Ministers' conferences on the Canadian constitution, NIB not only acquired a position of potential influence, but also acquired considerable prestige which itself is significant in certain other respects. First, it should temporarily relieve the pressure for the aforementioned status victories. In addition it clearly demonstrates that within government circles, NIB's legitimacy is something which ebbs and flows; it was only a relatively short while earlier that NIB had experienced diminished legitimacy as a result of its withdrawal from JNCC and its issuing of "report cards" on the DIAND Minister and other parliamentarians during the campaign for the 1979 federal election. However, NIB's increased legitimacy cannot be taken for granted, for it is sometimes undermined by internal dissent within NIB.[7] Although government officials do seem to recognize that Indian interests are every bit as complex as federalism is for Canada itself, they often expect Indians to be able to forge and enforce amongst themselves a national consensus—an almost superhuman political feat which flies in the face of the record of nonIndian politicians on nonIndian issues. Yet when NIB fails to achieve such a national consensus, its claim to being the national spokesman for Indians loses credibility in government eyes. Thus, for NIB it has proven to be the case that legitimacy with government must be won and re-won.

In delivering an overall assessment of NIB, former president George

Manuel said in 1979, "We're powerless, but we're doing a damn good job of bluffing!" This reference to powerlessness pertains to NIB's inability to mobilize Indian *communities* to take political action, which in turn is a reflection of NIB's low profile on reserves. However, NIB very clearly does have other kinds of power resources at its disposal. Among these are its sense of determination and its developing sense of self-consciousness. Important also are its external contacts ranging from international agencies (e.g., the United Nations) to foreign governments (e.g., Libya) to other pressure groups (e.g., labour unions) and sources of technical and professional expertise (e.g., consultants in universities). Indians have the backing of the Pepin-Robarts Task Force on National Unity in the struggle to obtain full negotiating status in Canadian constitutional talks. Further resources are the moral legitimacy provided by the churches and the possibility of victory in the courts. Some support has even been expressed by large corporations (e.g., Foothills Pipelines Ltd.). Finally, we must not lose sight of the fact that, at least over the short term, the government will continue to need NIB and NIB will continue to have the power to embarrass the government.

On the other hand, NIB is itself highly dependant upon government financing. It can also be co-opted or subtly circumvented by government. It is also faced with the extremely difficult task of aggregating and articulating the demands of a very heterogeneous constituency and has shown itself to be quite capable of creating severe problems for itself by being unable to control internal dissent. Thus, although NIB has the potential to build upon its successes to date, it is also quite possible that those gains could in large measure be wiped out. This is the dialectic which NIB's leaders face on an on-going basis.

NOTES

1. This figure includes salaries, travel, printing, and the unit's share of administrative overhead, rent, light and heating.

2. According to Ticoll and Persky (1975), the Communist Party of Canada (Marxist-Leninist) was also involved in the Caravan, almost from the outset. Additional communist supporters joined in the demonstration on Parliament Hill.

3. For a discussion of Cabinet committees, see Robertson (1971).

4. One senior government official implied that in refusing such permission the government was attempting to protect The Hudson's Bay Company and other corporations that might be implicated in Indian claims. The argument over the power of subpoena occupied most of 1976.

5. In addition to the aforementioned allegation that DIAND tried to subvert the Joint Committee, a senior NIB elected official also alleged that DIAND undermined the JNCC at the Joint Working Group level by tampering with

the minutes of previous JWG meetings. Specifically, he cited the omission of some items from the minutes and the downplaying of other items.

6. The frustration of Indian leaders can be understood when they are confronted with a situation where the government simultaneously refuses to negotiate with non-elected Indian leaders (e.g., the American Indian Movement), yet also refuses to grant legitimacy to the elected Indian leaders (NIB Executive Council). It is unclear to what extent government was aware of dissent on the NIB Executive Council prior to the NIB withdrawal from JNCC. An awareness of such dissent could have been the reason for the failure of government to accept the legitimacy of the NIB mandate.

7. The reliance upon expressive, rather than strategic tactical considerations can also erode NIB's legitimacy in government eyes.

Part IV

NonIndian Support Organizations

Chapter 10

Clerics, Philanthropists, and Liberals: Organizational Support for Indians

While NIB and DIAND represent the major actors or political camps in Indian affairs, there are also a number of minor actors on the stage, actors which are neither Indian organizations nor agencies of the federal or provincial governments. Some, like the churches, have been involved in Indian affairs for generations, although their contemporary role bears little resemblance to that played in the past. Others, like the Canadian philanthropic foundations, at present play a minor role but do show some potential for the future. Still others, epitomized by the Canadian Association in Support of the Native Peoples, illustrate both the difficulties that nonNative organizations have in grappling with Indian affairs, and the likely declining role of such organizations in the future. It is, then, to these less important yet interesting actors, that we turn in this chapter.

THE CHURCHES

HISTORICAL BACKGROUND

The role and history of the Christian churches in the colonization of Indians in Canada has been well documented (e.g., Hendry, 1969; McCullum and McCullum, 1975; Fumoleau, 1976) and need not be detailed here. Consistent with the prevailing ethnocentric ideology of the late eighteenth, nineteeth, and early twentieth centuries, the churches sought to "civilize" the Natives. This meant converting them to Christianity, wiping out their languages (by force when necessary) and much of their culture, and forcibly instilling in them the fundamentals of Eurocanadian culture. The insensitive and often brutally punitive way in which this policy was pursued, particularly in the church-operated mission schools (Hendry, 1969:23), produced a legacy of resentment and bitterness to which the churches seemed oblivious until the 1960s. The policy was often carried out in an atmosphere of interdenominational competition for the souls of Native "converts," while in the process sight was lost of the humanity of the Natives. Furthermore, a paternalistic orientation permeated missionary activities, such that Natives of all ages were treated like children and the capacity for independent action was greatly diminished.

Thus, in a peculiar but not unprecedented perversion of the basic tenets of Christianity, the policies and practices of the churches for the most part fit like hand and glove with the colonial designs of the government of the day. Indeed, this fusion of church and state persisted into the second half of the twentieth century, for it was not until 1969 that concerted, large-scale efforts began by the churches to both disentangle themselves from government and launch a new relationship with Native people. (With respect to the supply of educational services to Natives, the government was at the same time trying to disentangle itself from the churches.) Although the reversal of roles which the building of that new relationship necessitated is not yet fully accepted within the churches, the extent of the change to which the churches have committed themselves is truly remarkable. Rather than paving the way for the economic exploitation of Indian lands—as they did when they helped convince Indians to sign Treaty 8, for instance—the churches are now actually challenging some of the basic tenets of capitalism and interposing themselves between industrial capitalists and the managers of the state apparatus who in the past have facilitated the exploitation of Indian lands.

The leadership for this "about-face" came from the Anglican church, the Christian denomination with the largest number of adherents on reserves. Partly as a result of pressure from Native Anglican clergymen (of whom there were about two dozen at the time), Charles Hendry, the Director of the University of Toronto's School of Social Work, was commissioned to conduct an assessment of the church's role in Native affairs, and to make recommendations for change. In 1969 Hendry issued his report, entitled *Beyond Traplines*. It proved to be a watershed for the church, a catalyst for major change in both the internal affairs and external relations of the church. Internally, it called for (1) a much greater involvement of Native people in the church's decisions and activities related to Native people; (2) a concerted effort to change individuals' attitudes towards Natives; (3) a continuing effort to keep the church constituency informed about Natives' needs; (4) a reorganization of church structures; and (5) augmentation of church funds for Natives. With regard to the church's external relations, the Hendry report called for:

(6) the abandonment of interdenominational competition in the Native peoples realm and the adoption of co-operative approaches instead; and, significantly, (7) determined political lobbying action aimed at influencing the policies of governments and industry.

Roman Catholicism, the branch of Christianity most prevalent among Natives as a whole, was slower than the Anglican church in adapting to the winds of change. Central to the Catholic involvement in this area is a particular subdivision of the Catholic clergy, the religious order called the Oblates of Mary Immaculate, whose more than five hundred priests and brothers have focused upon the Native people as their primary area of concern.

In 1970 the Canadian Conference of Oblates undertook to reevaluate its involvement with Native people, and in 1971 it published the results of that study. Entitled *The Religious Situation of the Canadian Native People*, the report did help to bring about some needed attitudinal and programatic changes and to interest the Oblates and the church in general in new, less paternalistic forms of ministry to Native people. However, it lacked sufficient activist orientation and political "clout" to shake the Catholic church to its foundations in the way which the General Synod's adoption of Hendry's recommendations had in the Anglican church.

For the Catholic church, these two missing ingredients were provided by the Canadian Catholic Conference of Bishops (CCCB), an assembly of all of the Catholic bishops in Canada. In 1975 a subcommittee of the conference, the Social Affairs Commission under the leadership of Bishop R. J. DeRoo of Victoria, had undertaken an exercise in re-examining and re-formulating the church's priorities in the realm of social affairs. The events surrounding the James Bay dispute between Natives and government led the commission of seven bishops to examine the situation of Native people in other areas of Canada where industrial development was being launched (e.g., the Mackenzie Valley). Along with the Oblates in the Mackenzie Valley who had been working closely with the Dene there, the Social Affairs Commission was instrumental in convincing the CCCB that the church had to take a firm stand in support of the Native people of the North. Thus, in their collective Labour Day address of 1975, the bishops threw their spiritual and political force behind the Native people in a statement entitled "Northern Development: At What Cost?"

The bishops' lengthy address, which was read that day by parish priests in pulpits across the country, was an extraordinary document. It presented a critique of Canadian society which, in its analysis, was probably at least as radical as any previously offered by Native leaders themselves. The address focused on the issues of ethics, justice, and responsible stewardship of energy resources, and around them wove a critique which penetrated to the very core of the principles of contemporary industrial capitalism. It pointed, by specific names, to multinational corporations engaged in a continental struggle to gain control over new energy resources, and raised the fundamental issue of how northern energy resources are to be developed—i.e., by whom and for whom.

The address also pointed a finger at colonialism and exploitation in the North and explicitly drew the parallel to the plight of peoples in Third World countries. It alluded to conspiracies by governments and corporations and cited the maximization of consumption, profit, and power as the idols and operating principles of our society. It criticized "patterns of relentless consumption" and "the extravagant consumption of energy," and unabashedly called for "fundamental social change" whereby Catholics and other Canadians "change the profit-oriented priorities of our industrial system" and stand "in solidarity with the Native peoples of the North in a common search for more creative ways of developing the 'last frontier' of this country."

The address also made numerous recommendations for actions to be taken. Foremost among these was that a just settlement to Native land claims be reached before any decisions be made to proceed with specific projects for Northern development. Linked to this was a call for: (1) effective participation by Native peoples in shaping regional development; (2) adequate measures to protect the environment in Northern development; and (3) adequate controls to regulate the pace of extraction of energy resources from the North. The bishops' address also prescribed a role for Catholics and other Christians to take, including such actions as: (1) collaboration (in place of prior competition) with other churches; (2) changing wasteful patterns of energy consumption; (3) actively supporting Native peoples' organizations; and (4) raising ethical issues of industrial development with governments and corporations.

The Catholic and Anglican churches are by no means the only churches which have been closely involved with Native people. Unfortunately, however, space limitations preclude an extensive canvass of the Canadian churches. We will thus focus the remainder of our discussion, as indeed we focused our data collection efforts, on the Anglican church which, in the Native peoples field, has played a leadership role.

THE NEW ERA

In selecting "The New Era" as the title for this section of the chapter, we do so advisedly. That is, we are convinced that major differences have emerged in the way in which the Anglican and other churches, as organizations, relate to Native people. That is not to say, however, that paternalism has been totally banished, nor that the "rank and file" membership of the churches is fully in step with the thinking and actions of church leadership on Native people matters. In this section, then, we shall both substantiate our claim of the existence of a new era and sketch some of the limits and countervailing forces to that change.

"A Transforming Influence" is the title of a position paper issued in 1977 by the Anglican church. The title captures the essence of the Anglican church's role in Native affairs ever since the adoption of the Hendry report and the withdrawal from residential schools in 1969. The church has moved to adopt a new role as a *facilitator* for Native people. Support for this role was widespread within the church and no single individual is solely responsible for the momentum it gained during the 1970s. However, the leadership exhibited by the titular head or Primate of the Anglican Church of Canada, Archbishop Ted Scott, was of major importance. Scott took office in January 1971, and although the comment of one of our United Church respondents that Scott has "based his Primacy on his relation to the Native peoples" may be slightly exaggerated, it is clear that the plight of aboriginal peoples at home and abroad is a very high priority for him. Indeed, this is totally consistent with his career background, which includes years of experience with Native people.

Perhaps Scott's most visible leadership in the Native peoples realm was associated with his duties as Moderator (Chairman) of the Executive Committee of the World Council of Churches (WCC) during the last half of the 1970s. For instance, in 1978 the WCC's Committee to Combat Racism made an extremely controversial $85,000 (U.S.) donation for humanitarian purposes to the "terrorist" Patriotic Front in Zimbabwe, Africa (*Canadian Churchman*, December 1978:9,12). Another example of Scott's leadership is to be found in the Primate's World Relief and Development Fund (PWRDF), the major Anglican fund-raising and fund-disbursing mechanism. Although Scott does not himself make the individual grant decisions, it is probably safe to say that in the minds of most Anglicans the grants carry his imprimatur. These grants also illustrate the very concrete forms of assistance which are part of the facilitator role. Grants to Native organizations in Canada, which number about fifteen per year, usually amount to $75,000-$100,000 per year and represent about ten percent of the funds dispersed by the Fund. Some specific examples from the political realm are a grant to the Nishga Indians of B.C. to pursue their landmark aboriginal rights case in the Supreme Court of Canada and a loan to the Dene to replace moneys withdrawn by the federal government (McCullum and McCullum, 1975:187). Grants of a non-political nature have been received by such organizations as the Wandering Spirit Survival School, the Calgary Inner City Indian Street Workers Program, and the Canadian Association in Support of the Native Peoples.

A second general role adopted by the Anglican church has been that of an *advocate* for Native people. This role has been adopted in direct response to both the 1969 Hendry report and the 1972 report of J. W. Frei's Task Force on the (Anglican) Church in the North. Both reports raised the issue of lobbying governments and industry, and the Hendry report pushed hard for this. Thus, in an interview at the end of 1977, the Primate estimated for the authors that he had met personnally with the various DIAND Ministers a total of about ten times since taking office himself. A more recent interview with his Native affairs advisor, Rev. Adam Cuthand, revealed various letters in which the Primate lobbied both Cabinet Ministers and presidents of certain industrial corporations on behalf of indigenous peoples in Canada and abroad.

As a result of the aforementioned Task Force and of a 1975 report by the General Synod's Unit on Public Social Responsibility, the Anglican church decided to make a major commitment to involvement in the Canadian North. The discovery that the Anglican church shared with several other churches an interest in and commitment to the peoples of the North led to the formation in September 1975 of "Project North." Launched by the Anglican, Catholic, and United Churches, Project North within eighteen months had expanded its base to include the Presbyterian, Lutheran, and Mennonite churches, and became the central vehicle for these churches' involvement in the North.

The project has two main objectives, the first of which is to support Native people engaged in land claims and economic development struggles in the North, especially in communicating their struggle to people in southern Canada. The second objective is to mobilize the church constituency in southern Canada in response to the moral and ethical issues in Northern development. The specific activities in which the Project North team has become involved include lobbying both the DIAND Minister and members of the Opposition on behalf of the Dene, participating in Congressional hearings in Washington in an attempt to foster American awareness of northern Natives' position on northern pipelines, establishing relationships with environmental and other public interest groups, arranging news conferences in southern Canada for northern Native groups, and participating in church conferences. Notwithstanding some of these activities, staff member Karmel McCullum reported that those associated with Project North do not view it as a lobby group. Instead they see the Project as an *amplifier* of Native messages and as a vehicle for *raising* (and sustaining) *the consciousness and interest* of southern Canadians in the moral and ethical issues attending Northern development.

Not surprisingly, Project North has served as a lightening rod for opposition to the churches' involvement in the realm of social, economic, and political issues. The main opposition to such involvement is embodied in the Confederation of Church and Business Persons (CCBP), a

Toronto-based organization said to be led mainly by Anglicans. Says McCullum:

> We have been roundly denounced by [CCBP] . . . They see us as dark political forces inside the Church [and as] trying to overthrow the democratic system. They see us as a splinter group making decisions for the Church. I stress that we are working within the Church, with Church support, which CCBP is not.

It is argued by some members of CCBP that the actions of the churches in endeavours such as Project North are counterproductive, in the sense that when industrial development projects are blocked the Native people lose out on employment opportunities. Consequently, considerable pressure was applied to individual denominations to terminate their involvement in Project North, especially when its original mandate expired in 1977. However, the churches officially reaffirmed their commitment and the Project was given an extended life.

One reason for the churches' reaffirmation of support is that despite the very secular appearance of staff members' daily activities, those activities are guided by religious principles. Said staff member Karmel McCullum,

> There's quite a substantial theological component to Project North. Its present in almost everything we do and it comes out in almost all board meetings.

This observation is buttressed by the comment of a board member, who emphasized to the authors that

> Spirituality is not divorced from social action. To know God is to seek justice for the poor and the oppressed.

Thus, in providing support to Native peoples, the churches simultaneously *provide moral legitimacy* to the Natives' causes.

As indicated in the second objective of Project North, the churches have also taken on the role of *mobilizer of public opinion*. Part and parcel of this role is the task of disseminating information, as is illustrated in the Anglican church's publication of three books (McCullum and McCullum, 1975; Melling, 1967; McCullum, McCullum and Olthuis, 1977) dealing with Native people in the North. The point of view, towards which much of the effort at mobilizing public opinion in the mid-1970s was directed, was that a moratorium should be imposed on Northern industrial development until just settlements had been reached on aboriginal land claims.

A final role to be cited here involves the Anglican church's attempt to *bridge the gap between Native peoples*. One example of this is the financial contributions which the PWRDF has made to international meetings of aboriginal peoples both on secular topics (e.g., the World Council of Indigenous Peoples) and on religious topics (e.g., the annual Indian Ecumenical Conference at Morley, Alberta).

CONCLUSIONS

While carrying out the various roles we have identified, the churches have by no means enjoyed "smooth sailing." We have already made reference to a storm of criticism surrounding Project North and the WCC's Committee to Combat Racism. Reference could also be made to the initial resistance to the Hendry report and to the Catholic bishops' Labour Day address. These, however, are not the only problem areas. For instance, within the Anglican church tensions at one point arose between those who were promoting church involvement on the reserves and those promoting the concerns of Indians in urban areas. The more active role of the churches has also increased the danger of them being drawn into political disputes among Indians, such as in the case of the United Church's support for Indian rights for Indian women. Finally, the churches' encouragement of the revival of Indian religions may also create problems. The difficulty here is not so much because of any turning away from Christianity, for the relationship of the Christian church to Native religions may well develop in a co-operative direction similar to that found in contemporary relations between the church and Jewish organizations. Rather the difficulty comes because certain Native religions may reappear with some of the controversial ceremonies that led the churches to oppose them years ago.

To return to the contention that the churches have entered a new era in their relations with Native people, we believe that we have demonstrated this to be true of the Anglican church. Those interviews which we did conduct in other churches revealed very similar orientations, although not always as extensive an involvement. Those interviews also revealed some pronounced similarities among the staffs of different churches' Native programs, particularly with respect to a mixing of political astuteness with ethical, and/or theological training. While certain administrators and missionaries of the past may also have shared these characteristics, the contemporary church staff members are set apart by their willingness to put these skills at the service of Native people and to let the Native people themselves make the decisions. We find further evidence of the churches turning their backs on paternalism not only in their "no strings attached" assistance to Natives, but also in their willingness to challenge the economic and political elite rather than serve as their agents. The willingness of church leaders to stand firm in their support for Native people in the face of vigorous attacks from inside and outside the church is also relevant here.

Notwithstanding the above, we should not expect that a pattern which flourished for a century will be erased in a decade. Similarly, it is our strong impression that most churches have made very little progress in recruiting Indians to the ministry and that Indians have made few inroads in the committee structures of the various churches. Finally, Karmel McCullum has suggested, some of the "grass roots" parish-level support for Native people in the 1970s was offered without a full appreciation of the potential deleterious implications for the self-interests of those supporters. As those implications become more readily apparent and as other nonNative issues (e.g., fiscal restraint, energy) push to the forefront of public concern, ground already gained may be partially lost.

PHILANTHROPIC FOUNDATIONS

BACKGROUND

The estimated one thousand philanthropic foundations in Canada, taken together, are an enormously wealthy sector of society. Their combined assets total in excess of one billion dollars, while the three largest (J. W. McConnell Foundation, W. Garfield Weston Foundation, and the Griffith Foundation) alone account for over $400 million of that total (Arlett, 1973; 1978). At least fifteen foundations dispense one million dollars or more per annum in donations, while the largest three probably each disburse over six million dollars annually. Their wealth and their location at the very heart of the Canadian economic establishment place these foundations in stark contrast to the economically marginal majority of the Native population of the country. In this section we shall explore the nature of the relationship between these two sectors of society. Our primary concern will be with the kind and amount of support which foundations provide to Native people. The observations stem from an exploratory study which the senior author conducted in 1978-79.[1]

Most family[2] foundations derive their wealth from industrial, commercial, or publishing entrepreneurs whose businesses netted them large or small fortunes. Although not all of these individuals are well known, their companies usually are. The following list provides but a few examples of foundations of various sizes, along with the original bases of wealth or fame of the primary benefactor of each:

1. J. W. McConnell Foundation: St. Lawrence Sugar, Ogilvie Flour, Montreal Star newspaper

2. W. Garfield Weston Foundation: Loblaws, Weston Bakeries, William Nelson Ltd.
3. Atkinson Foundation: Toronto Star newspaper
4. S. & S. Bronfman Foundation: Distillers Corp.—Seagrams
5. Eaton Foundation: Eaton's department stores
6. McLean Foundation: Canada Packers
7. Molson Foundation: Molson's Breweries

AMOUNT AND NATURE OF SUPPORT

Regrettably, the amount and nature of the financial support which foundations provide to Native peoples cannot be stated with precision due first to the extreme secrecy of a minority of the foundations in our sample (e.g., the Weston and McConnell foundations) and secondly to "loopholes" in the public reporting provisions of the Income Tax Act. Such data as are available for our sample, however, are reported in Table 10.1.

Table 10.1 reveals that in the few years preceding our study, two foundations—Donner and Bronfman—consistently dominated philanthropic efforts in the Native peoples realm.[3] Peculiar circumstances[4] also led to a conspicuous profile for certain other foundations—Molson and R. & J. Ivey—in a particular reporting year, but they would not otherwise be considered among the dominants in the field. Several other foundations—Lee, McLean, Muttart, Richardson, and Vancouver—are also quite "active" in the Native peoples field, where "active" is defined as having made donations in this field in excess of $25,000 during the designated reporting year.

Clearly, those foundations which we have labelled as "dominant" or "active" collectively have the potential to make a significant impact upon the Native peoples field. Their combined grants in this field for the designated reporting year exceed $860,000 (excluding those of the Weston and McConnell Foundations[5]). Inclusion of the grants of the Molson Foundation and the R. & J. Ivey Fund bring the total to over one and one-third million dollars. Given the existence of other large and moderate sized foundations both within and outside our sample, there undoubtedly exists a potential to markedly increase this figure.

The donations cited in Table 10.1 were made in support of a wide variety of projects. Since the work of foundations is not well understood outside of foundation circles, we illustrate below some of the projects which they have funded in the Native peoples realm. These can be divided into four broad types according to the purpose of the grant.[6]

The first type of grant has as its purpose the preservation of Native culture. Grants by the Donner Canadian Foundation for post-secondary programs in Native Studies and Education would fall under this rubric. These grants, which totalled $1,490,400 between 1970 and 1977, went to nearly a dozen post-secondary institutions in support of Native Studies and Education programs, a Native Law Centre (The University of Saskatchewan), a Native component in the Carleton University School of Social Work program in social policy and administration, and a Communications Program for Native People in the School of Journalism at the University of Western Ontario. Also falling under this rubric would be various grants by the Bronfman Family Foundation to such Native organizations as the Association for Native Development in the Performing and Visual Arts and the Festival of Native Music. Libraries, museums, and art galleries are other mechanisms for preserving culture, and many grants have been made to them (e.g., by the Koerner Foundation) to increase their holdings of Native art objects.

A second type of grant consists of those which, broadly speaking, are intended to enhance the sociological integration of a community. These grants encompass such matters as the legal system, interracial relations, recreational facilities, leadership training, and communication. Included here would be a $48,000 Donner Canadian Foundation grant for the Regina Native Race Relations Association in an attempt to improve relations between Natives on the one hand, and police, landlords, merchants, etc., on the other hand. Included also would be $10,000 grants from the W. Garfield Weston Foundation towards the costs of constructing a community hall in various predominantly Native communities in the Canadian North.

A third type of grant consists of those related to defining and attaining what may be broadly termed "political" goals (e.g., gaining legal recognition of aboriginal rights, removing sex discrimination in the Indian Act). Although many foundations are wary of supporting such political goals for fear of jeopardizing their own tax-exempt status, some grants of this third type have been made. For instance, the Laidlaw Foundation made a $15,000 grant to the Union of Nova Scotia Indians for the purpose of hiring a lawyer to assist with land claims. On a larger scale, the Canadian Arctic Resources Committee (CARC) has received extensive support from foundations, particularly the R. and J. Ivey Fund ($20,000 in each of 1973, 1974, and 1975, and a pledge of $250,000 for the 1977-82 period), the Bronfman Family Foundation, and the Molson Foundation ($150,000). CARC's intervention to provide a critical and independent review of development projects in the North certainly places its activities squarely in the political realm.

The fourth and final type of grant consists of those which are designed to improve the health, security, comfort, or economy of Native people. Economic development projects have not received widespread foundation support, perhaps because of the involvement of the federal govern-

TABLE 10.1
Financial Profile of Foundations in Sample, With Donations in Most Recently Available Years

NAME OF FOUNDATION	Base Reporting Year	Location	Assets ($ million)	TOTAL DOLLARS GRANTED			NATIVE PEOPLES GRANTS		AVERAGE GRANT SIZE		AVERAGE GRANT SIZE OVER TWO PREVIOUS YEARS		% of All Donated Money in Prior 2 Years Allocated to Native Area
				A. All Areas ($ million)	B. Native Area ($ thousand)	'B' as % of 'A'	Number	As % of all grants	All Areas ($ thousand)	Native Area ($ thousand)	All Areas ($ thous.)	Native Area ($ thous.)	
Atkinson Charitable	1977	Tor	18	1.377	15	1%	3	2%	7.1	5.0	7.2	7.6	2%
J. P. Bickell	1977	Tor	23	1.451	9	1%	1	n.a.	7.2**	9.0	n.a.	n.a.	n.a.
S.&S. Bronfman Family	1977	Mtl	18	1.355	244e	18%x	20	n.a.	6.0x	n.a.	n.a.	n.a.	n.a.
Donner Canadian	1978	Tor	40	1.607	378	24%	5	26%	84.6	75.6	92.8	64.2	31%
Eaton	1976	Tor	10	.710	3e†	<$1/2$%	5†	2%e	3.1x	.6†	n.a.	n.a.	n.a.
Richard Ivey	1977	Ldn	10	.930	8	1%	1	1%	46.5	7.5	33.8††	6.5	<$1/2$%
R. & J. Ivey Fund	1977	Ldn	9	1.146	358	31%	3	13%	49.8	119.2	30.8	14.3	5%
L. & T. Koerner	1977	Van	2	.171*	12	7%	7	5%	1.2	1.7	2.6	6.3	13%
Laidlaw	1977	Tor	11	.745α	9α	1%	3α	7%	18.2	3.1	16.6	2.9	<$1/2$%

Law Foundation of B.C.	1977	Van	3	1.828	19	1%	1	2%	43.5	19.4	42.6	14.5	<1/2%
Clifford E. Lee	1978	Edm	3	.403	58	14%	6	11%	7.3	9.6	4.7	10.3	16%
J. W. McConnell	1977	Mtl	150e	7.254	25e	<1/2%e	4x	n.a.	n.a.	6.3e	n.a.	n.a.	n.a.
McLean	1977	Tor	6	.413	30	7%	4	4%	4.6	7.5	3.5	2.8	5%
Muttartπ	1977	Edm	n.a.	.456	45e	10%	n.a.	n.a.	n.a.	n.a.	n.a.	n.a.	n.a.
Molson	1978	Mtl	6	.772†	150	20%e	1	n.a.	42.9†	150.0	n.a.	2.8	<1/2%e
Mrs. James Richardson	1978	Wpg	2	.300x	30x	10%x	n.a.	n.a.	n.a.	n.a.	n.a.	n.a.	6%x
Vancouver	1977	Van	63	3.191	71	2%	12	4%	10.8	5.9	12.4	5.8	2%
W. Garfield Weston	1977	Tor	150e	n.a.	500e	10%	50x	n.a.	n.a.	10.0x	n.a.	n.a.	n.a.
Winnipeg	1978	Wpg	15	1.011*	24	2%	10	6%	6.5	2.4	6.8	55.0	6%

e   denotes estimated

x   denotes approximately (more precise than "estimated")

†   denotes 1977 data

†† denotes one previous year only

n.a.   denotes not available

*   denotes excludes scholarships and bursaries

∝   denotes figures from a two year reporting period divided in half

** denotes inclusion of only those 109 grants listed as "education" or "general" in the two year reporting period 1975-77

π   It is known that in 1978 and 1979 this foundation made grants of $50,000 and $67,500 to fund a Native Counsellor for three years at each of two Alberta post secondary education institutions.

Source: Ponting (1979b)

ment in this area. But two examples of those which have received foundation support would be a job training project for unemployed Natives in Edmonton (Donner, $75,000; Lee, $30,000; and Bronfman) and Stanbury et al.'s (1975) study of economic adaptation of urban Indians in British Columbia (Donner, $40,000). The Donner Canadian Foundation has also been involved in numerous innovative projects related to Native health.

CONCLUDING REMARKS

By our estimate the philanthropic foundations (including both those in our sample and those not) annually inject about two million dollars into the Native peoples field, a substantial sum of money. It should be borne in mind, however, that not all grants go directly to Native people (e.g., grants to museums, grants to academics). Second, even if the entire two million dollars did go directly to Native people, it would constitute less than one percent of the IIAP budget. Spread over such a wide variety of grants, private philanthropy will clearly never be a substitute for government funding.

Hypothetically, foundation grants might be highly attractive to Native people in several ways. First, and foremost, such grants can provide a degree of valuable autonomy from government agencies. Second, foundations can provide funds for projects in which government cannot appropriately become involved or refuses to become involved. Third, foundations often provide money on virtually a "no-strings attached" basis. Yet despite these attractions, there is a low incidence of utilization of foundations on the part of Native people. The reasons for this, we suspect, are several—not the least of which may be that seeking charity from foundations is seen as demeaning by some Native leaders. Other reasons probably include Natives' lack of awareness of foundations, and the reputation of foundations as being both conservative in ideology and demanding in their application and accountability procedures. (The former aspect of foundations' reputation appears to be fairly accurate, while the latter is rather exaggerated.)

We conclude, therefore, that foundations are not presently being utilized to their full potential. Yet it is not for us to advocate their greater utilization, for only Native applicants themselves can determine whether the returns are likely to be greater than the costs. We shall instead confine ourselves to a brief consideration of how the utility of foundations might be enhanced *if* Native leaders do so decide.

The resources of foundations can be turned to the benefit of Native peoples in several ways. First, rather than prolonging their dependence upon outsiders by seeking charity from foundations, Indian organizations and bands could approach foundations on a business-like basis wherein foundations would provide low interest loans (in addition to grants) for Indian economic development projects. Second, if ways could be devised (See Ponting, 1979a) for involving more foundations in funding policy-oriented projects, the recent Native ventures in policy development might be made to yield fruit more quickly. Third, foundations could be utilized as a mode of access to the Canadian elite. Foundation directors and senior staff members could open doors for Natives by helping them make initial contacts with other elite members, both on and off the boards of directors of the foundations. We note with interest that Indian organizations have successfully penetrated the Canadian religious elite (e.g., the Roman Catholic bishops), political elite (e.g., the Joint NIB/Cabinet Committee), and to a lesser extent the economic elite (e.g., NIB's establishment of a working relationship with a senior echelon of the Bank of Nova Scotia). Foundations, through their highly placed contacts, provide another vehicle for reaching the political, civil service, economic, and cultural elite of Canada.

Finally, the possibility must be raised of attempting to politicize philanthropy in Canada. By this we refer to political pressure which could be generated and applied to foundations so as to have more of their donations channelled into Native projects. Under law, foundations' funds are committed to serving public purposes and their relationship with the public, of which Natives are a part, is a fiduciary one. Foundations' donors have received income tax deductions or exemptions and that taxation income foregone by government is, in a sense, made up by other Canadian taxpayers (Arlett, 1978:16-17). Thus, in light of the taxation privileges which foundations and their donors receive, it is incumbent upon them to be sensitive to the views of the public. To date, Natives have not put the foundations to the test in any concerted way, and as a result it is not known how sensitive foundations really are to the views of the public in the realm of Native affairs. Only if Natives decide that such a testing should be pursued, articulate their views and needs to foundations, and press foundations to take on a larger funding role vis-à-vis Native people, will we know for sure if governmental legislative intervention is needed in this realm of private philanthropy.

Indian organizations have succeeded in politicizing the government's and the churches' administration of Indian affairs and in so doing have all but eliminated the notion that Indians should take what they are offered and be grateful for it. While the situation with foundations is not identical to that of government and the churches, there are parallels, and efforts at politicizing philanthropy could lead to similar successes. Once again, however, this is a strategy decision for Native politicians, not for nonNative academics.

THE CANADIAN ASSOCIATION IN SUPPORT OF THE NATIVE PEOPLES

The Canadian Association in Support of the Native Peoples (CASNP) was one of only a few nonNative bodies formally organized to provide support resources explicitly for Native peoples. Its small "l" liberal philosophy attracted a membership of about twenty-one hundred individuals and one hundred and ten organizations (as of 1978) from across the country. In this section of the chapter we present a detailed case study of CASNP, a case study that offers interesting insights into the kinds of problems which inhere at the organizational level when a liberal philosophy comes to grips with colonization and decolonization.

HISTORICAL BACKGROUND

CASNP, formerly known as The Indian-Eskimo Association of Canada (IEA), traces its origins to a 1957 committee of the Canadian Association for Adult Education. On January 29, 1960 that committee, the National Commission on the Canadian Indian, gave birth to the autonomous IEA. At that time there were very few Native organizations and no national Native organizations in existence in Canada. Thus, IEA included many Native persons within its general membership and its Board of Directors, and adopted as one of its main objectives the task of assisting Native people to establish their own organizations. The other main objective adopted was that of combatting, through public education, the vast pool of ignorance and misunderstanding which existed in the nonNative population.

The main activities of the early IEA were of two types. The first involved providing a platform (e.g., conferences and workshops) for Native peoples to speak out for themselves, an innovative approach which replaced the previous pattern of having missionaries, social scientists, and others speak on "the plight of our Native peoples" at various gatherings. The second involved lobbying the federal government, sometimes using findings of research sponsored by IEA itself. These lobbying efforts involved such concerns as the establishment of an Indian Claims Commission, the removal of the Indian Affairs Branch from the Department of Citizenship and Immigration, the improvement of Indian housing conditions, Indian Hunting Rights, and the establishment of Hawthorne et al.'s inquiry into the social, economic, and educational situation of Indians in Canada.

As a social movement the IEA faced a major crisis of legitimacy in 1968 when it came under attack from the very people whom it was supposed to be helping, the specifics of which will be discussed below when we examine the association's relations with Native organizations. The outcome was that the IEA entered into a transition period in which its role underwent a significant change, such that rather than functioning in a leadership capacity it moved more into the background as a support organization.

The transition period (1968-72) did see progress made on research and education aspects of the new role, as in the publication of the book *Native Rights in Canada* (Cumming and Mickenberg, 1970) and the holding of educational workshops for teachers and social workers. Examples of other activities conducted during this period include the operation of a Native speakers bank, operation of a library and reference centre, presentation of a joint brief with NIB to the Special Senate Committee on Poverty, and provision of assistance to several provincial and one national (Inuit Tapirisat) Native groups in their efforts to organize politically and to become formally incorporated.

Despite these activities, the association hovered on the brink of financial collapse and most of the staff had to be laid off. Furthermore, the locating of the association's headquarters (and Library and Information Centre) in Toronto rather than in Ottawa militated against its effectiveness in liaising with the Ottawa-based national Native organizations or in lobbying the politicians and bureaucrats in the nation's capital. Finally, in a "last-ditch" effort to survive, the association in 1972 once again subjected itself to an evaluational and direction-seeking exercise at the hands of the national Native organizations, changed its name, and moved its headquarters to Ottawa. Yet without the emergence of a major issue, specifically the controversial hydroelectric development project which adversely affected Indians in the James Bay region, the association might well have died at that point. This high profile controversy breathed new life into CASNP and generated new revenues for its empty coffers. After 1972 the association tended to function on an issue-oriented course. As issues arose, CASNP responded with specific programs. Just as many Indian organizations have in the past been characterized as crisis-oriented (Patterson, 1972:175), so too in many respects was CASNP.

In 1979 CASNP again faced an organizational watershed. Both federal and provincial government funding had been cut back, and the organization faced yet another acute financial crisis. Office space was reduced, staff was laid off, publications were cut back, and the Executive Committee met at its own expense. During the same year CASNP adopted an amended set of aims and objectives which, if anything, implied an expanded range of activities. By the fall, financial constraints had cut through any organizational fat to the bone and muscle. All permanent staff was laid off, the Ottawa office was closed, the Speaker's Bank was turned over to volunteers, and the operation of the CASNP library was suspended while the organization sought a new sponsor and adopted home for the library collection. At the time of writing, CASNP was on the verge of dissolving into a loosely organized network of locally-based volunteer working groups. To say that the future of CASNP is bleak would be unduly optimistic.

INTERNAL ENVIRONMENT

Although local nucleus groups did exist in various centres across the country, the CASNP membership was concentrated in Ontario, especially in Toronto (700). This made it difficult for the organization to be as truly national as its name implied. The demands placed upon the membership, many of whom were school teachers, tended to be minimal and only about one-seventh were active in projects.

Most of the activity of the association was carried out by the salaried staff under the general direction of the elected and unpaid board of directors. In practice, the executive director was the key individual, representing the association in relations with other organizations, developing broad policies for the consideration of the board, appointing and developing the staff, and generally making administrative decisions.

The board of directors of the IEA was a cumbersome body of sixty persons. Illustrative of the many prominent Indians who sat on the IEA board in its early years were Guy Williams of British Columbia, who later became a federal senator, Ralph Steinhauer of Alberta who became Lieutenant Governor of Alberta, and Omer Peters of Ontario who later became vice-president of the National Indian Brotherhood and Chairman of its Council of Elders. Prominent nonNatives were also sought out to serve as president or as board members and to lend further legitimacy to the association in the eyes of the government. The CASNP nominating committee, however, in later years tended to shy away from highly prestigious nominees who might have little time available to devote to the association, in favour of less well-known persons who would work actively on the board. The size of the board was also reduced to twenty persons.

At one point CASNP was nearly a half million dollar operation. After 1973, when its revenues plummeted to little better than half of the previous year's, the association experienced a steady increase in revenue, such that by the 1977-78 fiscal year its gross income was almost $450,000 and its deficit had dwindled to about $5000. However, during the 1978-79 fiscal year government, upon whom CASNP had become increasingly reliant (government grants accounted for 57% of CASNP revenues in 1978), reduced its spending, such that CASNP once again entered a period of crisis. In response, a directive from the board of directors suspended CASNP's fund-raising assistance to Native organizations and much of the time and effort of senior staff was diverted to attempts to raise funds for the association itself. Consequently, the year 1978 witnessed a diminished impact of the association. The association could not escape a "boom and bust" financial cycle which not only militated against its own effectiveness but which also led to friction with Native organizations.

RELATIONS WITH NATIVE ORGANIZATIONS

One of the main objectives of the early IEA was that of facilitating the development of Native organizations, and in this regard the association was quite active in the mid-1960s and early 1970s. This facilitating role was manifested in many ways, such as fund-raising, offering workshops on practical aspects of operating an organization, paying the salary of a field worker, and even providing a field worker/pilot (Wally Firth) and a Cessna airplane to facilitate communications among the widely scattered Native settlements of Northern Canada. The list of specific organizations which benefitted from these various forms of support in their nascent stage includes numerous Indian friendship centres, Inuit Tapirisat of Canada, and six other Northern Native associations such as the Yukon Association of Non-Status Indians.

Although new Native organizations were still being formed in the 1970s, a large number had emerged in the 1960s. With the emergence and development of these Native organizations, IEA found itself in the untenable and probably unintentional position of being in competition with Natives, especially insofar as funding was concerned. Furthermore, some well-established Native associations, like the Indian Association of Alberta, not having benefitted from IEA, were rather hostile towards it. Such was the state of affairs in September 1968 when the board of directors of IEA met with the boards of the National Indian Brotherhood and the Canadian Métis Society (CMS) in order to receive opinions of Natives as to the roles and directions which IEA should take in the future.

The transcript of this extraordinarily frank meeting reveals several sources of strain, some of which were in rather sensitive areas. In particular, some Métis organizations complained that the very existence of IEA meant that IEA was competing with them for nonstatus members, especially as they attempted to organize initially. In addition, the name of the IEA was seen as falsely implying that the association was a Native organization. The Indian Association of Alberta complained that the IEA Alberta Division had sought a $151,000 grant from the Edmonton Social Planning Council to do research on Indians in the city without even consulting with the IAA. The further allegation was made that the IEA used Indian people on the board of directors as "window dressing" when raising funds. Finally, the always sensitive issue of Indian spokespersons was also raised. It surfaced in the form of two grievances: first, that Native appointees to the IEA board of directors are arbitrarily chosen, and second, that any twenty individuals can form a local branch of IEA. The essence of the complaints was that in both cases there was no assurance that the people so chosen (or self-selected) would be true representatives of Native people.

Many of the concerns expressed at that important meeting were alleviated, and a commitment was made by the IEA leaders to redress the grievances raised. However, some of the needed changes were slow in coming. One of the changes implemented was that a certain number of positions on the IEA's board of directors were reserved for appointees selected by national Native organizations (e.g., NIB, CMS, and later NCC and National Association of Friendship Centres). This provided those organizations with an opportunity for on-going input into the association's policies and programs.

The story of the use and non-use of the two CASNP board positions allocated to the National Indian Brotherhood is an interesting one, for it provides a useful reflection of the state of relations between IEA/CASNP and the organization which serves as spokesman for status Indians across Canada. The relationship under NIB President Walter Deiter was cordial and both positions were filled. However, under George Manuel as NIB president, the relationship was very strained, largely because of further instances of competition for funds, including funds from IIAP. CASNP eventually adopted a policy of never applying to IIAP (nor to the Native Secretariat of the Department of the Secretary of State) for funds and of withdrawing if ever in competition for funds with a Native organization. Finally, in 1978 relations thawed somewhat as NIB President Noel Starblanket offered to ask the NIB General Assembly to review its decision of years earlier to boycott the CASNP board seats. The offer, however, was made contingent upon CASNP actively supporting the World Council of Indigenous Peoples (WCIP). This move on Starblanket's part was very much a case of putting CASNP to the test. As one NIB staff member said during our interview:

> If CASNP can't deliver the bucks (for WCIP), then they can die a slow and natural death, as far as I'm concerned. It's our first assignment to them. It's a test of their relevance and ability to produce money from their corporate contacts. . . . I've got a lot of personal respect for [the CASNP executive director] and they're into some good projects, but the main consideration was to get the bucks to WCIP.

Starblanket's call for CASNP to support WCIP was also calculated to have political, as well as economic, payoff. That is, the WCIP was a high priority project of George Manuel who had been one of its founders. In calling for CASNP to support WCIP, Starblanket was repaying a political debt to Manuel, who, as we noted earlier, had swung the British Columbia delegation behind Starblanket in Starblanket's very narrow victory in the NIB presidential election but a few weeks previously.

CASNP's response to the NIB challenge was more symbolic than material. The constitution of the Association was amended to include the objective of "endeavour[ing] wherever feasible to provide international support for the indigenous peoples of the world". This response was conditioned both by CASNP's own financial problems and by its policy of not taking sides with rival groups. This need for diplomacy at the international level was tied to the existence of the International Treaties Council, which is not only a rival of WCIP but is also strongly backed by the American Indian Movement in the U.S.A. (CASNP enjoyed cordial relations with AIM in Canada.)

In marked contrast to the relationship with NIB is CASNP's relationship with the Inuit Tapirisat of Canada (ITC). As the focus of this book is upon Indian affairs, suffice it to say here that CASNP provided important assistance in the original formation of ITC, that during its early years ITC was in many ways dependent upon CASNP, and that that dependency was eventually overcome and was replaced with a very amicable and co-operative working relationship between the two associations.

Standing in an intermediate position between the NIB and ITC cases is CASNP's relationship with the National Association of Friendship Centres (NAFC). In the early years IEA held workshops to train friendship centre workers in the operation of the centres. However, in later years the relationship deteriorated as NAFC, still in need of a certain degree of CASNP support, found its requests going unanswered and threatened to boycott CASNP. A concerted and successful effort by the CASNP executive director in 1976 to secure financial support for the NAFC's new magazine, *The Native Perspective*, was instrumental in markedly improving the relationship. In 1978, at the request of the NAFC, the one discretionary seat which it held on the CASNP board was changed, by a CASNP constitutional amendment, to two seats to which it was automatically entitled.

Local friendship centres and their national organization were very important to CASNP as they transcended legal distinctions among Native people by serving not just status Indians, but also nonstatus, Métis and Inuit populations, as did CASNP itself. Thus there was a natural convergence of interests between friendship centres and CASNP. In some local situations this convergence advanced to the point where the two often shared the same facilities, the staffs overlapped, and assistance to the friendship centre was the main activity of CASNP. At the national level a symbiotic relationship existed.

The other major national Native organization is the Native Council of Canada (NCC), which represents Métis and nonstatus Indians. CASNP's relations with NCC were amicable but not extensive. Unlike NAFC, NCC did not have to rely upon CASNP for fund-raising. Nor did NCC place a high priority on another commodity which CASNP could deliver, favourable nonNative public opinion. Finally, NCC preferred, in general, to work autonomously.

ACTIVITIES AND PROGRAMS

The support that CASNP supplied to Native organizations and individuals can be discussed using the same four-fold classification of types of support that was used with philanthropic foundations. The first type of support is that related to the preservation of Native culture. Relevant activities of CASNP in this regard included its teacher-training workshops and curriculum development projects. CASNP workshops on the mechanics of operating a friendship centre are also relevant here, inasmuch as one of the goals shared by most friendship centres is the fostering of Native culture.

The second type of support involves the enhancement of the sociological integration of local level communities, and encompasses a diverse array of more specific fields of endeavour including interracial relations. The cental purpose behind most of the educational projects which CASNP undertook for nonNative audiences was the improvement of interracial relations between Natives and nonNatives. Included under this rubric would be several of its publications, its speakers banks program (through which approximately 350 speaking engagements were filled in 1978 by 141 speakers, almost 90% of whom were Natives), many aspects of its Library and Information Centre, and much of its communications program.

The third type of support relates to the defining and attaining of what may be termed political goals. For many years CASNP's official statement of purpose explicitly referred to this third type of support, which was couched in terms of the promotion of awareness and understanding among nonNative Canadians of "just Native objectives." CASNP staff were well aware of the inappropriateness (from a Native point of view) of a nonNative organization becoming involved in the definition of Natives' goals. Thus, the association's involvement in providing this third type of support was largely confined to providing support for the attainment of objectives (e.g., special status) which Natives themselves had chosen.

In promoting Native goals, CASNP entered the political arena, both directly and indirectly. An example of the latter form of involvement was its Ontario North Today project, which increased awareness among Ontarians about proposals for industrial development in Northern Ontario and generated citizens' submissions to the Hartt/Fahlgren Royal Commission on the Northern (Ontario) Environment. More direct lobbying did occur, but not frequently. Examples of direct lobbying designed to support Native objectives would be CASNP's own submission to the Berger Commission on the Mackenzie Valley pipeline, and its brief to the Pepin-Robarts Task Force on National Unity.

Despite such activities, CASNP publications explicitly referred to the association as non-political. This was reflected in the orientation of the association's executive director who, in one of our interviews stated: "I don't see a need to cultivate a relationship with him [the Minister of Indian Affairs and Northern Development]. I don't honestly know what I'd talk about with him." Similar feelings were expressed with regard to relations with senior bureaucratic personnel in the department itself.

The issue of the relative prominence of the educational and lobbying roles of CASNP arose periodically as a point of disagreement on the CASNP board of directors. It is not difficult to understand why. On the one hand, there already existed lobby groups for the status Indian (NIB), Métis and nonstatus (NCC), and Inuit (ITC) populations, and CASNP had committed itself to intervening with politicians only in response to these organizations' requests for assistance. On the other hand, under certain conditions Ministers are responsive to public opinion, and by going to its membership CASNP could probably have generated hundreds of letters of support for a Native stance.

Turning finally to the fourth type of support, we might here express it in somewhat more general terms than those used in discussing foundations. Thus, we refer to it here as the provision of resources, facilities, and other means used in the pursuit of Native goals. Most of CASNP's fund-raising efforts for Native individuals (i.e., for scholarships) and organizations fell under this rubric, as did its publication of "how to" books which instruct Native organizations in the mechanics of such matters as fund-raising, bookkeeping, media relations, and operating a library or a speakers bank. Certain workshops which it held for Native organizations, such as the workshop on management techniques, also illustrate this fourth type of support.

THE DEMISE OF CASNP

There are so many factors involved in the demise of CASNP that we can provide neither a complete enumeration nor a rank-ordering of their importance. The factors discussed below, however, strike us as both germane and interesting for the light they shed on some more general issues of Indian affairs quite apart from the fate of CASNP itself.

The internal character of CASNP was the source of a number of problems. For example, the association eschewed membership drives which
could have significantly strengthened its resource base and national profile. For the members that it did attract, CASNP failed to provide sufficient participation gratification; people drawn into the association by the
desire to help others found too few opportunities. Moreover, the association failed to completely shed a charity orientation that had been an important factor in its formation two decades earlier. Related to this was a
failure to recognize the need for politicization. Reluctant to enter the
political arena, CASNP saw itself relegated to the sidelines and then to
the bench in what was becoming an increasingly politicized contest.

CASNP was not alone in its efforts to build bridges between the Native
and nonNative communities in Canada, and to provide support for
Native organizations and individuals. Implicitly at least, CASNP was in
competition in this respect with other organizations such as the churches.
The latter, however, possessed vastly greater resources than did CASNP.
Moreover, they were not single-issue organizations; their membership
base and resources were sustained quite independently of their involvement in Indian affairs.

In a sense, CASNP became redundant as other organizations moved
into Indian affairs, and because it was so much weaker organizationally
than its competitors, the redundancy was fatal. Put another way,
CASNP failed to find a distinctive ecological niche in the growing system
of Native support organizations. The foundations have such a niche
through the financial resources they control, as do the churches in their
capacity as a moral authority. CASNP, however, was a much more
amorphous organization. Its educational work became largely supplanted by the educational system's new awareness of Indian issues, an
awareness that CASNP did much to induce. CASNP had little or no
financial resources to disperse, and the moral authority of the association paled beside that of the churches.

Throughout, CASNP tried to bridge the government-created legal
divisions within the Native community and, as noted above, the friendship centres were a vital component of this strategy. However, not only
did this spread the resources and attention of CASNP very thinly, but it
also aroused the ire of Native organizations. Native organizations have
been built upon the legal distinctions that CASNP sought to bridge, and
in defending their own turf they have been suspicious of pan-Native
orientations and organizations. CASNP ran into particular trouble with
NIB on this issue, with the consequence that NIB challenged the very
legitimacy of the association. CASNP's alienation of NIB president
George Manuel weakened its relationship with other Indian leaders who
quite correctly reasoned that it was more important to court Manuel than
CASNP.

To a large degree, CASNP sowed the seeds of its own destruction. Its ideology made it inevitable that it would be co-opted by Native associations rather than looking out for its own organizational well-being. CASNP refused to compete with Native organizations for funds and, in an era of increased financial constraints, found alternative funding more and more difficult to attract. Funding agencies preferred to give funds directly to Native organizations rather than to intermediary organizations such as CASNP, an approach that Native organizations, of course, supported themselves. CASNP was caught in an ever-tightening financial squeeze: for ideological and practical reasons it could not compete directly with Natives for funding; alternative sources that were not being tapped by Native organizations were few and far between; government funding was drying up; and the membership base of CASNP was too small to sustain its activities without external support.

While it is going too far to say that CASNP died of success, there is an important kernel of truth in such a statement. One of the original goals of CASNP was to foster the growth of Native organizations, and this growth has indeed occurred regardless of to what degree CASNP was responsible. By the end of the seventies, the Native organizations dwarfed CASNP in their size, staff, financial resources, professionalism, and political expertise. The additional contribution that CASNP could make became analogous to a drop in a bucket. CASNP, then, became outstripped by events. It was born to fill a void in Native affairs and died as an anachronism. Natives no longer need a spokesman such as CASNP. Still, when one compares the strength of Indian organizations today to the situation when the IEA was formed, surely the founders would see the demise of CASNP as indicative of a much greater success.

CONCLUSION

This chapter has shown that the role of Indian support organizations has changed considerably over time. The moral authority of the churches is no longer used as an instrument of social control, but is being used more and more to facilitate the efforts of Indians to obtain the goals that they themselves have defined. Philanthropic foundations may be emerging as an important means by which some of the accumulated wealth of the Canadian society can be placed at the disposal of Native organizations. And organizations such as CASNP, which sought to provide organizational resources to Natives that were once in desperately short supply, have found their role eclipsed by the new organizational strength of the Native community.

The history of CASNP and the churches illustrates the shift in emphasis in support organizations from paternalism to a more facilitative role. Support organizations now play a sharply diminished role in setting the agenda of Native organizations. This change was not brought about without internal tension in both CASNP and the churches, and it has been unevenly carried out with respect to the foundations. It is a change, however, that is irreversible.

Unless support organizations are utilized much more heavily by Natives in the future than they have been in the past, they will remain at the periphery of Native affairs. This is not to say, however, that the contributions they will make will be unimportant. Indeed, support organizations may play an expanded role in the future, but at the same time will see their relative contribution offset by the continued growth of Native organizations.

NOTES

1. The study involved in-depth in-person interviews with one or more senior officials of nineteen foundations located from Vancouver to Montreal. Foundations included in the study were those which by self-definition or reputation were considered to have a major funding interest in Native peoples. Because the study examined the potential role which foundations could play, several other large foundations were also included even though they did not have a major interest in Native peoples. Results of the study are reported in detail in Ponting (1979b), available from the author. A summary providing detailed information on individual foundations for grant applicants is available from the Research Branch of IIAP, which funded the study.

2. In addition to the family foundation there are three other commonly identified types: the commercial or corporate foundation, the community foundation, and the special interest foundation. Of these four, our sample contains sixteen of the first type, none of the second, two of the third, and one of the fourth.

3. For a grant to be designated as falling within the "Native peoples realm" it had to meet one or more of the following criteria:
   (a) the recipient agency or organization has the word "Indian", "Native", "Métis", "Inuit", "Eskimo", "Aboriginal", or "Indigenous" in its official name;
   (b) aboriginal people constitute at least 50% of the clientele or membership of the recipient organization;
   (c) aboriginal people are explicitly cited in the grant application as beneficiaries of the grant; or
   (d) aboriginal people or their culture is the focus of the project for which the grant is given (e.g., a Native Studies program at a university).

4. Reference here is to grants made in support of the Canadian Arctic Resources Committee's campaign to raise one and one-half million dollars as operating funds for a five-year period.

5. Despite their respective profiles in Table 10.1, the author hesitates to classify the Weston Foundation as "dominant" or the McConnell Foundation as

"active" due to a concern over the accuracy of the data provided by these two foundations. For both foundations, the data on Native peoples grants consist only of estimates from a foundation official.

6. Readers familiar with Parsonian theory in sociology will recognize that the typology is derived from Talcott Parsons' four needs, or functional requisites, of a social system (Parsons, 1965).

Part V

Conclusion

Chapter 11

Conclusion

SUMMARY

The 1970s were years of enormous change in Indian affairs, despite the policy inertia which characterized the decade. The changes of this period can be grouped under several themes and we shall discuss each in turn.

INDIANS' EMERGENCE FROM IRRELEVANCE

The 1960s ended with a thunderclap as the government announced its White Paper on Indians; Indian protests against it reverberated from one end of the country to the other. The government's proposals galvanized Indians to action, producing an unprecedented level of pan-Indian unity in the process. As the decade progressed, Indian political organizations were consolidated and strengthened at both the provincial and the national levels such that Indians came to have articulate and forceful Indian advocates of their interests. These advocates were not content to acquiesce in the colonial state of affairs which prevailed and which had relegated Indians to a position of economic, political, social, and geographic irrelevance vis-à-vis the larger Canadian society. Pushing their demands for the recognition and enforcement of Indian rights and claims through institutionalized lobbying and uninstitutionalized protest actions, they succeeded in forcing the government to take notice of them. Through an escalation of demands and the power of embarrassment they forced the government to make concessions upon which they later built. Government imposition of policy was replaced by consultation and negotiation. Indians' ability to obstruct large-scale nonIndian economic development projects (e.g., in the James Bay and Mackenzie Valley areas), coupled with moral victories in the courts and the press conferred new power upon them, and Indians became a power with which industry and government had no choice but to reckon.

INDIAN POLITICAL DEVELOPMENT

The decade of the seventies witnessed phenomenal developments in Indian politics. First, Indian politics became "nationalized." That is, with the formation of the National Indian Brotherhood, political cleavages and rivalries which had previously been played out in other forums (e.g., provincial associations) now were raised at the national level along with the new and old interregional and intertribal rivalries. Indian leaders thus found themselves confronted with the task of articulating Indian needs in the context of a very heterogeneous constituency.

Another development in Indian politics was the considerable learning experience which Indians underwent as they confronted and co-operated with the government and its bureaucracy. The lessons learned included such matters as how to photocopy a "leaked" government document without getting the source of the leak fired, how to use the deliberate leak, the real power of the DIAND/IIAP bureaucracy, the limits to the power of the DIAND Minister, and the ins and outs of the larger government bureaucracy. In addition, Indians learned how to use the international arena to their advantage.

The 1970s also saw the emergence of a "new breed" of Indian politician. This new breed tended to be young, highly educated, strident in its rhetoric and somewhat technocratic. To an unprecedented extent they succeeded in gaining access to the senior politicians and in forcing the government to at least consider—indeed, actively seek—Indian input to policy decisions.

Over the course of the decade the character of one of these Indian associations, the National Indian Brotherhood, changed noticeably. From an organization which was in significant part oriented to the internal development of the broad Indian community, it became at once a formalized lobby group and an extra-parliamentary opposition to the government. As part of that opposition and acting on behalf of Indian bands, it competed with the government for the authority to make policy affecting Indians. By the end of the decade this was extended to the point where Indian bands were unilaterally asserting their sovereignty in certain jurisdictional realms, rather than seeking concessions from the government in those realms.

INCREASING COMPLEXITY

A third feature of the 1970s was that the level of political and bureaucratic complexity of Indian affairs increased significantly. Indian interests were represented not only by NIB, but also by other national associations, provincial organizations, bands, tribal associations, and nonIndian support organizations. The courts and investigative commissions also came into play, as increasingly did the provincial governments (with attendant constitutional problems) and private sector industrial corporations. Indian affairs also became quite expensive and Indian issues became entangled with others (e.g., environmental conservation, energy, sex discrimination). Furthermore, a number of other departments and central agencies (e.g., PCO, PMO, Treasury Board) in the federal government also demanded a voice in Indian affairs.

In terms of politics, Indian administrators both inside and outside government found themselves operating not in a two or three dimensional political space, but rather in a *six dimensional* political space. That is, not only were party politics involved in Indian affairs, but so too were Indian-government politics, federal-provincial politics, Indian-Indian politics, bureaupolitik, and inter-departmental politics. Thus, to say that the political environment of Indian affairs is exceedingly complex is no overstatement.

WEAKENING OF COLONIALISM

During the 1970s colonialism and the ideology which accompanied it were dealt severe body blows, although the knock-out punch was never delivered. One of the earliest blows came with the decline of the charity and paternalistic orientations in support organizations such as the churches, for this removed much of the moral legitimation upon which colonialism had been built. The increased nonIndian emphasis upon civil liberties, equality, and ethnic pluralism, coupled with a spread in the ideology of self-determination, provided a second blow to colonialism. Then the "we know what is best for Indians" view which government administrators had long held, became unfashionable after being denounced by highly politicized and often highly educated Indian leaders. Indeed, the fact that large numbers of Indians were now receiving post-secondary training meant that Indians were now better equipped to manage their own affairs, resulting in such developments as the adoption of the policy of Indian control of Indian education and the government's efforts to recruit Indians into IIAP (and the larger public service).

Another important force of the 1970s which weakened the colonial approach to administering Indian affairs was the introduction into the IIAP bureaucracy of the dialectic between the "new guard" and the "old guard". Although this introduction was achieved in the 1960s as part of the community development program, the new guard did not become a power to be reckoned with until the 1970s. Once it did become established, though, it operated within the bureaucracy to challenge old attitudes and procedures, to demand greater Indian input, and more generally, to instigate and lubricate change. Yet notwithstanding the entry of the new guard into the bureaucratic fray, colonial vestiges were by no means eliminated.

NEW MODES OF ADMINSTRATION

By the 1970s the old form of interpersonal control which Indian agents often exercised had already vanished. The 1970s witnessed an evolution to a less personalized, and often more subtle form of social control over Indians—namely, what we have called "socio-fiscal control." At the same time, however, the government advanced and supported models and proposals which involved a loosening of its control over the lives of Indian people. Some of these amounted to little more than a bureaucratic extension of IIAP, such that band employees administered programs and delivered services which were designed by IIAP. Some others, though, were broader in scope and had a much greater potential for significantly increasing Indians' self-determination.

The IIAP bureaucracy itself took on a new, much more technocratic face during the 1970s, to the point where the danger arose that technocratic features might intrude on the government-Indian relationship and exacerbate the already poor state of communication between Indians and government. This technocratic orientation, which was promoted by a new, highly-skilled, and professionally-oriented breed of senior IIAP official, in some respects replaced the earlier moral arguments (e.g., white man's burden) as a legitimator of IIAP actions towards Indians.

Thus, the picture of Indian affairs which emerges at the end of the decade is a highly complicated one which is riddled with contradictions. Those who subscribe to the value of Indian self-determination can find sources of hope in that picture and government officials can point to new experiments and initiatives undertaken. Yet it should be noted that the same colonial, control-oriented Indian Act was in effect at the end of the decade as at the beginning. Indian leaders, too, can point to major gains which Indians made during the decade, but they cannot overlook the fact that their people still suffer in large numbers from socio-economic privation and discrimination.

SUGGESTIONS FOR FUTURE RESEARCH

The foregoing are some of the main findings of our own research. That research has made us aware of other aspects of Indian affairs which stand in need of further research. It is to a consideration of these which we now turn.

One of the weaknesses of the current research is its lack of a comparative dimension. Thus, our first, and most general suggestion is for the inclusion of such a comparative approach in future research. Such comparisons, it should be noted, need not deal only with instances of decolonization in other countries. Other potentially fruitful domestic comparisons could be made between status Indians, on the one hand, and nonstatus Indians or Inuit on the other hand, particularly in their dealings with their constituents, with government, and with government departments. A quite different set of comparisons could also be made between IIAP and various other government departments (or parts thereof) in terms of the ideologies, strategies, and norms governing their interactions with their respective clienteles. Examples which come readily to mind are the Departments of Veterans' Affairs, Labour, Regional Economic Expansion, Secretary of State, and Health and Welfare.

Beyond this more methodologically-oriented first suggestion, numerous substantive realms can be identified for futher research. On the Indian side we need to examine other organizational vehicles which Indians are using to move out of irrelevance. Included here are the provincial and territorial member organizations of NIB, tribal and district associations such as the Dakota-Ojibway Tribal Council, management advisory boards such as the Ontario Regional Liaison Council, and economic enterprises of various sorts. The organizational strengths, weaknesses, and problems of these various bodies, and their relations with other levels of Indian organization, have gone largely unexplored by social scientists, yet the one major exception to this rule—the Joint NIB/Cabinet Committee—suggests that much could be learned from their experiences. But one example of a specific research question suggested in this area by our study of NIB is the question of how such Indian organizations build and sustain their legitimacy.

Related to this is the matter of Indian politics and leadership styles. Politics and leadership are absolutely central to the future unfolding of Indian affairs; yet studies to date, including our own, have only scratched the surface. So far we have scant knowledge of how Indian political leadership and processes are similar to and different from those of other ethnic groups (including the dominant ethnic groups), of how far politicization of the grass roots constituency (particularly the youth) has progressed, of the role of class and clan cleavages in the Indian polity, or of the role of communications mechanisms such as the moccasin telegraph.

Another important area for study is suggested by the emphasis of some Indian leaders upon self-reliance and the internal development of the Indian community. In this regard our research has found that among different Indian leaders there exist quite different approaches to the task of mobilizing resources; the time may be approaching for assessing those different approaches.

While most attention has been focused on Indians' penetration of the federal government's bureaucratic and political elite, little attention has been devoted to the establishment of relations between Indians and the economic elite of Canadian society. This is a newly expanding realm of activity which not only certifies Indians as having unquestionably moved out of irrelevance, but provides opportunities for social scientists to study a phenomenon from near its inception.

On the side of government and its departments and agencies, one of the areas in most need of research is that of the relations between IIAP and central agencies such as the Treasury Board and the Privy Council Office. Close behind in importance would be relations between IIAP and other federal departments. Weaver's forthcoming study of the formulation of the 1969 White Paper has clearly demonstrated the importance of the central agencies, while the importance of other departments has been shown by Cardinal's (1977) writing on the funding of Indian organizations and by some of our own discoveries with regard to the strain towards an over-arching "Native peoples" policy within the federal government.

Also emerging from our study was a striking similarity in ideology among senior IIAP (and DIAND) officials, and a fear of repercussions from dissent on the part of more junior officials. This suggests that a study of the informal socialization processes within IIAP would prove highly interesting, as would a study of the informal mechanisms of social control (negative sanctions) used by senior and intermediate staff vis-à-vis their junior staff and their Indian clientele.

Our study of the bureaucracy revealed definite tensions and rivalries, such as those between senior DIAND officials and the Minister's office and those which led field staff in the regions to occasionally subvert the policies and directives issued from headquarters. These are well worth exploring, in our opinion.

Finally, the decade of the 1970s witnessed an expanded role for provincial governments in the domain of Indian affairs, which opens up yet another new realm for study. Included here could be questions as to the political motivations and strategies of the various parties to these negotiations, the "trade-offs" made, and the impact of the resultant arrangements upon Indian people. Indeed, federal-provincial politics is just one of the six different dimensions of arenas of politics which we identified earlier; a study of the relative salience of these respective political arenas, or of what happens when an issue cuts across several of these arenas and simultaneously mobilizes political actors in each, would be valuable.

UNDERLYING THEMES IN INDIAN AFFAIRS

Much of this book has dealt with one or another of the various aspects of the policy-setting phenomenon in the realm of Indian affairs. However, an obvious, albeit difficult question which remains is: "Who is in control?" Who dominated the policy process during the late seventies and who is likely to do so in the 1980s? In the conclusion to Chapter One we suggested that the rejection of the White Paper ended an era where policies could be unilaterally imposed by the federal government, and that the direction of Indian policy was "up for grabs." Yet if the federal government is no longer in control, who is? To answer this question, and to enable the reader to relate Indian affairs to current events with which the reader may well be more familiar, we draw an analogy between Indian affairs and the major preoccupation of Canadian politics during the 1970s, federal-provincial relations.

FEDERAL-PROVINCIAL RELATIONS

Contemporary federal-provincial relations have been aptly characterized (Smiley, 1976) by the term "executive federalism." While the term is broad in its scope, there are three features that are of particular relevance to the analogy with Indian affairs. The first is that neither level of government—federal or provincial—can be said to be in control of public policy. The second feature follows from the first: the unilateral exercise of power is replaced by a continual process of bargaining, compromise and negotiation between governments. The third feature is that the bargaining process takes place among the political executives of the governments involved—cabinet ministers, first ministers, and senior civil servants. The House of Commons and the provincial legislatures come into play only to rubber-stamp decisions that have already been hammered out between the federal and provincial governments, and public opinion imposes only the broadest form of electoral constraint on the policy process.

If we apply the analogy of executive federalism to Indian affairs, the correspondence is instructive, although not complete. First, we note that neither Indian organizations nor the federal government can be said to be in control of Indian policy development. While the federal government has generally recognized that it cannot unilaterally impose policies, Indian organizations also have great difficulty acting unilaterally, for they lack the constitutional power and necessary resources. Indians and the government act effectively only when acting in concert; neither can be effective acting alone and each can stymie the other.

Since neither side can be forced to act against its will, more subtle means of influence must be employed. This leads to the second part of the analogy: the rise of a bargaining relationship. In Indian affairs this bargaining process has become very complex as the number of players has expanded to include not only IIAP and its ministers on one side and NIB on the other, but also NIB's member organizations, Indian bands, chiefs, tribal associations, central control agencies of the federal government, provincial governments, and so forth. Nevertheless, in correspondence with the executive federalism analogy, the central interaction takes place between the national Indian organization (NIB) and the senior officials of DIAND and IIAP. On the government side, the House of Commons is at best marginally involved, and the constraints of public opinion are both loose and flexible. In this instance, however, the analogy breaks down somewhat on the Indian side, for NIB lacks the power and the political authority of provincial governments. Unlike the latter, NIB is engaged in a continual struggle for legitimacy, and the resources at its disposal are dwarfed by those of even the smallest provincial governments. Furthermore, some Indian issues have been treated like "political footballs" by the federal and provincial governments, especially insofar as they involve constitutional disputes, and rather than participating as full negotiating partners, Indian organizations are at times virtually relegated to the sidelines during these discussions.

The aspirations of Indians in the policy development process bear a striking similarity to the aspirations of provincial governments in the executive federalism model. Indians, like the provincial governments, seek to roll back existing federal government intrusions into their lives. Second, just as provincial governments are constantly wary of new federal government intrusions into provincial areas of jurisdiction, so too are Indians constantly on guard for new governmental infringements—federal or provincial—upon Indian rights. Third, Indians seek to expand the application of traditional Indian rights just as provincial governments seek to expand their legislative jurisdiction into new policy areas. In this respect the quest for Indian governments and for the transfer of federal government fiscal resources to them also parallels many federal-provincial disputes. Fourth, both Indians and provincial governments seek greater input into federal government policy making; both are unwilling to tolerate unilateral federal government action that impinges upon their respective turf. Finally, just as the provinces have resented being treated like junior governments and have insisted upon being recognized as equal partners with the federal government in confederation, so too have Indians sought equality with the federal and provincial governments on constitutional matters, albeit with much less success.

The analogy of executive federalism thus provides a useful handle on contemporary Indian policy making. It suggests that Indian policy evolves through complex political interaction and that Indian organizations will continue to play a vital role in its future evolution. It also suggests a second analogy which sheds valuable light on the broader course of social and political change within Indian affairs—an analogy provided by the events that have transformed Quebec society and politics during recent decades.

AN INDIAN "QUIET REVOLUTION"

Since the Second World War, Quebec has been transformed in a number of fundamental ways (Posgate & McRoberts, 1976). The so-called "Quiet Revolution" has permeated virtually every aspect of Quebec society. A formerly rural society has been rapidly urbanized, and traditional rural norms have been lost. Accompanying urbanization has been the secularization of Quebec, including the breaking of the Catholic church's near monopoly on francophone education, trade union organizations, and ideological thought. With urbanization and secularization, the birth rate in Quebec has plummetted from the highest to the lowest in Canada, a change which threatens the long-term position of the francophone minority in Canadian society and politics. Since 1960 a modern secondary and post-secondary educational system has been put in place and has yielded francophone graduates with a full array of industrial, technological, and managerial skills. The mass media has expanded in scope and vitality, and has become a potent force in the preservation of French Canadian culture. French Québécois have overcome a longstanding distrust of government, a distrust founded on Catholic political thought and the domination of the Canadian state by English Canadian interests. The powers of the state, including a large, highly skilled and politically ambitious provincial civil service, are being widely used for the protection of the French language and culture. The Quebec labour force, private and public, has been unionized and radicalized. Linking all these changes together has been the emergence of a new, assertive Québécois nationalism that draws strength from movements of national liberation that have been occurring throughout the world.

These and other changes have in turn transformed Quebec politics. Successive Quebec governments have sought to wrest more and more power away from the federal government, and have indeed brought into question the legitimacy of the federal govenment in speaking for the interests of Quebec. While political demands have ranged from a renewed federalism and special status to sovereignty-association and outright independence, there has been a common underlying theme—the desire to increase the autonomy of Quebec.

There are many parallels between social changes in Quebec and those presently at work within the Indian community in Canada. In the latter case, rapid urbanization has also been occurring in the sense of a large scale migration from reserves to the cities. The Indian educational system has been secularized and partially placed under Indian control,[1] and the proportion of Indians with secondary and post-secondary educations is increasing dramatically. In step with urbanization and educational change there has emerged a new Indian middle class, proportionately smaller than that in Quebec but in attitudes, skills and aspirations not unlike the new Quebec middle class that has been such a driving force for social and political change. Like the Québécois, Indians have been exposed to movements of national liberation throughout the world, and the examples have exerted an influence on Indian political thought, demands, and rhetoric. As Québécois nationalists have stressed and defended the territorial sovereignty of Quebec, so too have Indians repeatedly emphasized the importance of Indian land, and of Indian control of Indian land. In addition, Indians, like the Québécois, are stressing their unique cultural identity and are challenging the existence and value of a pan-Canadian nationality. Finally, demands for Indian government, or the transfer of the political authority of the federal government to Indian hands, parallel, in many respects, the proposals for sovereignty-association.

Of course there are differences between changes in Quebec and those occurring within the Indian community. The Indian birth rate is not falling as low as Quebec's and, unlike Quebec, Indians face the problems associated with a burgeoning population. The character and extent of urbanization is very different, and the reserves remain the key component of the contemporary Indian situation, compared to an ever-declining rural influence in Quebec. Indians, unlike the Québécois, lack a macro level government that they themselves can control, and Indians thus have not shed their distrust of government. Furthermore, Indians lack a bureaucracy—apart from those of NIB and the PTOs—that is controlled by Indians and can be turned to the protection of Indian interests and culture.

Nevertheless, leaders of both Indians and Québécois seek a transfer of federal government powers to their own control. Both challenge the right of the federal government to speak for their interests, and by implication challenge the Canadian "political community" (Easton, 1965). Both seek to protect traditional rights, and to expand the applicability of those rights in the modern world. Both feel that the most important political changes are those that come from within, and both espouse an increasingly assertive ethnic nationalism.

Indians, however, lack the resources—numbers, votes, money, territorial concentration—to have a similar degree of influence on Canadian politics to that exerted by the Québécois in recent years. Internally, the Indian situation is much more complex: the Indian community is territorially fragmented; the legal basis of Indian rights is contentious; uncertainties exist as to who should be, or will be in the near future, considered to be Indian; and there is no direct counterpart to the unifying force of the French language in Quebec. Perhaps most importantly, Indian political demands, except perhaps in the Far North, do not yet challenge the survival of the Canadian state; there is nothing that carries with it the same degree of threat as does the potential separation of Quebec from Canada. This, combined with the small size of the Indian electorate, makes Indian demands less urgent in the eyes of government. As a result, Indian affairs have not been able to gain a priority comparable to that awarded in recent years to political problems emanating from Quebec.

The foregoing by no means exhausts the relevant points of comparison between Indians and Québécois. For instance, in bargaining to promote group or collective rights Indians and Québécois have run head on into a wall of federal political resistance. Indeed, certain victories by Quebec in surmounting that resistance have unquestionably made it more difficult for Indians to make similar progress. That is, the federal government adopted a policy of retrenchment and felt that it could not make concessions to Indian nationalism, for such concessions would have to be met by further concessions to Quebec. One of the central issues in both of these conflicts has been one which is also central to most other ethnically or racially pluralistic societies—namely, how the racial or ethnic group is to be *integrated* or *incorporated* into the larger society. We turn now, therefore, to a consideration of the nature and extent of Indians' integration into Canadian society, after which we consider the ideological roots which underlie the conflict between Indians (and French Québécois) and the federal government on the issue of how the former are to be incorporated into Canadian society.

INDIAN INTEGRATION WITH CANADIAN SOCIETY

As the 1970s came to a close, in some important respects Indians found themselves to be in, *but not a part of*, Canadian society. Inasmuch as Indians were long ago relegated to the sidelines, the contemporary social scientist studying Indian affairs finds relatively few threads that bind Indians into the patchwork quilt that is Canada. Canadians concern themselves unceasingly with national unity in terms of English-French relations and the interprovincial relations; yet the integrative bonds between provinces, regions, and English and French are strong in comparison to those between the Indian and nonIndian sectors of society. Indeed, the Indian-nonIndian relationship may be characterized more by malintegration than by integration, as we shall argue below.

At the outset it should be emphasized that when we speak of societal integration we are not primarily referring to assimilation nor to the spatial proximity (e.g., in schools or residential neighbourhoods) of different racial or ethnic groups. Instead, the reference is to social cohesion; that is, to bonds that bring the parts of the societal whole together in relationships or to take co-ordinated action in the pursuit of some shared goals. The term "societal integration" therefore is closely akin to what in more colloquial terms is called "national unity," although the significant difference between our usage and the popular usage is that we make no value judgement as to whether a high degree of national unity or societal integration is desirable or undesirable. Below we shall consider various factors which social scientists have viewed either as requisites for societal integration or as means for bringing about such integration.

For much of this century social scientists believed that a consensus on values was a prerequisite for societal integration. Although that belief has been dispelled (e.g., van den Berghe, 1967, Chapt. 11), value consensus is still recognized as being one potentially important contributor to societal integration. In Canada the range of issues on which there is consensus between Indians (as represented by NIB) and nonIndians (as represented by the federal government and its functionaries) is narrow. The NIB-government relationship, as we have seen, is an adversary relationship characterized more by conflict than by consensus. On the fundamental issues of land, rights, and government, the two sides are far apart: government insists on extinguishing aboriginal title to land while Indians seek to preserve it; government offers privileges while Indians seek inalienable rights; government seeks an increased scope for band councils while NIB condemns that as tokenistic "sandbox politics." Indeed, the two sides cannot even agree on who should be considered to be an Indian. Furthermore, at the cultural level Indian and Eurocanadian cultures clash on such emphases as co-operation versus competition, mastery of nature versus living in harmony with nature (Frideres, 1974:95), and most importantly, as we shall discuss later, individualism versus collectivism.

A second factor which has been identified as fundamental to the integration of a social system is legitimacy (Schermerhorn, 1970:68ff); the view held by parts of the system that the distribution of power, wealth, privileges, and authority is right and proper. Despite the role of Christianity in legitimating ethnic stratification in Canada in the past[2], it is probably safe to say that few Indians now view as legitimate the domination which nonIndian society has exercised and in some respects continues to exercise over them. The federal government's violation of treaty promises and trust responsibilities and its failure to adequately address such basic needs as housing, while simultaneously rendering foreign aid abroad, also do little to enhance the legitimacy of the federal government in Indian eyes. Furthermore, as we have seen in earlier chapters, through NIB Indians are now challenging the legitimacy of the very authority of the federal government to make Indian policy. Bluntly put, history has taught Indians not to trust nonIndian policy-makers and to always question their motives.

We can gain a more systematic understanding of this crisis of legitimacy if we break the polity down into four different levels, as Posgate and McRoberts (1976:2-3) (in their analysis of Quebec) and Easton (1965) did. At the first level is a *policy* of a given government. At the second level are the *incumbents* in political office. At the third level is the *regime* or constitutional structures and division of powers between governments. At the fourth and highest level is the *political community*, or the sense of territory and peoplehood upon which the state is based. By the end of the 1970s Indians had challenged the legitimacy of the status quo on all four of these levels. For instance, Indians rejected such policies as the extinguishing of aboriginal title in land claims settlements, not to mention any policy which was reminiscent of the 1969 White Paper. At the level of incumbents, Indians have repeatedly called for the resignation or replacement of various Ministers of DIAND, of various DIAND and IIAP officials, and initially seemed pleased at the 1979 ouster of the Trudeau Liberals. At the level of the regime, Indians reject the notion of the pervasive authority of the Minister of Indian Affairs and rejected the division of powers suggested in the federal government's proposals (the band constitution system of Indian government) for amending the Indian Act. Finally, lacking a strong identity with Canada and guided by ethnic nationalism, Indians partially rejected the existing Canadian political community in favour of ethnically based political jurisdictions (e.g., the Dene nation) for themselves. In light of these various levels of challenge to the legitimacy of the status quo, it is clear that yet another fundamental thread for weaving together disparate elements of society is lacking in the Indian-nonIndian relationship.

A third potentially integrative factor in society is a shared identity. Inasmuch as Eurocanadian society pushed Indians to the economic, political, social, and geographic periphery, it can hardly expect Indians to share and cherish an identity as Canadians. Instead, reports suggest that Indian identity is anchored in tribal and band affiliations, in the relation to the land, and for some, in the individual's relation to the Great Spirit. Efforts at propagating a pan-Indian identity in Canada or even a Fourth World identity internationally also militate against the adoption of a Canadian identity by Indians. With Indians taking on greater control over the school as an institution of socialization, under the policy of Indian control of Indian education, this separateness of identity may become even more pronounced.

Certain other means of integration are commonly found in some societies, but not in the Indian-nonIndian relationship in Canada. For instance, employment by a government which transcends ethnic divisions can bind together members of different ethnic groups under a commitment to some shared goals and ideals. Yet Indians in Canada, to the minimal extent that they are employed by the federal state at all, tend to be employed at the junior and menial levels—levels where commitment is not likely to be engendered. Political patronage can also serve integrative functions; yet the electoral impact of Canadian Indians has been almost negligible, with the result that federal politicians have viewed patronage towards Indians as unnecessary. In the absence of all else, economic exchange and interdependence (sometimes coupled with coercion) have proven sufficient to integrate some societies (e.g., South Africa). In Canada, even this has been only partially operative, for Indian-nonIndian economic exchange has for over a century been highly asymmetrical, with Indians in the dependent position. Finally, as Mazrui (1969:346) has argued, "The crucial capacity to be cultivated in the integrative process is the art of conflict resolution." However, in Indian affairs in Canada, conflicts have often been left unresolved (e.g., Indian Act revisions in the 1970s), or have been resolved only through the imposition of the will of the dominant nonIndian sector (e.g., treaties) or through the imposition of a settlement by a third party arbitrator (e.g., the courts). Rare have been the occasions where the two sides have successfully gone through the give and take of compromise. Thus, Indians and nonIndians in Canada lack the cumulative experience of conflict resolution—experience which can provide precedents, momentum, and motivation for resolving new conflicts as they arise.

The foregoing is not intended to suggest that Indians are totally unintegrated with the larger nonIndian society, for integration is both multifaceted and a matter of degree. Turning now to the ways in which Indians *are* integrated into Canadian society, we note that integration has occurred at the level of individuals through extensive intermarriage and co-habitation (Chapter Two), through assimilation, through the establishment of patron-client relations (Dosman, 1972:56) with IIAP officials, or through other types of economic dependency. As discussed in earlier chapters, co-optation of Indian individuals and organizations into the nonIndian power structure (bureaucratic or political) has also been attempted by IIAP, albeit with variable success. In addition, Indians' involvement in lobbying government is evidence of a certain degree of integration with the larger society. (Yet even here there are definite limitations to the extent of Indian-nonIndian integration, but one illustration of which is the resort by Indians on several occasions to other political arenas outside Canada.[3])

Valentine (1978) has identified yet other means through which attempts have been made to integrate Indians into the larger nonIndian society. He notes, for instance, that the 1969 White Paper tried to integrate Indians by denying them special legal status and by including them within the ambit of regular provincial responsibilities and services. To a degree this is happening today (although the federal government retains its financial obligations). Indian capitalism is another integrative mechanism cited by Valentine and it can be seen at work in IIAP-sponsored Indian economic development projects as well as in provisions of certain land claims settlements. Finally, Valentine cites what he calls "incorporation through bureaucratic extension," one modern example of which would be the Indian administration of IIAP programs which we described in Chapter Six.

Thus, the Indian and nonIndian sectors of Canadian society are integrated to a certain degree, and in their importance to the elites of that larger society, Indians have unquestionably moved from the sidelines of Canadian society back onto the main stage with the other players. Indians *have* moved out of irrelevance. However, the Indian performance is played by different rules and for a different audience. That performance is unpredictable and unsettling to the directors of the larger nonIndian society who in the 1980s have the task of trying to bring Indians into the fold where their actions will be more predictable, and therefore more co-ordinated with those of nonIndians and less capable of disrupting or embarrassing the nonIndian elite and the larger nonIndian society. Such a task, of course, harkens back to our earlier discussion of the social control functions of IIAP.

LIBERALISM AND MODES OF ETHNIC INCORPORATION

The matter of the integration of Indians into the larger Canadian society can be pursued at a more abstract level using the concept of "modes of incorporation." The sociological literature has identified three main modes of incorporating racial or ethnic groups into a larger society (Smith, 1969:430ff). The first, called *differential incorporation*, involves the differential distribution of civil and political rights among different racial or ethnic groups. In its extreme form this institutionalized and legalized discrimination can be found in South Africa today, but in a milder form it also characterized Indian-nonIndian relations in Canada from at least the early nineteenth century onwards. The second mode of incorporation is called *universalistic* (or *uniform*) *incorpora-*

tion. Here individuals are incorporated directly into the public domain as co-equal individuals, without any intermediary role being played by any membership in a racial or ethnic sector or organization. Significantly, Smith himself (1969:435) has described this as radical political individualism which is inherently assimilative in both its orientation and its effect. In seeking to root out the discrimination of the prevailing differential mode of incorporation, the Trudeau government's 1969 White Paper opted for this universalistic mode of incorporation. Finally, there is *equivalent incorporation*, which Smith (1969:434) has described as a consociation of complementary or equivalent, but mutually exclusive, racial or ethnic groups; membership in one of which is a prerequisite for citizenship in the wider political unit. Thus, in this third mode of incorporation there exist *group rights*, while in the second mode there exist only *individual rights*.

The fundamental conflict of Indian affairs in Canada, which will have to be addressed in the 1980s, is between the desire of the nonIndian political elite (and of their constituents[4]) to incorporate Indians into Canadian society on a *universalistic* basis, and the desire of at least the Indian political elite for Indians to be incorporated into Canadian society on the basis of the *equivalency* (consociational) mode. To understand this we have to understand the liberal ideology or philosophy which, as Marchak (1975) notes, is the dominant ideology of North America. The description of that philosophy, which Jones (1972:144ff) relates preparatory to his analysis of its role in the Quebec situation, is as useful for our purposes as it was for his. Accordingly, we draw primarily from him in discussing that philosophy below.

Under the philosophy of liberalism, individual rights are supreme and group rights are an anathema, particularly in the sense of special rights being granted on the basis of racial criteria. To the liberal, government ("the state") is first and foremost an instrument for maintaining law and order, achieving economic and social progress, and creating the conditions of individual liberty. Based on reason and rationality, it is the antithesis of the emotionalism which underlies the notion of the "nation state." For the liberal the state also has social obligations such as ensuring that material goods and rights are distributed in a rational and just fashion among its citizens. On the other hand, the nation state, which is to say the governing body of a political unit whose boundaries are coterminous with those of the ethnic group, distinguishes certain types of individuals—calling them "nationals"—and in pursuing its primary obligation of protecting their best interests is bound to discriminate against non-nationals. The liberal is particularly concerned that that discrimination by the nation state will be of an authoritarian character. Furthermore, the liberal points out that the individual in the nation state has other interests (e.g., those stemming from his/her occupation, education, social position, etc.) than those which stem from his/her ethnicity. The nation state is thus seen by the liberal as being unrealistic in expecting to be able to exact from the individual full devotion to the ethnic cause. Finally, liberal philosophers believe that the nation state is bound to destroy itself because minorities will continually be discovered within a majority and those minority groups will then develop a sense of ethnicity and will seek to secede to form their own new nation state.

Pierre Trudeau firmly adheres to this liberal philosophy. It now seems clear that the kinds of ethnically-based political organization which Indian leaders sought in the 1970s (e.g., in the Dene Declaration reproduced in Appendix B) and still seek in the 1980s, are seen by Trudeau and his intellectual followers as moving in the direction of the nation state, particularly in northern Canada. The Trudeau government could not philosophically bring itself to accept the notion of a Dene nation in the Canadian North, for it feared for the individual rights of the non-Dene who would be included within the territory of such a quasi nation state. Similarly, in southern Canada local government by Indian bands could only be allowed to reach certain limits before the nation state would, to a degree, be approximated in a de facto sense.

It is precisely those limits which are one of the main foci of Indian-government conflict today. The Trudeau government and its representatives in the senior echelons of DIAND and IIAP were prepared to grant to Indians a form of cultural pluralism with certain social and structural concomitants. They were prepared also, in accordance with liberal philosophy, to grant Indians participatory democracy and to help Indians attain their "rightful place" in Canadian society. In their world view, that "rightful place" falls far short of political autonomy for Indians. Indeed, even the Hawthorn report's advocacy of a "citizens plus" status for Indians does not fit well with the liberal ideology. Resigning themselves to the realities of our historical legacy, government officials instead made the fulfillment of the government's "lawful obligations" one of the cornerstones of its Indian policy of the 1970s and 1980s. While any policy shying away from fulfillment of such lawful obligations would have been unthinkable political suicide, it is nevertheless worth noting that the restrictive, past orientation of the lawful obligations policy contrasted markedly with what Indians were seeking, namely a far greater political autonomy more along the lines of sovereignty-association[5] than mere cultural pluralism or participatory democracy. The "tinkering" with the status quo which policies of cultural pluralism and participatory democracy offered was clearly unacceptable to Indians, who as we noted earlier in this section, were rejecting certain parts of the very political regime and political community of Canada.[6] Furthermore, if Peter (1979) is correct in his critique of the government's cultural pluralism policy ("multiculturalism within a bilingual framework'') as being primarily intended to exclude the non-British and non-French from the positions of real power at the top of society, then Indians' rejection of this policy being applied to them emerges as being politically very astute.[7]

We have already stated our belief that despite its denials, the Trudeau government had made the conscious decision to adopt a "Native policy" encompassing status Indians under the same rubric and programs as Métis, nonstatus Indians, and Inuit people. Indications from the early days of the Clark regime are that this policy lived on, at least in the bureaucracy. Inasmuch as we do expect it to be implemented (albeit in a subtle and piecemeal fashion) during the 1980s, we cite it here as but one example of the marriage of the universalistic mode of incorporation and the liberal philosophy—a marriage which is also embodied in some other policies and practices in the Indian affairs realm.

The basic feature, then, of the Native policy is the eroding of the special *group* rights and privileges of registered Indians and their replacement by specific programs (e.g., the 1978 Native participation program of Treasury Board) for all Native *individuals*. That is, the policy sidesteps the issue of the unique legal rights of registered Indians and treats the overall "Native peoples problem" as a social problem afflicting not a legally constituted racial or ethnic group, but rather an aggregate of individuals. Of course, if the situation were to become defined and structured in these terms, then the way would be paved for status Indians to be treated just like any other provincial citizens in terms of their eligibility for the receipt of provincial government services and to be treated just like any other ethnic group in terms of the federal government's multiculturalism policy. The cynic might add that the way would also be paved for the federal government to withdraw from or pull back on its funding agreements with the provinces, thereby leaving Indians "out in the cold," caught in the middle between two feuding levels (federal and provincial) of government. However, for the Native policy to make it to first base, so to speak, it is necessary for the federal government to blunt the opposing thrust by status Indians for retrenchment of special rights and status in the Canadian constitution.

By early 1978 the federal government and the NIB had reached a stalemate; the Joint NIB/Cabinet Committee had broken down, not coincidentally, on the matter of whether Indian demands should be treated as matters of fundamental group rights ("You have not convinced us" said the Liberal Cabinet Minister Marc Lalonde.) or as matters of special privileges and "maximum access" for Indian individuals. The stalemate was still in effect at the time the Trudeau Liberals were ousted from office in 1979. With the change in incumbents, Indian hopes for moving out of that stalemate were raised and a new sense of opportunity for progress prevailed at NIB. However, the standoff continued, in part because the senior bureaucrats advising the government changed very little, but in larger part because the liberal philosophy of individualism and universalistic incorporation is the prevailing ideology of most of North America, not just of the Liberal Party of Canada.

INDIAN AFFAIRS IN THE 1980s

As we embark upon the 1980s it is impossible to predict with any certainty either how the fundamental conflict between the universalistic and equivalency modes of incorporation will be resolved, if at all, or what shape Indian affairs will assume during the decade. In concluding we offer some thoughts on some possible accommodations and their determinants.

First and foremost, the future of Indian affairs depends upon the nature of Indian leadership. What our research has not permitted us to discern is the extent to which the current Indian political elite, which is pressing Indian nationalism so hard, is in tune with the grass roots level Indian community. It may be that the contemporary Indian political elite is not in tune with the grass roots. For instance, a senior IIAP official reported late in 1979 that it has been his experience that Indians at the band level do not attach a high priority to the constitutional revisions which NIB has been aggressively pursuing as one of its top priorities. Although he found that bands did not oppose NIB's efforts vis-à-vis the Canadian constitution, the bands are, he says, more interested in such matters as achieving a reduction in IIAP's daily control over band affairs. In addition, such events as the outcome of the 1979 referendum on the Blood reserve in Alberta raise the question of the extent to which, or at least the circumstances under which, the collectivistic orientation which underlies so much of NIB's efforts is actually shared by individual band members.[8]

If the national Indian leaders are not in tune with the grass roots, and if these leaders are challenged by other Indian politicians who promise greater grass roots benefits through working in co-operation with the government rather than engaging in confrontational politics, an entirely new Indian political leadership may come to the fore. Such an eventuality would likely mute Indian nationalism and relegate many of the remaining nationalistic demands to the realm of public posturing.

It is quite likely, especially under this first scenario, that the functions of the Indian and Inuit Affairs Programme of DIAND will shift drastically. Provincial governments and other federal government departments will likely come to deliver most services to Indians. Although continuing to administer the Minister's trust responsibilities and perhaps also Indian lands, the primary mandate of an IIAP much reduced in size will probably be to provide advice and support to bands, to co-ordinate the services of other federal government departments, and in Valentine's (1978:36) view, to serve as a mediator or conflict manager in disputes between Indians and provincial agencies.

Another major determinant of Indian affairs in the 1980s will be various developments in relations between Quebec and Canada. Notwithstanding Indians' objections to being compared with Quebec, the progress of Indians towards *negotiated* Indian sovereignty will, in our opinion, be very much affected by Quebec's progress towards sovereignty-association. If the Quebec referendum opens the flood-gate to constitutional change and succeeds in establishing in Canada a political ethos of experimentation and flexibility—and we can by no means be assured that it will—Indians too should benefit. If, however, the Canadian response to the Quebec referendum is one of retrenchment or the development of a view of the remainder of Canada as a monolithic Anglo society, it is difficult to imagine how Indians could buck the tide and negotiate significantly greater nationalistic autonomy.

Yet it is also difficult to imagine Indians not seeking to expand the scope and authority of local Indian government in the 1980s. The Indian baby boom children will be entering the labour force equipped, in increasing numbers, with a post-secondary education, high aspirations, and a sense of cultural pride. With the cities having lost some of their glitter, it is reasonable to expect that large numbers of Indians will choose to stay on the reserves. Thus, in parallel fashion to the provincial government for Québécois, local band or tribal government will likely emerge as a major employer of this new aspiring middle class of Indians. To meet those needs there will likely be strong pressures to expand the scope and authority of such local governments. Furthermore, such pressures will also arise from the efforts of bands to compete with off-reserve employers for those highly skilled Indians who might otherwise be less attracted to employment on the reserves and more attracted to off-reserve urban employment.

Notwithstanding our earlier reference to the referendum on the Blood reserve, it is our belief that Indians in Canada in the last decades of the twentieth century are going to be highly involved in the local counterpart of a developmental process known as "nation building."[9] By this we refer to the development of social solidarity, of shared collective goals, and of an institutional and economic base that will enable the sociopolitical unit (e.g., the band or group of bands) to exercise a much greater degree of self-determination. This involves a transfer of meaningful powers from the federal government to the local band or tribal level, especially to local level Indian governments. For it to be successful, Indians are going to have to capture or otherwise build a *resource base*, which thus stands as another crucial determinant of the shape of Indian affairs in the 1980s.

We use the term "resource base" very broadly to refer not just to natural resources, but also to other tools—such as money and legitimacy—which can be used to promote Indian development. There are several potential sources for such a resource base. For instance, these resources can be amassed through claims settlements, from the private sector (e.g., foundations and corporations), from the exploitation of natural resources, and from agencies external to Canada. However, one of the most potent sources of all is the Indian population itself. As one provincial Indian leader said to the authors in a discussion about the potential funding role of philanthropic foundations,

> I tell my people "If you want to go to outside sources like foundations that's fine, but make sure beforehand that you've got a plan of action for how you're going to get the project done by yourself anyway if they refuse you the money".

This philosophy of self-reliance is an invaluable tool in the "nation building" or "band-building" phenomenon, in part because it is simultaneously one of the goals of the development phenomenon.

That same Indian leader told us that he tells his people, "If something must be done, go out and *do* it if you have to, regardless of the legality of it." This is precisely how we expect Indian development to proceed in the 1980s if success is not achieved in attempts to negotiate greater sovereignty for local level Indian govenments. That is, if government continues to resist explicit constitutional recognition of Indian rights and sovereignty, Indians will *unilaterally assert* such sovereignty, as has already been done by some bands on fishing and tax (toll) collecting matters. While IIAP may acquiesce in such de facto local sovereignty, other federal departments (e.g., Fisheries) are not likely to. Similarly, past history suggests that within Indian communities, disputes will arise as aggrieved or aspiring clans or individuals challenge the actions of band governments[10] and seek to draw the government into local disputes. These clashes involving band or tribal level governments against the federal government have already entered the courts and may well only be resolved at the level of the Supreme Court of Canada. Alternatively, or subsequently, Indians may attempt to go outside the domestic legal and political arena to some external body such as the United Nations in an attempt to counter the federal government. Our interviews suggest that this is not a remote possibility. With the "Third World" dominance of the contemporary United Nations, such a move could mark the beginning of a whole new era in Indian affairs in Canada.

CONCLUSION

The foundations upon which Canadian society was constructed are today rather shaky. The structures (e.g., Act of Union, BNA Act, treaties, Indian Act, and Macdonald's "National Policy") erected in the nineteenth century to benefit economic and political special interest groups (McInnis, 1959; Clement, 1975) defied certain realities of geography, race, ethnicity, language, and culture. Canada was built upon the *conquest* of the French and the *colonization* of the aboriginal peoples. Just as the conquest is indelibly etched in the psyche of French Canadians, so too is white racism indelibly imprinted in the psyche of Indian people. There it festers and generates a deep distrust, skepticism, and sometimes even hatred of whites and their government. In such a situation, band-aid solutions are futile. What is necessary is radical surgery—in this case the construction of a whole new relationship between Indians and the larger society. The pillars of the old structures of accommodation are crumbling (Gibbins and Ponting, 1978:52-3) and Indians are demanding a new accommodation be struck between Indians and the larger society. In reaching those new accommodations, especially to the extent that they are de jure rather than de facto, enormous problems will be encountered. As the IIAP director of policy observed,

> There's so much to be done. It's like an avalanche of issues. . . . It's like trying to move a ship with your two baby fingers. . . . It requires an almost unbelievable orchestration of forces like a finale at a concert where all the instruments come into play at once. If any one musician is out of tune—any one Minister or Assistant Deputy Minister of NIB member organization—then the whole thing falls flat.

The title of this book identifies it as being merely an introduction to the field. Thus, we have identified only some of those many issues and "musicians" to which the director of policy referred, and have explored only some of the structures and dynamics underlying them. Much remains to be done by academics and by practitioners. Some of the problems, especially the fundamental underlying problems, may in fact not be solvable within the present institutional context at the local and societal levels. It is the hope of the authors, though, that this book will directly or indirectly prove useful to those who are willing to try to develop new and more facilitative institutional structures and processes.

NOTES

1. Data provided by IIAP in late 1979 indicate that under the policy of Indian control of Indian education there are now 3 Indian provincial school

boards, 104 band school authorities with total control, and 405 band school committees exercising partial control.

2. The reference here is to the Christian (particularly Roman Catholic) emphasis upon accepting one's lot in this life in expectation of reward in the after-life (e.g., "The last shall be first and the first shall be last").

3. Examples of Indians resorting to external political arenas include the attainment by NIB of Non-Governmental Organization status at the United Nations, NIB's involvement in the formation of the WCIP, and the Chiefs' lobbying trip to England in July 1979. Other indications of the limits of Indian integration into the Canadian political system can be found in the lack of organized Indian participation in contributing to the election campaigns of the major parties, and perhaps even in the frequent use of issue-oriented lobbying rather than institutionalized lobbying. (See Chapter Nine.)

4. That the larger nonIndian society favours a universalistic mode of incorporation for Indians is suggested by responses to one of the questions in our national survey. Eighty-seven percent of our respondents agreed with the statement "the federal government should treat all Canadians alike, regardless of their ethnic background." Conversely, a plurality (44% vs 36%) of respondents in that same survey agreed with the statement "Indians, as the first Canadians, should have special cultural protection that other groups don't have."

5. Although Indian political aspirations are in some respects similar to sovereignty-association, one significant difference emerges with regard to taxation. Whereas the Quebec version of sovereignty-association involves expanded powers of taxation for the Quebec government within Quebec, Indians seek control of revenues raised outside the Indian polity.

6. Although Indians were rejecting parts of the political regime and community of Canada, that rejection by no means extended to the entire Canadian regime and community. For instance, Indians continued to stress the importance of treaty and other legal and constitutional obligations of the Canadian federal government towards them, and to seek entrenchment of special Indian rights in the constitution (a form of equivalent incorporation).

7. According to Peter (1979), the federal government's bilingualism and multiculturalism policies are containment strategies which try to take the aspirations for power on the part of the non-English and deflect those aspirations into linguistic or cultural forms of equality. The multiculturalism policy would be seen as being designed to buy off the compliance of the non-English non-French ethnic groups and thereby legitimize and justify the bilingualism policy.

8. The referendum, which was forced upon the band council by a petition circulated on the reserve, was on the issue of what to do with $11.4 million in revenues from the sale of exploration permits and oil and gas leases. Band members voted by a ten-to-one margin in favour of distributing the money directly to individual band members (almost $2,200 to every man, woman and child), rather than investing it in collective enterprises of the band. However, this referendum cannot be taken as a litmus test for the presence of the individualistic versus collectivistic orientation as the band has a history of investing band revenues in band collective enterprises. Some of those who voted in favour of the per capita distribution simply wanted to

ensure that they would benefit from the windfall rather than having the windfall invested in new economic development projects which, like some of the earlier ones, might fail to turn a profit.

9. Québècois have referred to a very similar phenomenon as building "une société globale". Richards and Pratt (1979), in referring to the development of Western Canada, use the term "province building" in a somewhat similar way.

10. Such challenges are particularly likely in those situations in which there emerges the very authoritarianism that liberal philosophers fear—bands which, in Harold Cardinal's terms, are ruled by "village tyrants".

Bibliography

Adams, Howard, 1975. *Prison of Grass: Canada From The Native Point of View*. Toronto: General Publishing.

Anonymous, 1978. "Special Edition: Discussion Paper for Indian Act Revision." *Indian News*. Ottawa: IIAP.

Arlett, Allen (ed.), 1973. *A Canadian Directory to Foundations and Other Granting Agencies*. Third Edition. Ottawa: Association of Universities and Colleges of Canada.

Arlett, Allen (ed.), 1978. *A Canadian Directory to Foundations and Other Granting Agencies*. Fourth Edition, Ottawa: Association of Universities and Colleges of Canada.

Badcock, William T., 1976. *Who Owns Canada: Aboriginal Title and Canadian Courts*. Ottawa: Canadian Association in Support of the Native Peoples.

Bernard, Howard, 1978. "New H.Q. for D.O.T.C." *Indian News*. 19, 7:1.

Berry, John, W., Rudolf Kalen and Donald M. Taylor, 1977. *Multiculturalism and Ethnic Attitudes in Canada*. Ottawa: Minister of Supply and Services.

Bibby, Reginald W., 1975. "Code Book for Project Canada: A Study of Deviance, Diversity, and Devotion in Canada." Lethbridge: University of Lethbridge, Mimeo.

Breton, Raymond and Gail Grant Akian, 1978. "Urban Institutions and People of Indian Ancestry." Montreal: Institute for Research on Public Policy, Mimeo.

Brown, Dee A., 1971. *Bury My Heart at Wounded Knee: An Indian History of the American West*. New York: Holt, Rinehart, and Winston.

Brown, Marion C., 1978. *Native Claims: Policy, Processes, and Perspectives*. Ottawa: Office of Native Claims, DIAND.

Canadian Association in Support of the Native Peoples, 1978. "Factsheet #4: Native Health." Ottawa, Mimeo.

Canadian Press, 1975. "Natives Want Own House Style." *Calgary Herald*. March 11:10.

Canadian Press, 1978a, "NIB Withdrawal is Cop-out: Faulkner." *Calgary Herald.* April 14:D15.

Canadian Press, 1978b, "Spending Cuts May Spark 'White Backlash', Indians Fear." *Calgary Herald.* Sept. 20:A10.

Canadian Press, 1979a, "Parole Tougher for Native Males." *Calgary Herald.* March 6:D15.

Canadian Press, 1979b, "Legal Fees Unsettled After James Bay Pact." *Calgary Herald.* April 24:B13.

Cardinal, Harold, 1969. *The Unjust Society.* Edmonton: M. G. Hurtig.

Cardinal, Harold, 1977. *The Rebirth of Canada's Indians.* Edmonton: M. G. Hurtig.

Chamberlin, J. E., 1975. *The Harrowing of Eden.* Toronto: Fitzhenry & Whiteside.

Clement, Wallace, 1975. *The Canadian Corporate Elite: An Analysis of Economic Power.* Toronto: McClelland and Stewart.

Coles, Robert, 1964. "Social Struggle and Weariness." *Psychiatry.* 27, 4:305-315.

Community Services Branch, 1979. *Housing Needs Analysis Survey, 1977.* Ottawa: IIAP.

Corporate Personnel Group, 1979. *Action Plans For Increased Native Employment in DIAND.* Ottawa: DIAND.

Costo, Robert and Jeanette Henry (eds.), 1970. *Textbooks and the American Indian.* San Francisco: Indian Historical Press.

Cumming, Peter and Neil Mickenberg, 1972. *Native Rights in Canada.* Don Mills: General Publishing and CASNP.

Department of Finance, 1979a. *Public Accounts of Canada, 1977-78.* Ottawa: Department of Supply and Services.

Department of Finance, 1979b. *Estimates, 1979-80.* Ottawa: Department of Supply and Services.

Department of Indian and Northern Affairs, 1977. "Management Information Package: Indian, Metis, Nonstatus Indians and Inuit Employment." Ottawa Mimeo.

Doerr, A. D., 1974. "Indian Policy." pp. 36-54 in G. Bruce Doern and V. Seymour Wilson (eds.), *Issues in Canadian Public Policy.* Toronto: Macmillan.

Dosman, Edgar, 1972. *Indians: The Urban Dilemma.* Toronto: McClelland and Stewart.

Dunning, R. W., 1962. "Some Aspects of Governmental Indian Policy and Administration." *Anthropologica.* 4, 1:209-232.

Easton, David, 1965. *A Systems Analysis of Political Life.* New York: Wiley.

Franks, C. E. S., 1971. "The Dilemma of the Standing Committees of the Canadian House of Commons." *Canadian Journal of Political Science.* 4, 4:461-476.

Frideres, James S., 1974. *Canada's Indians: Contemporary Conflicts.* Scarborough: Prentice-Hall.

Frideres, James S., 1978. "Indian Identity and Social Conflict." pp. 217-234 in Leo Dreidger (ed.), *The Canadian Ethnic Mosaic: A Quest For Identity.* Toronto: McClelland and Stewart.

Frideres, James S., "Native People in Canada: A Structural Analysis," in S. Bolaria (ed.), *Oppressed Minorities in Canada: Colonized People and Non-White Immigrants.* Scarborough: Butterworths, forthcoming.

Fumoleau, Rene, 1976. *As Long As This Land Shall Last.* Toronto: McClelland and Stewart.

Gamson, William A., 1968. *Power and Discontent.* Homewood, Ill.: Dorsey.

Gibbins, Roger and J. Rick Ponting, 1976a, "Public Opinion and Canadian Indians: A Preliminary Probe." *Canadian Ethnic Studies.* 8, 2:1-17.

Gibbins, Roger and J. Rick Ponting, 1976b, "Public Opinion Cartography: The Native Peoples Issues in Canada." Paper presented to the Canadian Political Science Association, Quebec, Quebec.

Gibbins, Roger and J. Rick Ponting, 1977. "Contemporary Prairie Perceptions of Canada's Native Peoples." *Prairie Forum.* 2, 1:57-81.

Gibbins, Roger and J. Rick Ponting, 1978. "Prairie Canadians' Orientations Towards Indians." pp. 82-102 in Ian Getty and Donald Smith (eds.) *One Century Later: Western Canadian Reserve Indians Since Treaty Seven.* Vancouver: University of British Columbia Press.

Goffman, Erving, 1959. *Asylums: Essays on the Social Situation of Mental Patients and Other Inmates.* New York: Doubleday.

Government of Canada, 1969. *Statement of the Government of Canada on Indian Policy.* Ottawa: DIAND.

Green, Leslie C., 1969. *Canada's Indians—Federal Policy, International and Constitutional Law.* Edmonton: Government of Alberta.

Guillemin, Jeanne, 1978. "The Politics of National Integration: A Comparison of United States and Canadian Indian Administrations." *Social Problems.* 24, 3:319-332.

Harper, Allan G., 1945. "Canada's Indian Administration: Basic Concepts and Objectives." *America Indigena.* 4, 2:119-132.

Harper, Allan G., 1946. "Canada's Administration." *America Indigena.* 5, 3:297-314.

Harper, Allan G., 1947. "Canada's Indian Administration: The Treaty System." *America Indigena.* 7, 2:129-140.

Hawthorn, Harry B., Cyril S. Belshaw and Stuart M. Jamison, 1960. *The Indians of British Columbia: A Study of Contemporary Social Adjustment.* Toronto: University of Toronto Press.

Hawthorn, Harry B. et al, 1967a, *A Survey of the Contemporary Indians of Canada: A Report on Economic, Political, Educational Needs and Policies, Volume I.* Ottawa: Queen's Printer.

Hawthorn et al, 1967b, *A Survey of the Contemporary Indians of Canada: A Report on Economic, Political, Educational Needs and Policies, Volume II.* Ottawa: Queen's Printer.

Hendry, Charles E., 1969. *Beyond Traplines.* Toronto: Anglican Church of Canada.

Hoople, Joanne, 1976, *And What About Canada's Native Peoples?.* Ottawa: CASNP.

Indian Chiefs of Alberta, 1970. *Citizens Plus.* A Presentation to Right Honourable P. E. Trudeau, Prime Minister, and the Government of Canada.

Jamieson, Kathleen, 1978. *Indian Women and the Law in Canada: Citizens Minus.* Ottawa: Ministry of Supply and Services Canada.

Jamieson, Roberta, 1979. "Viewpoints on Indian Government." pp. 23-35 in Jessica Mahkewa and Gail McDonald (eds.), *Indian Government Development Conference.* Ottawa: National Indian Brotherhood.

Jefferson, Christie, 1976. "Justice For Natives Exposed." *Discussion.* 4, 4:9-10.

Jenness, Diamond, 1960. *The Indians of Canada.* Fifth Edition, Ottawa: National Museum of Canada.

Jones, Richard, 1972. *Community in Crisis: French Canadian Nationalism in Perspective.* Toronto: McClelland and Stewart.

Kroeber, Alfred L., 1939. *Cultural and Natural Areas of Native North America.* University of California Publications in American Archaeology and Ethnology: 38. Berkeley: University of California Press.

Lachance-Brulotte, G., 1975. *La nuptialité des indiens inscrits du Canada, 1966-74.* Mémoire présenté à la Faculté des Etudes Supérieures en vue de l'obtention de la maîtrise en sciences (démographie). Montreal: Départment de Démographie, Université de Montreal.

Levy, Charles J., 1968. *Voluntary Servitude: Whites In The Negro Movement.* New York: Appleton-Century-Crofts.

Lipset, Seymour M. and Earl Raab, 1970. *The Politics of Unreason: Right Wing Extremism in America, 1790-1970.* New York: Harper and Row.

Little Bear, Leroy, 1979. Address to XXth Annual Meetings of the Western Association of Sociology and Anthropology, Lethbridge, Alberta.

Lyman, Peter, 1979. "A Challenge for Tory Ministers: Find the Key to the Bureaucracy." *Globe and Mail.* June 12:7.

Lysyk, Kenneth, 1967. "The Unique Constitutional Position of the Canadian Indian." *Canadian Bar Review.* 45, 3:513-553.

Lysyk, Kenneth, 1968. "Human Rights and the Native Peoples of Canada." *Canadian Bar Review.* 46, 4:695-705.

Macdonald, R. St. J., 1970. *Native Rights in Canada.* Toronto: Indian-Eskimo Association.

Macdonnell, James J., 1976. *Report of the Auditor General of Canada to the House of Commons for the Fiscal Year Ended March 31, 1976.* Ottawa: Department of Supply and Services.

Macdonnell, James J., 1978. *Report of the Auditor General of Canada to the House of Commons for the Fiscal Year Ended March 31, 1978*. Ottawa: Department of Supply and Services.

MacInnes, T. R. L., 1946. "History of Indian Administration in Canada." *Canadian Journal of Economics and Political Science*. 12, 3:387-394.

Mackie, Marlene M., 1974. "Ethnic Stereotypes and Prejudice: Alberta Indians, Hutterites, and Ukrainians." *Canadian Ethnic Studies*. 6, 1-2:39-52.

Manuel, George, 1972. "President's Report to the General Assembly." Ottawa: National Indian Brotherhood, Mimeo.

Manuel, George and Michael Posluns, 1974. *The Fourth World: An Indian Reality*. Toronto: Collier Macmillan.

March, Roman R., 1974. *The Myth of Parliament*. Scarborough: Prentice-Hall.

Marchack, M. Patricia, 1975. *Ideological Perspectives on Canada*. Toronto: McGraw-Hill Ryerson.

Maslow, Abraham H., 1965. *Eupsychian Management*. Homewood, Illinois: Irwin and Dorsey.

Mazrui, Ali A., 1969. "Pluralism and National Integration." pp. 333-349 in Leo Kuper and M. G. Smith (eds.), *Pluralism in Africa*. Berkeley and Los Angeles: University of California Press.

McCarthy, John D. and Mayer N. Zald, 1973. *The Trend of Social Movements in America: Professionalization and Resource Mobilization*. Morristown, N.J.: General Learning Press.

McCullum, Hugh and Karmel McCullum, 1975. *This Land Is Not For Sale*. Toronto: Anglican Book Centre.

McCullum, Hugh, Karmel McCullum and John Olthuis, 1977. *Moratorium: Justice, Energy, The North, and the Native People*. Toronto: Anglican Book Centre.

McDiarmid, Garnet and David Pratt, 1971. *Teaching Prejudice: A Content Analysis of Social Studies Textbooks Authorized For Use in Ontario*. Toronto: Ontario Institute For Studies in Education.

McInnis, Edgar, 1959. *Canada: A Political and Social History*. Toronto: Holt, Rinehart and Winston.

McWorter, Gerald A. and Robert L. Crain, 1971. "Subcommunity Gladiatorial Competition: Civil Rights Leadership as a Competitive Process." pp. 105-123 in James A. Geschwender (ed.), *The Black Revolt: The Civil Rights Movement, Ghetto Uprisings, and Separatism*. Englewood Cliffs, New Jersey: Prentice-Hall, Inc.

Medical Services Branch, 1978. *Health Data Book*. Ottawa: Department of National Health and Welfare.

Medical Services Branch, n.d. *Suicide Prevention Among British Columbia Indians: Guidelines For Helpers*. Vancouver: Department of National Health and Welfare.

Melling, John, 1967. *The Right To A Future: The Native Peoples of Canada*. Toronto: Anglican Book Centre.

Miller, Kahn-Tineta et al, 1978. *Historical Development of the Indian Act.* Ottawa: Department of Indian and Northern Affairs.

Native Council of Canada, 1976. *Pilot Study of Canadian Public Perceptions and Attitudes Concerning Aboriginal Rights and Land Claims.* Ottawa.

National Indian Brotherhood, 1978, "A Review and Critique of Bill C-60, An Act to Amend The Constitution of Canada." Ottawa.

Oliver, Christine et al, 1977. *A Strategy For The Socio-Ecomonic Development of Indian People: National Report.* Ottawa: National Indian Brotherhood.

Olsen, Marvin E. and Mary Ann Baden, 1974. "Legitimacy of Social Protest Actions in the United States and Sweden." *Journal of Political and Military Sociology.* 2, (Fall):173-189.

Ontario Regional Liaison Council, 1978. *O.R.L.C. Mandate.* Internal document, December 14.

Palmer, Howard, 1976. "Mosaic Versus Melting Pot?: Immigration and Ethnicity in Canada and the United States." *International Journal.* 31, 3:488-528.

Parsons, Talcott, 1965. "An Outline of the Social System." pp. 30-79 in T. Parsons, E. Shils, K. D. Naegele and J. R. Pitts, (eds.), *Theories of Society: Foundations of Modern Sociological Theory.* New York: The Free Press.

Patterson, E. Palmer II, 1972. *The Canadian Indian: A History Since 1500.* Don Mills: Collier-MacMillan.

Patterson, E. Palmer II, 1978. "Andrew Paull and the Early History of B.C. Indian Organizations." pp. 43-54 in I. A. L. Getty and D. B. Smith (eds.), *One Century Later: Western Canadian Reserve Indians Since Treaty 7.* Vancouver: University of British Columbia Press.

Peter, Karl, 1979. "The Myth of Multiculturalism and Other Political Fables." Paper presented to the Biannual Meetings of the Canadian Ethnic Studies Association, Vancouver, B.C.

Pfeffer, Jeoffrey, 1976. "Beyond Management and the Worker: The Institutional Function of Management." *The Academy of Management Review 1,* 2:36-46.

Ponting, J. Rick, 1979a, "A Preliminary Assessment of Canadian Private Foundations As Potential Sources of Funding For Projects By or About Native People: Final Report." Ottawa: Department of Indian and Northern Affairs, Mimeo.

Ponting, J. Rick, 1979b, "Private Charitable Foundations and Their Role in the Native Peoples Field." Paper presented to the XXth Annual Meeting of the Western Association of Sociology and Anthropology, Lethbridge, Alberta.

Ponting, J. Rick and Roger Gibbins, "English Canadians' and French Quebecers' Reactions To Contemporary Indian Protest." *Canadian Review of Sociology and Anthropology.* Forthcoming.

Posgate, Dale and Kenneth McRoberts, 1976. *Quebec: Social Change and Political Crisis.* Toronto: McClelland and Stewart.

Presthus, Robert, 1974. *Elites in the Policy Process.* London: Cambridge University Press.

Programme Support Group, 1979. *Listing of Information Relating to the Housing Needs Analysis, 1977.* Ottawa: IIAP.

Programme Reference Centre, 1965, 1975. *Post-Secondary Courses for Indian Students,* Ottawa: IIAP.

Programme Reference Centre, 1965, 1970, 1975. *Registered Indian Population By Age, Sex, and Residence For Canada.* Ottawa: IIAP.

Pross, A. Paul (ed.), 1975. *Pressure Group Behaviour in Canadian Politics.* Toronto: McGraw-Hill Ryerson.

Quasar Systems Ltd., 1977. "Performance Measurement in the Indian Programme." Ottawa: Department of Indian and Northern Affairs, Mimeo.

Rich, Pat, 1978. "NIB Withdraws From 'Useless' Committee." *Indian News.* 19, 2:1.

Richards, John and Larry Pratt, 1979. *Prairie Capitalism: Power and Influence in the New West.* Toronto: McClelland and Stewart.

Robertson, Gordon, 1977. "The Changing Role of the Privy Council Office." pp. 373-387 in Paul Fox (ed.), *Politics Canada.* Fourth Edition, Toronto: McGraw-Hill Ryerson.

Rocher, Guy, 1972. *A General Introduction To Sociology: A Theoretical Perspective.* (Trans. Peta Sheriff) Toronto: Macmillan of Canada.

Romaniuk, Anatole and Victor Piché, 1972. "Natality Estimates For The Canadian Indians by Stable Population Models, 1900-1969." *Canadian Review of Sociology and Anthropology.* 9, 1:1-20.

Ryan, Joan, 1978. *Wall of Words: The Betrayal of the Urban Indian.* Toronto: Peter Martin Associates.

Safety and Fire Prevention Services, 1977. *Report on Fire Losses in DIAND.* Ottawa: Engineering and Architecture Branch, Administration Programme, DIAND.

Sanders, Douglas, 1978, "The Unique Constitutional Position of the Indian." *Indians and the Law Conference.* Ottawa: National Indian Brotherhood, Mimeo.

Saskatchewan Human Rights Commission, 1974. *Prejudice in Social Studies Textbooks: A Content Analysis of Social Studies Textbooks Used in Saskatchewan Schools.* Saskatoon.

Schermerhorn, Richard A., 1970. *Comparative Ethnic Relations: A Framework for Theory and Research.* Toronto: Random House of Canada.

Schmeiser, Douglas A., 1974. *The Native Offender and The Law.* Ottawa: Information Canada.

Scott, Duncan C., 1914a, "Indian Affairs, 1840-1867." pp. 331-364 in Adam Shortt and Arthur G. Doughty (eds.), *Canada and Its Provinces, Volume V.* Toronto: Glasgow, Brook and Company.

Scott, Duncan C., 1914b, "Indian Affairs, 1867-1912." pp. 593-628 in Adam Shortt and Arthur G. Doughty (eds.), *Canada and Its Provinces, Volume VII.* Toronto: Glasgow, Brook and Company.

Sealey, D. Bruce and Antoine S. Lussier, 1975. *The Metis: Canada's Forgotten People*. Winnipeg: Manitoba Metis Federation Press.

Sellar, Don, 1977. "Statistics Show Death By Fire on Canadian Indian Reserves Is Nine Times National Average." *Calgary Herald*. August 29:70.

Shorter, Edward, 1978. "The Private Life of the Ruling Class." *Saturday Night*. October:21-28.

Simpson, Jeffrey, 1978. "Setup of House Committees Makes Progress Difficult: Analysis." *Globe and Mail*, August 3.

Smiley, Donald V., 1976. *Canada in Question: Federalism in the Seventies*. Second Edition, Toronto: McGraw-Hill Ryerson.

Smith, Derek, G. (ed.), 1975. *Canadian Indians and the Law: Selected Documents, 1663-1972*. Toronto: McClelland and Stewart.

Smith, M. G., 1969. "Some Developments in the Analytic Framework of Pluralism." pp. 415-458 in Leo Kuper and M. G. Smith (eds.), *Pluralism in Africa*. Berkeley and Los Angeles: University of California Press.

Special Committee on Procedure, 1968. *Report of the Special Committee on Procedure*. Ottawa: Queen's Printer.

Stanbury, W. T. et al., 1975. *Success and Failure: Indians in Urban Society*. Vancouver: University of British Columbia Press.

Standing Committee on Indian Affairs and Northern Development, 1978. *Minutes of the Proceedings and Evidence*. May 4: Issue No. 3.

Starblanket, Noel V., 1978a, "Report by the President of the NIB to the Ninth Annual General Assembly of the NIB." Ottawa: National Indian Brotherhood, Mimeo.

Starblanket, Noel V., 1978b, "Presentation to The Joint Senate/House of Commons Committee on Bill C-60," Ottawa: National Indian Brotherhood, Mimeo.

Starblanket, Noel V., 1978c, "Brief to the Special Senate Committee on the Northern Gas Pipeline (Bill C-25)." Ottawa: National Indian Brotherhood, Mimeo.

Statistics Canada, 1971. *Census of Canada*. Ottawa: Department of Supply and Services.

Statistics Canada, n.d., *Social Security: National Programs, 1976*. Catalogue No. 86-201.

Statistics Canada, 1977. *Perspective Canada II: A Compendium of Social Statistics, 1977*. Ottawa: Department of Industry, Trade, and Commerce.

Statistics Division, 1978. *Registered Indian Population by Sex and Residence, 1977*. Ottawa: Programme Reference Centre, IIAP. (A publication up-dated yearly.)

Stauss, Joseph, Bruce A. Chadwick and Howard M. Bahr, 1976. "Indian Americans: The First is Last." pp. 221-253 in Anthony G. Dworkin and Rosalind J. Dworkin (eds.), *The Minority Report: An Introduction to Racial, Ethnic and Gender Relations*. New York: Praeger Publishers.

Stymeist, David H., 1975. *Ethnics and Indians: Social Relations in a Northwestern Ontario Town*. Toronto: Peter Martin Associates.

Swanson, Guy E., 1971. *Social Change*. Glenview, Illinois: Scott, Foresman & Co.

T.A.P. Associates Ltd., 1979. *Review of Community Social Services to Indians in Ontario*. Toronto. (Consultant's report available from Program Evaluation Branch, IIAP, Ottawa.)

Ticoll, David and Stan Persky, 1975. "The Native Peoples' Caravan." *Canadian Dimension*. 10, 6:15-31.

Treasury Board and Public Service Commission, 1978. *Increased Participation of Indian, Metis and Nonstatus Indian and Inuit People in the Public Service of Canada*. Circular #1978-49. Ottawa.

Trudeau, Pierre Elliott, 1968. *Federalism and The French Canadians*. Toronto: Macmillan.

Turner, Ralph and Lewis Killian, 1972. *Collective Behaviour*. Englewood Cliffs, N.J.: Prentice Hall.

Upton, L. F. S., 1973. "The Origins of Canadian Indian Policy." *Journal of Canadian Studies*. 8, 4:51-61.

Valentine, Victor, 1978. "Native Peoples and National Unity: A Profile of Issues and Trends." Ottawa: Carleton University Department of Sociology and Anthropology, Mimeo.

van den Berghe, Pierre L., 1967a, *Race and Racism: A Comparative Perspective*. New York: Wiley & Sons.

van den Berghe, Pierre L., 1967b, *South Africa: A Study in Conflict*. Berkeley and Los Angeles: University of California Press.

Warden, Kathryn, 1979a, "Indian Housing Budget Falls Far Short of Needs." *Calgary Herald*, March 22:84.

Warden, Kathryn, 1979b, "Indian Resource Revenues to Double." *Calgary Herald*, December 24: A1.

Warden, Kathryn, 1979c, "Oil Cash Gives Indian Bands 'Sense of Pride'." *Calgary Herald*, December 24: B1.

Weaver, Sally M., 1973. "Segregation and the Indian Act: The Dialogue of Equality vs. Special Status." Paper presented to the Canadian Ethnic Studies Association National Conference on Canadian Culture and Ethnic Groups, Toronto, Ontario.

Weaver, Sally M., 1976. "The Role of Social Science in Formulating Canadian Indian Policy: A Preliminary History of the Hawthorn-Tremblay Report." Mimeo.

Weaver, Sally M., 1978. "Recent Directions in Canadian Indian Policy." Paper presented to the Annual Meetings of the Canadian Sociology and Anthropology Association, London, Ontario.

Weaver, Sally M., *The Hidden Agenda: Indian Policy and the Trudeau Government*. Toronto: University of Toronto Press, forthcoming.

Weber, Max, 1947. *The Theory of Social and Economic Organization*. (A. M. Henderson and Talcott Parsons, trans.; Talcott Parsons, ed.). New York and London: Free Press and Collier-Macmillan.

White, Geoff, 1978. "Cardinal's Charges Will Serve Long-term Interests of All." *Calgary Herald*, September 30:A7.

Wright, Gerald, n.d., "Professionalism in Private Philanthropy." Toronto: The Donner Canadian Foundation, Mimeo.

Wuttunee, William I. C., 1971. *Ruffled Feathers*. Calgary: Bell Books.

Zey-Ferrell, Mary, 1979. *Dimensions of Organizations*. Santa Monica Calif.: Goodyear.

Construction of the Knowledge Index

	Index Score	% Total Sample	% Anglo-phones	% Franco-phones
1. "What percentage of Canada's total population would you estimate is native Indian?"				
A. One to five percent	+3	24	26	23
B. Less than one percent, six to ten percent	+2	16	16	15
C. More than ten percent, don't know, can't estimate	+1	60	58	62
2. "To the best of your knowledge, what level of government has the *major* responsibility for dealing with Canadian Indians?"				
A. Federal government	+3	56	60	54
B. Both federal and provincial	+2	19	15	26
C. Both federal and municipal	+1	1	*	1
D. Federal, provincial and municipal	+1	6	7	2
E. Provincial	+1	7	8	6
F. Municipal	+1	1	1	*

	Index Score	% Total Sample	% Anglo-phones	% Franco-phones
G. Both provincial and municipal	+1	1	1	*
H. Other, don't know	+1	11	9	12
3. Meaning of the word "Inuit".				
A. Eskimo	+3	13	15	12
B. Northern native, "Eskimo word", "Eskimo half-breed"	+2	6	6	8
C. Other, not familiar with the term, don't know	+1	81	79	81
4. Meaning of the word "Metis".				
A. French-Indian half-breed, Indians of mixed ancestry (e.g., "halfbreed", "part Indian")	+3	42	47	38
B. Non-treaty Indian, non-status Indian, non-registered Indian, native woman married to a non-native, Indians of Western Canada	+2	4	4	*
C. Other, not familiar with the term, don't know, no opinion	+1	55	49	61
5. Meaning of the difference between 'status' and 'non-status' Indians				
A. Status Indians come under the jurisdiction of the federal government (Indian Act), while non-status Indians do not (sic)	+3	*	*	*
B. Status Indians receive government support, N-S Indians do not	+3	3	4	*
C. Status Indians registered with the government, N-S Indians do not	+3	2	2	2

	Index Score	% Total Sample	% Anglo-phones	% Franco-phones
D. Non-status Indians include native women who marry a non-native	+3	4	7	*
E. Status Indians live on reserves, N-S Indians do not	+2	11	16	3
F. Status Indians have treaty rights, N-S Indians do not	+2	4	8	1
G. N-S Indians include half-breeds, while status Indians are full-blooded	+2	2	3	*
H. Other, don't know, not familiar with the term	+1	73	59	93
6. Meaning of the term "aboriginal rights".				
A. The rights of the original inhabitants of Canada to occupy or use the land from which they made their living when whites first came	+3	5	7	1
B. The rights of Indians and/or Eskimos to control their own lives	+3	1	1	1
C. General rights of the first people here (ancestral rights, birthrights)	+2	12	15	6
D. Treaty rights of Indians	+2	3	4	1
E. The first people in Canada (no mention of rights), other, not familiar with the term, don't know	+1	80	74	92

The Dene Declaration

We the Dene of the N.W.T. insist on the right to be regarded by ourselves and the world as a nation.

Our struggle is for the recognition of the Dene Nation by the Government and people of Canada and the peoples and governments of the world.

As once Europe was the exclusive homeland of the European peoples, Africa the exclusive homeland of the African peoples, the New World, North and South America, was the exclusive homeland of Aboriginal peoples of the New World, the Amerindian and the Inuit.

The New World like other parts of the world has suffered the experience of colonialism and imperialism. Other peoples have occupied the land—often with force—and foreign governments have imposed themselves on our people. Ancient civilizations and ways of life have been destroyed.

Colonialism and imperialism are now dead or dying. Recent years have witnessed the birth of new nations or rebirth of old nations out of the ashes of colonialism.

As Europe is the place where you will find European countries with European governments for European peoples, now also you will find in Africa and Asia the existence of African and Asian countries with African and Asian governments for the African and Asian peoples.

The African and Asian peoples—the peoples of the Third World—have fought for and won the right to self-determination, the right to recognition as distinct peoples and the recognition of themselves as nations.

But in the New World the Native peoples have not fared so well. Even in countries in South America where the Native peoples are the vast majority of the population there is not one country which has an Amerindian government for the Amerindian peoples.

Nowhere in the New World have the Native peoples won the right to self-determination and the right to recognition by the world as a distinct people and as Nations.

While the Native people of Canada are a minority in their homeland, the Native people of the N.W.T., the Dene and the Inuit, are a majority of the population of the N.W.T.

The Dene find themselves as part of a country. That country is Canada. But the Government of Canada is not the government of the Dene. The Government of the N.W.T. is not the government of the Dene. These governments were not the choice of the Dene, they were imposed upon the Dene.

What we the Dene are struggling for is the recognition of the Dene Nation by the governments and peoples of the world.

And while there are realities we are forced to submit to, such as the existence of a country called Canada, we insist on the right to self-determination as a distinct peoples and the recognition of the Dene Nation.

We the Dene are part of the Fourth World. And as the peoples and Nations of the world have come to recognize the existence and rights of those peoples who make up the Third World the day must come and will come when the nations of the Fourth World will come to be recognized and respected. The challenge to the Dene and the world is to find the way for the recognition of the Dene Nation.

Our plea to the world is to help us in our struggle to find a place in the world community where we can exercise our right to self-determination as a distinct people and as a nation.

What we seek then is independence and self-determination within the country of Canada. This is what we mean when we call for a just land settlement for the Dene Nation.

INDEX

Aboriginal rights, 102
Accountability, 100, 125-126, 147, 168
Act for the Gradual Civilization of the Indian Tribes in the Canadas, 6
Administrative evolution of Indian affairs, 14-16
Administration Programme, DIAND, 97, 99
  Corporate Policy Group, 99, 100
  Corporate Personnel Group, 100
  Finance and Professional Services, 100
Agriculture, 3
Ahenakew, Dave, 200
Alcohol abuse, 58-60
Allmand, Warren, 154, 173, 174, 209, 248
American Indian Movement, 272-273
Andras, Robert, 118, 143
Anglican church, 284-285, 287
  Task Force on the North, 288
Anglophones, 86, 87, 89-90
Arlett, Allen, 291, 297
Assimilation, xvii, 5, 6, 7, 10, 11, 13, 17-19, 29, 326
Auditor-General, 100, 109, 116, 131, 159, 168, 170
Authority, concentration of, 11-12

Baby boom, 39
Backlash, public, 83
Band councils, 241
Bands, Indian, xv
  delivery of services, 182
  geographical location, 34-36
  membership, 184
  population, 34-35
  relation with IIAP, 181-188
Barber Lloyd, 154, 260
Basford, Ron, 255, 260

Beaver, Jack, 150
Begin, Monique, 240
Bennett, R. B., 15
Berger, Thomas, 209
Bernard, Howard, 153
Berry, John W., 69
Bibby, Reginald, 70
Bill of Rights, 25
"Block funding", 117, 125-126
Blood reserve referendum 1979, 331
"Boundary maintenance" mechanisms, 10
Brant, Dan, 224, 238-239
British Columbia, 16, 58
British North America Act, 6, 8, 9, 182, 184, 190, 213, 214
Brown, Dee, 205
Brown, Marion C., 101
Brown, Rod, 128, 157, 186
Buchanan, Judd, 127, 175, 258, 260
Budget, DIAND/NIB, 97-98, 115-127, 212, 213, 226
  Indian input, 117-118
  socio-fiscal control, 124-127
Bureaupolitik, 104, 156

Canadian Association in Support of the Native Peoples, 172, 269, 298-308
Canadian Indian Constitutional Commission, 211
Canadian Indian Rights Commission, 260
Canadian Press, 50, 60, 145, 265
Capitalism, Indian, 327
Cardinal, Harold, 9, 10, 11, 14, 20, 24, 28, 29, 55, 100, 103, 115, 125, 144, 147-151, 188, 198, 200, 202 205, 220, 227, 260, 318
Central Mortgage and Housing Corporation, 170